HUMAN RELATIONS IN MANAGEMENT
A Behavioral Science Approach

THE IRWIN SERIES IN MANAGEMENT

Consulting Editor JOHN F. MEE *Indiana University*

HUMAN RELATIONS IN MANAGEMENT
A Behavioral Science Approach

Philosophy, Analysis, and Issues

BY WILLIAM G. SCOTT, D.B.A.

PROFESSOR AND CHAIRMAN
MANAGEMENT DEPARTMENT, COLLEGE OF COMMERCE
DE PAUL UNIVERSITY

RICHARD D. IRWIN, INC.

HOMEWOOD, ILLINOIS · 1962

First Printing, March, 1962
Second Printing. September, 1963
Third Printing, August, 1964

Library of Congress Catalogue Card No. 62–11286

PRINTED IN THE UNITED STATES OF AMERICA

TO *Julie*

AIDE: I see they have painted the streetcars in Detroit.

PRESIDENT COOLIDGE: Yes. At least on one side.

An observation attributed to President Coolidge while riding through a street in Detroit.

Preface

SIR D'ARCY WENTWORTH THOMPSON regarded the preface of his book *On Growth and Form* as redundant, for he felt that the entire book was in reality a preface to the subject. Most textbook writers concur with this view. All that a textbook imparts to readers, besides a few facts which easily become outdated, is a framework for thinking about the subject. The framework developed by an author is one which he feels adequately amalgamates the research, the analysis, the issues, and the criticisms of the field it represents. Writing, as he is, a "preface" to a field of thought, an author cannot be accountable for failing to include every last research piece and ideological nuance. But he is accountable if he fails to stimulate some readers to research, to read more, or to reflect at least on the main streams of development of the field surveyed.

This book is written for business school students. It was begun in the "innocent" days before Ford and Carnegie Foundation reports on the state of higher education in business. It was begun at a time when human relations and administrative practice courses were about as close as many business school students got to the behavioral sciences. But as this book was being written, the Ford and Carnegie reports, the behavioral sciences, and exciting areas of study such as organization theory combined to challenge business schools to do something about the way in which the crucial areas of individual and organizational behavior were being handled in their curricula. This book, changed in detail in response to emerging demands, but preserving the basic design of its original intent, is an effort to weld the analytical, critical, and philosophical implications of the behavioral sciences into a framework having meaning for a student who one day may occupy a managerial position.

The main objective of this book is the relating of the behavioral sciences to the management process from the standpoints of philosophy, conceptual and analytical tools, and major issues. However, for the sake of balance, it must be said that both management and the behavioral sciences are relatively young and unseasoned. These areas are evolving; consequently, they contain little that can be presented and accepted as matters of immutable truth. A book of this type, being a synthesis of the "good and beautiful" in management and the behavioral sciences, might actually compound the shortcomings in these fields. Yet, this risk must be taken for at least two reasons.

First, management and the behavioral sciences are *disciplines* that contribute to the intellectual development of the student. The informed business school student should be able to *think* in terms of the behavioral sciences, as he should be able to think in quantitative terms. Modern society, which includes business, requires of its leaders the ability to conceptualize the behavioral processes that are the core of social action.

Second, the student, as a candidate for executive positions in business in the future, needs to appreciate the relevant contributions of the behavioral disciplines. This need is tied directly to the effectiveness of executive performance. The concrete problems of human behavior and organizational relationships are as much of the executive's world as production, marketing, and finance. The behavioral sciences can illuminate vital organizational activities with insights of considerable value for the manager.

The preface of a book is usually delayed by the author until the last. Psychologists might interpret this as a desire to avoid a shattering blow to the ego. Because it is in the preface that the author acknowledges that he alone had not sufficient wit to create all that appears in subsequent pages.

I am deeply in the debt of Professor John F. Mee, Mead Johnson Professor of Management, Indiana University. He dangled the motivational carrot with uncanny intuition at times of particular difficulty. Beyond his help with this book, Professor Mee's strength as scholar and practitioner in management shaped my commitment to this field in graduate school days when my objectives were "unstructured" to say the least.

Professor Wilmar F. Bernthal, the Department of Management, University of Colorado, read the entire manuscript in semifinished form. His recommendations on the general orientation of the book and specific treatments of topics in it were exceedingly valuable in the final preparation.

True to his national and philosophic heritage, following the Greek school of stoicism, Professor Gus Economos, Department of Marketing, De Paul University, endured many excruciating hours of discussion with me on a variety of topics covered in this book. Without his critical sensitivity many obscurities would not have been overcome.

Dean James A. Hart of the College of Commerce, De Paul University and Reverend John T. Richardson, Executive Vice-President of De Paul University offered encouragement and resources which materially eased the burdens associated with writing this book.

I wish also to acknowledge the hundreds of authors, scientific and critical, whose work provides the backbone of this text. Specifically, I want to express my appreciation to the authors and publishers who have granted their permission to reproduce and quote diagrams and passages of significance to certain topics of this book.

Finally, thanks are in order to my family, three generations of them, who graciously put up with four years of my manic-depressive cycles associated with progress or lack of it. Special appreciation is due to my mother who aided me in the final stages of preparation. My children, however, have had more intimate connection with this book than the rest. They have gotten more ink on their fingers from my typewriter than the manuscript pages.

W.G.S.

Chicago
1962

TABLE OF CONTENTS

PART I. PHILOSOPHY

PART II. ANALYSIS

INDEXES

PART I

Philosophy

CHAPTER 1

A Philosophy of Human Behavior at Work

ARISTOTLE said, "He who is unable to live in society or who has no need because he is sufficient for himself, must be either a beast or a god. . . ."[1] In this statement, Aristotle noted the fact of dependency of people on one another. In Aristotelian thought it was difficult, if not impossible, to be human outside of social relationships.

Man's need for human association stems from a variety of want-satisfying activities such as family life, recreation, education, government, and ordinary companionship. This book deals with one particular form of human association—work. People's behavior on their jobs, their motives for employment, and the satisfactions or dissatisfactions they experience in work have long been topics of speculation. However, serious study of man's behavior in his work environment through the use of "scientific tools" is of rather recent origin.

New avenues of thought and investigation were opened as the behavioral sciences matured and the behavioral scientists became interested in the work environment as a legitimate field of study. Since work is, indeed, a way of life in our civilization, the study of job behavioral patterns yields useful information to students of society. But more important, at least for the purposes of this book, the behavioral sciences offer to *management* relevant insights into the processes of individual and group behavior in the organizational setting.

At one time or another most have seen the phrase "human relations." It is applied to many areas in which human interaction is critical. Human relations problems are treated in such contexts as race relations, education, family life, religious life, and so on. Human relations is also an established field of study in management. In this respect human relations operationally refers to *processes of effective motivation of individuals in a given situation in order to achieve a balance of objectives which will yield greater human satisfaction and help accomplish company goals.* For the here and now of American management, human relations embraces matters of

---

[1] *Politics*, Book I, chap. 2.

3

philosophy and practice. It promises higher productivity; greater organizational effectiveness; and happy, satisfied employees.

For certain fields of endeavor to be valuable they must be based on research and deductive analysis. Human relations is one such field. So in addition to its acceptance by many practicing executives, human relations is allied with academic activities of scientific investigation. A great deal of the body of knowledge of human relations is drawn from such behavioral sciences as anthropology, sociology, psychology, social-psychology, and political science. By making fundamental contributions to human relations these disciplines are, in turn, aiding management to improve administrative practice in the vital areas of human motivation and organization.

However, too frequently sprinkled clichés and slogans pertaining to human behavior and company "human relations policies and programs" appear in management literature and in the public statements of executives. Management wants good human relations! Management will do everything in its power to promote good human relations! But "good human relations" can hardly be obtained by wishing it into existence or by muttering a magic formula.

Unfortunately, unsophisticated approaches to human relations by well-meaning managerial practitioners or by opportunistic consulting witch doctors have undermined its stature in the eyes of operating executives and students of the field. Even the name "human relations" strikes a sour note with some managers and scholars in the behavioral sciences. For many today, the field of human relations represents at best a rather pedestrian effort and at worst a cynical attempt to manipulate people.

This disenchantment with human relations is not of recent vintage. But in spite of the criticism leveled at it, human relations as a movement still stands for a philosophy and a point of view which are widely accepted in management circles. Those managers who are inclined in spirit toward human relations as a field of study and practice will find much in the current literature to absorb their interests. However, if one examines the trends in the field of management over the last five or six years, changes are observable indicating new directions for management in the analysis of human behavior at work.

In the forefront of the "new wave" are the behavioral sciences. However, the reader should discover as he moves through this book that the behavioral sciences are not new. They have contributed, and will continue to contribute, to human relations, organization theory, decision theory, management, and to other areas which can be illuminated by them. The behavioral sciences stand in relation to these areas somewhat in the same way as the natural sciences relate to medicine.

The major significance of this new direction in management thought is one of attitude. Specifically, this attitude is manifested by practicing managers as a desire to know more in depth about human behavior. It is manifested by educators in business schools as a desire to lead students into areas which will challenge their potentials to conceptualize problems of human behavior in the business setting. And finally it is manifested by many scientists from the behavioral disciplines in their recognition of the value derived from focusing their powers of research and analysis on the business organization.

Briefly, the new direction in management thought demands treatment of human motivation and organizational behavior on higher conceptual levels. This demand requires more extensive consideration of research and generalizations in the behavioral sciences plus more penetrating analysis of the ethical implications of administrative practice in the management of human interrelationships. But to ignore the field of human relations in the frantic effort to adopt the guise of behavioral science frontiersmanship is to ignore a movement which, though maligned, is nevertheless deeply ingrained in management philosophy. Yet, at the same time, the relevant contributions of the behavioral sciences must be introduced in management regardless of whether the vehicle is human relations or some other approach which may appear more appropriate. So this book is about the behavioral sciences applied to management. And this book is also about human relations because it has come to achieve the status of an integral segment in the philosophy of management.

Management is in a particularly critical position in our society. It must respond sensitively to the challenges created by social changes (discussed in the following pages of this chapter). Not only must management satisfy the desires of stockholders, customers, and the public, it must also be concerned with the needs of the employees in the company. In this respect, management is advised by the human relationists to create a work environment designed both to prevent the occasions of destructive organizational conflict and to promote the personal development and satisfaction of employees.

Human relations, as a combination of practices, policies, scientific theories, and philosophies, is considered in modern management thought as the key which will solve many of business' vexing "people problems." Through the behavioral sciences—which contribute the substantive content of human relations—management is provided with the intellectual and practical equipment necessary to understand and perhaps to settle conflict situations as they occur in the concrete reality of the business setting.

Thus this book is a study of an area popularly known as human relations. But this is not a human relations book in the conventional sense. The reader will find little of the "cookbook" human skills approach between the covers. Nor will he find uncritical acceptance of human rela-

tions proverbs. However, the reader will discover much about the
behavioral sciences and about the issues and assumptions inherent in a
subject treating such a volitile area as human interactions at work.

The first two chapters of this book deal with the philosophy and
history of management's "human relations" point of view. The third
chapter contains a discussion of the essential features and assumptions of
human relations. This chapter also presents a critique of the human
relations perspective. These first three chapters comprise Part I.

The second part of this book analyzes the relevant segments of the
behavioral sciences as they apply to the management process. Part III
examines current issues in management which are susceptible to discussion
and analysis in behavioral science terms.

This chapter focuses on a philosophy of human behavior at work, a
topic which is intimately associated with the evolution of human relations
in management thought. The philosophical point of view set out in this
chapter has two demensions. The first is the function of the clinical
dimension of human relations as it relates to management. The clinical
approach stresses the concrete realities of human behavior on the job and
the steps management can take to influence human behavior toward the
accomplishment of organizational goals on the one hand and individual
satisfactions on the other. The second dimension of the human relations
movement relates to its ethical overtones. Justification of the human
relations movement is sought in this dimension.

THE CLINICAL DIMENSION

Human relations is the term commonly applied to the process of
focusing the methodology and findings of a number of behavioral science
disciplines on human problems. The human relations approach to problem solving is, therefore, labeled *interdisciplinary*. Management uses human relations to determine a course of action for unraveling problems of
human conflict and human satisfactions in business. *Management action
through human relations requires the application of behavioral science
principles to promote human collaboration and social solidarity within the
social system of the business organization.* This definition has four elements which must be explained.

1. The phrase *social system* means that the organization is a complex of
mutually interdependent but variable factors. Every organization is
composed of individuals acting both independently and in groups. Each
group has a pattern of interrelationships, including job activities and
social activities. Separate organizational groupings are related to each
other and are contained in the total physical, economic, social, and
psychological environment of the company. Therefore, each group is a
system in and of itself which in turn is woven into a broader organiza-

tional pattern or system.[2] Management whenever possible should promote the internal harmony of the group; but, more important, management must secure the co-ordination of *all* the factors contributing to the goals of the organization.

2. The idea of *balance*[3] logically follows from a discussion of the social system. Balance means a resolution of forces; it is a state of harmony among the various elements of the social system. Attitudes, activities, and personal interactions of the members of the system must be compatible, or at least not in conflict, for a situation of balance to prevail *on the level of the small group.* For the large group or the total organization balance should be sought among the objectives of individuals, informal groups (cliques), the various jobs being performed, and the policies of the organization as a whole.

In short, balance is the opposite of conflict in the subsystems of small groups and in the larger organizational system. Balance is an operative concept through which management preserves the harmonious relationships among the many factors which make up the social system.

3. *Collaboration* is co-operative effort expended by people who are joined together in the pursuit of common goals or objectives. Collaboration is not necessarily spontaneous. Frequently it must be consciously sought by management.

4. *Social solidarity* means a oneness of purpose in human relationships. Social solidarity includes the ideas of the social system, and of collaboration, and more. It requires that people engaged in a common undertaking, such as employment in a certain company, have purpose, permanence, continuity, and stability in their associations. Management should interpret social solidarity in its company as involving:

a) Human interaction, both in the performance of jobs *and* in personal relations which are not always job oriented.

b) Communications, both formal and grapevine.

c) Personal employee objectives which are not always consistent with organizational goals.

d) Job roles which will both yield individual satisfaction and have the capacity of expanding in accordance with an individual's ability.

In summary, it must be stressed that management's technical skills in running a business must be backed by human skills so that co-operative action and social solidarity will emerge without the loss of an individual's identity. This is a large order, but the advocates of the clinical approach feel it will produce these desirable outcomes.

---

[2] A comprehensive treatment of the social system is given in John B. Knox, *The Sociology of Industrial Relations* (New York: Random House, 1955), chaps. 11–13, 15.

[3] The term "balance" is frequently referred to as "equilibrium" in the literature of human relations.

In a classic statement of the clinical approach, F. J. Roethlisberger outlines two sets of questions for managers. They are:

1. A Useful Way of Thinking about Individuals in a Business Organization
  a) What is the individual bringing to the work situation?
  b) What is the work situation demanding of the individual?
  c) What is the resulting equilibrium?
2. A Useful Way of Thinking about the Interactions of Individuals in a Business Organization
  a) What are the formal patterns of behavior in a group?
  b) What are the informal patterns of behavior in a group?
  c) What are the major schemes in terms of which individuals are being evaluated?
  d) What is the resulting equilibrium?[4]

If the above questions are to be answered honestly the manager is forced to view human interactions in the system concretely and specifically. The manager has to accept the fact that problems of human behavior are not purely individual matters but often involve the individual plus the group, plus job requirements, plus formal and informal criteria against which the behavior of the individual is measured. *The manager must look at his organization as a social system.*

Roethlisberger's questions are good for a start. But a more complete understanding of the clinical dimension can be had from reviewing Donald R. Schoen's guides for a manager in human relations practice.

1. He should understand and accept people as they are.
2. He should be aware and sensitive to another's point of view—along with an ability to maintain his own position.
3. He should be willing to understand and to respond to the feelings and attitudes of others which might not be purely logical from his own frame of reference.
4. He should be aware of himself and appreciate the scope of his influence of others.
5. He should appreciate the social structure or social system in which he is involved.
6. He should be realistic about his authority and status and aware of how they affect others.
7. He should attempt to predict (although the probability of occurrence of the outcomes he predicts may be low) how the organization will respond to a change he introduces.
8. He should make use of experience and abstract generalizations about social phenomena in taking action.[5]

Through the clinical approach the manager takes a hard look at the human situation in which he is involved and then acts in this situation following experience, intuition, and behavioral science data and principles

   [4] F. J. Roethlisberger, *Management and Morale* (Cambridge: Harvard University Press, 1941), pp. 118–24.

   [5] Donald R. Schoen, "Human Relations: Boon or Bogle?" *Harvard Business Review*, November–December, 1957, pp. 43–45.

as guides. *The essence of the clinical philosophy is using human tools and data to solve concrete human problems in the situation where they occur.* The results of this approach in terms of management action have already been shown to be minimization of conflict, the encouragement of collaboration, and the promotion of solidarity in the social system.

Some human relations clinicians wish to divorce their approach from the sphere of "moral" philosophy.[6] Yet certain values are bound to underlie the clinical approach to human relations. Specifically, the clinical approach answers the question of "how" good human relations will be achieved; the ethical approach answers the question of "why" human relations is necessary in the first place. These questions prepare for the following discussion of the ethical dimension of human relations.

THE ETHICAL DIMENSION

Human relations is more than techniques; it is also a system of management values. It has a history and has undergone an evolution in content. Human relations is a segment of management thought which emerged during the transition of America to an industrialized, urbanized society.

Management thought does not exist in its own little world. It is responsive to and has influence upon the main currents and substreams of social philosophy. Management thought did not remain static when America was changing from a rural to an industrial nation. Management literature over the last sixty years reveals a steadily increasing influence of the human relations point of view on management philosophy.

Two Ethical Systems which Influence Management Thought: a Description

Frequently, "management philosophy" is used synonymously with "value systems" to denote the base upon which the objectives and policies of an organization are built. Ethics in turn provide operational values for the management of the organization. As a result of this view of ethics, it is appropriate to ask what system of values management embraces. The answer is most probably that management values are not fundamentally different from the values of society. Broader social values, however, are modified and adapted in specific forms by management to fit into an operating philosophy consistent with the purposes of the organization.

The *individualistic ethic* and the *social ethic* are two broad value systems which have a profound effect on management thought. These ethics are like "super value systems" for management. They supply the ethical points of departure from which management formulates its own specific systems of values, such as scientific management, human relations, merit incentive plans, and so on.

---

[6] *Ibid.*, p. 42.

Value systems constructed on an ethic of individualism or on a social ethic are not new in our society. They have been discussed since people first began theorizing about the nature of man. These philosophical arguments are often concerned with whether or not man's nature is essentially individualistic or collectivistic. Modern value systems based on either the social ethic or the individualistic ethic can be traced through the historical traditions of such philosophic speculations. Yet even today there is no consensus on what view should be taken by management in regard to this basic problem.[7]

The Individualistic Ethic. The individualistic ethic, from the standpoint of its place in management thought, springs from the ideals of economic freedom. These ideals, in turn, are rooted in liberalism,[8] the Protestant ethic,[9] and the American frontier.[10] Liberalism (sometimes referred to as the doctrine of natural liberty) and the Protestant ethic were European in origin. The frontier in America was a phenomenon which deeply influenced national and, hence, management thought during the history of this country. The frontier gave an American twist to the doctrines of human freedom inherited from Europe.

A precise definition of the individualistic ethic is useless because the result would be a history, not a definition. At best, it can be said that *the individualistic ethic is a conglomeration of ideas pertaining to personal freedom and the pre-eminence of individual action.* The European intellectual foundations of individualism were framed in an American context because of the frontier. The ability to "go West" if the press of civilization in the East became too great was part of the meaning of the frontier in America.

---

[7] For a wide expression of views on this point see "A Faith for Modern Management," *The Atlanta Economic Review*, September, 1958, pp. 1–7.

[8] Liberalism as a concept of economic freedom is founded in the notion of "natural liberty." Within this philosophy personal liberty, private property, and freedom of contract are of central importance. Versions of this doctrine run from "man has a right to do what he will with his own" to "every man is free to do that which he wills, provided he infringes not on the equal freedom of any other man." For an analysis of the natural-liberty question see Henry M. Oliver, Jr. *A Critique of Socioeconomic Goals* (Bloomington: Indiana University Press, 1954), chap. 1.

[9] Of all the works dealing with the idea of religious approbation of business behavior, Max Weber's *The Protestant Ethic and the Spirit of Capitalism* (New York: Charles Scribner's Sons, 1930) is the best known and the most influential. The thesis of this essay is that Protestantism formed an ethical base for capitalism. From this base, profit making, and the accumulation of material goods found approval in the sight of God. In this sense, worldly possessions were evidence of divine favor and eventual salvation. Most significant, however, is that economic individualism flourished as an outgrowth of the Protestant reformation.

[10] There have been a number of ideas pertaining to the significance of the frontier as a shaper of American attitude and philosophy. One of the best known is the "safety-value doctrine." This theory is stated in Frederick Jackson Turner, *The Frontier in American History* (New York: Henry Holt and Co., 1920), p. 259. Turner's work is a classic, revealing how the presence of a frontier affected life, thought, and economic development in America.

The Social Ethic. The social ethic is as solidly founded in the history of ideas as is the individualistic ethic.[11] In the largest sense, the social ethic centers on the *collectivity* and the corporate well-being of society. This ethic emphasizes the value of harmony and solidarity in interpersonal and intergroup relationships. The social ethic has grown as a dominant current in social thought during the twentieth century because of increased human interdependency.

The urbanization and industrialization of America must be underscored in this respect. With the changing economic and social aspect of America came a civilization of specialized, urbanized, dependent employees.[12] This change began shortly after the Civil War but proceeded at a much more rapid pace in this century.

The magnitude of this change cannot be dismissed lightly. Old values no longer seemed particularly appropriate when management was faced with the problems that resulted from the American industrial revolution. The fact of human proximity and dependency required a new base of interpretation and ethical rationalization. The modern forms of social organization and, of course, business organizations needed justification for the tendency toward collectivism and control characteristic of twentieth-century civilization.

The social ethic provided a source of justification. Indeed, when people are dependent on each other for employment, the necessities of life, and even the discharge of their job functions, the collectivistic aspect of human nature is forced to the forefront of ethical consideration. Interdependency requires a social philosophy directed toward collaboration and solidarity rather than competition and conflict.

Unfortunately, hardly anything exists that can be called a coherent body of management social ideals. To put the point more clearly, no one body of social ethics has had the impact on management philosophy as the traditional ethic of individualism.

In the social sense management philosophy is composed of a polyglot of ideas that give points of departure for solving social problems caused by industrialization. The behavioral sciences are called upon to answer such questions as: what do people want from their jobs? How can people be made happy in their work? How can people be motivated to meet organizational objectives but remain content and derive job satisfaction at the same time? Presumably, the individualistic ethic had answers for these questions. However, the answers were incomplete. Psychology, sociology, and the newer disciplines like social-psychology, organization

---

[11] For a short history of the backgrounds to the contemporary social ethic see Harry Elmer Barnes (ed.), *An Introduction to the History of Sociology* (Chicago: The University of Chicago Press, 1948), chap. 1–2, esp. pp. 71–76.

[12] The problem and implications of dependency in employment are discussed in Peter Drucker, "The Employee Society," *American Journal of Sociology*, January, 1953, pp. 358–63.

theory, and decision theory had to be consulted for more comprehensive answers to the problem of human motivation and satisfaction in an industrial civilization.

To summarize, the reference point of the social ethic is the collective nature of man. The social ethic affirms the value of human collaboration and social solidarity. The individual is, of course, not neglected. But individual satisfactions are seen as resulting from participation in a social environment characterized by oneness and harmony.[13] Berrien comments that the prerequisite for individual self-realization comes from ". . . the development of close relationships which anchor the individual securely in some stable, continuing group."[14]

In contrast, the individualistic ethic starts with the person as the ultimate source of individual and social values. The "atomistic" person acting intelligently in pursuit of his own self-interest will eventually contribute the most to the good of the group.

The social ethic has not supplanted the individualistic ethic in management philosophy. These two ethics are found side by side today. In fact, some writers feel that management is torn in its allegiance between these ethics. They argue that lip service has to be given to the symbols of individualism while collectivism is the practical and acceptable form of management practice.[15]

It is, however, presumptuous to make an "either-or" case for the natures of man supposedly reflected in these two "super value systems." Man is neither purely individualistic nor purely collectivistic. As Demant points out, "The community and the individualist propensities are part of man's *natura* in dialectical interplay. . . ."[16]

In Demant's sense, man has both social and individualistic tendencies, and the dominance of either tendency results from man's environment, or, more generally, man's "web of culture." Thus it appears that adjustment to the dilemma created by these ethics is a personal thing. Maybe some managers develop a split personality by attempting dual allegiance to these ethics. But if man's nature is really a complex of individualistic

---

[13] Sigmund Diamond has an interesting side light on this point with respect to obituaries of major businessmen. In the early nineteenth century greater stress was placed on the personal, unique qualities of the individual businessman. More recently Diamond finds the values expressed in the obituaries place greater reliance upon the "system" and on the nonbusiness characteristics of the businessman, emphasizing not what set him apart but rather the qualities he had in common with all persons. See Sigmund Diamond, *The Reputation of the American Businessman* (Cambridge: Harvard University Press, 1955), pp. 178–82.

[14] F. K. Berrien, *Comments and Cases on Human Relations* (New York: Harper and Bros., 1951), p. 236.

[15] For example see William H. Whyte, Jr., *The Organization Man* (New York: Simon and Schuster, 1956).

[16] V. A. Demant, *Religion and the Decline of Capitalism* (New York: Scribner's Sons, 1952), p. 139.

and collectivistic propensities it would appear that management can roll quite satisfactorily with the transition to the social ethic.

In conclusion, the conditions existing in pre–twentieth-century America caused an ethic of individualism to make sense for management. Equally, the changed conditions in twentieth-century America created a climate in which the social ethic has progressively enlarged its role in management philosophy. The events which caused this shift in value emphasis are investigated next.

Two Forces behind Social Change

The process of social change is enormously complicated. In order to simplify the analysis only two major forces at work in American history have been selected for application. These forces are called the expansion factor and the collision effect.

The Expansion Factor. The expansion factor is intimately connected to the geographical frontier which existed until around 1900. The meaning of the frontier has been clouded by symbolic usages such as educational frontiers, the frontiers of science, religious frontiers, and so on. The part played by a physical, geographic frontier, however, has particular significance in American social thought.

The frontier meant expansion into a new land and an opportunity for relatively unhampered individualistic expression. The expansion factor placed a premium on individualism. In addition, with room to expand, the competitive social and economic environment in the highly populated part of the country was diluted. It was possible for an individual to get away if his life became unbearable.[17] An illusion of competition without brutality was present when the expansion factor was operative.

The effect the expansion factor had on the attitude of the American people was even more important. Anything seemed possible as long as the individual had enough tenacity to endure hardships. Success was measured by the individual's ability to tap the material wealth abounding in expanding frontiers.[18]

This optimistic spirit was not limited to those who sought opportunity

---

[17] It is noted by Krooss that the frontier did not necessarily provide a "safety valve" for oppressed urban populations and that booms on the frontier took place during periods of prosperity instead of during periods of depression. Herman E. Krooss, *American Economic Development* (Englewood Cliffs: Prentice-Hall, Inc., 1955), pp. 108–12. As explained further on in this section, the "safety valve" is as much a psychological doctrine contributing to national optimism in individualism as it is an explanation of the economic forces which were active in the growth of the American economy.

[18] For some interesting comments on the West as related to the expansion factor see Merle Curti, *The Growth of American Thought* (New York: Harper and Bros., 1943), chaps. 11, 19. For a study of the influence of the frontier on American economic development and foreign policy see William Appleman Williams, *The Contours of American History* (New York: The World Publishing Co., 1961).

on the frontier. The halo of optimism covered even those in the more densely populated regions. The glamour of a golden horizon conditioned the individualistic philosophy of the nation. As a result, management almost unequivocally accepted the individualistic ethic in the nineteenth century.

The Collision Effect. The collision effect is characterized by conflict. The collision effect results from environmental conditions which draw people into inescapable *proximity* and *dependency* on one another. The frontier was not infinite; its closing, coupled with *technological* and *population dynamics*, contributed to an intensifying collision effect. These two dynamics are explored further.

1. *Technological dynamics.*

a) Industrialization. The causes underlying American industrialization are many-faceted. Industrialization required new power sources, a program of mechanization, the growth of capital-goods industries (machine tools and precision instruments), financial sources, and an innovative spirit behind the development of processes, materials, and methods. The economic history of the United States records how these factors and others combined to change America from a handicraft and rural economy to a major industrial nation in the twentieth century.

b) Standardization. One key feature of industrialization is standardization. Uniformity in performance is necessary for complex, large-scale business enterprise to exist. The necessity for uniformity applies to policy matters throughout the company as well as to interchangeability of parts and equipment. Thus, the concept of standardization applies equally well to administrative activities as to the physical uniformity of parts and equipment required by mass-production techniques.

c) Division of labor and job specialization. The division of labor is the breaking down of work into smaller elements or parts so that an employee may "specialize" in a simplified task rather than "generalize" in a fairly complicated job. The division-of-labor process has often been called the rationalization of work.

The division of labor is, in one sense, an extension of the idea of standardization to job performance. Control over many aspects of the production process is simplified when jobs are reduced to their most basic elements—made routine.

Job specialization and the division of labor often refer to operative jobs at the point of production. However, the treatment can be easily extended to apply to executive functions. The vertical growth of a business through the subdivision of management jobs is a case of specialization in the line functions. The horizontal growth of a company by the addition of staff is an example of specialization through advisory and facilitative services for the line organization.

It follows that no matter where the division of labor occurs—at the operative or administrative levels of the organization—all the subdivided functions are closely interrelated in terms of the total operation of the company. The result is that co-ordination of the parts is a paramount need. Further, the processes of industrialization, standardization, division of labor, and specialization are linked inseparably; and in this combination they contribute greatly to the proximity and dependency features of the collision effect. Specifically, the increase in the number of functions to be performed requires more people and thus contributes to proximity; and the increase in the interrelation of these functions contributes to dependency.

d) Improved communication and transportation. Adam Smith observed that the division of labor was limited by the extent of the market; that is, the degree to which industry can be rationalized is limited by the available market outlets for the goods produced.

Market extension was, of course, facilitated by the dramatic growth of the transportation and communication networks. Besides enlarging the market for industrial output, the effect of this development in American industrial growth was to tie people even closer—and thus aggravate the collision effect.

2. *Population dynamics.*

a) Population growth trends. Population growth added to the intensification of the collision effect.

Population increase is shown in the census figures in Table 1–1. It

TABLE 1–1

THE GROWTH OF AMERICAN POPULATION
1790–1960

Year	Population	Year	Population
1790	3,929,214	1880	50,155,783
1800	5,308,483	1890	62,947,714
1810	7,239,881	1900	75,994,575
1820	9,638,453	1910	91,972,266
1830	12,866,020	1920	105,710,620
1840	17,069,453	1930	122,775,045
1850	23,191,876	1940	131,669,275
1860	31,443,321	1950	150,697,361
1870	38,558,371	1960	179,323,175

Source: Bureau of the Census.

is interesting to observe that before 1890—the date the Bureau of the Census declared the frontier officially closed—the population was around 59 million. Since that time it has increased by 120 million.

Up until recently, space (or population density) has not been a matter of very great concern. However, because of the rapid increase in population, note is being taken now of the mounting competition for available space, particularly in strategically located urban areas. The raw data on American population trends serve to re-enforce the validity of the proximity aspect of the collision effect.

b) Urbanization trends.   Significant also to population dynamics is the location of people. According to the 1960 census of population:

> In 1790, 1 out of every 20 of the 3,929,214 inhabitants of the United States was living in urban territory. In every decade thereafter, with the exception of that from 1810 to 1820, the rate of growth of the urban population exceeded that of the rural population. By 1860, 1 out of 5 persons was included in the urban population. The process of urbanization continued in the following decades, and by 1920 the urban population had exceeded the rural population. In 1960 about 5 out of every 8 persons were living in urban territory.[19]

The relationship of rural to urban population is illustrated in Figure 1-1.

Most urban dwellers are aware of the closeness of their neighbors and of their dependence on others for the supply of essential goods and services. Urbanization coupled with population increase has accentuated the problems arising from the proximity and dependency of people. Additionally, no end seems to be in sight to expanding urban populations. Hence, on the score of population dynamics plus contributions to proximity and dependency made by technological dynamics, the collision effect would appear to be an intensifying rather than an abating process.

3. *The significance of technological and population dynamics.*

The key social and technological developments in our society during this century are those which have tended to make people more dependent upon and proximate to each other. These ingredients make the collision effect thrive.

The collision effect, *if left unharnessed*, would breed brutal competition, then conflict, to end in the degeneration of society. However, this cycle did not occur as the collision effect matured. Simultaneously with the growth of the collision effect a change in values began which was necessitated for survival reasons. This is another way of stating the sociological process of competition, conflict, and accommodation.

The American industrial revolution spawned the collision effect; and in turn the collision effect generated its own countervailing ethical force —the social ethic. The "pure" principles of the individualistic ethic lost realism with the diminishing expansion factor. The individualistic industrial buccaneer in the expansion period could not be the hero of the new order.

The values which shored him up, indeed even glorified him, were becoming obsolete at the beginning of this century. The industrial in-

---

[19] Bureau of the Census, *Census of Population: 1960* (Washington, D.C.: U.S. Government Printing Office, 1961), Vol. I, p. xiv. These comparisons are based on the definition of "urban territory" used prior to the 1950 census.

dividualist was replaced, slowly at first, by the professional managerial "relationship expert." The competitive struggle as a vital force *within* an organization was soft-pedaled. Group solidarity as a goal began to be substituted for competition with the expectation that a social philosophy would lead to industrial harmony and human satisfaction.

FIGURE 1–1

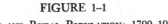

URBAN AND RURAL POPULATION: 1790–1960

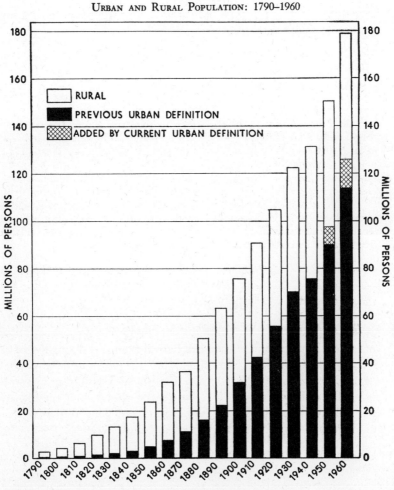

Source: Department of Commerce, Bureau of the Census.

The novel is often a good reflection of prevailing sentiments. Regarding the purpose of business, in 1905 Upton Sinclair wrote the following about the meat packers:

Here was Durham's, for instance, owned by a man who was trying to make as much money out of it as he could, and did not care in the least how he did it; and underneath him, ranged in ranks and grades like an army, were managers and superintendents and foremen, each one driving the man next below him and trying to squeeze out of him as much work as possible. And all the men of the same rank were pitted against each other; the accounts of each were kept separately, and every man lived in terror of losing his job, if another made a better record than he. So from top to bottom the place was simply a seething caldron of jealousies and hatreds; there was no loyalty or decency anywhere about; there was no place where a man counted for anything against a dollar.[20]

Mirroring the modern change in attitude about the purpose of a business, Bernard Lester, in 1956, says:

First of all the objective of a business should be to attain abiding satisfaction for all those persons who are a part of it irrespective of position of relative responsibility. . . .
With this objective for the superstructure, the foundations are men. They support everything. . . . Two families exist in the industrial world today. They are the home-family with its duties and relaxations, and the company- or factory-family with its responsibilities to be gladly and cogently performed. We can't measure accomplishments with a yardstick but each act in each family must give life meaning and reality. . . .
The best equipped plant will drag in production or even periodically come to absolute rest simply because men don't continue to work harmoniously together. . . . Industrial leaders . . . have emphasized competition, and a ruthless approach to that. . . . This approach to efficiency is misleading; the false gods deceive, for the efficiency of men can never be plotted on a curve when they have been robbed of the personal satisfaction of their work . . . .[21]

These quotations suggest the changed philosophy in management thought. Sinclair speaks of competitive individualism; Lester extoles the values of human satisfaction and company harmony.

Two Models of Management Thought: a Summary

Four rather involved points have been covered in this discussion of the ethical dimension of human relations. Figure 1–2 illustrates the connections among the individualistic ethic, the social ethic, the expansion factor, and the collision effect. This figure also shows how these forces and ethics, in combination, have significantly influenced management thought. Figure 1–2 may be interpreted as follows:

1. The expansion factor operating in the nineteenth century—in part because of the frontier—established the necessary setting for the flowering of the ideals of economic freedom. These ideals were based on the Protestant ethic and the doctrine of liberalism.

2. As a result, the philosophy which emerged was the individualistic ethic since it provided the justification for a form of behavior demanded by circum-

---

[20] Upton Sinclair, *The Jungle* (New York: The Viking Press, 1946), pp. 59–60. Used with permission.

[21] Bernard Lester, *Weatherby Crisis* (New York: Twayne Publishers, 1956), pp. 220–21. Used with permission.

stances in pre-twentieth-century America. Individualism consequently had its impact on management thought.

3. The character of society began to change around 1870. By 1900, the new face of society was clearly one of human dependency and proximity. The older order of the pre-eminence of individual action—or, in its pathological form, individualism without a conscience—was becoming outdated.

4. The developing conditions of proximity and dependency, and thus the collision effect, were accelerated by the closing frontier, advancement in all forms of technology, and the movement to the city of large segments of the rural population and waves of immigrants.

5. The escape valve provided by the frontier was no longer available. Competition could turn into conflict. The alternatives resulting from this situation were two—social degeneration or accommodation.

6. Accommodation requires a change in values to offset the effects of conflict. A change of values did occur with a shift toward the social ethic to counter the collision effect. Management, in its own way, has been and is increasingly susceptible to the point of view of the social ethic.

FIGURE 1–2

MANAGEMENT THOUGHT IN A CHANGING CULTURE

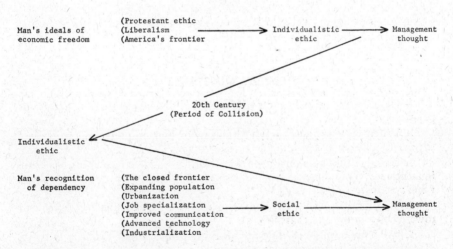

The serious shortcoming of a descriptive model is the difficulty of introducing a dynamic quality into it. This failure might be overlooked when certain historical processes that are over and done with are being described. The lack of a dynamic attribute, however, becomes downright misleading when an explanation of contemporary events is needed. The collision effect is still going on. And, consequently, greater refinements in the concrete applications of the social ethic are being sought.

Human relations is an example of a specific modification of the social ethic adopted by management to understand and to influence a certain form of human association which is peculiarly sensitive to the collision effect. This form of human association refers, of course, to people gathered in a work environment. Human relations is a useful way of looking at and affecting the conflict-biased sociological and psychological processes involved in any organizational effort.

A RECONCILIATION OF THE ETHICAL AND CLINICAL DIMENSIONS

Usually when a reader sees that something is about to be reconciled he becomes wary that a dark and mysterious undertaking is afoot. This section is, perhaps, mistitled because there is nothing incompatible between the ethical and clinical dimensions of human relations philosophy. They are, in fact, part of the same thing. The ethical side of human relations is a rather abstract justification for management's endorsement of the social ethic in the operation of its company. The clinical aspect of human relations provides management with the concrete tools necessary to be effective in administering human situations. The clinical approach is the more "practical" and the ethical approach is the more "theoretical." Thus, human relations philosophy cannot be criticized on the basis of inconsistencies between its ethics and its applications. Rather, to be meaningful criticisms have to be directed toward the social ethic itself.

REVIEW QUESTIONS

1. Describe the main features of the clinical dimension of human relations philosophy.

2. When viewing the concrete problems of human interaction why must the manager think in terms of the social system?

3. Contrast the individualistic ethic with the social ethic. What are their foundations? What is meant by the statement that these ethics constitute "super value systems"?

4. Why is the social ethic in a certain sense a justification for tendencies toward collectivism and control?

5. "Man has both social and individualistic propensities." Evaluate in terms of management's human relations philosophy.

6. Describe and contrast the essential characteristics of the expansion factor and the collision effect.

7. Outline the technological and population dynamics which caused the intensification of the collision effect.

8. Comment on the observation that, "The key social and technological developments during this century caused the collision effect to thrive."

9. How does the social ethic as a system of values act to offset the collision effect?

10. Summarize the interrelationships found among the expansion factor, the collision effect, the social ethic, and the individualistic ethic.

SUPPLEMENTARY READINGS

DRUCKER, PETER. "The Employee Society," *American Journal of Sociology,* January, 1953, pp. 358–63.

KNOX, JOHN B. *The Sociology of Industrial Relations,* chap. 15. New York: Random House, 1955.

ROETHLISBERGER, F. J. *Management and Morale.* Cambridge: Harvard University Press, 1941.

WHYTE, WILLIAM H., JR. *The Organization Man,* Part I. New York: Simon and Schuster, 1956.

CHAPTER 2

Management Approach to Human Motivation: A Historical Overview

INDUSTRIALIZATION creates special human problems which require for their solution a distinctive philosophy and combination of techniques. Management's decisions on the choice of a philosophy and techniques, out of a wide range of alternatives, depend on assumptions about the nature of human behavior and human motivation. The question underlying the formulation of such assumptions is: what sort of job situation best affords employees work satisfaction but also stimulates them to act so as to accomplish company objectives?

There is a scarcity of a management point of view concerning human motivation in pre–twentieth-century literature. However, a few early commentators on the industrial scene were attracted to problems which can be considered motivational. The early views of motivation can hardly be called the "human relations" approach familiar to modern management. Yet the nineteenth-century background that follows provides a necessary introduction to the greater sophistications later introduced into management thought.

EARLY CONTRIBUTIONS

The contributions of Andrew Ure and Charles Babbage to management thought appeared in the early to middle 1830's.[1] The imprint of Adam Smith and his *Wealth of Nations* is indelibly impressed on the philosophy in these works. While Ure and Babbage quibbled with Smith on some minor issues they accepted the master economist's doctrine on major points. But for their purposes Babbage and Ure interpreted Smith as saying:

---

[1] Andrew Ure, *The Philosophy of Manufacturers* (London: Charles Knight, 1835); and Charles Babbage, *On the Economy of Machinery and Manufacturers* (3d ed.; London: Charles Knight, 1833).

22

1. The greatest social good will result from each person operating in his own intelligent self-interest.

2. Wages are the primary motivating force behind employee action.

3. The profits of employers and the wages of employees are geared to productivity.

The synthesis of these three assumptions is best expressed by the term *mutuality of interests*. This concept means that the well-being of the worker and of the employer is inextricably allied. For example, it is in the best interest of the employee to work hard because higher productivity means more money, and money is the main source of his satisfaction and happiness. At the same time, of course, the employer profits from increased productivity. Babbage, it appears, was the first to note the significance of this theory for manufacturers.[2] He observed that workers should be more concerned with producing for the mutual benefit of themselves and their employers rather than combining in unions against their employers. A union of operatives, Babbage felt, would not further the objectives of either the employees or the employers.

Ure also accepted the money-and-motivation equation and the mutuality-of-interests concept. He went beyond Babbage, however, in describing other benefits of industrial employment not directly associated with wages.

Ure discussed the salutary moral, health, and educational influences of industrial employment upon operative employees. These "fringe benefits" of factory employment, plus high wages, were to Ure important motivational features. His account of the "salubrious" conditions in factories seems overdrawn and naive in the face of evidence concerning the life of an industrial worker in early nineteenth-century England.[3] But Ure's purpose in writing his book was in part to contrast factory life with the expiring cottage system of production. Perhaps from this point of view life in a factory was preferable to starvation in a garret or to consumption in a damp basement.

Ure's and Babbage's attitudes toward human motivation and happiness in manufacturing were simple and optimistic. Labor was deemed a commodity which responds to immutable economic laws. Money and motivation were synonymous. The economic man was paramount. The individualistic ethic was a source of inspiration; if people were left free to seek their own interests the maximum in material and nonmaterial benefits would accrue to the individual and also to the community.

---

[2] As he states, "A most erroneous and unfortunate opinion prevails amongst workmen in many manufacturing countries, that their own interest and that of their employers are at variance." Babbage, *op. cit.*, p. 250.

[3] Book the Third entitled the "Moral Economy of the Factory System" in Ure's *Philosophy of Manufacturers* contains his interesting descriptions of the life of factory "inmates." See Ure, *op. cit.*, pp. 277–429.

Not much of particular interest for management appeared between the time of Babbage and Ure and the first contributions of the scientific management writers. This period was roughly fifty years; it was ended by papers before the American Society of Mechanical Engineers. These papers were reproduced in the *Transactions* of the society. The beginning of the scientific management movement was an address by Henry R. Towne, "The Engineer as Economist," in 1886.[4] After Towne's plea to the engineers to build a management literature of "science and practice" several other contributions were made by W. E. Partridge, Towne himself, and F. A. Halsey.[5] Frederick W. Taylor's paper delivered in 1895 was significant because it anticipated his later work in scientific management.[6]

These writers reduced the problem of human motivation and satisfaction in industry to money. Interestingly enough, the fundamental philosophy of these writers was not essentially different from the philosophy expressed by Babbage and Ure. They endorsed the concept of mutuality of interests. High wages, high productivity, and greater human happiness were viewed as interconnected elements in the philosophic framework of industrial efficiency.

The central problem with which these writers were concerned was elevating wage systems to a scientific plane. The older forms of piecework wage plans were criticized by the writers because they did not result in the desired motivational outcomes. Taylor commented, "The ordinary piece-work system involves a permanent antagonism between employer and men . . . even the best workmen are forced continually to act the part of hypocrites to hold their own in the struggle against the encroachments of their employers."[7] Taylor claimed exactly the opposite results for his system, the differential piecework system, which ". . . makes each workman's interests the same as that of his employer."[8]

Taylor's plan to induce proper worker motivation was a revolutionary form of piecework payment; Towne and Halsey proposed programs of premium wage payments. These latter plans were designed to give workers monetary rewards directly in relation to time saved in the per-

---

[4] Henry R. Towne, "The Engineer as Economist," *Transactions*, American Society of Mechanical Engineers, Vol. 7 (1886), pp. 428–32. All subsequent references in this chapter to the transactions of this society will be identified by the initials ASME. The page numbers include the major paper, and discussions of the paper where appropriate.

[5] W. E. Partridge, "Capital's Need for High-Priced Labor," *Transactions*, ASME, Vol. 8 (1886–1887), pp. 269–94; Henry R. Towne, "Gain Sharing," *Transactions*, ASME, Vol. 10 (1889), pp. 600–26; and F. A. Halsey, "Premium Plan of Paying for Labor," *Transactions*, ASME, Vol. 12 (1891) pp. 755–80.

[6] Frederick W. Taylor, "A Piece-Rate System," *Transactions*, ASME, Vol. 16 (1895), pp. 856–903.

[7] *Ibid.*, p. 856.

[8] *Ibid.*, p. 856–57.

formance of jobs. Although these plans were *not* suggested as substitutes for older forms of piecework pay methods they did attempt to introduce another economic incentive into a wage-payment structure. One of the members of the society, a Professor Denton, commented that Towne's "gain-sharing" plan answers the question of: "How can we at once get the workman to squeeze a little more out of himself and at the same time be good-natured in doing it?"[9]

These early wage-system proposals were efforts to objectify the remuneration of the "economic man." The major assumption—that man was primarily motivated by and received work satisfaction from economic gain—was not questioned. Given this premise the next logical and scientific step was to quantify, as far as possible, the economic contribution of a man to the firm and the firm's reward for the contribution.

Money was the nineteenth-century answer to the "motivation-satisfaction" question posed at the start of this chapter. This attitude was amplified to some extent by introducing systems to determine "fair" wages and techniques to promote "mutuality of interests." But management's understanding of human motivation did not progress very far in this century. Economic man was still rattling his coins. Contrasted with the lean years of the nineteenth century, management literature proliferated during this era. Along with it, management thought grew more sophisticated.

THE SCIENTIFIC MANAGEMENT MOVEMENT

The social and technological changes underway in America in the late nineteenth century accelerated in the twentieth century. As noted earlier, these changes were felt in the form of the collision effect. The result was that management needed new values more consistent with the proximate and dependent condition of people in an industrial society, and it also needed better methods to cope with more complex technology and business organization.

The scientific management pioneers[10] sought answers to this twofold problem. They realized a new approach was required to accomplish too tightly knit goals: (1) higher industrial efficiency through improved management practice and (2) greater collaboration among those working in industry. The pioneers hoped to achieve this second goal through the promotion of a true mutuality of interests.

Testifying before a Special House Committee, Taylor had the following to say about scientific management:

---

[9] Towne, *op. cit.*, p. 616.

[10] Frederick W. Taylor, Frank and Lillian Gilbreth, Morris L. Cooke, Henry L. Gantt, and Harrington Emerson.

Scientific management is not an efficiency device . . . not a system of figuring costs . . . not a piecework system . . . not a bonus system . . . not a premium system . . . it is not holding a stop watch on a man and writing things down about him . . . it is not time study, it is not motion study . . . it is not any of the devices which the average man calls to mind when scientific management is spoken of. . . .

. . . In its essence scientific management involves a complete mental revolution on the part of the workingmen . . . and it involves an equally complete mental revolution on the part of those on the management's side. . . .

The great revolution that takes place in the mental attitude of the two parties under scientific management is that both sides take their eyes off of the division of the surplus as the all-important matter, and together turn their attention toward increasing the size of the surplus until this surplus becomes so large . . . that there is ample room for a large increase in wages for the workmen and an equally large increase in profits for the manufacturer.[11]

Taylor's testimony clearly revealed the goals of scientific management. Scientific management was more than techniques; it was a way of thought. The early advocates of this movement felt it was truly a revolution in management values—a revolution through which the pioneers saw a way to obtain a mutuality of interests among those dependent on business for a living. The immediate objectives of a mutuality of interests were visualized as human collaboration in the organization effort and ever-increasing productivity accompanied by a wider, more equitable distribution of an economic surplus.

The pioneers felt that if these proximate objectives could be realized the ultimate objectives of industrial harmony and human work satisfactions would be forthcoming. Looked at in this way, scientific management was a philosophy reflecting the social ethic, and the scientific management pioneers were crude human relationists. Scientific management was an idea which attempted to reconcile the paradox of the need for co-operation among people in industry with the philosophy of individualism.[12]

Taylor made it explicit that the philosophy of scientific management should not be confused with its mechanisms. In the following

---

[11] "Special House Committee to Investigate the Taylor and Other Systems of Shop Management," reprinted in Frederick W. Taylor, *Scientific Management* (New York: Harper and Bros., 1947), pp. 26, 27, 29–30. These quotes were presented in this form by Reinhard Bendix, *Work and Authority in Industry* (New York: John Wiley and Sons, Inc., 1956), p. 276.

[12] Taylor characterizes scientific management by four elements: (1) science, not rule of thumb; (2) harmony, not discord; (3) co-operation, not individualism; (4) maximum output, not restricted output. Frederick W. Taylor, *Principles of Scientific Management* (New York: Harper and Bros., 1919), p. 140. Taylor's third characteristic might appear contrary to the individualistic ethic. This point is cleared up when he says, ". . . All great things will be done by that type of co-operation in which each man performs the function for which he is best suited, each man preserves his own individuality and is supreme in his particular function, and each man at the same time loses none of his originality and proper personal initiative."

sections, the major areas of scientific management which have broad human implications are discussed. The mechanisms, such as specific wage plans, or motion and time study, which fall into these areas are avoided so that just the major issues are developed. No one area constitutes the total philosophy of scientific management. They are all part of an inclusive format which is like a simultaneous equation designed to solve the problem of human collaboration.

Work and Wages

Taylor, his disciple Gantt, and the Gilbreths labored extensively with the problems connected with the analysis of work and the setting of the "right" wage. Taylor's approach to work was an enormously significant step in the science of management. Work was taken for granted for thousands of years. No one really attempted to deal with the elements involved in the performance of a task. Taylor tackled this problem.

The right wage was an explosive issue that grew out of an industrialized economy. Taylor felt the wage paid must be related in some way to the work done. To find the relation, he formulated time-study experiments to measure work. Taylor's work was refined and expanded by the Gilbreths' method analysis and Gantt's task and bonus system.

It is apparent that these writers considered the analysis of work and the payment of wages crucial elements of industrial harmony. In essence, their theory ran that given a fair wage, scientifically set in relation to a fair amount of work, an employee would be induced to see his objectives for higher wages as mutually compatible with the employer's objectives for profit. Thus, the reasons for unions to protect workers from exploitation would be eliminated and organized labor would have no reason to exist.[13]

This theory of work and wages makes a good deal of sense, given the unwavering nature of the motives of economic man. An honorable worker, according to Taylor, will soldier (loaf) only if he feels he is not going to be properly rewarded for work. But if his efforts are honestly evaluated and fairly paid the worker will be only too happy to extend himself to get greater rewards.

The Standardized Man

Standardization, to the pioneers, went beyond the mere standardization of parts, equipment, and methods. Standardization was a concept applicable to all the personnel in the organization. The "quest for the one best way" led the Gilbreths to the systemization of personnel prac-

---

[13] Hoxie, one of the first major critics of scientific management, did not see it this way. While he felt the theory of scientific management was acceptable, he thought many abuses would appear in practice. See Robert Franklin Hoxie, *Scientific Management and Labor* (New York: D. Appleton and Co., 1915).

tices, notably selection and training. The theory is that a standardized system of personnel techniques will produce a standardized man. This standardized man is an integral part of the theory since by studying him the most reliable motion and time data are obtained.[14] And these data are basic to process engineering, work simplification, and wage payment.

Standardization was applied to employee levels above the operative. Functional foremanship was Taylor's unconventional view of organizing personnel in the most effective way. Without running the course of Taylor's arguments, it should be enough to say that work was to be divided so that men with certain abilities (specializations) could be placed where their talents would be best utilized. Taylor felt that under the military-type organization a foreman was required to have too many specialized tasks to supervise. Functional foremanship allowed concentration on a few specializations within a job toward which each foreman had some individual bent. Of course, the concept of functional foremanship could be applied to higher levels of management as well. The result would be a high degree of standardization and specialization in all managerial positions.

Gantt, Emerson, and Cooke saw from several points of view the benefits resulting from standardization. Gantt was interested in standardization for establishing "habits of industry." Habits of industry meant conditioning workers for industrial life. It included management planning, training of workmen, and noting the influence of the informal organization on job behavior. Emerson assigned a major role to standardization in his efficiency principles which he visualized as guides for management. Cooke applied the concept of standardization to public administration.[15]

Standardization was a necessary part of scientific management. From the human standpoint it is interesting to observe that the pioneers did not feel that standardization would result in less incentive or greater feelings of anonymity for employees. Indeed, their attitude was that standardization increased employee happiness and self-realization.[16]

---

[14] L. M. Gilbreth, *The Psychology of Management* (New York: Sturgis and Walton Co., 1914), p. 152.

[15] For representative examples of these three authors' viewpoints see H. L. Gantt, "Training Workmen in the Habits of Industry and Cooperation," *Transactions*, ASME, Vol. 30 (1908), pp. 1037–63; Harrington Emerson, *The Twelve Principles of Efficiency* (New York: The Engineering Magazine Co., (1913); and Morris L. Cooke, *Our Cities Awake* (New York: Doubleday, Doran and Co., 1918).

[16] For example, see Gilbreth, *op. cit.*, chap. VI. Mrs. Gilbreth used the same reasoning as the eminent sociologist Emile Durkheim in justifying standardization in humanitarian terms. Durkheim felt that the division of labor with its subsequent specialization and standardization was a source of solidarity. He said, "The division of labor presumes that the worker, far from being hemmed in by his task, does not lose sight of his collaborators, that he acts upon them, and reacts to them." Emile Durkheim, *On the Division of Labor in Society* (Glencoe: Free Press, 1947), p. 373. (The date of the original work was 1893.)

Prosperity and Productivity

The prosperity and productivity ideals of the scientific management pioneers were closely related to their notions of work and wages just discussed. Gantt noted that the utilization of resources is more effective through scientific management. As a result, greater wealth would be created, contributing to national social and economic well-being.[17]

Taylor was convinced an individual's prosperity can only be maximized when national prosperity is maximized, in the long run of course. In this respect, as noted before, the interests of workers and employers would be allied. If workers produced as much as possible, and managers managed scientifically, relatively higher degrees of prosperity would be enjoyed by all. "Relative degrees" is an important modification. Taylor realistically believed that many factors contributing to prosperity were outside the control of the scientific manager. However, he insisted that firms run scientifically would fare better than others, even in periods of economic decline.

The immediate goal of scientific management was a productivity closely tied in with the profit and service objectives of a business. But the pioneers were so strong in their faith in scientific management that they felt other business objectives could be realized through it as well. These other objectives were the broader considerations of social welfare. Again, this is the mutuality-of-interest idea applied on a much wider scale; that is, the goals of society, industrial employees, consumers, and owners of businesses are mutual and can be realized by the same device—scientific management.

Scientific Management and Welfare

Frank and Lillian Gilbreth working as a team made important contributions to scientific management. Lillian Gilbreth is a psychologist by training, and one of her early books dealt with the scientific application of psychology to management. One section of this book is interesting in its revelations of what scientific management can do to improve the welfare of employees. In short, Mrs. Gilbreth said scientific management provides for:

1. Physical improvement of workers (increased health, better color and general appearance).
2. Mental development (wider interest, deeper interest, increased mental capabilities).
3. Moral development (personal responsibility, responsibility for others, appreciation of standing, self-control, "squareness").
4. Contentment, brotherhood, and the "will to do." (These developments are natural consequences of item three—moral development.)[18]

---

[17] H. L. Gantt, "Efficiency and Democracy," *Transactions*, ASME, Vol. 40 (1918), pp. 799–808.

[18] Gilbreth, *op. cit.*, chap. 10.

These effects of scientific management predicted by Mrs. Gilbreth are somewhat reminiscent of the "salubrious" benefits industrial employment had on factory "inmates" observed by Ure almost eighty years before.

Gantt and Emerson also forecast welfare consequences of scientific management, but they made their predictions on an international scale.[19] They considered the efficiencies resulting from scientific management as the cornerstones of national strength. The nations most proficient in industrial efficiency would rise to international supremacy. Gantt pointed out that in a successful industrial nation the industrial leaders will move into positions of national power. He underscored the necessity for American business leaders to develop an attitude of social consciousness not only in dealing with employees but also in supplying services to the community. Only in this way, Gantt felt, could the menace of socialism be overcome.

The Implication of Scientific Management

The scientific management movement laid the foundation for the professionalization of management. While the pioneers may have recognized this point, they did not exploit it to its fullest possibilities. The key idea, however, was presented in 1913 by Edward D. Jones as a result of a historical study of famous administrators of the past. Jones observed that, ". . . The dominant problem now is one of originating and formulating a science of administration."[20]

Jones singled out for special emphasis:

1. The trusteeship role of management, occasioned by the separation of ownership from control.
2. The duality of administrative skills, human skills, and process skills.
3. The development of a "whole new race of executives."

Jones concluded that scientific management was just a tool for professional management. This "new breed" of management by necessity would have to look beyond the simple dictums of profit making and economic man in order to make decisions which would enhance industrial social solidarity. The "new manager" had to be a leader of men.[21] An understanding of the complex interrelationships of people, groups, methods, firms, and industries had to come within the scope of executive decision making.

---

[19] H. L. Gantt, *Work, Wages, and Profits* (New York: The Engineering Magazine Co., 1911), esp. chap. 9; and Emerson, *op. cit.*, chap. 1, 2.

[20] Edward D. Jones, *Industrial Leadership and Executive Ability* (New York: The Engineering Magazine Co.; 1920), p. 5. (First edition appeared in 1913.)

[21] Gantt was very much aware of Jones' work, and agreed with his views. See H. L. Gantt, *Industrial Leadership* (New Haven: Yale University Press, 1916), chap. 1.

Jones was ahead of his time. His work makes an excellent transition into the next periods because he anticipated much of what was to happen. Up until 1920, the history of management thought was dominated by scientific management. This movement provided a new set of management values that acted as a transition from the individualistic ethic to the social ethic.

CHANGES IN THE 1920's

The bulk of the pioneers' contributions to scientific management was made before World War I. After the war these contributions were expanded in depth and breadth. The depth expansions appeared in the form of more analytical approaches to the mechanisms of scientific management. Many refinements in motion and time study, cost analysis, and wage measurements were offered. The breadth expansion included the wholesale introduction and use of psychology in management practice.

The economic work motive stressed by the pioneers began to decline in popularity. Money and motivation, it was recognized, were not synonymous. Psychology offered suggestions for the satisfaction of work motives which were essentially noneconomic in nature. Personnel policies were designed to meet such employee needs as recognition, participation, accomplishment, security, and so on.[22]

It must also be recognized that the 1920's were the period of the "open shop" or "American plan" movement. This movement was geared to defeat organized labor by giving workers directly what they had to get indirectly through the union and the process of collective bargaining. Better wages figured into the American plan, but this program also included many fringe benefits and organized worker activities. The success of the American plan was demonstrated by the decline in union membership during the 'twenties. However, the movement collapsed in 1929 for obvious reasons.

The mutuality-of-interests objective as the source of human collabora-

---

[22] The 1920's were heydays for pseudo and real industrial psychologists. It was popular to think that people naturally do not like to work and that more and more money will not yield more and more happiness. A flood of literature during this time showed the "broader" applications of industrial psychology. The following are some books of the period with indicative titles: Cecil D. Burns, *Industry and Civilization* (New York: Macmillan Co., 1925); Stuart Chase, *Men and Machines* (New York: Macmillan Co., 1929); L. Frankel and Alexander Fleisher, *The Human Factor in Industry* (New York: Macmillan Co., 1920); J. D. Houser, *What the Employer Thinks* (Cambridge: Harvard University Press, 1927); W. D. Scott, *Science and Common Sense in Working with Men* (New York: Ronald Press, Co., 1921); John H. Van Deventer, *More Work per Man: Tested and Selected Methods of Managing Men* (New York: Engineering Magazine Co., 1921); W. Eugene, *Human Engineering* (New York: Appleton and Co., 1921).

tion was not changed, although the content of scientific management was broadened to include both material and nonmaterial motives for work. But probably of greater significance from the standpoint of human relations was the beginning of experiments in human relations at the Hawthorne plant of Western Electric in the 1920's. The findings of this research did not have much effect on management philosophy until the 1930's, so it will be discussed in the next section.

DEVELOPMENTS IN THE 1930's

It is odd that the general disenchantment with business resulting from the depression in the 1930's did not prevent this period from being one of the most fruitful in the production of management ideas. Several strands of thought solidified in this decade and the direction of future thought in management was established. A full appreciation of this period involves the discussion of a number of related developments. These developments are treated in this order:

1. The professionalization of management.
2. The business plan.
3. The organization.
4. The human relations movement.

The Professionalization of Management

Ownership and Control. The separation of business ownership from control and the numerical increase of people in managerial functions contributed to the management professionalization trend. Berle's and Means' masterly analysis, *The Modern Corporation and Private Property*,[23] was like a manifesto for the professionalization of management. It was the contention of Berle and Means that the modern corporation upset the traditional theory of property in which ownership and control of property were inseparable qualities. In many companies the stockholders, while legal owners, were for all practical purposes deprived of the privilege of control over their property.

This peculiar by-product of the corporation device placed management in a stewardship position. Stewardship can be visualized as management running a corporation to achieve the objectives of the owners. Basically, management acts as an intermediary between the corporation on one hand and the owners of the corporation on the other hand. This concept of stewardship resembles a "pure theory." The corporate structure allows management to operate fairly independently of the controls traditionally associated with the ownership of property. This situation often places management in a good position to exploit an or-

---

[23] Adolf A. Berle, Jr., and Gardiner C. Means, *The Modern Corporation and Private Property* (New York: The Macmillan Co., 1932).

ganization's resources for ends not necessarily owner oriented.[24] The idea of exploitation also applies in cases where management's inside knowledge of a special situation allows it to profit although no damage is done to the corporation.

These exploitive opportunities might overstate the case somewhat; the ethics of the management of every corporation must be judged on the merits of the situation. The realistic point of view is that professional managers, in the modern, complex world, are often better able to handle an owner's property than is the owner himself. The point of key significance is that economic decision making has tended toward centralization, while the broad base of democratic business ownership is a matter of propaganda, not of fact.[25]

Organizational Size. Another phenomenon contributing to the professionalization of management was expansion in organizational size accompanied by a rapid increase in administrative personnel. The problem of size and bureaucracy had started to unfold early in this century and by 1930 was in urgent need of analysis. Measurements of bureaucratic growth indicated that the numbers of administrative personnel in business organizations were expanding at a faster rate than were the so-called production employees.[26] The ratio of administrative employees to production employees in 1937 stood at 17.7 per cent, while this same ratio in 1899 was 7.7 per cent.[27]

Thus, more managers were appearing with specialized functions. The division of labor in management required consideration of internal coordination. The framework of business organization was becoming exceedingly complicated and needed explanation.

In summary, the impetus to management professionalization was provided by:

1. An accelerated use by business of the corporation device which, in turn, created a climate that made the stewardship concept very significant.[28]
2. The rapid growth in organizational size, accompanied by the appearance of more and more employees in management jobs.

The embryonic management profession did not have a particularly inclusive or sophisticated body of thought from which to deal with the

---

[24] *Ibid.*, p. 354. Berle's and Means' observations on this point anticipated a more extensive analysis of managerial exploitation by Burnham. See James Burnham, *The Managerial Revolution* (New York: The John Day Co., 1941).

[25] For a recent treatment of this point see Victor Perlo " 'People's Capitalism' and Stock-Ownership," *American Economic Review*, June, 1958, pp. 333–47.

[26] Bendix, *op. cit.*, chap. 4. This chapter gives an excellent account of the bureaucratization process.

[27] *Ibid.*, p. 214.

[28] The reader should not interpret this to mean that the corporation device was peculiar to the 1920's and the 1930's. The rush to incorporate was begun by businesses in the late nineteenth century.

technical and human problems created by these changes in the business institution. There were, to be sure, the philosophy and the techniques inherited from the scientific management pioneers. But these contributions did not entirely meet professional needs. The philosophical aspects of early scientific management had almost utopian overtones. But when the pioneers considered specifics, the application was generally to the operative levels of the organization.

A professional approach needed a rather high level of abstraction, plus universality and practicality in explaining what management does and how an organization works. Two routes were followed to meet this need for a professional philosophy: the technical and the human routes.

The Business Plan

Ralph C. Davis' *Industrial Organization and Management* is probably one of the most enduring and representative examples of the technical route to a modern management philosophy.[29] The quality of this work is in its comprehensiveness. Davis deals with the universality of business elements. Starting with a philosophy, he derives business objectives, ethics, policies, and the role of leadership in business. From here he moves to the business functions of creation, distribution, and finance, and then to an analysis of the management functions of planning, organizing and controlling. All these elements are woven into a business plan.

Davis was not the first to write about industrial management but he was the first to generalize the management process. Although he discusses specifics such as quality control, maintenance, supply, and the like, these find direction in the fundamentals laid out at the beginning. This work, coming as it did in the 1930's, filled a definite need for management since it was professionally oriented.

The Organization

Another aspect of the technical route to a management philosophy was the study of organization. And to organize is to establish a co-operative system.[30]

This statement has dual implications. The first is a notion of action —*organizing;* the second is the result of organizing action—*organization.* This duality created difficulties for a theory of organization. Organizing, as a management function, can be dehumanized. That is, the relationships among work, the work place, and the people who do the work can be established without reference to personality. However, the product of

---

[29] See Ralph C. Davis, *Industrial Organization and Management* (New York: Harper and Bros., 1939).

[30] This concept of the organizing process is based upon the work of Barnard. See Chester I. Barnard, *The Functions of the Executive* (Cambridge: Harvard University Press, 1938), esp. chaps. 6, 7.

the organizing activity—organization—cannot be managed without considering the people involved.

Many of the attempts to explain the organizing process and organization were fuzzily handled because of the duality problem. Both Dennison[31] and Dutton[32] offered thoughts on the organization question early in the 1930's. They began with the premise that the organization was a system and then they interpreted the effect the system has on the individual.

Henry Dennison, in particular, was concerned with the human side of organization. Such matters as social environment, leadership, teamwork, co-ordination, and mutuality of interests are found in his book. Both Dennison and Dutton devoted much space to showing how the individual can be adjusted to the demands of the organization system by managements' use of fairly conventional personnel techniques like training, job analysis, and placement. Neither of these works, however, posed an integrated picture of organization, nor did they put forth a clear exposition of the process of organizing as connected to the functions of management in an organization.

The outstanding work which seemed to solve the duality problem was *Onward Industry* by Mooney and Reiley.[33] Mooney's and Reiley's main hypothesis was the distinction between organizing as a depersonalized process and the day-to-day personalized administration of an organization. Organizing activities, in the authors' views, takes place before administration of the organization. Thus, organizing is placed on the level of a science whereas administration they consider an art.

Mooney and Reiley were not concerned with techniques, however. They developed a sequential arrangement of broadly applicable principles to demonstrate the meaning and logic behind functional relationships in formal organizations. The first of these principles is the co-ordinative principle. Defined, this principle means an "orderly arrangement of group effort, to provide unity of action in the pursuit of a common purpose."[34] Essential to this principle are doctrine, discipline, and mutual service. Later, Barnard made much the same point in describing the foundations of the formal organization as communication, willingness to contribute action, and common purpose.[35]

The second principle is the scalar principle, which is merely the grad-

---

[31] Henry Dennison, *Organization Engineering* (New York: McGraw-Hill Book Co., 1931).

[32] Henry P. Dutton, *Principles of Organization* (New York: McGraw-Hill Book Co., 1931).

[33] James D. Mooney and Alan C. Reiley, *Onward Industry* (New York: Harper and Bros., 1931). Later revised by Mooney and published under the title *The Principles of Organization* (New York: Harper and Bros., 1947). All subsequent references to this book will be made to the later edition.

[34] *Ibid.*, p. 5.

[35] Barnard, *op. cit.*, chap. 7.

ing of duties according to degree of authority and corresponding responsibility.

The functional principle is the third; it involves the differentiation of kinds of duties performed in the organization.

Mooney and Reiley did not have too much to say about running the organization once organizing activities were completed. The task of deciphering the problems of day-to-day administration was left to Elton Mayo and his associates. The experiments conducted by this research group set the stage for revolutionary changes in management philosophy. The Hawthorne studies were the beginning of the human relations movement; as such they merit considerable attention here.

The Hawthorne Studies

The Western Electric experiments at its Hawthorne plant began as a straightforward attempt to determine the relationships between work environment and productivity. For example, the experimenters sought to discover the connection between the intensity of light on a job and the output. It was thought that the relationship would be a direct one: as the light was decreased output would also decrease. However, as the experiments progressed the results were disconcerting. The workers in the experimental situation were behaving the opposite of how they "should." In one case, as the light was decreased by set increments the output increased until the employees could no longer see.

The results of the illumination and other experiments conducted at the Hawthorne plant led the researchers to conclude that they were dealing with classes of sociological and psychological phenomena which could not be adequately explained with the tools of analysis developed up to this time. The formal organization of the company was revealed to be merely a "blueprint" of the economic logics upon which a business is structured. The Hawthorne studies exposed many management misconceptions. An organization, it was shown, is more than a formal arrangement of functions. *It is a social system.* The company is a system of cliques, grapevines, informal status systems, and rituals; it is also a mixture of logical and nonlogical behavior.

Further, the Hawthorne experiments demonstrated that the people in the company want to participate and to be recognized. They are not rabble but individuals with psychological drives and social yearnings.[36]

Pareto and the Human Relationists. Through the research and writings of the human relationists[37] the importance of human skills in dealing

---

[36] A complete report of the Hawthorne studies may be found in F. J. Roethlisberger and William J. Dickson, *Management and the Worker* (11th printing; Cambridge: Harvard University Press, 1956).

[37] Elton Mayo, F. J. Roethlisberger, William J. Dickson, T. N. Whitehead, and L. J. Henderson.

with human situations was hammered home to management. The results of the Hawthorne experiments provided a fountainhead of philosophy which influenced contemporary management attitudes in human relations.

Yet the theoretical edifice built by the Harvard human relationists was not new. Knox points out, "Pareto's treatise on general sociology provided the major theoretical framework for the Western Electric research."[38] Thus Pareto, one of the last great sociological system builders, contributed a steppingstone toward a modern philosophy of administration.

The Pattern of Pareto's Influence. Following Knox, it appears that Pareto's theories found in his *The Mind and Society*[39] were introduced informally to Mayo, Roethlisberger, and their associates by Lawrence J. Henderson, a physiologist on the Hawthorne research team. Knox's case is that, aside from Henderson, the Hawthorne researchers were not aware of the extent to which they were influenced by Pareto.[40]

Parallelisms. A comparative analysis of Pareto's general sociology and the major works of the Hawthorne human relationists reveals striking similarities in the theoretical systems. Table 2–1 presents the central ideas flowing from the Hawthorne experiments. This figure also shows some of the most evident parallels found in Pareto's work and in the work of the human relationists. The concepts of the social system, logical and nonlogical behavior, equilibrium, the functions of language, and the circulation of the elite are the essential features of the theoretical scheme of Pareto and the human relationists.

From the experiments and the theoretical explanation of the findings of the experiments, the Hawthorne researchers dramatically showed the fallacy of early management attitudes regarding the motivation of people. The atomistic, self-seeking economic man was effectively dispatched. A new era and a new philosophy focusing on the human skills of management were introduced.

The Administrator

The professionalization of management followed two routes to arrive at a modern philosophy which met the tests of universality and practicality. Davis, Mooney and Reiley made basic contributions to a technical philosophy of management; the Harvard human relationists con-

---

[38] John B. Knox, "Sociological Theory and Industrial Sociology," *Social Forces*, March, 1955, p. 242.

[39] Vilfredo Pareto, *The Mind and Society*, trans. and ed. Arthur Livingston (New York: Harcourt, Brace and Co., 1935).

[40] Henderson's study of Pareto is demonstrated by his essay. See Lawrence J. Henderson, *Pareto's General Sociology* (Cambridge: Harvard University Press, 1935).

TABLE 2–1

PARALLELISMS: PARETO AND THE HAWTHORNE HUMAN RELATIONISTS*

Pareto†	The Human Relationists‡
1. The social system	**1. The social system**
Pareto's definition of a system is mutually dependent variations of variables. Society is a cluster of interdependent, but variable, units. The concept of interdependence of the units in a social system is a key part of Pareto's theoretical framework (see pars. 2060–66; 2079–104).	"By 'system' is meant something which must be considered as a whole because each part bears a relation of interdependence to every other part" (ref. A, p. 551). The concept of the social system plays an essential part in the philosophical orientation of the Hawthorne researchers. The significance of the interdependence of the social and physical components of the work environment is noted also in ref. B, Chap. X, esp. pp. 184–87, and in ref. C, p. 256. Roethlisberger and Dickson note their indebtedness to Pareto for the concept of the social system in ref. A, p. 272.
2. Logical and nonlogical behavior a) By logical behavior Pareto means logical actions that conjoin means to ends not only from the standpoint of the subject performing them but from the standpoint of other persons who have more extensive knowledge (par. 150). b) Nonlogical behavior was dealt with by Pareto under the term "residues," or sentiments (par. 145–248). At times Pareto treats sentiments as manifestations of residues; at other times he uses the terms "residues" and "sentiments" interchangeably. Rationalizations of nonlogical behavior were termed "derivations" by Pareto (pars. 249–367). Nonlogical conduct originates in definite psychic states, sentiments, subconscious feelings, inclinations, preconceptions, and so on. These residues or sentiments are essential to the equilibrium of the social system. Nonlogical conduct is contrary to logical behavior in that the objective ends of nonlogical actions differ from the subjective purpose of such actions. Residues or sentiments change slowly; they tend to persist. Derivations or rationalizations change rapidly. (For further references see pars. 1397–686.)	**2. Logical and nonlogical behavior** a) In trying to separate fact from sentiment in human actions (or verbalizations of such actions), the human relationists defined a fact as ". . . a statement from experience involving sensory processes and physical and logical operations, such that if the statement is challenged there exist certain generally accepted procedures by means of which the statement can be tested. . . ." The connection between this approach and Pareto's definition of logical behavior is evident when tied in with human conduct (ref. A, chap. XII). b) Nonlogical behavior and the concept of sentiments are a basic aspect of the human relationists' analysis. Sentiments mean the same thing to the human relationists as residues mean to Pareto (ref. B, chap. II, and ref. C, chap. 15). Whitehead analyzes some experimental results of the Hawthorne study in terms of certain of Pareto's classes of residues—for example, persistence of aggregates and instinct for combination (ref. C, pp. 226, 232). Relative to Pareto's concept for derivations, Roethlisberger observes: "One of the most time-consuming pastimes of the human mind is to rationalize sentiments and to disguise sentiments as logic" (ref. B, p. 91).

TABLE 2-1 (continued)

Pareto†	The Human Relationists‡
3. Equilibrium	**3. Equilibrium**
Pareto defines equilibrium in the following way: ". . . the state of X is such a state that if it is artificially subjected to some modification different from the modification it undergoes normally, a reaction at once takes place tending to restore it to its real, its normal, state" (par. 2068).	The human relationists treat equilibrium in much the same way as Pareto handles it. Roethlisberger and Dickson, following Henderson (who in turn follows Pareto), define social equilibrium as ". . . an interaction of sentiments and interests in a relation of mutual dependence, resulting in a state of equilibrium such that if that state is altered, forces tending to re-establish it come into play" (ref. A, p. 365; for further reference on this point see ref. C, pp. 225, 257, ref. B, chap. X).
The social system, residues, and equilibrium are integrally connected in Pareto's general sociology. Equilibrium is a logical and operative necessity of a system as Pareto conceives it. Residues function to maintain social equilibrium by acting to resolve social forces. (For further reference see pars. 2067–78, 2203–2236.)	Equilibrium has a value connotation to the human relationists in that the administrator functions to maintain equilibrium and thereby preserve social values of the co-operative system (ref. B, p. 193).
4. The functions of language	**4. The functions of language**
Language to Pareto is simply a vehicle for expressing (reflecting) logical and nonlogical actions in terms of words. (See Index-Summary of the Theorems, pp. 1927–30.)	The human relationists talk of language as functioning in logicoexperimental, emotive, and daydreaming capacities. Logicoexperimental language is associated with logical forms of behavior; emotive language is connected with nonlogical behavior (ref. B, pp. 88–92).
5. The circulation of the elite	**5. The circulation of the elite**
The elite is defined by Pareto as the ruling class in society. The circulation of the elite is a process whereby the quality of this class is maintained. The function of the elite class is to provide imaginative leadership. (See pars. 247?–85).	Mayo made much of this concept. He considered the function of the elite as maintaining equilibrium through successfully dealing with problems associated with gaining greater human collaboration. Mayo considered the elite of his time (1933) as the "elite of yesterday." To handle modern problems, he felt, the present elite must circulate and be replaced by those more capable of administering human situations (ref. D, chap. VIII).

* The references noted in discussing the five parallels should be taken as suggestive, not exhaustive. Space does not permit cross references among the human relationists themselves or elaborate cross references between the human relationists and Pareto.

† Unless noted in the text of Table 2–1, all references to Pareto are made in terms of his paragraph numbers. The source used is the American edition translated and edited by Arthur Livingston. See Vilfredo Pareto, *The Mind and Society* (New York: Harcourt, Brace and Co., 1935).

‡ The key for references to the human relationists is as follows:
Ref. A: F. J. Roethlisberger and William J. Dickson, *Management and the Worker* (Cambridge: Harvard University Press, 1939; seventh printing, 1956).
Ref. B: F. J. Roethlisberger, *Management and Morale* (Cambridge: Harvard University Press, 1941, twelfth printing, 1956).
Ref. C: T. N. Whitehead, *The Industrial Worker* (Cambridge: Harvard University Press, 1938), Vol. I.
Ref. D: Elton Mayo, *The Human Problems of an Industrial Civilization* (2nd ed.; Boston: Graduate School of Business Administration, Harvard University, 1946).

tributed the human aspects of a management philosophy. The concept of the administrator evolved from a merger of these routes.

Two sets of skills are needed by an administrator. The first is composed of those skills which enable him to practice competently such functions as planning, organizing, and controlling. These functions include the human element, of course. But people in the light of these functions are only one of a number of productive factors which must be co-ordinated for the administrator to be effective in achieving the organization's objectives.

The second set includes those skills uncovered by the findings of the human relations experiments at the Hawthorne plant. The conclusions of these experiments focused on the administrator as a motivator of people. To be adequate in this capacity the administrator needs to be equipped with more than the "logical" skills inherent in the functions of planning, organizing, and controlling. Additionally, the administrator has to view the organization as a system of relationships. He has to approach, concretely and with a clinical attitude, such matters as the informal organization, communication, status, social and psychological needs of employees, and social roles and personality. *In short, the administrator has to be an expert in understanding and handling the variety of technical and human relationships in an organization's social system.*

A LOOK BACK

This chapter has reviewed over 100 years of history—roughly, from 1832 to 1940. It is a history of a search for philosophy, values, and techniques to be used by management in governing its relations with employees. It is also a history of an evolution in management thought regarding human motivation. There is quite a contrast between Babbage's and Ure's approach to motivation compared with the findings of the Hawthorne researchers,

Building on the scientific management movement, Jones' prediction of the professionalization of management began to materialize in the 1930's. Along with the professionalization trend came management philosophies oriented toward the social ethic. The concept of the administrator and his human skills amply demonstrates the impact of the social ethic on management thought. The administrative notion was in large part a product of a search for values to offset the collision effect, in the same way as scientific management was an early approach to this same problem. Such terms as plans, co-ordination, leadership, the human factor, teamwork, collaboration, social system, equilibrium, and so on are symbolic of a philosophy reflecting an ethic rooted in a social value system.

The social ethic grew vigorously because the collision effect did not abate in the 1930's. The ascendancy of the professional manager was an unparalleled event. In the face of growing technical and human problems he had to prove himself not only from the standpoint of his company but also to society in general. The new manager had to emphasize peace and harmony in the industrial system. Only in this way would business make a positive contribution to a society characterized by proximity and dependency.

Contemporary human relations is an outgrowth of the past. But it has been a fruitful past because the human relations point of view is firmly grounded in modern management philosophy. The next chapter deals with modern human relations in terms of its assumptions and perspective.

REVIEW QUESTIONS

1. What assumptions did Babbage and Ure make regarding human motivation? Who did they rely on for these assumptions? How did these assumptions influence the philosophy of the scientific management pioneers?

2. Identify and explain the objectives of the scientific management movement.

3. Distinguish between the philosophy of scientific management and its mechanisms.

4. Discuss the role of standardization in the scientific management scheme.

5. In what ways did the scientific management pioneers relate scientific management to national welfare and prosperity?

6. "Scientific management was in some respects a crude human relations movement." Evaluate. How was scientific management a manifestation of the social ethic?

7. Discuss the transitions in American business which gave rise to new directions in management thought in the 1930's.

8. What factors contributed to the "professionalization" of management? How did the "business plan" and new approaches to organization theory relate to the professionalization movement?

9. Outline the main contributions of the human relations movement to management thought.

10. Discuss the parallels between the framework of the human relationists and Paretian analysis.

11. What is the concept of the administrator which emerged from the evolution of management thought?

SUPPLEMENTARY READINGS

BARNARD, CHESTER I. *The Functions of the Executive,* Part IV. Cambridge: Harvard University Press, 1938.

BURNHAM, JAMES. *The Managerial Revolution,* chaps. 6–7, 13. New York: The John Day Co., 1941.

DAVIS, RALPH C. *Industrial Organization and Management,* chaps. 1, 3, 4. New York: Harper and Bros., 1939.

GANTT, H. L. *Industrial Leadership.* New Haven: Yale University Press, 1916.

GILBRETH, L. M. *The Psychology of Management.* New York: Sturgis and Walton Co., 1914.

JONES, EDWARD D. *Industrial Leadership and Executive Ability.* New York: The Engineering Magazine Co., 1920.

KNOX, JOHN D. "Sociological Theory and Industrial Sociology," *Social Forces,* March, 1955, pp. 240–44.

MAYO, ELTON. *The Human Problems of an Industrial Civilization.* 2d ed. Boston: The Graduate School of Business Administration, Harvard University, 1946.

ROETHLISBERGER, F. J., AND DICKSON, WILLIAM J. *Management and the Worker,* chaps. 24, 25. 11th printing. Cambridge: Harvard University Press, 1956.

TAYLOR, FREDERICK W. *Scientific Management,* pp. 23–33 in the "Testimony." New York: Harper and Bros., 1947.

CHAPTER 3

A Critical View of the Modern Human Relations Movement

HUMAN relations could incorporate everything or nothing, depending on management's point of view. Nearly all matters of concern to management would fall into the area of human relations if the mere presence of the "human element" is the only criterion for selecting a perspective. Or there is nothing for management in human relations if the field is just a neat batch of platitudes and slogans.

Human relations has to be associated with business in a practical and useful way if management is to derive benefits from it. This chapter is a critical analysis of the field of human relations. It begins with a straightforward presentation of an operational definition of human relations for the purpose of establishing a common orientation to the subject.

AN OPERATIONAL DEFINITION OF HUMAN RELATIONS

The following definition of human relations was offered in Chapter 1. It is pertinent now to consider this definition in depth.

Human relations is a process of effective motivation of individuals in a given situation in order to achieve a balance of objectives which will yield greater human satisfaction and help accomplish company goals.

This definition has four parts:

1. The process of effective motivation.
2. The given situation.
3. The balance of objectives.
4. The human satisfaction and the accomplishment of company goals.

Each of these elements is discussed below. Some aspects of the definition are given rather cursory treatment because they are subjects for more extensive analysis in later chapters.

Human Relations as a Process of Effective Motivation of Individuals

Motivation is a management function. It stimulates people to accomplish company goals. As a management function, the motivation process aims at gaining desired results through human effort. The motivational approach has to be selected and applied as the result of a manager's evaluation of an individual's propensity, feeling, or attitude toward his part in the accomplishment of organizational objectives. Two limiting cases may be identified in this respect. The first case is that people willingly and spontaneously pursue organizational objectives. The second is that people have to be induced to pursue these goals.

The first case is another way of stating the idea of mutuality of interests. In the last chapter it was found that people do not always view their own interests in the light of organizational interests. Ideally, if mutuality of interests existed the motivation of people could be achieved without much conscious effort by management. People would be self-motivating.

The second case is however, more pertinent in the discussion of motivation. Stated simply, in most cases management must consciously strive to motivate people. Motivation is a job to be done, not an outcome automatically obtained. *The essence of motivation is stimulating people to action toward the accomplishment of objectives which may or may not be compatible with their own objectives.*

Management has at its disposal two categories of action-producing methods which take the form of *positive* and *negative* incentives. Positive incentives to action, commonly called "positive motivation," involve the cultivation of a co-operative attitude among subordinates so that organization goals will be striven for with whole-hearted acceptance and approval. Numerous techniques promote positive motivation. Two obvious ones are participation and democratic leadership.[1]

Stimulating people to action through fear is the foundation of negative incentive or "negative motivation." This type of motivation is based on the fact that often people will work toward the stated organizational objective because they have no other *reasonable* alternative, not because they are convinced of the goal's inherent good or value. What an employee considers a "reasonable alternative" is purely an individual matter—the fear of disciplinary action, ranging from a simple reprimand to loss of a job, may be a sufficient negative motivating force to cause the individual to move in the directions established by the company. Put another way, negative motivation forces the individual to make a selection between two undesirable alternatives. Theoretically, he will select the least undesirable. So if losing one's job is more undesirable than pursuing an unpleasant company project the individual will grit his teeth and work toward completion of the project.

Negative motivation has many shadings; another one lies in the area of leadership. Unilateral or authoritarian leadership frequently has been

---

[1] For another approach to positive motivation see Manley Howe Jones *Executive Decision Making* (Homewood, Ill.: Richard D. Irwin, Inc., 1957), pp. 101–7.

interpreted as connoting negativism. The authoritarian leader does not invite participation in decision making, either in setting objectives or in determining means for achieving the objectives. Instead, the leader sets the goals and spells out the course of action to achieve the goals without any reference to group opinion. In a leadership situation such as this the element of fear as described above may be so deeply submerged in superior-subordinate relationships as not to be of great significance. Negative motivation in this sense is simply the use of authoritarian leadership. It is the opposite of positive leadership which applies participation and a democratic decision-making climate.

Some fairly complex problems of values are connected with these two aspects of motivation. These problems turn on the results management seeks and on the criteria used for measuring the success of one motivational method versus the other. If the criteria are human happiness and job satisfaction it would be fair to say that positive motivation is appropriate in most situations. If success, however, is measured in terms of productivity and efficiency, the selection of the motivational method is merely a practical matter; the technique chosen logically must be the one which produces the greatest output. It is a fortunate by-product if this technique increases employee satisfaction also.

Research seems to show that management can have its cake and eat it too. Numerous studies indicate positive motivational policies and techniques produce not only greater human satisfaction but also higher productivity. In one research study, Likert concludes, ". . . *pressure-oriented, threatening, punitive management yields lower productivity, higher costs, increased absence, and less employee satisfaction than supportive, employee-centered management which uses group methods of supervision coupled with high-performance expectations.*"[2]

Situational Analysis

Part of an executive's job is understanding and dealing with the environment where human relations problems occur. A manager must handle each human problem on its own merits and within the context of the situation. Slogans are not adequate to facilitiate leadership or to solve human relations problems. An executive faced with a specific human problem must use human means for solving it. The particular means he selects are the result of careful analysis and evaluation of the situation confronting him.

Situational analysis is frequently viewed as a drab methodological procedure, but intelligent action is impossible without it. Following are several questions which form a usable guide to situational analysis.

---

[2] Rensis Likert, "Measuring Organizational Performance," *Harvard Business Review*, March–April, 1958, p. 45 (author's itals.).

Questions to Focus the Analysis

1. What is the problem?
2. Who is involved in the problem?
3. Is it a problem of individual motivation, or collective (group) behavior?

Questions to Ask about the Employee and Yourself

1. What are the employee's attitudes and motives in this case?
2. Are the attitudes of the employee self-generated or have they resulted primarily from the influence of his associates on the job?
3. How do I feel about the employee's motives and attitudes?

Questions to Ask about the Work Situation

1. What factors on the job situation are important to the problem *other* than the employee's attitudes and motives and his fellow workers? (For example, supervision; the physical conditions of the job.)
2. How does company policy affect the problems and the decisions which may be rendered to solve the problems?
3. Will any outside organizations affect the problem? (For example, a union; other companies; professional associations.)

These questions are summarized and placed in relation to an approach toward human relations decision making in Figure 3–1. Note that

FIGURE 3–1

SITUATIONAL ANALYSIS AND HUMAN RELATIONS PROBLEM SOLVING

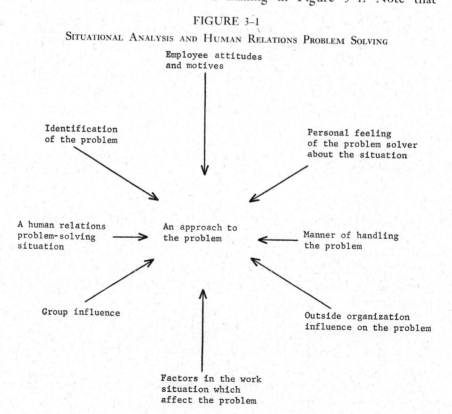

answers to these questions suggest an *approach* to handling the situation. This in turn should give rise to a method. While situational analysis, properly used, will offer suggestions for an approach and a method in dealing with human problems, *it cannot guarantee results.*

Using human relations tools for solving a particular problem is a matter of skillful application by the executive. It is an art. One might study painting for years and never create a masterpiece, let alone an acceptable painting. In much the same way, situational analysis will help an executive diagnose a problem and find a route to take for a solution, but it will not directly improve the executive in the art of interpersonal relations.[3]

Balance of Objectives

The subjects of the social system and balance were introduced in Chapter 1. It was observed there that a resolution of forces is a logical necessity in the concept of a system. Any system is comprised of mutually dependent elements. In an organization, four basic elements are present.

1. The *individuals* in the organization.
2. The *jobs* being performed.
3. The *informal* organizations (cliques or friendship groups).
4. The *formal* organizations (the over-all structure of the company which relates the specific jobs, departments, and divisions to one another).

From this, a definition of balance is derived easily. *Balance is a condition in a company where there is accord among the objectives of individuals, the informal organization, jobs, and the formal organization.* The relationships among the four elements in the definition can be shown in a simple way as illustrated in Figure 3–2. The subject of balance is discussed further in chapter 11.

FIGURE 3–2

PATTERNS OF BALANCE

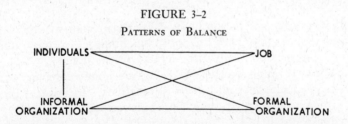

Human Satisfaction and the Accomplishment of Company Goals

The fourth part of the definition sets out the objectives of human relations. Probably one of the most comprehensive reviews of human

---

[3] For a more extensive treatment of situational analysis see Lowell Julliard Carr, *Situational Analysis* (New York: Harper and Bros., 1948); and Paul Pigors and Charles A. Myers, *Personnel Administration* (New York: McGraw-Hill Book Co., 1956), chap. 4.

relations goals is found in a series of papers submitted by members of the International Committee for Scientific Management.[4]

Objectives for human relations expressed in the reports of the various participating countries fall into two broad categories. The first goal, emphasized in the Swiss report, is that the product of human relations should be employee *satisfaction on the job*. The second representative objective is stressed in the Dutch report which recognizes contentment and happiness in work as important, but also notes the necessity for human relations to promote another objective of parallel significance— *increased production*.

The objectives of employee satisfaction and increased productivity are not fundamentally opposed. Indeed, as the Dutch report states, the productivity and human-satisfaction objectives supplement each other. It would be naive, however, to overlook the fact that the basis of many business' human problems stem from a conflict between these two objectives. Methods which improve on-the-job efficiency may cause a decline in the satisfactions employees obtain from their jobs, and vice versa.

Frequently management must compromise these objectives to meet the practical demands of the situation. The long-run stability of the company is determined by short-run, day-to-day decisions. Management cannot shortchange the interests of owners or customers for the sake of a permissive, employee-centered company environment. At the same time, however, management has to set a leadership pattern which will create, overall, a positive atmosphere where people will work.

At any one period, and in some one department, it is possible to find "too much" human relations or an overemphasis on efficiency and productivity. In proper perspective these "maladjustments" are probably part of the exigencies of management which may be adjusted through time.

People who make a career in business are usually fairly "savvy" about the facts of business life. They are not so much impressed by "too much" human relations or "too much" productivity orientation at any one point in time. They are impressed, however, by the honest attempts of management to reconcile the satisfaction-productivity objectives within the structure of a realistic philosophy of employee relations.

The clinical orientation of this definition is evident. Human relations, as a part of management philosophy, is action oriented. Its purpose is to get the most and the best out of people in areas of business where administrative expertness in handling human affairs is highly critical.

But management does quite a bit more than "dealing with people."

---

[4] For a digested report see Earl G. Planty (ed.), "Management Methods of Improving Human Relations: A Report of the 10th International Management Congress," *Personnel*, May, 1954, pp. 507–16.

Fifty years ago this statement would be considered just as simple-minded as it is today. However, it has to be made because the current emphasis on human relations in management literature, college courses, and executive-development programs might lead one to believe that the only thing management does is to try to get along with people.

The purpose of the next section is to set out in the form of an uncomplicated model a view of the basic elements which comprise an organized enterprise, and then to show those elements in which human relations activities have a major role.

THE PERSPECTIVE OF HUMAN RELATIONS IN TERMS OF THE BUSINESS ELEMENTS

The business elements in the model diagrammed in Figure 3–3 are universal to all organized enterprises. The model is an effort to put these universal organizational factors into a logical arrangement. Thus, at the outset of this discussion it should be observed that the *right* to do business is forthcoming from *organized society*, and the *purpose* of business is the *satisfaction of human needs*. However, the rights and purposes of business are not actually elements of business. They are the beginning and end points, the reasons for being, of business. The following outline identifies and defines the elements themselves.

Objectives

Objectives are general goals or values sought by the organization. Defined, the *major* business objectives are:

Primary	Collateral
1. *Profit*—pecuniary returns after costs, either retained by the company or distributed to owners.	3. *Social*—general values created by the company in the interest of the public from which no monetary reward is anticipated.
2. *Service*—the obligation of a company to provide the values in a product which the customer has the right to expect, consistent with the price paid.	4. *Personal*—the obligation to create an atmosphere conducive to satisfying employee needs.

The objectives of *economy and efficiency* are subordinate to the above major objectives; they relate to the effective operation of the organization so that the major objectives can be achieved in an optimum fashion.

Leadership

Objectives are accomplished through leadership which can assume three forms in an organization:

FIGURE 3–3
BASIC BUSINESS ELEMENTS

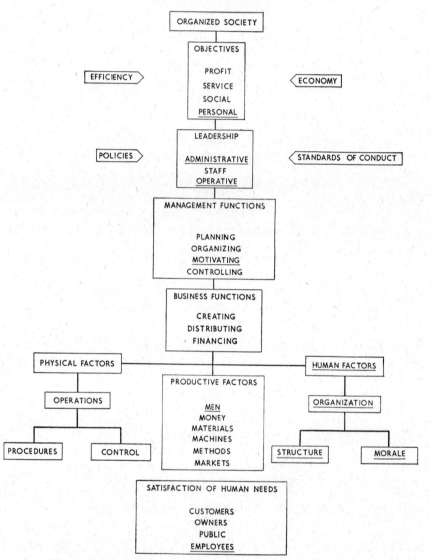

Source: Adapted from a basic business factor chart developed by members of the Management Department of Indiana University.

1. *Administrative*—the management of other managers in a line organization. This form of leadership extends from the president down to the first line of supervision.

2. *Staff*—while the staff includes some elements of line leadership, in this case staff leadership refers to the effective performance of advisory and facilitative services for the line.

3. *Operative*—the management of employees at the point of the creation of goods or services. This form of leadership is often referred to as first-line supervision.

The activities of leaders are guided and circumscribed by organizational policies and standards of conduct—ethics.

Management Functions

Management functions give leadership direction. They are a convenient way of describing the activities performed by management in the content of its job.

1. *Planning*—considering and establishing related facts in advance to achieve desired results. The essence of planning is the selection of alternatives and standards to set and guide a future course of action.
2. *Organizing*—establishing the proper relationships among work, people, and the work place.
3. *Motivating*—stimulating people to action toward objectives through the application of sanctions (incentives).
4. *Controlling*—insuring that the action taken proceeds according to previously established plans.

Business Functions

Management functions bring life to the functions of a business. These functions are called organic because they are so vital that the business ceases to exist unless they are performed.

The Productive Factors

A business creates, distributes, and finances goods and services through the media of management co-ordination and direction of the productive factors. The physical and human factors, which include men, money, materials, methods, machines, and markets, are merged in a company by organization and operations.

The Satisfaction of Human Needs

The direction which all business activity takes is the satisfaction of the needs of people. It must be noted that the objectives listed as the first element in the business plan coincide with those categories of people interested in the functioning of a business. For example:

Service objective—customers.
Profit objective—owners.
Social objective—public.
Personal objective—employees.

Human Relations and the Business Elements

The business elements described in the foregoing outline and illustrated in Figure 3-3 clearly show that an organization is a combination of human and nonhuman factors and processes. The factors underlined in Figure 3–3 are those that most directly involve the application of human skills by management. They are the personal objective, leadership guided by personal and human relations policies, the management function of motivating, and the human factors in organization.

Such matters as general policy making, planning, organizing, and controlling do not exclude the human factor, of course. The point is that to accomplish effectively the nonunderlined factors in the business plan more is required than the use of human skills; technical skills are required, and overwhelmingly at times.

A case is not being built for a conflict between technical skills and human skills. Quite to the contrary, an executive needs both. The relative degree of importance to him of human skills versus technical skills depends upon what function he performs in the organization. Ideally, the executive should be competent in both skill areas, because the need for their use is apparent in practically every part of the business organization. *The skillful executive is one who can blend the human factors with the nonhuman so that the organization can meet its objectives without a loss of dignity among the employees serving it.*

To have meaning in terms of its clinical applications in business, human relations as an area of research and practice must be based on assumptions regarding behavior and motivation. The next section considers the key assumptions of human relations.

THE PERSPECTIVE OF HUMAN RELATIONS
IN TERMS OF ITS ASSUMPTIONS

It is a matter of record that the assumptions drawn from the "economic man" hypothesis of human motivation and behavior affected management practice in the realm of employee relations policies. In the same way, different assumptions, following the human relations line, also affect management practice. Therefore, it is necessary to isolate the assumptions of modern human relations in order to understand fully their implications in management practice.

The General Assumption of Human Relations

The general assumption states that human relations is an interdisciplinary subject; but what is more, human relations is uniquely greater than the sum of the disciplines which make it up. The benefits which flow from an interdisciplinary approach to understanding the behavior of people qualify human relations to solve problems of human conflict more adequately.

The whole being greater than the sum of its parts is a *Gestalt* or configurationist method of analysis. The study of a painting serves as an example of the meaning of this theory. When one looks at an oil painting from a distance, say of one foot, all that is seen is a mass of paint blobs and a certain texture. But as the viewer moves back the painting assumes a structure, a form, a contour. The configuration which emerges as the subject of the canvas is, indeed, more than the sum of the blobs of paint which make it up. Paint and canvas are only the media through which art is expressed.

The configurationist approach is the central feature of the general assumption of human relations stated above. Human relations amalgamates behavioral science disciplines and focuses their theories, data, methods, and findings *in combination* on human problems. The problem-solving virtue of human relations may be expressed as "two plus two equals five." The extra "one" in the formula comes from the special twist that human relations problem solving gets by using the inter-disciplinary method. Human relations, as a result, contributes different and singularly useful insights into human problems. Human relations attempts to overcome the shortsightedness of specialists working independently on a problem.[5]

The disciplines of anthropology, political science, sociology, psychology, and social-psychology make up the backbone of human relations. But this list is expanding through the incorporation of other fields. Semantics and cybernetics are being utilized to improve the communication processes in organizations.[6] The human relations over-tones of the decision-making process are being studied not only by behavioral scientists but also by mathematicians and philosophers. The traditional theories of economics are being reinterpreted in the light of more advanced knowledge in the behavioral sciences.[7] Even the literature of business fiction is being analyzed to gather observations on the behavior of people in business from a heretofore untapped source.[8]

No attempt has been made so far to associate the general assumption of human relations to business in particular. This omission is intentional because the scope of the assumption encompasses management in many forms of organized endeavors. The general assumption of human relations is appropriately applied to government, organized labor, and the neighborhood garden club.

The general assumption is a point of departure. From the standpoint

---

[5] A statement and criticism of the interdisciplinary assumption may be found in William H. Knowles, *Personnel Management*, (New York: American Book Co., 1955), pp. 102–6.

[6] Norbert Weiner, *Cybernetics* (New York: John Wiley & Sons, 1948).

[7] Herbert A. Simon, "Theories of Decision-Making in Economics and Behavioral Science," *American Economic Review*, June 1959, pp. 253–83.

[8] A. D. Van Nostrand, "Fiction's Flagging Man of Commerce," and "After Marquand, the Deluge," *English Journal*, January, 1959 and February, 1959.

of business management practice, however, certain action-designed assumptions are especially crucial. These assumptions, taken up next, are
again not the exclusive property of management in business enterprises.
But they have fallen on the most willing ears in this sphere of organized activity.

The Action-Designed Assumptions

Action-designed assumptions are necessary for management to cultivate a realistic human relations philosophy from which operating objectives and policies may be derived. The eight operating assumptions
described—uncritically—below appear to represent a consensus among
writers on effective measures to improve and promote successful management human relations practice.

1. *Good human relations practice is the product of the manager
using experience, intuition, and interdisciplinary generalizations to guide
him in the action he takes.*[9] This assumption is the essence of the
clinical dimension of human relations. It is the most inclusive; the remaining assumptions are more or less corollaries or tools for implementing
good human relations practice.

2. Employee *participation* is often essential to higher productivity and
greater human satisfaction. Employees will be happier if they have something to say in affairs that affect their destinies on the job. Companies
have applied this assumption in the forms of allowing operative employees a chance to engage in the decision-making process on their
jobs,[10] and in development schemes which promote more "involvement"
of managers in the problems of their company.[11]

Another aspect of the participation assumption is the leadership climate
which elicits participation. *Democratic leadership,* where leader seeks out
group advice, is considered essential for establishing a "permissive" environment in which participation can flourish.[12] For purposes of contrast, democratic leadership can be compared with authoritarian
leadership characterized by unilateral decisions on the part of the manager.

3. The *role* assumption stems from the variety of demands an individual faces at work.[13] Two general categories of roles are identifiable:

---

[9] F. J. Roethlisberger, *Management and Morale* (Cambridge: Harvard University
Press, 1941), pp. 138–41.

[10] Lester Coch and John R. P. French, Jr., "Overcoming Resistance to Change,"
Human Relations, 1948, pp. 512–32.

[11] William B. Given, Jr., *Bottom-up Management* (New York: Harper and Bros.,
1949).

[12] A. Bavelas, cited in N. R. F. Maier, *Psychology in Industry* (Boston: Houghton
Mifflin Co., 1946), pp. 264–66.

[13] For a more comprehensive treatment of the subject of roles see Mason Haire's
comments in Arthur Kornhauser, Robert Dubin, and Arthur M. Ross (eds.), *Industrial Conflict* (New York: McGraw-Hill Book Co., 1954), pp. 381–82.

the "job-oriented role" and the "informal group-oriented role." In a sociological sense roles are institutionally determined—for example, the role of the company president, the role of the staff specialist, the role of the foreman, and the role of the operative employee. Social psychologists approach the subject of role in terms of the individual's niche and function in small groups.

From the standpoint of the executive the operating aspect of the role concept is linked to his understanding of an individual's behavior as a product of the demands made on him from the different directions in a business organization. These demands can be called expectation forces. Thus an individual's behavior is partially a result of the expectations of the job and the company, and also the expectations of those with whom the individual associates at work. The first group of expectations may be termed *formal;* the second group is frequently *informal,* which means the expectations are social and not necessarily part of the demands of the job itself.

4. *Communication* has often been referred to as the nervous system of the organization. Anything which impairs the functioning of the communication system will limit organizational effectiveness in terms of the accomplishment of business objectives. The "good communication" assumption is not entirely in the province of human relations. It may, in some cases, be a technical or engineering matter relatively immune from human manipulation. However, communication is largely a human problem, subject to human foibles. Therefore, good communication has become the main point of attention for theories and practices designed to unclog communication channels.[14]

5. The next assumption is that *teamwork* is an indispensable element of management practice for organizational survival. The substance of teamwork is put formally by Simon as follows: ". . . in a cooperative pattern both participants prefer the same set of consequences; hence if each anticipates the other correctly, they will both act so as to secure these consequences. In a competitive pattern, the optimum outcome for the first participant is not the optimum for the second. Hence the realization by the first participant of the consequence he prefers will frustrate the other participant. . . ."[15]

Thus, teamwork is a matter of mutual anticipation and agreement on goals. Teamwork and co-operation go hand in hand; one stimulates the other in a situation where employees are striving to obtain the same set of desired outcomes.

---

[14] The need for good communication is emphasized in Keith Davis, *Human Relations in Business* (New York: McGraw-Hill Book Co., 1957), chaps. 13, 14.

[15] Herbert Simon, *Administrative Behavior* (New York: Macmillan Company, 1954), p. 72. Another approach to teamwork may be found in Peter Drucker, *The Practice of Management* (New York: Harper and Bros., 1954), pp. 170–78.

6. Man is *diversely motivated;* he has a hierarchy of needs which are quite changeable. This assumption is the opposite of the money-and-motivation, economic-incentive notion. Employee work satisfaction, according to this assumption, is not entirely money directed.[16] People derive work satisfactions from job accomplishment, recognition, participation, and the like. Very frequently employee morale and contentment are based not on the paycheck but on the social and psychological

TABLE 3–1

TRADITIONAL VERSUS HUMAN RELATIONS ASSUMPTIONS CONCERNING HUMAN BEHAVIOR

Traditional Assumptions	*Human Relations Assumptions*
	1. *From psychology*
	a) Man is diversely motivated.
	b) Man is not always rational; he often behaves nonlogically in terms of the rewards he seeks from work.
	c) Man is interdependent, and individual behavior frequently must be explained in terms of the social setting at work.
	d) An executive can be trained in "good" human relations practice.
1. People try to satisfy one class of need at work—*the economic need.*	2. *From sociology*
	a) The social environment on the job affects and is affected by those in the situation and not only by management.
2. There is an automatic sharing of goals in an organization; that is, no conflict exists between individual and organizational objectives—*mutuality of interests.*	*b)* The clique or informal organization is a reality, and it affects and is affected by the formal organization.
	c) Job roles are more complex than job descriptions suggest because of personal and social factors inherent in job functions. They are usually excluded in job analysis techniques, however.
3. People try to maximize rewards—*rationality.*	*d)* The organization must be realistically viewed as a social system composed of numerous interacting parts.
	3. *From social psychology*
	a) People are not always anxious to see their objectives in the light of organizational objectives. People have to be influenced.
	b) Communication channels carry information relating both to the logical-economic functioning of the company *and* to the feelings and sentiments of the people who work in the company.
	c) Participation in the decision-making process has a positive effect on morale and productivity.
	d) Teamwork is essential for co-operation and sound technical decisions.

Adapted from Leavitt's comments on organization theory in Harold J. Leavitt, *Managerial Psychology* (Chicago: The University of Chicago Press, 1958), pp. 291–303.

---

[16] For descriptive illustrations of the point see William F. Whyte, *Money and Motivation* (New York: Harper and Bros., 1955).

conditions of employment. This assumption questions the core of the traditional theory of human behavior, which assumes economic rationality and the maximization of monetary rewards by people at work.

7. The seventh assumption is that the plant or office is a *social system*. Viewing the work situation as a network of variable and interrelated elements is a major feature of modern human relations practice for the executive.[17] The executive must be a relationship expert to maintain the balance (equilibrium) of the social system in which he is involved.

8. The capstone assumption states that *executive skills in human relations practice can be developed*. This assumption means that the executive's clinical ability can be improved so that he will be equipped to handle concrete human problems successfully. The executive can be trained to be aware, sensitive, and competent to cope with the human problems of the organization.

Listings always present the danger that each item will be regarded as a discrete, independent unit. This is far from true in the case of the above assumptions. They are all tied into each other, and *together* make a fairly complete picture of modern human relations. Table 3–1 summarizes the operating assumptions relating them to the particular behavioral science area which has contributed to their development. The table also compares the modern assumptions regarding human behavior to the more traditional assumptions.

The general assumption and the action-designed assumptions of human relations have been presented without critical comment. Each assumption could be shown to have shortcomings and inconsistencies. But a detailed analysis is not within the scope of this chapter and will have to be delayed until later in the book. However, for the sake of perspective two rather general criticisms of human relations are considered next.

Modern Human Relations: a Case of Introversion and Shortsightedness?

Introversion. If the assumptions just discussed are treated as a whole they add up to guides for management action bordered by the rather rigid limits of the day-to-day problems with which a manager must deal. Taken as such, the assumptions are a useful way to view a *certain class of problems*. These are the problems a manager faces when he turns inward to minimize conflict, to motivate, and to promote co-operation among his subordinates in the organization.

According to some writers this treatment of the plant or office workforce "community" is not adequate for solving conflict problems which arise from larger institutional settings. Sheppard, for one, is severely critical of the failure to treat unions as a fundamental determinant of in-

---

[17] This assumption was discussed more extensively in Chapters 1 and 2, but it bears repeating here. The basic character of the assumption was noted by the researchers in the Hawthorne experiments. F. J. Roethlisberger and William J. Dickson, *Management and the Worker* (Cambridge: Harvard University Press, 1939), chap. 24.

dustrial harmony, because of the "tight little social system" attitude expressed in the human relations assumptions.[18]

Sheppard has four indictments of modern human relations which are profitable to summarize.

1. Human relations is a "systematic underestimation . . . of economic and political determinants of industrial peace, either within, or external to, the factory."

2. Human relations restricts the area of observation to the factory "as if in a vacuum." It does not look beyond the social system of the organization for causes of harmony or conflict.

3. Minimization of conflict by the employer or manager does not come from redistribution of decision-making power or concessions to employee demands but from the application of social (manipulative) skills. The direction of manipulation is to get employees "to reinterpret their complaints in such a way as to eliminate the company as the object of hostility. . . ."

4. Thus, industrial relations in the human relations perspective reduces itself to "person-to-person relations, primarily between worker and worker, worker and supervisor." The main source of conflict is found at this level.[19]

Sheppard's criticism has a good deal of universality to it. Human relations could be misleading unless its introverted nature is recognized. For example, the agonies of assimilating recently migrated racial or national groups into large urban areas could involve numerous conflict situations on the job. These problems are not likely to be solved by application of human relations skills in the limited sphere of the work environment; job conflicts may be merely symptomatic reactions to the foreign and frequently antagonistic life in which the migrants find themselves.

Human relations is not a palliative for all human problems. The perspective of modern human relations in business is not readily adaptable to settling problems of the broader variety just described.

Shortsightedness. Evidence relating to the shortsightedness of human relations assumptions can be assembled from three points.

First, Peter Drucker made a devastating attack on human relations when he observed that *it lacks adequate focus on work.* Human relations places undue emphasis on interpersonal relations and the group. It is not the job that determines employee happiness, only the employee's relations to fellow workers, according to Drucker's interpretation of human relations. He feels, however, that the functions people perform in an organization *are* major determinants of happiness and that analysis of work and job is the sensible place to begin developing positive motivations for the people working in the organization.[20]

Second, *modern human relations tends to neglect the economic di-*

---

[18] Harold L. Sheppard, "Approaches to Conflict in American Industrial Sociology," *British Journal of Sociology*, December, 1954, pp. 324–41.

[19] *Ibid.*, p. 327.

[20] Drucker, *op. cit.*, pp. 278–80.

mension of work satisfaction. This shortcoming of human relations is in part a result of a number of research studies which have "proven" that the modern employee does not place wages at the top of his hierarchy of needs.[21] In other words, social and psychological satisfactions have been found to be more important than money to employees.

The primacy of social and psychological needs is not very surprising, given a generally high level of income coupled with the fact that large numbers of employees have their wages and salaries relatively fixed for fairly long durations. When the economic needs of employees are translated into union contracts or employment agreements for executives not much can be done about wages until the time arrives for a renegotiation of the economic terms of employment. Thus, it would seem natural for individuals to be inclined during periods of wage stability to stress less tangible job satisfactions. This is much like saying man does not live by bread alone, once he has bread.

Economic man should not be buried too deeply. Whyte in this regard brings up his "face-value" theory of human behavior.[22] Essentially, this theory is that people often do what they do because of perfectly rational reasons and not because of deep complexes or subconscious motives. Thus, workers go out on strike because they want more money, not because of a Freudian reaction against the father symbol of authority.

Human relations offers numerous psychological and sociological tools for probing human behavior. But ill-conceived sociological or psychological explanations for conflict or human dissatisfaction may be just as dangerous as assuming that behavior is completely rational in an economic sense. Economic motivation is exceedingly strong, and in many cases economic explanations are quite appropriate for understanding human behavior.

The third cause of human relations shortsightedness is the structure of human relations research. Most of what is known empirically about human behavior at work is a product of human relations research at the operative or, at best, the first level of supervision in the company. Further, much human relations research has been done in the factory, in the military services, or in college classrooms using captive sophomore subjects. The findings of this research—some of which have been translated into generalizations—are considered satisfactory explanations of behavior at higher levels of management. Little effort has been expended to determine whether or not these generalizations *are* appropriate.[23]

---

[21] For example, see "What Do Workers Want Most?" *The Management Review*, June, 1954, p. 362.

[22] William H. Whyte, Jr., *The Organization Man* (New York: Simon and Schuster, 1956), p. 40.

[23] For a discussion of the paucity of research into the behavioral patterns of management see Mason Haire, "Psychological Problems Relevant to Business and Industry," *Psychological Bulletin*, May, 1959, pp. 187–88.

It may certainly be assumed that people usually like to participate, be recognized, and feel a sense of accomplishment no matter what their job happens to be. But these conclusions, obtained from studies of non-managerial behavior, are not necessarily useful when an executive seeks to motivate subordinates who frequently are other managers, or perhaps engineers and scientists.[24]

Additionally, these studies are especially disappointing for the outside observer who wants to learn about managerial behavior. In this latter case, students of management may ask such questions as: how do managerial expectations and motivations differ from those of operative employees? How does the manager's view of himself condition the role he plays and the satisfaction he expects from his job? How do the structure and culture of a management group affect the decisions it makes? What can the data and methodologies of political science offer for an understanding of managerial behavior in large, bureaucratic-type organizations?

Research outside the management context cannot give satisfactory answers to these questions. The psychologists took a step forward when they stopped making generalities about people from the study of rats and started studying the people themselves. If human relations seeks generalizations about management these generalizations should come from the study of management.

In spite of its more apparent shortcomings, the field of human relations is accepted by many executives in a rather matter-of-fact way, simply because its clinical elements are valuable in management practice. But this observation provides little more than a pragmatic justification for the existence of a "human relations movement." Perhaps a more idealistic approach to the legitimacy of human relations is in order.

HUMAN RELATIONS AND THE DEVELOPMENT OF THE "WHOLE MAN"

Not long ago at an executive-development seminar the conference leader proposed to the men attending that management was obligated to develop the whole employee. The argument ran that management's responsibility toward employees did not end with the simple provision of tools, good wages, adequate leisure time, and proper training to perform jobs. Management must also be concerned with providing the type of environment conducive to extending each employee's scope beyond the narrow confines of the job he was performing. Management had to consider the moral, educational, psychological, and social well-being of the

---

[24] An illuminating article on the motivation of engineers and scientists may be found in L. E. Danielson, "Management's Relations with Engineers and Scientists," *Proceedings of the Industrial Relations Research Association*, 1957, pp. 314-21.

whole man. The employee needed to be treated as a "bio-psycho-spiritual organism."

This position was immediately challenged. Some conferees wondered if the conference leader had a very realistic view of superior-subordinate relationships. They asked if it were not enough for management to provide good tools and working conditions, decent wages, and sufficient time to enjoy a higher standard of living. After all, the comments ran, these are the things American management knows how to do best. Why try to convert managers to combination social workers, psychologists, ministers, and teachers?

The positions of the conference leader and those conferees questioning him were both rather extreme, but they do illustrate a point. Business is a fundamental institution in society, and management is the human instrumentality through which the institution is brought to life to serve a socially useful purpose. This purpose is to provide goods and services for the consuming public by the allocation of human, financial, and material resources into productive channels. The inescapable conclusion is that business still exists to perform an economic function in society.

Management is responsible for seeing that this function is carried out with a certain degree of dispatch consistent with the major objectives of the organization. Management may decide to adopt the human relations behavioral assumptions and tools in order to facilitate the accomplishment of economic goals; but this decision in no way changes the character of the business organization's reason for being. The introduction of a "human" approach toward the people in a company may simply be a result of a cold, calculated, economic decision on the part of the policy makers in the organization. As a character in a business novel puts it, speaking of a human relations program in his company, "It's the only form of practical Christianity I know that pays at least ten per cent."[25]

Naturally, these observations should not be taken as generalizations on management's motives for the promotion of good human relations. Indeed, management could stand behind the human relations program as both necessary for human dignity and the proper spiritual thing to do. *The motive depends on the aspiration.*

Human Relations Aspirational Levels

The motives underlying human relations practice can be found in any one—or their combination—of three aspirational levels: (1) the materialistic productive efficiency, (2) the humanistic, and (3) the theological. They are interpreted as follows.

The materialistic productive efficiency level of aspiration has already been implied in preceding sections. Its meaning is closely associated with

---

[25] Nigel Balchin, *Private Interests* (Boston: Houghton Mifflin Co., 1953), p. 5.

the practice of human relations as good business policy. Through the use of human relations, people are motivated to strive for the profit and service objectives. They are made willing and efficient contributors to the productive goals of the company. Since the result of most company activity is either directly or indirectly in the material order, this aspiration is termed materialistic.

The *humanistic* aspirational level is based on dignity. Human relations practice at this level is motivated primarily by the fact that the employee is a human being who deserves respect. The humanistic level is not primarily framed in terms of what the employee can or cannot contribute to the materialistic ends of the company.

The *theological* aspirational level has as its foundation the spiritual destiny of man. Human relations practice derived from this source stems from more than a personal dignity derived from being human. This aspirational level results from a belief that man is the ultimate achievement of creation; and, further, that man's stay on earth is temporary before receiving final judgment. The theological aspirational level is based in the Judeo-Christian ethic.

These aspirations can exist as levels, abstractly independent of one another. But more than likely they are tightly interwoven in an almost infinite variety of patterns.

An interpretation of the relationships among the aspirational levels could run as follows: a management philosophy which aspires for the materialistic level cannot hope to achieve the productive efficiency goal without recognizing the human dignity of all employees—the humanistic level. It is then just a step from this proposition to the next. Human dignity is firmly rooted in the Judeo-Christian tradition which places great weight on the worth of the individual and the brotherhood of man. Therefore, the theological attitude is that good human relations, motivated by Christian love, has divine approval.

Ordering the Aspirational Levels. In the traditions of Western culture, these aspirational levels have an order of importance or value. The lowest aspirational level is the materialistic. The next is the humanistic; and the highest is the theological. Thus, few, if any, management practices done in the name of productive efficiency could find justification if the outcome violates human dignity or is opposed to Judeo-Christian doctrine.

Though this observation is somewhat platitudinous it does bring up the acceptability of management practice if the conditions were reversed. Could management practice done in the name of human dignity or theological doctrine have acceptance and justification if such practice violates the productive efficiency aspiration?

The "Automaticity Notion." Few human relations practitioners have come to grips with the foregoing question. It is brushed away by the convenient "automaticity notion." This notion assumes that successful accomplishment at one aspirational level will yield desirable outcomes at another. For example, the scientific management pioneers felt that if the productive efficiency aspiration could be attained the humanistic aspiration could also be attained. Again, some human relationists believe that realizing the humanistic aspiration will go far toward achieving the productive efficiency aspiration. Or, finally, the theological aspiration automatically satisfies the humanistic aspirational level which, in turn, has positive effects on the productive efficiency level.

While this description of the automaticity notion has been oversimplified its implications are fairly evident. The scientific management pioneers in their approach to obtaining the goal of human collaboration have been branded by some as naive for thinking in terms of an equitable division of the economic surplus. But is it not just as naive to assume, as some modernists do, that a humanistic focus will necessarily result in productive efficiency?

A theory of an automatic relationship among the aspirational levels tends to distort the picture of the nature of management's function in society. When a conflict of choice occurs (human dignity *or* productive efficiency, Christian principles *or* materialistic expediency) a decision has to be made by management, and management has to accept the consequences of its decision. Heaven is the only place where all aspirational levels are mutually agreeable and consistent. One function of management is to choose goals from an aspirational level which will not always be compatible with alternative goals available in other aspirational levels. This is decision making.

From all of this, certain concluding observations can be drawn. The "whole man" approach asks management to operate on all aspirational levels at the same time. In addition to being outside the practical limits of human ability this demand also appears to be a misdirection of energy when viewed from the standpoint of other management jobs. Our society is specialized, and it is not management's primary role to make other managers and operative employees happy. Fortunately, or unfortunately as the case may be, human relations programs which are supposed to yield employee happiness are only justifiable if the true economic function of the business organization is not impaired.

The curious thing is that some people consider management responsible for the development of the "whole man" in the first place. The argument usually given is that work is a way of life; a man's most important (productive) years are spent on the job. Therefore, management should do what it can to extend an employee's range, to develop him into a better person.

One wonders how other institutions which also are supposed to make people better fit into this picture. Could it be that education, religion, or

even the family are so ineffectual that the necessity for human development must fall on management in business? If the answer to the question is
"yes" the assumptions of modern human relations should be reconsidered
and the conception of the business organization in terms of its objectives
and functions should be revolutionized. Indeed, the perspective of modern human relations would have to be changed from that of a tool to help
management achieve business ends to that of human relations as a major end
in itself.

Fortunately, business organizations have not acquired the character of
"total institutions" requiring management to fulfill all the "inmates' "
needs. Modern human relations is largely a product of the social ethic. It
is a value system aimed at the reduction of conflict and the motivation of
people in a dependent environment. Human relations as such is a logical
extension of management thought, because management must administer
complex, conflict-loaded situations. Human relations provides the intellectual and practical concepts and skills necessary to do the job.

All this is not to discount the higher levels of motivation management
might have in the practice of "good human relations." It is simply an admission that it is impossible to separate the concrete, practical advantages
of the sound administration of human affairs from the idealisms of human
dignity and spirituality. Management, of course, is conscious of these latter concerns because it participates in a culture which holds human dignity
and man's supernatural destiny as fundamental theses. But management
also has a functional economic obligation which stresses material objectives. And it is the fulfillment of this functional responsibility through
human effort that occupies management's immediate attention. So, in this
respect, the purpose of the next part of this book is the investigation of the
behavioral sciences in order to conceptualize their role and contribution to the management process.

REVIEW QUESTIONS

1. In what ways is the operational definition of human relations clinical and
action oriented?

2. How may the objectives of human relations given in the operational
definition conflict?

3. Discuss the functions of situational analysis and balance as administrative
tools.

4. Review and outline the basic business factors. Which of these factors appear to be most strategic for the application of human skills? Why does an
executive need to be competent in *both* human skills and technical skills?

5. "The general assumption of human relations has a *Gestalt* implication."
Discuss.

6. Outline the action-oriented assumptions of human relations.

7. Evaluate the criticisms of shortsightedness and introversion as they apply
to the human relations movement.

8. "The character of motives behind the use of human relations depends on an executive's level of aspiration." Discuss.

9. Evaluate the human relations notion of the development of the "whole man."

10. Discuss the nature of the automaticity notion.

SUPPLEMENTARY READINGS

CARR, JULLIARD. *Situational Analysis.* New York: Harper and Brothers, 1948.

DANIELSON, L. E. "Management's Relations with Engineers and Scientists," *Proceedings of the Industrial Relations Research Association,* 1957, pp. 314–21.

HAIRE, MASON. "Psychological Problems Relevant to Business and Industry," *Psychological Bulletin,* May, 1959, pp. 169–94.

LEAVITT, HAROLD J. *Managerial Psychology.* Chicago: The University of Chicago Press, 1958.

SHEPPARD, HAROLD L. "Approaches to Conflict in American Industrial Sociology" *British Journal of Sociology,* December, 1954, pp. 324–41.

PART II

Analysis

CHAPTER 4

Introduction and Overview

Part I provides the backdrop for the study of behavioral sciences. The purpose of this part of the book is to develop an analytical and conceptual framework into which are fitted both empirical and deductive results of a considerable amount of work in the behavioral sciences. Part II is organized in eight chapters which cover five analytical areas in human relations.

The areas of analysis are:

1. Motivation, Chapter 5.
2. Status and Role, Chapter 6.
3. Organization, Chapters 7 and 8.
4. Communication, Chapters 9 and 10.
5. Balance and Change, Chapter 11.

While these analytical areas cover a large number of topics, they are united by two common themes—the individual and the organization.

1. The *individual* is the fundamental unit in business. The human person is a self-contained, discrete entity, which can determine its own course of action. The individual has attitudes, motives, and aspirations which constitute a unique personality structure. Personality is modified by organizations, but it is not entirely a product of them. Man is not a creature of his work environment; he is a distinct being and not a creation of the organization with which he works.

This statement is as much one of philosophy as it is of fact. It is too easy to fall into the trap of thinking of the individual as an "organism" passively reacting to the "stimuli" provided by the organization. Man is self-determining and possesses an individuality and dignity which sets him apart from the nonhuman segments and processes of the organization. It is important to keep these thoughts in mind, particularly when the abstract and impersonal notions of organization are brought up for study.

2. *Organization* is the second main theme. Thinking of a company, or for that matter of any organized enterprise, as a social system is especially fruitful. The system is made up of interrelated, variable parts. The functions performed by each part have reciprocal affects on other parts

throughout the system. Impersonality in system analyses stems from the fact that while they are dependent on people to vitalize them, they are not dependent on *particular people*. The so-called "human element" is a "part" of the total system.

Systems seem to have a life of their own. They are self-maintaining and have a built-in propensity for survival through adaptation to change. Like living organisms, social systems incorporate features of feedback and control through a communication network containing decision centers. Systems, also, have goals. It is well known that the goals of the business organization need not be the same as those of the people who work in it. The cleavage between organizational goals and individual objectives is a matter of considerable interest to a number of writers in the behavioral sciences. That there is at times disagreement between the individual and the organization is one of the facts of life brought out in Part I. This problem is carried over into this part where it is treated in some detail in several of the chapters.

These main themes have subthemes which constitute specific topical areas covered in the following seven chapters. Associated with individual attitudes and motives is the subject of morale and productivity. Related also to the main theme of individual behavior, but forming a bridge to the theme of organization, is the analytical area covering status and role. Drawing from sociology and social psychology, status and role systems in organizations are analyzed. The subject of role is concerned largely with the interaction between the individual and the organizations (formal and informal) with which he comes in contact. The problems raised by the expectations of various organizations, in terms of demands on the individual, provide a useful transition to the main theme of organization itself.

There are a number of points of view about the subject of organization. Currently, three dominant theories of organization are identifiable: the classical, neoclassical, and modern. This classification is somewhat artificial because the boundaries separating these theories are not clear. However, a division of this kind introduces order into the analysis, and serves as a framework for studying the major concepts in the organization theme.

Consideration is given throughout the discussion of organization to the social system, its parts, and forms of interaction among the parts. Singled out for intensive investigation in separate chapters are two organizational processes—communication and balance. Change is treated in Chapter 11 as the last subtheme of this part to be discussed. Table 4–1 summarizes the themes and subthemes analyzed in the following chapters.

This brief preview of the next seven chapters is, of course, lacking in detail, and it skips some important topics. The intention, however, is to show that all the following chapters are interrelated. This requires

TABLE 4–1

THEMES AND SUBTHEMES ANALYZED IN PART II

Major Themes	*Subthemes*

1. The Individual
  A. Attitudes
  B. Motives
  C. Aspirations
	1. Morale and Productivity
	
	2. Status and Role Systems ⎱ Transition to
	                             ⎰ the Organizational
	3. Formal and Informal Expectation Forces ⎰ Theme

2. Organization—the
Concept of the Social
System
	1. Contemporary Views of Organization
	  A. Classical
	  B. Neoclassical
	  C. Modern
	
	2. Parts of the System and Their Interaction
	  A. Individuals
	  B. Formal Organization
	  C. Informal Organization
	  D. Physical Environment at Work
	  E. Status and Role Expectancy Systems
	  F. Organization Processes
	
	3. Organization Processes
	  A. Communication
	  B. Balance
	
	4. Change

frequent reference throughout these chapters to matters previously covered or subjects coming up. While frustrating, the reader should understand that the topics analyzed are part of a pattern.

The organic unity of the topics analyzed in this part of the book is best described as the business organization as a whole, made up of parts, interacting internally among themselves and externally with their environment. But it must also be clear that some of the components of the business organization exhibit great propensity for variety and independence of action. The people in a company fall into this category. In many ways, the over-all theme of this part is characterized as people acting in the surroundings of the organization. The resulting human interaction of individuals with other personalities, with groups, and with organizational processes constitutes a large segment of the behavioral sciences.

This part also has continuity with the subjects discussed in the preceding chapters. The analytical areas are firmly rooted in both the clinical and ethical dimensions of human relations. A key feature of the clinical approach, it is recalled, is management's awareness and use of the research findings and abstract generalizations derived from the behavioral sciences. The mission of the next chapters is to provide the material for such an awareness. Figure 4–1 shows the relationship of the analytical areas to the clinical dimension.

As Figure 4–1 illustrates, the data supplied by the analytical areas provide management with a basic understanding of human behavior and organizational processes. With this information, management should have the technical insight necessary for the diagnosis, prevention, or cure of many human problems in business.

FIGURE 4–1

ANALYTICAL AREAS AND CLINICAL DIMENSIONS OF HUMAN RELATIONS

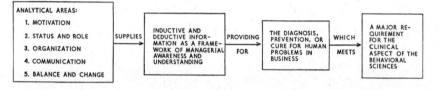

However, all these analytical chapters can really give are the elementary "tools" of analysis and research findings. Knowing this information does not guarantee successful administrative practice any more than knowing about paint, colors, brushes, and technique is sufficient for an artist to produce a masterpiece. Applying the "tools" of the behavioral sciences successfully is an administrative art. But the foundations of the art of administration are grounded in science. The scientific underpinnings of successful management practice relating to human interactions are found in the following chapters. The art of application comes with experience and the development of an executive into an informed, mature, and responsible person.

Chapter 1 brought out the dichotomy which exists between the ideologies of the individualistic and the social ethics. It is inevitable that the analytical areas reflect this division. Probably the most pressing philosophical problem faced by management is preserving individual dignity and integrity while at the same time integrating people into an effective, coordinated organization directed toward achieving the aims of the company.

The diversity of personality and its clashes with organization have already been mentioned in this chapter. Throughout the analytical areas frequent reference is made to the individual versus the organization in terms of specific conflict situations. Indeed, Chapter 11 on "Balance and Change" treats the problem of organizational harmony. But this chapter also deals with the subject of conflict, noting that clashes can serve a positive function in maintaining a vital, and even stable, organization.

In any event, the pervasive influence of organization is always present and is a threat in some cases to individual integrity. Another danger is the unscrupulous manipulative use of the analytical tools by clever individuals in order to accomplish their own ends. Such is the problem of all scientific work which is, in itself, ethically neutral. It can be used as means to achieve ends which are either ethically good or bad.

Like it or not, it is impossible to divorce the behavioral sciences from their ethical implications. Management practice, to repeat, is more than the scientific use of tools. By its nature it requires judgments which often involve ethical issues. Even though the analytical tools are crude at their present stage of development, they are powerful enough to subvert people to the dictates of organization, and to gain ends for the user which are ethically questionable.

The history of management thought, traced in Chapter 2, singled out the 1930's as the time when administration became identified with two sets of skills—the technical skills and the human skills. Each of these areas of skill carries a connotation of competancy in the sense of mastery over the technical (nonhuman) aspects of an executive's job and the ability "to deal" successfully with people at work. Of course, it is hoped that the analytical areas will help improve management's ability on the level of the so-called human skills. Recently, however, a skill of overriding importance has been brought to the forefront of management thought. It is the conceptual skill.

Business is a framework in which the behavioral sciences have application. They combine anthropology, sociology, psychology, social psychology, political science, and economics to offer a point of view of human behavior. Business is a vehicle in which behavior is subjected to the scrutiny of analysis to derive data and generalizations. From these data and principles, the executive may find information useful to him for understanding, predicting, and motivating human action.

But the immediately applicable, "cookbook" skills are not the real promise of the behavioral sciences. Instead, the behavioral sciences offer a special way of looking at business. The information obtained from them relates to personality structure and behavior of man as an individual, small-group processes, and the functioning of larger aggregates of people in organizations. In addition to this, certain synthesizing areas like communication and cybernetics, decision theory, and balance and change present relevant abstractions and principles which also throw light on human organizations.

The behavioral sciences have established principles and pioneering vistas. It is true that it is a little early to render final judgment on the ultimate value to management of work in modern organization theory which incorporates much advanced research in human behavior. However, regardless of what time proves about the specifics of the pioneering work, it will implant one very important heritage in management thought. It will force development of management's conceptual skills in thinking about human behavior.

Recent strides in the behavioral sciences focus on processes which are integrative and conceptual in nature. They appear to go beyond the traditional technical and human skill requirements of managers. Future applications of the behavioral sciences to business will insist on a conceptual-analytical base. The chapters in this part are written with this idea in mind.

The behavioral sciences are not altogether pioneering, however. The reader should not get the impression that all which follows is a résumé of current work on the frontiers of knowledge. A good deal, if not most, of the "body of knowledge" of the behavioral sciences is drawn from writing that is not of recent date. For example, the Hawthorne studies still provide the spiritual fountainhead for many students of human relations. Thus, the analytical areas are a blend of the old and new.

A summary of the objectives of this part is the last thing that is left to be accomplished in this chapter. The objectives are:

1. To present an integrated view of behavior in the social system in such a way that it is relevant to management practice.

2. To underscore that because the individual is discrete and complete in himself conflicts often arise between him and the organization in which he finds himself.

3. To pinpoint some ethical problems as well as to scrutinize the clinical aspects of the analytical areas.

4. To synthesize current and "established" behavioral concepts into a framework of analysis.

5. To stress the conceptual aspects of the behavioral sciences.

CHAPTER 5

Motivation, Morale, and Productivity

THE basic human unit of organization and, of course, of satisfaction and productivity is the individual. It is reasonable, therefore, to start the analysis with a chapter devoted mainly to this primary unit. Groups are not motivated by management; and there is some question among psychologists of whether or not groups have morale. It seems, then, that management motivates *individuals* and concerns itself with the morale of *individuals*.

Psychology is consulted for the foundations of individual behavior. Why did Bob act this way? Why does Joe act another way under almost identical circumstances? Management is conscious of behavior; but underlying behavior are layers of attitudes and motives which condition it. To understand behavior, management must first fathom the prompting causes.

ATTITUDES

Roethlisberger, in discussing the Hawthorne studies, frequently refers to the researchers' interpretation of attitudes. When the studies began, a simple, direct connection was assumed between a given change on the one hand and a predictable response on the other hand. As experimentation progressed the stimulus-response relationship was found to be neither direct nor predictable. People did not respond to a certain stimulus as it was predicted they would. The often-cited illumination experiments at the Hawthorne plant are an example.

The purpose of this experiment was to determine how productivity would vary under different light-intensity conditions. The design of the experiment was fairly simple—change the brightness of the light and measure the amount of output at different intensities.

Intuitively, it might be thought that there would be a certain optimum or "normal" range of light intensity which would correlate significantly with higher levels of productivity. As the light intensity approached, then went beyond the upper and lower limits of the optimum range, productivity would start to drop.

This bit of a priori prediction sounds quite reasonable, but the experiments did not have these results. Summarizing the third illumination experiment, it was said:

After the level of illumination in the test group enclosure changed to a lower value, the efficiencies of both the test and control groups increased slowly but steadily. When the level of the illumination for the test group finally reached three foot-candles, the operatives protested, saying that they were hardly able to see what they were doing, and the production rate decreased. The operatives could and did maintain their efficiency to this point in spite of the discomfort and handicap of insufficient illumination.[1]

The moral of this story (and of the other Hawthorne experiments) is that people did not do what they were supposed to do according to the simple stimulus-response postulate. The researchers hypothesized that some unaccounted-for, purely human factor must be acting as an intermediary between the stimulus and the response. This factor was called attitudes or sentiments.

Roethlisberger developed his "X" chart, shown in Figure 5–1, to portray the relationship of attitudes to behavior.

FIGURE 5–1

THE "X" CHART

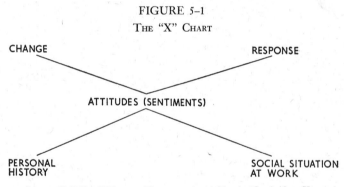

Source: F. J. Roethlisberger, *Management and Morale* (Cambridge: Harvard University Press, 1941), p. 21. Reprinted with permission.

The chart is interpreted as follows:

So that a response to a change may be understood, much less predicted, the attitudes of the individual involved must be known. Attitudes are in themselves products of a person's background (personal history) and the total work environment (the social situation at work).

It is easy to see how an enormous variety of responses could be found among individuals in similar stimulus situations. Recognition of this fact has led psychologists to formulate the *Principle of Individual Differences.* This principle is another way of labeling the phenomenon noted by

---

[1] F. J. Roethlisberger and William J. Dickson, *Management and the Worker* (Cambridge: Harvard University Press, 1939), pp. 16–17.

Roethlisberger. People act differently—if you will, unpredictably—because of different environmental experiences. These differences, in turn, cause each person to view the work situation in a manner not quite like his fellow employees.

Human differences, in the psychological order, are crystalized in attitudes. Attitudes are mental states which precede actions or responses. The sort of response which results from an environmental change is largely dependent on the individual's attitudes regarding the total situation in which the change takes place.

Psychologists have given much attention to the subject of attitudes, and a number of formal definitions are readily available in the literature. Cattell and Baggaley define attitudes as ". . . a readiness to respond with a defined course of action, in relation to an object, in a given stimulus situation."[2] Or, if you prefer, Adams defines sentiments (attitudes) as ". . . a part of a personality identified by its reference to an object."[3]

One point emerges dominant from these definitions of attitudes. Attitudes are habit structures which, as part of an individual's personality, must come before action toward a goal. As Viteles puts it, attitudes are ". . . a fundamental state of readiness for motive arousal or a reaction in a characteristic way to certain stimuli or stimulus situations."[4]

Thus, attitudes are first in a series of steps which precede overt human behavior. They are prejudices, predilections, habits of thought, or mental dispositions. Further, attitudes are intimately associated with human motives, which are eventually manifested in behavior directed toward a goal. For example, a person might have a fear of financial insecurity in old age which would motivate him in a quest for security. Overt behavior in this regard could be frugality in his younger years, coupled with employment by a company with an adequate pension program.

FIGURE 5–2

THE RELATION OF ATTITUDES TO BEHAVIOR

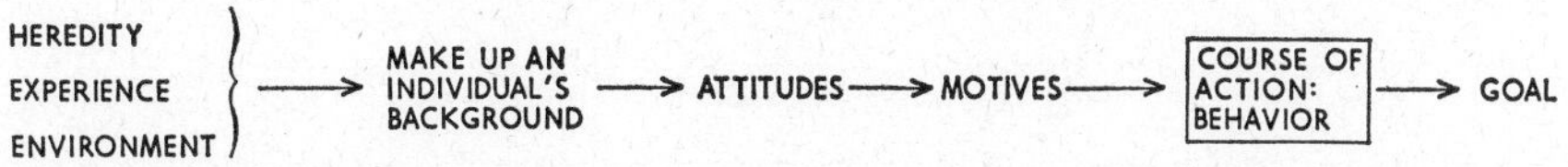

Attitudes and their ultimate effect on behavior can be visualized by Figure 5–2.

---

[2] Raymond B. Cattell and Andrew R. Baggaley, "The Objective Measurement of Attitude Motivation: Development and Evaluation of Principles and Devices," *Journal of Personality*, 1955–1956, p. 421.

[3] Donald K. Adams, "The Organs of Perception: Sentiments," *Journal of Personality*, 1953–1954, p. 53.

[4] Morris S. Viteles, *Motivation and Morale in Industry* (New York: W. W. Norton and Co., 1953), p. 74.

Referring to Figure 5–2, attitudes result from experience, heredity, and environmental influences. An individual's attitudes will determine his motives and, thus, his response to a given stimulus in a certain situation.[5] The response takes external form in a course of action which is behavior. Behavior is directed toward the accomplishment of a desired goal. It may be noted, however, that the individual may perceive a goal he deems desirable as a result of his attitudes, and will select a form of behavior out of a wide range of alternatives so as to accomplish the goal. The line between attitudes and successful goal achievement is not straight; it usually is jagged and discontinuous because of trial-and-error efforts to reach an objective.

Types of Attitudes

Attitudes are thought to fall into two general classifications—logical and nonlogical. This method of classification was proposed by Elton Mayo and associates who were involved in the Hawthorne studies. But even before these studies were conducted, Pareto had suggested a similar classification of attitudes. The debt owned to Pareto by the Hawthorne researchers has been mentioned in Chapter 2. Since the concept of attitudes is a cornerstone of the Hawthorne studies, it is necessary to consider the topic of attitude type in some detail.

Logical Attitudes. Logical behavior is prompted by logical attitudes. Logical behavior is such that means are united directly with ends in the ultimate pursuit of a goal. Logical behavior, according to Pareto, must meet the test of outside, objective criticism from someone, besides the acting subject, who knows more about the objective situation. A chemistry professor, for example, is in the position of an outside observer who can evaluate the degree of logic in a student's behavior when the student is performing an experiment.

Thus, when one acts logically the means and subordinate ends are welded to one another for both the objective and subjective purposes of achieving a goal. To illustrate:

$$\boxed{\text{MEANS}} \longrightarrow \boxed{\text{ENDS}} \longrightarrow \boxed{\text{MEANS}} \longrightarrow \boxed{\text{ENDS}} \longrightarrow \boxed{\text{GOAL}}$$

Nonlogical Attitudes. Nonlogical conduct, based on nonlogical attitudes, states objective purposes which are different from the subjective purpose of such action. This Paretian idea was adapted by the experimenters at Hawthorne to provide an explanation for the fact that people often give quite logical verbal reasons for their behavior, while they *really* behave as they do for different reasons.

A man may quit his job, and give inadequate pay for the cause. The

[5] For a study of the relationship of job attitudes to job performance see Joseph Weitz and Robert C. Nuckols, "Job Satisfaction and Job Survival," *Journal of Applied Psychology*, 1955, pp. 294–300.

reasoning would be considered by many as quite logical. In reality, however, the man might *actually* have left because of a nonacceptance by fellow employees, or dissatisfaction with supervision, or lack of recognition for accomplishment, and so on. This type of behavior may be illustrated as follows:

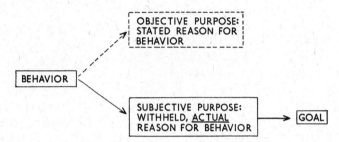

Management and Attitudes

The management implications in the above discussion of attitudes are threefold. First, *very little of human conduct is logical.* Most human conduct, says Pareto, is nonlogical and originates in psychic states, inclinations, preconceptions, and subconscious feelings. Thus, management must be aware that people are not logic machines, rationally conjoining means with ends in the relentless pursuit of some goal.

Second, the most usual form of behavior is a nonlogical one based on feelings and prejudices. The attitudes underlying nonlogical behavior have been long established and are brought by the employee to the company. Additionally, other attitudes of a nonlogical variety may be formed after employment. Attitudes in this sense are socially produced in the work situation.

Nonlogical attitudes are subtle and varied, but they are no less a reality than logical attitudes. Management needs to know their nature and to channel them, if not change them, in directions which are conducive to accomplish the objectives of the company.

Third, it is often a purely relative matter whether attitudes are logical or nonlogical. It is not enough to consider our attitudes as logical and the other fellow's as nonlogical—a bias which management frequently has. If any employee fails to respond to an incentive system, management might consider him as acting completely at variance with a perfectly logical method of wage payment. But, the employee might think of his actions as quite logical, feeling that it is management's lack of insight into his motives for work which causes him to behave as he does.

WORK MOTIVES

Man is not born with a desire to make money, any more than he is born with a love of liberty or a sense of responsibility and justice. Motives are learned. Work motives also are learned, but they constitute only a small segment in a very broad range of human motives. Therefore, any analysis of work motives must follow a more general discussion of motives viewed in the larger sense.

Referring back to Figure 5–2, it is seen that motives appear between attitudes and response. At the risk of repeating, attitudes pave the way for the development of motives, and then, depending on the particular motive, a certain response is chosen.

The pure meaning of motive is associated with *directed behavior*. That is, an individual perceives a goal and responds with a form of behavior directed toward obtaining it. This treatment specifically excludes physiological needs, such as hunger, thirst, and fatigue, from the category of motives. Most basic biological needs are automatically, or at least partially automatically, satisfied. The key point is that the satisfaction of physiological needs is not completely a matter of individual will, whereas the satisfaction of motives is a matter of individual volition. Again, *motives imply that resulting behavior will be consciously directed toward a goal.*[6] The goal may be viewed as a specific satisfaction for a specific motive.

Motives can be satisfied through numerous forms of activities including religion, education, social service, family life, and many more. Of course, work is a channel of satisfaction for a number of learned human motives.

Figure 5–3 shows a system of classification of work motives illustrating their relationship to primary drives, basic motives, and their ultimate requirement of satisfaction.[7] Figure 5–3 is interpreted as follows:

Primary drive. The biological drive, already mentioned, requires the satisfaction of those basic needs essential to maintain physiological integrity—organic survival. The nature of satisfaction for this drive is specifiable. The need for food, water, rest, air, and elimination is necessary for the survival of the human organism, even though the level of satisfaction of these biological requirements differs from person to person.

Basic motives. There are two basic motives—psychological and social. The psychological motive results in a quest by an individual to maintain his mental integrity or balance. The social motive stems from the natural gregariousness of man, and his need to associate with his fellow man.

Unlike the biological drive, it is impossible to generalize and predict the specific routes individuals will follow to satisfy these motives. Further, the satisfaction of basic motives is volitional. Although it was said that the social motive is basic for man in general, the example of a hermit or recluse comes to mind immediately to demonstrate the volitional character of this category of motives.

---

[6] For a general discussion of motives see Viteles, *op. cit.*, pp. 69–71.

[7] Kornhauser observes that the classification of motives has become unpopular among social psychologists, but he does defend and use such classifications in his work. See Arthur Kornhauser, Robert Dubin, and Arthur M. Ross (eds.), *Industrial Conflict* (New York: McGraw-Hill Book Co., 1954), pp. 67–72.

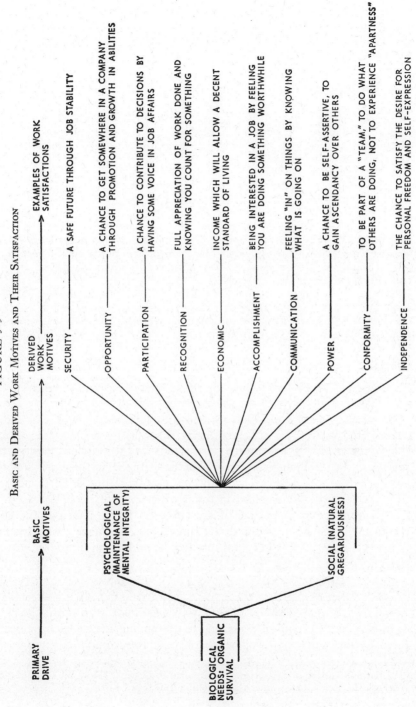

FIGURE 5-3

BASIC AND DERIVED WORK MOTIVES AND THEIR SATISFACTION

Derived (work) motives. This last category provides the richest source of motives underlying human behavior. The ten derived work motives are only a few of many possible reasons why people work. These motives are derived from the basic social and psychological motives. But they are not connected in a specific way to one or the other basic motives. Who can say with any degree of certainty that the recognition motive is social or psychological in origin? The only possible way to find out is by studying an individual, not by generalizing to a whole population.

Derived work motives have the interesting characteristic of being highly dynamic in nature. In this regard, (1) each person at a point in time has a certain hierarchy, a special ordering of importance of the derived motives; and (2) when the motive which is first on his "list" is satisfied, it slips in urgency and another motive takes its place.

Thus when research studies in worker motives turn up the "discovery" that money is not top of the list of motives for a group of employees, the obvious conclusion is *not* that money is no longer important. Money is still vital *but it is not the only reason for working.* Once the basic income requirement is satisfied, other motives supercede it on the list of motives, for a time at least.

The requirement of satisfaction. Management is in part responsible for the satisfaction of derived work motives. The satisfactions listed in Figure 5–3 are suggestive; and some satisfactions appear to be mutually exclusive of others.[8] Each individual may interpret his requirement for the satisfaction of a particular motive differently. One job of the manager who is attempting to improve his motivational ability is to determine what his subordinates expect in terms of satisfaction for their unique motives.

Generalizations will not accomplish this job, nor will statistical studies of the hierarchy of employee motives. No substitute exists for managerial insight and sensitivity when it comes to perceiving the type of motive satisfaction required by each employee. Understanding individual motives is a day-to-day task.

The discussion of work motives, which is based on Figure 5–3, may be summarized in these terms. The primary drive of survival requires primitive forms of satisfaction. When this drive is satisfied higher motives, the social and the psychological, emerge to dominate the personality. Derived work motives are associated with the basic motives; but the derived motives are highly individualized in terms of specific forms of satisfaction and their ordering in personal hierarchies. So far as it is possible and reasonable, satisfaction of the derived motives is a management responsibility in the work environment. More will be said on this in the following section.

MOTIVATION

Motivation, in a more traditional sense among management writers, means a process of stimulating people to action to accomplish desired goals.

---

[8] For another list of satisfactions see Lyndall F. Urwick, "How the Organization Affects the Man," *Management Review,* July, 1957, pp. 54–61.

Although many words are substituted for motivation (such as "actuating" and "directing") the meaning of the process is reasonably clear. Motivation is a function which a manager performs in order to get his subordinates to achieve job objectives.

While this point of view is valid and useful, there is another side of the coin of motivation. Instead of viewing motivation as a management process it is profitable to look at it from the standpoint of the individual who is motivated. Psychologists call individual motivation a *state of tension*.

Motivation, so considered, represents an unsatisfied need which creates a condition of tension or disequilibrium causing the individual to move in a goal-directed pattern toward restoring a state of equilibrium by satisfying the need.[9]

Management should be aware that the strength of tensions, and therefore the strength of motivations, vary. Atkinson[10] views motivation strength in the form of an equation—motivation = f(motive × expectancy × incentive). The strength of motivation to perform some act is a function of:

1. *The strength of the motive* which is the position of a motive in the individual's hierarchy of motives, representing a level of urgency for fulfillment.
2. *Expectancy* which is the probability that the act will obtain the goal.[11]
3. *The value of the incentive* which is the rewards hoped for by obtaining the goal. The greater the rewards, the greater will be the motivational strength, providing the other two factors remain equal.[12]

The equation can be portrayed as follows to give an example of motivational strength in several situations.

---

[9] Viteles, *op. cit.*, p. 73.

[10] John W. Atkinson, "Motivational Determinants of Risk Taking Behavior," *Psychological Review*, 1957, pp. 360–61.

[11] Deutsch reports, for example, that highest individual motivation would be found among individuals in highly motivated groups where the probability for success in achieving a goal was low. In these experiments, however, the authors focus on the degree of group integration (solidarity) which is achieved under varying stress situations. They conclude that groups which are highly motivated and which also perceive a small chance of obtaining a valuable goal will react by forming a greater degree of interdependency among themselves. See Morton Deutsch, "Some Factors Affecting Membership Motivation and Achievement Motivation in a Group," *Human Relations*, 1959, pp. 81–95. For similar conclusions, see Leonard Berkowitz, Bernard I. Levy, and Arthur R. Harvey, "Effects of Performance Evaluations on Group Integration and Motivation," *Human Relations*, 1957, pp. 195–208.

[12] In an earlier study, Kahn and Morse pointed out that motivational strength was dependent upon (1) the strength of the need served by the behavior, (2) availability of alternative behaviors to meet the need, (3) the extent to which behavior sets up opposing tensions to interfere with the satisfaction of other needs, and (4) the ratio of need satisfaction to required energy input—pleasure-pain. R. L. Kahn and N. C. Morse, "The Relationship of Morale to Productivity," *Journal of Social Issues*, 1951, p. 12.

Assume: A = motive strength which can be $\begin{array}{l} + \text{ high} \\ - \text{ low} \end{array}$.

         B = Expectancy which can be $\begin{array}{l} + \text{ high} \\ - \text{ low} \end{array}$.

         C = Incentive value which can be $\begin{array}{l} + \text{ high} \\ - \text{ low} \end{array}$.

Eight possible states of motivational strength can be illustrated from this simplified situation.

FIGURE 5–4

VARYING DEGREES OF MOTIVATIONAL STRENGTH

	A	B	C		A	B	C
1.	+	+	+	5.	−	−	+
2.	+	+	−	6.	−	+	−
3.	+	−	+	7.	+	−	−
4.	−	+	+	8.	−	−	−

The left side of Figure 5–4 shows degrees of relatively high states of motivational strength; the right side indicates various degrees of low motivational strength.

Again, it is the individual who perceives and assigns actual values to the plus and minus signs in the motivational equation. Naturally, management would prefer to see evidence of plus rather than minus signs of individual motivational strength toward company and job objectives. Such a situation would indicate individual tensions which could be satisfied by the pursuit of company established goals. However, as Ginsberg says, management has difficulty appreciating that organizational goals and the goals of employees are not the same.[13] Shades of mutuality of interests!

Motivation is not an automatic nor is it a one-sided management process. Individual motivational tensions are social, psychological, as well as economic in origin. Knowing the unmet motives, expectancies, and value systems of individuals provides management with the concrete information necessary to perform the *process* of motivation considered in the more traditional sense. An over-all approach to motivation may be visualized in Figure 5–5.

A manager faced with a motivational problem should seek a method of attack—an approach. As a beginning, he needs to find the answers to seven key questions. The first set of questions relates to the employee's attitudes,

---

[13] Eli Ginsberg, "Perspectives on Work Motivation," *Personnel*, July, 1954, pp. 43–44.

FIGURE 5–5

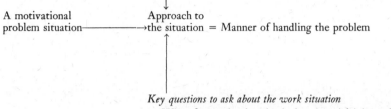

AN APPROACH TO MOTIVATION

Key questions to ask about the employee and yourself
1. What are the employee's attitudes?
2. What are the employee's motives?
3. What is the strength of his motivation?
4. How do I, as a manager, feel about his motives and attitudes?

A motivational problem situation ———→ Approach to the situation = Manner of handling the problem

Key questions to ask about the work situation
1. What factors in the physical and social job setting are relevant to the solution of this problem?
2. To what extent does company policy circumscribe actions that might be taken to solve the problem?
3. Are there any outside organizations, like a union, which may affect the problem?

motives, and strength of motivation; this set also contains a question regarding how he as a manager sizes-up the worth of the situation. The second set of questions is about the work situation, including an appraisal not only of formal policy which may bear on the case and union-management relations, but also of the social and physical setting of the problem. Answers to these questions, conscientiously obtained and realistically appraised, should yield an approach to the motivational problem.

Appropriately enough, Likert calls motivation the core of management. He concludes that ". . . the nature of human motivation shows that every human being earnestly seeks a secure, friendly, and supportive relationship which gives him a sense of worth in face-to-face groups which are most important to him . . . a supervisor should strive to treat individuals with dignity and a recognition for their personal worth."[14]

MORALE AND PRODUCTIVITY

The topic of morale and productivity is firmly rooted in the preceding discussion of attitudes and motives because, indeed, the will to produce and the satisfactions obtained from work are largely matters of attitudes and motives.

---

[14] Rensis Likert, *Motivation: The Core of Management* (American Management Association, Personnel Series, Number 155) 1953, p. 16.

For some time, people interested in the relationship between morale and productivity labored under the misapprehension of the Law of Effect.[15] This "law" proposed that morale and output would be low if job satisfactions are not found by the individual in the work situation. Conversely, it was assumed that production would be high if satisfactions from the job were forthcoming. Thus, morale and productivity are postulated to be directly related—high morale generates high productivity and low morale results in low productivity.

Recent research has questioned the generalty claimed by the Law of Effect. Studies have shown that a direct positive relationship between morale and productivity does not always prevail. Hence, it may be concluded that productivity is not a dependent variable operating as a function of morale. But this is getting a little ahead of the story. The next few pages summarize the complexities of morale-productivity studies.

Productivity

Productivity presents fewer problems of definition and measurement than morale. Productivity is usually quantifiable in terms of an input-output ratio for research purposes. As Kahn and Morse define it, "productivity is the number of units of work accomplished in a given period of time."[16]

This method of defining productivity is simple and direct. Furthermore, it is quite adequate for gathering data and making appraisals of work groups which are producing a tangible, measurable output in a given time period. However it must be noted that this approach to productivity is wholly inadequate when it comes to measuring the output of executive personnel. Typically, the executive, functioning in either a line or staff capacity, does not work under the rigorous demands of a production line.

The executive's output is often intangible and is frequently creative, which are two conditions that defy quantification. So, unfortunately, research in the morale-productivity relationship has been largely concentrated at the operative level. Any generalizations which are made on morale should be accepted as applying to production employees and not to employees at higher levels in companies.

Morale

While the matter of productivity can be treated rather summarily, such is not the case with morale. Definitional and methodological problems inherent in morale research and measurement result, it seems, from

---

[15] For a discussion and criticism of the Law of Effect see Arthur H. Brayfield and Walter H. Crockett, "Employee Attitudes and Employee Performance," *Psychological Bulletin*, September, 1955, pp. 396–424.

[16] Kahn and Morse, *op. cit.*, p. 10.

the lack of an explicit, universally acceptable definition of morale. In addition, widely varying sampling techniques and criteria measures of morale are probably a major reason for the conflicting findings of many research reports treating the morale-productivity relationship.

Three Approaches to the Problem of Definition. 1. *The "classical" approach* stems from the "needs psychology" school. Personal determinants of morale are emphasized in this approach. Needs are visualized as emanating from the ultimate problem of human survival. Thus, satisfaction of basic needs is seen as a primary morale factor.

2. *The psychological approach* stresses the hierarchial and dynamic nature of needs. When basic needs are satisfied, then higher motives, such as accomplishment, recognition, and participation, emerge to dominate an individual's behavior. High morale from this point of view results from a continual satisfaction of the so-called "higher" motives.

3. *The social approach* to morale is a product of the work of Elton Mayo and the Hawthorne researchers. Morale is considered as a social phenomenon caused by the strong desire of man to be associated with his fellow man. Thus, morale is determined by the social situation at work.[17]

A number of operational definitions of morale have resulted from these three basic approaches. For example:

a) "Morale is the extent to which an individual's needs are satisfied and the extent to which the individual perceives that satisfaction as stemming from his total job situation."[18]

b) "Morale is the sum of satisfactions which the individual experiences because of his membership and involvement in an organization."[19]

c) Morale is ". . . the attitudes of individuals and groups toward their work environment and toward voluntary cooperation to the full extent of their ability in the best interests of the business."[20]

d) "Morale is a predisposition on the part of persons engaged in an enterprise to put forth extra effort in the achievement of group goals or objectives."[21]

And on and on it could go! The probability of arriving at a generally accepted definition of morale is unlikely. However, for reasons of research and analysis of employee attitudes and morale it is necessary to have an operational definition, but with the realization that this definition would not be acceptable for other situations.

[17] The three approaches to defining morale are found in Melany E. Baehr and Richard Renck, "The Definition and Measurement of Employee Morale," *Administrative Science Quarterly*, 1958, pp. 159–60.

[18] Robert M. Guion, "The Problem of Terminology," *Personnel Psychology*, Spring, 1958, p. 62.

[19] Kahn and Morris *op. cit.*, p. 8.

[20] Keith Davis, *Human Relations in Business* (New York: McGraw-Hill Book Co., 1957), p. 444.

[21] Egon E. Guba, "Morale and Satisfaction: A Study in Past and Future Time Perspective," *Administrative Science Quarterly*, 1958–1959, p. 198.

The current feeling is that morale is multidimensional, no matter what definition is finally assigned to it. Zaleznik, Christensen, and Roethlisberger, for example, list five determinants which form morale dimensions. They are the technical (formal) organization of the group, the social structure of the group, individual task motivation (willingness to work), rewards for performance, and satisfactions from group acceptance.[22]

It is commonly held among authors that *morale is a result of a composite of factors including the personality structure of the individual, the social organization of the work situation, the type of leadership used, the formal nature of the job, company policy, incentive systems, and the physical environment of the job.*

The Four Factors Included in the Multidimensional Morale Approach. 1. *Personality structure.* The first morale factor, personality structure, brings attitudes and motives to the surface of the discussion again. Motives and attitudes underlie the will to work and, of course, productivity. The degree to which the existing work situation satisfies an individual's work motives will determine, at least in part, the state of his morale. The satisfaction of employee motives in the work situation crosscuts the entire range of human desires for work, including the social, psychological, and economic motives.

2. *The social organization on the job.* As stated earlier, one of man's strongest motives is to be associated with his fellow man. Identification of an individual with a group has considerable influence on his behavior and morale. The study by Zaleznik and associates has pointed out that workers who were being rewarded by the group with regular membership tended to be highly satisfied, regardless of their rewards by management. Those who were not rewarded by the group gave evidence of low satisfaction.[23] William C. Schutz, in another study, found high morale and group efficiency to be based on compatibility in interpersonal relations.[24]

3. *Leadership and supervision.* Any number of studies can be cited to support the direct relationship existing between morale and supervision. Notable work in this field has been conducted by Likert. The widely held view, which Likert champions, is that supportive, participative leadership elicits the highest morale-productivity situations.[25]

---

[22] A. Zaleznik, C. R. Christensen, and F. J. Roethlisberger, *The Motivation, Productivity, and Satisfaction of Workers: A Prediction Study* (Boston: Harvard University Press, 1958), p. 35. For other listings of morale dimensions see Gerald M. Mahoney, "Unidimensional Scales for the Measurement of Morale in an Industrial Situation," *Human Relations*, 1956, pp. 7-9; and Baehr and Renck, *op. cit.*, pp. 175, 176.

[23] Zaleznik, Christensen, and Roethlisberger, *op. cit.*, p. 285.

[24] William C. Schutz, "What Makes Groups Productive?" *Human Relations*, 1955, pp. 429-65.

[25] For example see Rensis Likert, "Measuring Organizational Performance," *Harvard Business Review*, March–April, 1958, pp. 41-50.

Much of the research Argyris summarizes backs up Likert's conclusions.[26] But it must be emphasized that the supportive-participative approach to supervision should not be taken as a "soft" approach. Indifferent leadership or leadership which casts aside all formal control patterns can produce low morale conditions.[27]

4. *Formal aspects of organization: job functions, company policies, and incentives.* In addition to the above factors, the formal aspects and demands of the work situation must not be overlooked as influential elements determining morale. Argyris has a thesis that the nature of the work done is a basic determinant of morale. Individuals derive greater satisfaction from challenging jobs rather than routine, monotonous ones.[28] Among others, Super supports this view in a research study from which he concludes that varied and interesting jobs prompt workers to express attitudes of greater satisfaction in what they are doing.[29]

Besides the job itself, morale is further affected by the over-all work environment set by management through the medium of company policy. Such policies cover the total employment situation. They include not only tangible "fringe" benefits but also statements of *operating* policy recognizing human dignity and individual worth.

Coupled with policy is the reward system of incentives endorsed by the company. Viteles defines incentives as "situations which function in arousing dynamic forces in the individual, or arrangements of conditions introduced with the expectation of influencing or altering the behavior of people."[30]

Incentives, so viewed, are considerably broader than "incentive pay plans" or "piecework plans." Incentives arouse motives by appeal to *all* the sources of human motivation.

Concluding Remarks on Morale

Three main points have to be underscored in conclusion. First, morale is closely connected with the satisfactions an individual hopes to derive from work. As noted earlier, need satisfactions do not have to be forthcoming immediately, but they have to be anticipated by the individual as quite probable of occurring.[31]

---

[26] Chris Argyris, *Personality and Organization* (New York: Harper and Brothers, 1957), p. 188 *ff.*

[27] Robert L. Kahn and Daniel Katz, "Leadership Practices in Relation to Productivity and Morale," in D. Cartwright and A. Zander, *Group Dynamics Research and Theory* (Evanston: Row-Peterson and Co., 1953), pp. 612–27.

[28] Chris Argyris, "The Individual and Organization: An Empirical Test," *Administrative Science Quarterly*, September, 1959, pp. 145–67.

[29] D. Super, "Occupational Level and Job Satisfaction," *Journal of Applied Psychology*, 1959, pp. 547–64.

[30] Viteles, *op. cit.*, p. 76.

[31] One writer feels that high satisfaction must precede high morale; that is, a person first has to have experience with satisfaction before he will have high morale. See Egon Guba, *op. cit.*, pp. 195–209.

Second, morale is often dependent on the relationship of the individual to the group. Group acceptance or nonacceptance frequently determines whether an individual has high or low morale. But membership in a group depends on the willingness of the individual to pursue group goals. The third conclusion arises as a corollary to this observation.

A problem which often arises in the work situation is a conflict between group and individual goals. Goal conflict frequently results in low morale for individuals. To illustrate this point, Stagner has four examples shown in Figure 5–6 which indicate various morale conditions.

FIGURE 5–6

Various Morale Situations Resulting from

Individual-Group Interactions

A

MAXIMUM MORALE

B

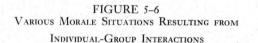

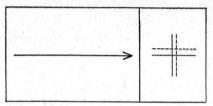
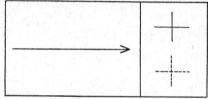

Group goal and individual goal achieved as part of the same process

Group and individual goals closely associated but not achieved simultaneously as part of the same process

C

D

MINIMUM MORALE

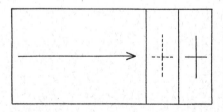
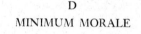

Obtaining group goal necessary before the individual's goal is achieved

Individual and group goals perceived as separate and are obtained separately

KEY: = INDIVIDUAL GOALS; --|-- = GROUP GOALS

Source: Ross Stagner, "Motivational Aspects of Industrial Morale," *Personnel Psychology,* Spring, 1958, pp. 67–68. Reprinted with permission.

Maximum morale results in condition "A" where group and individual goals are perceived as being the same, and where these goals can be achieved by the same process. The other cases result in lower morale. This leads Stagner to conclude, "The task of the person who wishes to raise morale within an organization is to create situations in which group and individual goals coincide to the maximum extent possible."[32]

Morale and Productivity

The question of the relationship of morale to productivity can be re-opened now that some of the intricacies of the morale problem have been investigated. The morale and productivity variables may exhibit four logically possible relationships. These relationships are shown in Figure 5–7.

FIGURE 5–7

RELATIONSHIPS BETWEEN MORALE AND PRODUCTIVITY

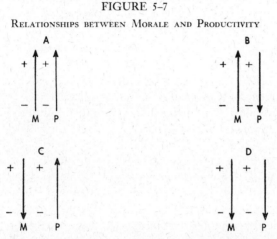

Situations "A" and "D"—high morale and high productivity, low morale and low productivity—are kinds of relationships predicted by the Law of Effect. Just because the Law of Effect has been shown not actually to be a law does not mean that it is unusual to find direct relationships between morale and productivity. Giese and Ruter, for example, using objective measures of morale, found a direct and slightly positive relation between morale and productivity for retail employees.[33]

Further, the findings in the Hawthorne study revealed a direct relationship between morale and productivity. An improved change in worker attitudes were reflected in productivity increase. The relationships found by Mayo and associates is not purely a matter of changing attitudes, however. Higher productivity is an outcome of the whole work environment where needs are met, where employees have satisfactory associations with fellow employees, and where the supervisor maintains informal social relationships.[34]

---

[32] Stagner, *op. cit.*, p. 70. It is evident that "group goals" refer to the goals of both the formal and the informal groups.

[33] William James Giese and H. W. Ruter, "An Objective Analysis of Morale," *Journal of Applied Psychology*, October, 1949, pp. 421–27.

[34] For example, Roethlisberger and Dickson, *op. cit.*, pp. 84–86.

Situation "B" represents a case of high morale and low productivity. As Davis observes, this condition results from a supervisor feeling that employees must be kept happy at all costs.[35] The consequence might well be falling production with soaring morale.

Situation "C" perhaps appears unusual because of the low morale-high productivity relationship. The cause of a condition like this results from an overwhelming emphasis on output and a disregard for the feelings of employees. Sustained production pressure through forced sign out of work and close supervision would produce this situation easily.

Goode and Fowler[36] report an interesting example of such practices. The company they studied failed to maintain its equipment adequately, and safety practices were neglected. New employees were given little training. They were fired if they did not achieve standard output in a given period of time. Wages were low. Workers also did not receive the usual fringe benefits common to the area. Finally, stability of the work force was absent—turnover was high.

These conditions would produce low morale if anything could. Nevertheless, output was high as measured by objective standards against similar companies. The authors concluded that in spite of poor working conditions, informal group pressure (brought about by key personnel placed by management among the operative employees),[37] and overt management action (produce or be fired), productivity was pushed to high levels.

Besides the four morale relationships just discussed, two other morale situations have been found to exist. The first of these two shows no relationship, neither direct nor inverse, between morale and productivity. Katz and associates report that a study of office workers reveals, "Neither intrinsic job satisfaction, satisfaction with the company, nor financial and status satisfaction was found to be directly related to productivity."[38]

The second additional morale situation can be called the circular relationship. In a study of small military units, Medalia and Miller concluded that, "Unit operating efficiency is a factor associated with morale . . . standing in a mutually reinforcing relationship to morale."[39] Lead-

---

[35] Keith Davis, *op. cit.*, p. 182.

[36] William J. Goode and Irving Fowler, "Incentive Factors in a Low Morale Plant," *American Sociological Review*, 1949, pp. 618–24.

[37] This situation is "human relations" in reverse. Management used the key personnel as informal leaders within operative ranks to motivate workers to high production levels. The informal leaders were agents of management rather than individuals selected by their peers through natural group processes.

[38] Daniel Katz, Nathan Maccoby, and Nancy C. Morse, *Productivity, Supervision and Morale in an Office Situation*, (Ann Arbor: Institute for Social Research, University of Michigan, 1950), p. 63.

[39] N. Z. Medalia and D. C. Miller, "Human Relations Leadership and the Association of Morale and Efficiency in Work Groups: A Controlled Study with Small Military Units," *Social Forces*, May 1955, p. 349.

ership may act to increase morale or efficiency, but the increase in efficiency then reacts to improve morale, which then acts to further improve efficiency, and so on.

Thus, under certain conditions morale and productivity are reciprocal. This point has also been noted by Haire and Gottsdanker when they say, "To be sure, as soon as we get into the problem we find that it is somewhat circular, for just as morale may lead to high production, high production may lead to good morale."[40]

It is fairly clear from the foregoing that high morale is no longer considered as a prerequisite of high productivity. But more than this, the *nature* of the relationship between morale and productivity is open to serious questioning. Is it direct? Is it inverse? Is it circular? Or, is there any relationship at all between the two; are they independent variables?

Generalizations are impossible to make. At best, the morale-productivity relationship is situational. Thus, morale and productivity must be studied in the specific work environment with research tools adapted to each situation.

WORK SATISFACTION AND MANAGEMENT RESPONSIBILITY

Sound management practice in human interrelationships is firmly committed to promoting both morale and productivity. Employee satisfaction and productivity are goals which management must seek. They are values of a high order. Recall that the operational definition of human relations selected for this book stresses the necessity of achieving greater employee satisfaction *and* accomplishing the objectives of the company.

The best route to achieving these dual objectives—which may be recognized as conflicting at times—is through an enlightened type of motivation. Enlightened motivation by management accepts the diversity of human motives and attitudes. It also attempts to work through the personalized forms of individual motivations (states of tension, unmet needs).

In addition, enlightened motivation takes the social structure of employee groups as a given factor. That is, management should recognize that such groups exist, and that efforts to destroy them could result in a morale crisis. Informal groups are in themselves molders of attitudes and conditioners of behavior. They carry values and forms of satisfactions for which management cannot offer substitutes.

Finally, morale and motivation at lower levels of a company reflect the morale, attitudes, and motives of executives at higher levels. Morale filters down from the top; the morale of a subordinate tends to be responsive to the morale of his immediate superior. Thus, the entire management corps must be conscious of its own morale. And what is more

---

[40] M. Haire and J. S. Gottsdanker, "Factors Influencing Industrial Morale," *Personnel*, May, 1951, p. 445.

important, policies and operating behavior must be a true expression of high morale throughout the executive ranks.

High morale is a goal in itself no matter what its relation to productivity. But the approach for achieving high morale must be consistent with the basic economic objectives of the firm. Reference to Barnard's concept of "effectiveness" and "efficiency" in an organization is appropriate for concluding this chapter.

An organization is effective if it accomplishes its ends. But the organization is efficient if it satisfies the derived work motives of the individuals in it. An organization can be either effective or efficient; however, an organization must be *both* effective and efficient to build a cooperative system.[41] The executive must be concerned with balancing efficiency and effectiveness by intelligent and sensitive application of his technical and human skills.

REVIEW QUESTIONS

1. Is the classification of attitudes as logical and nonlogical absolute? To what extent does such a classification depend on one's "frame of reference?"

2. What is "goal-directed behavior?"

3. How are attitudes, motives, and behavior related?

4. How does the conventional management approach to motivation differ from the psychologist's view of motivation?

5. What is meant by a hierarchy of work motives? Why is this hierarchy considered "dynamic?"

6. Is the "Law of Effect" really a law? Explain.

7. What are the underlying determinants of morale?

8. Has research "proven" anything regarding the relationship between morale and productivity? Discuss.

SUPPLEMENTARY READINGS

ARGYRIS, CHRIS. "The Individual and Organization: An Empirical Test," *Administrative Science Quarterly*, September, 1959, pp. 145–67.

BRAYFIELD, ARTHUR H., AND CROCKETT, WALTER H. "Employee Attitudes and Employee Performance," *Psychological Bulletin*, September, 1955, pp. 396–424.

GUION, ROBERT M. "The Problem of Terminology," *Personnel Psychology*, Spring, 1958, pp. 59–64.

HAIRE, M., AND GOTTSDANKER, J. S. "Factors Influencing Industrial Morale," *Personnel*, May, 1951, pp. 445–54.

LIKERT, RENSIS. "Measuring Organizational Performance," *Harvard Business Review*, March–April, 1958, pp. 41–50.

MASLOW, A. H. "A Theory of Human Motivation," *Psychological Review*, Vol. 50 (1943), pp. 370–96.

---

[41] Chester I. Barnard, *The Functions of the Executive* (Cambridge: Harvard University Press, 1938), pp. 19–21, 82–83.

CHAPTER 6

Status and Role

THE last chapter dealt mainly with individual behavior and how it is conditioned by attitudes and motives. However, additional understanding of behavior must be sought in a social context. Hans Speier observes, "A man's honor neither springs from his personality nor clings to his deeds. It depends upon other men who have the power to bestow honor on him and a will to pay it."[1]

This quotation is quite appropriate for the introduction of a chapter on status and role. Status is a matter of foremost concern in human consciousness. Achieving status positions is a goal toward which people devote countless hours and considerable energy. But unlike attitudes and motives, status is not generated by the individual. It is something, similar to honor, which is given to an individual by others. Status is socially defined and granted.

People are status conscious, although it is probably more accurate to say that people are conscious of the status symbols they possess or lack. Status symbols, however, are simply externalizations of a fundamental social process.

This chapter examines the basic concept of status, noting its application to business organizations. The latter part of the chapter deals with role theory.

STATUS

Status has two connotations. First, it may be thought of as a ranked system of rights and duties of the kind found in the formal structure of a business organization. This view of status is *objective*. Second, status can have a private, *subjective* connotation. For example, one in his own mind can judge another individual. This personal status judgment is not necessarily related to the formal status position that the person being judged holds in the organization.

Thus status may apply to a position in a social structure distinct from the individual who occupies it; or it may apply to a private evaluation of an individual by another. These status connotations are not unrelated, of

---

[1] Hans Speier, "Honor and Social Structure," *Social Research*, February, 1935, p. 74.

course, because a private evaluation of another may very well determine his position in the formal, or objective, structure of the business. This is particularly true when a superior forms opinions of his subordinates.

The Objective Connotation of Status

In the objective sense, status is often considered as a position involving rights and duties arranged in a structure of human interrelationships. A particular status is something apart from the individual who occupies it.[2]

Status systems refer to the total structure of an organization, including a hierarchial pattern of rights and duties. The rights and duties, and their relative position in status hierarchies, are determined by the value systems of institutions.[3] For example, a business organization has various positions carrying rewards, authorities, and obligations. Also, these positions are ordered in relation to each other according to the importance assigned to them by the company.

Thus, a president and vice-president have specific functions to perform, but the value placed on the president's job is greater than that given the vice-president's position. This example could be carried to all the positions in a business organization. The point to keep in mind is that both the *specific* obligations and rewards for status positions, as well as the relative values assigned to them, are determined by the company. *Management imposes the status hierarchy.*

The Subjective Connotation of Status

The subjective aspect of status is concerned with how people come to make status judgments of others. Man constantly evaluates those with whom he comes in contact. This behavior is a process of making *status judgments*. From these private judgments an individual receives a status in a plant, office, or executive group.[4] Status from this point of view is an individual's position in a social system resulting from the judgment of others regarding him.[5]

---

[2] Linton points out that role is the dynamic counterpart of a status position. An individual is given a status through a social process; but when he begins to discharge the obligations of this position he is said to be playing a role. Status and role, thus, are inseparable. Ralph Linton, *The Study of Man* (New York: D. Appleton-Century Co., 1936), pp. 113–14.

[3] The hierarchial aspect of status is discussed at length by Emile Benoit-Smullyan, "Status, Status Types, and Status Interrelations," *American Sociological Review*, April, 1944, pp. 151–61.

[4] The status one receives may be translated into a position in the formal organization, or a position in an informal organization, or it may simply remain one person's opinion of another.

[5] Status is approached this way by Herbert Goldhammer and Edward A. Shils, "Types of Power and Status," *American Journal of Sociology*, September, 1939, p. 179; and George C. Homans, *The Human Group* (New York: Harcourt, Brace and Co., 1950), p. 179. This method of viewing status presumes application to both formal and informal evaluations. That is, people are placed by the judgment of others into

The Criteria Underlying Status Judgments. People's status judgments are based on criteria. A judgment is a form of measurement through which status decisions are made by comparing an individual against certain standards. According to Talcott Parsons, five standards are used to measure status.[6] Briefly described they are:

1. *Birth*—a person may hold a certain status simply by being born into a particular family, social class, race, or sex. A president of a company may hold his position because a tradition passes the presidency through the family.
2. *Personal qualities*—one person may be differentiated from another, status-wise, because of age, strength, intelligence, or just being a "good guy."
3. *Achievements*—a person may be accorded status because of his accomplishments. A president of a corporation may hold a high status among his fellow businessmen because his leadership results in success for his company.
4. *Possessions*—"possessions" refer to an individual's belongings. The kinds and amounts of such belongings may be used as a basis for judging status.
5. *Authority*—authority is considered as the right to command action from others. The extent of authority is an important measure of status in business.

Not all individuals or groups at all places and at all times are going to weigh each of these standards the same. Different weights are assigned to these standards by the groups and individuals with whom one comes in contact. This accounts for the fact that a person can have a "high" status position in one group and a "low" status position in another.

The purpose of making status evaluations is to associate a person with a position on a "status scale" which ranges between two extremes—high and low. A person's position on the scale results from the "score" he makes when evaluated. The method of evaluation may be described as a comparison process. Each person brings to a social situation a "status profile," which is some weighted combination of the status-measuring characteristics mentioned above.

Now, the people with whom an individual associates have norms or standards also comprised of the same characteristics. The degree to which the "profile" of the individual matches the norms of the evaluating group determines the status of the person being measured. This rather complex process can be clarified by a diagram, shown as Figure 6–1.

Several remarks can be made about Figure 6–1. First, the profile the individual brings to the evaluating situation is, in this case, heavily weighted on "personal qualities." It might be inferred that this individual is a likeable sort, long on personality and roughly average on the other

___

status positions involving the rights and duties connected with their jobs. Also, people are ranked in terms of private evaluations of others regardless of their duties.

[6] Talcott Parsons, *Essays in Sociological Theory Pure and Applied* (Glencoe: The Free Press, 1949), pp. 171–72. Parsons also mentions a sixth category of power which is status achieved by illegitimate means.

four qualities. The boss evaluating this person is likely to rank him about average because the achievement factor emphasized by the boss is not predominant in the individual's profile. However, his fellow employees will probably give this individual a high status because of the close match of his profile with their measuring norms.

Second, the diagram suggests another important fact about status.

FIGURE 6–1

THE PROCESS OF STATUS EVALUATION

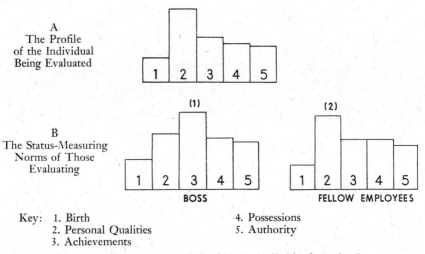

Key: 1. Birth   4. Possessions
       2. Personal Qualities   5. Authority
       3. Achievements

Many different statuses are possible for an individual. Indeed, a person can have as many different statuses as he has contacts with people.

Third, once a person has a status assigned to him he is not doomed forever to that particular status. He may change his profile in such a way so as to make it conform more closely with the norms of those doing the evaluating. For example, the mythical character in Figure 6–1 could improve his "achievements" and, with all the other factors remaining equal, raise his status in the eyes of his boss.

Fourth, as might be guessed, the process of making status evaluations is rather arbitrary. When evaluating others, people do not apply the status-measuring criteria in a uniform way. In other words, people's judgments of the profile of others vary even though the situation in which the evaluation takes place does not vary. Two individuals, for example, performing the same function in an office might be evaluated by their boss as having high status for different reasons. The boss may defer to one because he happens to be the son of the president of the company; the boss might respect the other because of his achievements on the job.

Fifth, status determination is not a unilateral process. An individual entering a status-evaluating situation can cause those measuring to readjust the weights placed on their evaluating norms, just as pressure from a group or individual can cause the individual being evaluated to modify his profile. This last point is associated with the reciprocal relationship which exists between the individual and the evaluating group. It is analyzed in greater detail under the topic of role.

Status Symbols

Once a status position has been assigned, "badges of office" are granted. These badges are status symbols and act as tangible evidence of the rank and function of people in a business organization.

The symbols of formal organizations are easiest to describe. In a company, titles serve as status indicators. The title "vice-president of sales" has a twofold message. First, "vice-president" says the individual occupies a high rank in the *chain of command*. Second, "sales" tells interested parties the function or job the individual performs in the company.

But titles relate only part of the story of an individual's status in a company. At best they are rough indicators, particularly when the middle-management "jungle" is viewed. Here other symbols tend to become more important. External trappings of office such as the size of the desk; name in the company telephone directory; a secretary; the floor on which the office is located; gold, silver, or brass spitoons—all are evidence of a rank in the formal structure. While subtle, these symbols are quite tangible. They show the shadings of status gradients in an organization.

A neat description of status symbols in a bank is given by John P. Marquand in his novel *Point of No Return*.

> Though you seldom talked of salaries at Stuyvesant, your social status was obvious from the *position* of your desk. Charles occupied one of the *two flat mahogany desks* that stood in a sort of *no man's land* between the *roll-top desks* of the officers and the *smaller flat-tops* of lesser executives and secretaries crowding the floor of the bank *outside* the cages. A *green rug* extended from the officers' desks, *forming a neat and restricted zone* that *just included* Charles's desk. . . ."[7]

Without knowing any more about Charles and the Stuyvesant bank than this passage reveals, it is still easy to pinpoint his position in the status structure of the company.

Although fun can be made of the elaborate forms and rituals connected with the use of status symbols in business, their importance as a social phenomenon must not be disregarded.[8] Few grasp the abstract meaning and the logic behind the concept and application of status in a business organization. But the tangible results of the process of making status judg-

---

[7] John P. Marquand, *Point of No Return* (Boston: Little, Brown & Co., 1949), p. 29. Reprinted with permission. Italics are mine; they indicate the symbols mentioned in this short paragraph.

[8] For a further discussion of status symbols see Erving Goffman, "Symbols of Class Status," *British Journal of Sociology*, December, 1951, pp. 294–304.

ments—status symbols—have real significance for those in business. Rewards often are made not only in terms of money but also in terms of symbols. (One executive wryly remarked, "We can amortize a larger office when we promote a man, but we are always stuck with a higher salary for him.") People weigh external evidence of success heavily. Accomplishments do not taste so sweet unless others know about them. Status symbols represent achievement; if symbols are not awarded, many would suffer from severe cases of "status anxiety."

Besides satisfying people's ego requirements, status symbols serve other major purposes in business.

1. *Motivation*—Status symbols act as honors or rewards for achievements. As such, they provide incentives to motivate people toward greater accomplishments.

2. *Identification*—Status symbols make it easier to determine who holds authority and performs differentiated functions in a company. The greater the degree to which specialization of functions is carried the more important status symbols become in order to identify who does what.

3. *Dignification*—Status symbols add dignity to a position and support an executive's authority in that rank.

4. *Stabilization*—Status symbols solidify rank, authority, and areas of work specialization, and this facilitates regularization of work patterns.

Status Systems

So far, the processes of assigning status and the use of symbols have been discussed. Next, and probably most important, is an analysis of the forms status structures assume in business organizations. Earlier it was said that a particular status may be thought of as a position relative to other status positions in a pattern or system.

Status systems incorporate all status positions in an organization into an over-all pattern of relationships. Every status position in a company can be plotted as a point on a matrix having both vertical and horizontal relationships to points representing other status positions.[9] The horizontal status system is called *functional;* the vertical status system is called *scalar.*

Functional Status Systems. Functional status is based upon the *job or task* done in a company. Functional status systems disclose which positions are on the same level in an organization. This type of system is in no way predicated on the right to command. A functional position has no authority over other positions on the same level. Again, functional status is derived from the job and its horizontal relation to other jobs of equivalent importance. Figure 6–2 depicts a horizontal status system.

Scalar Status. The essential feature of scalar status is that it carries the *right to command* others. Scalar status bestows command privileges on individuals occupying positions in a vertical system of relationships. The

[9] This treatment of status systems follows Chester I. Barnard, *Organization and Management* (Cambridge: Harvard University Press, 1949), pp. 207–44.

FIGURE 6-2

An Example of a Functional Status System

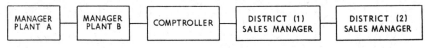

| MANAGER PLANT A | MANAGER PLANT B | COMPTROLLER | DISTRICT (1) SALES MANAGER | DISTRICT (2) SALES MANAGER |

president of a company has a higher scalar status than the vice-presidents. Hence the president has authority to command action from the vice-presidents, and so on through all the superior-subordinate positions down the line. This type of system is shown in Figure 6-3.

FIGURE 6-3

An Example of a Scalar Status System

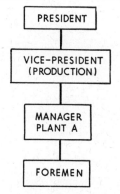

PRESIDENT

VICE-PRESIDENT (PRODUCTION)

MANAGER PLANT A

FOREMEN

The Status "Pyramid." A typical business organization is a combination of scalar and functional systems assuming a form roughly like a pyramid. The sample organization chart in Figure 6-4 demonstrates the pyramid character of the combined status systems.

This figure shows the functional levels of the organization and the scalar chain of command. Note that each executive position on the vertical hierarchy has both functional and scalar status. But observe the positions at the bottom of the chart shown in dotted lines. Obviously the positions occupied by operative employees, clerks, and salesmen have functional status. As for their scalar status, of course these positions do not carry the right to command. However, the concept of scalar status must not be narrowly restricted to include only the command privilege. Scalar status also should be interpreted to imply the obligation to report to a superior. This being the case, it is evident that the positions at the bottom level of the status pyramid simultaneously carry functional and scalar status.

Other Status Relationships. In addition to the basic status systems just discussed, other forms of ranked positions exist in a business organization. One example is the ranking of jobs according to pay grade determined by

job-evaluation methods. An employee could move from job classification "A" to classification "B" with an increase in pay and most likely a
change in function. This status arrangement, however, in no way implies
that a change in classification for pay purposes includes scalar authority
over employees in a lower classification.

The case of the "working supervisor" presents an interesting status

FIGURE 6–4

SAMPLE ORGANIZATION CHART COMBINING FUNCTIONAL AND SCALAR STATUS SYSTEMS

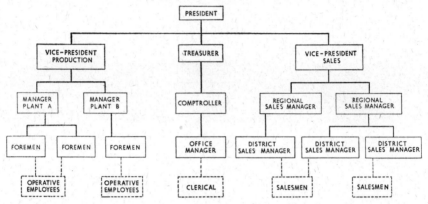

problem. This position goes by many names such as lead man, straw boss,
set-up man, and others. The working supervisor is between the foreman
and the operative employees. He is actually classified as operative employee, but his position is slightly senior to them. The position has scalar
authority including obligations for training new employees; setting-up
for production runs; and acting—by virtue of skill—as a "consultant" for
production problems which might occur on the line.

This position does not include other important scalar prerogatives such
as the right to discipline; fire; give pay increases; and so on. The working
foreman, thus, is in sort of a status never-never land.[10]

The formal structure of a business organization presents myriad cases
of hybrid status relationships, such as line-staff, the "assistant to," liaison
work, and master-apprentice systems. Obviously, all these problems cannot be discussed in this chapter.

**Several Additional Points on the Significance of Status Concepts in Busi-
ness**

Men are constantly making evaluations of others, ranking them according to criteria not always related to how well they are able to do a

---

[10] For a larger treatment of this subject see George Strauss, "The Changing Role
of the Working Supervisor," *Journal of Business*, July, 1957, pp. 202–11.

job. Many human problems and injustices can result from the ranking process when status decisions are incorporated, perhaps informally, into company policy. Just as one example, consider the criterion of "birth" mentioned before. Conflict and dissatisfaction frequently result from Negro versus white, or men versus women comparisons. Birth, not ability, becomes the heavily weighted status criterion which determines job opportunities.

In a very real sense, the status-evaluating standards endorsed by top management seep down through the organizational levels to set a tone throughout the company. Most top managers will agree that in "their" company it is the individual's *achievements* which will merit rewards and advancement for him. While this is undoubtedly true, achievements are not the only standard against which an individual is appraised. Often the individual's *personal characteristics* carry as much status weight as achievements. Personal characteristics mean, among other things, the individual's ability to maneuver in the social and political atmosphere of the company. This factor coupled with a well-considered show of tasteful *possessions* can often determine a person's future in business.

The significance of status systems to management is evident. The formal structure of the company is built on them. One further point, however, needs to be made regarding the functions of status systems. They act to facilitate the communication process. Barnard writes that status systems produce two types of authoritativeness. The first type is command authoritativeness, meaning that an order is backed by a status position on the scalar chain. Command authoritativeness has the reciprocal feature of making clear to whom one has the obligation to report. The second type of authoritativeness is functional. When a person communicates with functional authoritativeness he is doing so as an expert in his job or area of specialization.[11]

Thus, if management wishes to improve communication, a place to begin is with the status system. It is here that distinctions in command privileges and job jurisdiction are determined. If statuses overlap, if there are gaps between status positions, or if status relationships are generally muddled, the effectiveness of the communication process will be diminished accordingly. No one knows for certain who speaks with what kind and how much authority.

ROLE

At the beginning of this chapter, the inseparable nature of status and role was noted. Every status has a role, and every role has a status. While this point is straightforward enough, the concept of role is complex.

---

[11] Barnard, *op. cit.*, pp. 224–28.

Three Points of View on the Subject of Role

Role has three rather distinct connotations. These connotations stem from the particular behavioral science persuasion of the person discussing role.[12] If he is a sociologist, or perhaps an anthropologist, he will approach role as something outside the individual. Role would be considered as a set of social pressures which direct and support an individual in the action he takes in an organization. Coutu defines role in this sense. Role is a ". . . socially prescribed way of behaving in particular situations for any person occupying a given social position or status."[13]

If the social scientist has a psychological orientation, he probably will look upon role as an individual's conception of the part he plays in an organization. Using this point of view in an experimental situation, Gerard observes that in any social situation an individual will tend to evaluate the degree to which his behavior has fulfilled the expectations of the role he has played.[14] Role in this sense is highly personalized because it is based on how the individual visualizes what the role expects of him, and the individual's evaluation of his own actions in terms of these expectations.

The third view of role, which seems to be highly popular currently, is that of the social psychologist. The ". . . concept of role concerns the thoughts and actions of individuals, and, at the same time, it points up the influence upon the individual of socially patterned demands and standardizing forces."[15]

The reciprocal and normative nature of role is stressed in the social psychologist's point of view.[16] For example, a small work group has expectations of the type of behavior it anticipates from members of the group. These expectations are values or norms commonly held by members of the group.[17]

An individual who seeks association with a group must sense what its values are and modify his behavior accordingly. But, as Bakke observes,

---

[12] The three "usages" of role are adapted from Daniel J. Levinson, "Role, Personality, and Social Structure in the Organizational Setting," *Journal of Abnormal and Social Psychology*, March, 1959, p. 172.

[13] Walter Coutu, "Role-Playing versus Role-Taking: An Appeal for Clarification," *American Sociological Review*, April, 1951, p. 180.

[14] Harold B. Gerard, "Some Effects of Status, Role Clarity, and Group Goal Clarity Upon the Individual's Relations to Group Process," *Journal of Personality*, (25) 1956–1957, p. 475.

[15] Levinson, *op. cit.*, p. 170.

[16] See Aidan Southall, "An Operational Theory of Role," *Human Relations* (12), 1959, pp. 17–34.

[17] Frederick L. Bates, "Position, Role, and Status: A Reformulation of Concepts," *Social Forces* (34), 1955–1956, p. 319.

the individual is also capable of modifying the expectations of the group.[18] What results is a "fusion process" which changes both the group and the individual so that their separate values may be reconciled.

These three points of view of role are presented diagrammatically in Figure 6–5. Of course, this presentation is an oversimplification. Most behavioral scientists do not work in a vacuum that prevents them from adopting useful approaches from other areas. This is particularly true since the interdisciplinary study of human behavior has become popular. Nevertheless, within the orientations of the sociological, psychological, and social-psychological disciplines, the propensity exists for shading the consideration of the role concept in the directions noted in Figure 6–5.

Some Management Applications of Role Theory

For management purposes human behavior cannot be treated only in a sociological fashion which views an individual's actions as determined by social pressures. Further, the psychological approach of individual perception of role expectations is not a complete explanation of human behavior. Probably the most satisfactory point of view is the one offered by the social psychologists, which stresses the reciprocal relationship that exists between the individual and the role expectations.

Expectation Forces. Following this approach, the individual is influenced in his actions by two major sources of role expectations—the formal demands made by the company as spelled out in the job, and the informal ones made by the groups contacted by the individual in the work situation. Thus both formal and informal expectation forces make behavioral demands on the individual.

As a result of these demands, the individual attempts to structure the social situation and to define his place in it. This process is called *role definition*. Role definition, as Levinson notes, is an aspect of personality and is expressed in terms of basic values, opinion of one's self, objectives in life, and attachment to an occupation. The purpose of role definition is to guide the individual in his pursuit of goals and to help him obtain work satisfaction.[19]

This approach, however, is somewhat oversimplified. For as Sarbin observes, "role expectations are bidimensional. . . ." For every expectation a formal or informal group might have a reciprocal expectation or demand is made by the individual on these groups.[20] Additionally, as could

---

[18] E. Wight Bakke, "Concept of the Social Organization," in Mason Haire (ed.), *Modern Organization Theory*, (New York: John Wiley and Sons, 1959), pp. 60–61.

[19] Levinson, *op. cit.*, p. 178.

[20] Theodore R. Sarbin, "Role Theory," in Gardner Lindzey (ed.,) *Handbook of Social Psychology* (Cambridge: Addison-Wesley Publishing Co., 1954), Vol. I, p. 255.

FIGURE 6–5

<small>THREE USAGES OF THE ROLE CONCEPT</small>

(1)   (2)

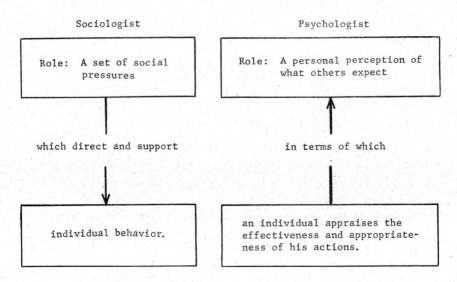

Sociologist   Psychologist

Role: A set of social   Role: A personal perception of
        pressures   what others expect

which direct and support   in terms of which

individual behavior.   an individual appraises the
                                      effectiveness and appropriate-
                                      ness of his actions.

(3)

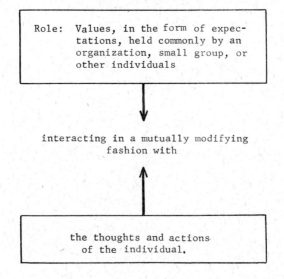

Social Psychologist

Role: Values, in the form of expec-
        tations, held commonly by an
        organization, small group, or
        other individuals

interacting in a mutually modifying
fashion with

the thoughts and actions
of the individual.

be anticipated, the groups themselves can be expected to interact, each affecting the other's expectations. Figure 6–6 shows the interacting of relationships these preliminary remarks suggest.

The outcome of the pattern indicated in Figure 6–6 is the fusion process, which, in turn, is a fragment of Bakke's total theory of social organization. He says that the reconciliation of expectancies brought by the

FIGURE 6–6

ROLE EXPECTATIONS AND THEIR INTERACTIONS

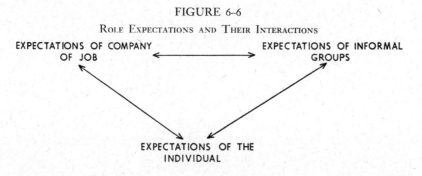

fusion process acts ". . . to maintain the integrity of the organization in the face of divergent interests of individuals, groups, other organizations, and the organization itself. . . ."[21]

Management should note several things regarding expectation forces:

1. The job is not the only force which makes demands on individuals. The informal organization acts as an expectation force as well. At times informal demands may seem more imperative to the individual than formal job requirements.

2. Each individual will attempt to define the roles expected of him. His "accuracy" in the definitional process can determine his satisfaction and performance on the job. Management can facilitate this process by clearly defining job requirements and company policy.

3. Management can anticipate that the three sources of expectations—formal, informal, and individual—will interact and modify each other.

The Significance of Empathy. Empathy refers to an individual's *role-taking* ability.[22] It is a process whereby an individual "puts himself in another's shoes." There are three general ways, listed by Turner, which an individual can empathize:[23]

1. An individual can *unwittingly* adopt the other's standpoint as his own. The role-taking individual identifies himself with the other.

---

[21] Bakke, *op. cit.*, p. 60.

[22] Role taking and role playing are distinct processes. Role playing refers to overt behavior in which an individual performs what he conceives to be the content of a role. Role playing also is the name of a training technique which is discussed in chapter 19.

[23] Ralph H. Turner, "Role-Taking, Role Standpoint, and Reference Group Behavior," *American Journal of Sociology*, January, 1956, pp. 318–21, 326.

2. The other person can remain as a purely *objective* consideration to the role-taking individual. He understands and interprets the other's role, but he does not allow the role to become his own. In this case the role-taking individual *does not* identify.

3. The role-taking person allows the attitudes of the other to become his own and *consciously* adjusts his behavior as he sees how the other is reacting to it. This is a reflexive or adaptive act in which one modifies his own behavior as he observes the counteraction of the other.

The ability to empathize is of obvious importance for a manager, because it allows for both motivation of others and adjustment to them.[24] If management is to motivate through the attitudes, motives, and satisfactions demanded by other employees, then management must understand the structure of the personality. Management should know the nature of individual expectations. The skill of empathizing—objectively or reflexively—is a powerful tool in achieving an understanding necessary for employee motivation.

Further, the fusion process is facilitated if management, through empathy, can anticipate the internal adjustments necessary for organizational survival. Empathy can be used to weld the diverse expectations in an organization into an internally sound structure. Empathy is one way to achieve organizational stability with flexibility.

Role Conflict.   Role conflict results when an individual is faced with two roles which are incompatible.[25] He cannot meet the expectations of these roles simultaneously, and thus a conflict ensues between them. The seriousness of the conflict depends on two factors:

1. The nature of the situation, including the degree to which the roles are incompatible, and the rigidity with which the expectations are enforced.

2. The personality of the individual, including his adjustment to the situation and his ability to ignore some of the demands of one role or the other.[26]

An individual in a business organization is required to play a number of roles. Traditionally, good management practice attempts to insure that role conflict does not occur in formal job requirements, because of the consequent inefficiencies and employee dissatisfactions.

As far as possible, well-managed companies spell out the functions required of employees and arrange that these functions are not incompatible. Also, the principle of unity of command[27] is framed to counteract the problems which would arise from a number of superiors having different role expectations from the same subordinates.

---

[24] Probably the empathizing forms most valuable to management are the objective and the reflexive since they require *conscious* interpretation and reaction to the role of others.

[25] See John T. Gullahorn, "Measuring Role Conflict," *American Journal of Sociology*, January, 1956, pp. 299–303.

[26] J. W. Getzels and E. G. Guba, "Role, Role Conflict, and Effectiveness: An Empirical Study," *American Sociological Review*, April, 1954, pp. 164–66.

[27] A person should have one, and only one, superior to whom he is responsible.

However, modern business organizations are so complex that it is practically impossible to eliminate all sources of role conflict. One example is the production foreman who is faced with certain productivity demands by his immediate line superior. At the same time, a staff organization—quality control, for instance—is making demands on him in terms of quality expectations. Frequently these two demands are inconsistent and the foreman is faced with a quality-or-quantity dilemma. Whichever route he chooses, someone is likely to label him as incompetent.

In addition to role conflict between functions within the formal organization, there is also the problem of role conflict between the expectations of the formal versus the expectations of the informal organizations. Output restriction is a convenient example of this situation. Output restriction is a deliberate effort, informally enforced by the group, either to produce below standards set by management or not to produce as much as possible under the standard for fear it may be unfavorably revised.

An individual coming into such a situation is faced with two sets of demands. Management wants as much output as possible. The informal organization pressures the individual to restrict his output to some limit that they, not management, consider appropriate. Hence role conflict results!

What does the individual do? On the one hand he may go to either extreme. He can join forces with the output restricters, or he can commit himself to be a rate-buster. On the other hand, the individual may vacillate or try to find a niche somewhere between these two extremes. In speaking of restricters and rate-busters Whyte notes that by far the majority of employees in a particular situation studied by him were "men in the middle." They were pulled in one direction by the goal of higher productivity and in the other by the goal of the restricting work group.[28]

Role conflict, no matter what its origin, is a source of individual frustration and a threat to the integrity of the organization. Management has a greater opportunity to iron out problems of role conflict when they are caused from unclear job definitions or chain-of-command relationships: direct action to adjust the organizational structure is possible. But adjustments are less clear and direct when role conflict is caused by line-staff jurisdictional questions or from formal versus informal demands on the individual.

Part of the answer for settling role conflict in line-staff relationships lies in improved communication and better understanding. One company found a tangible increase in tolerance between the line and staff as a result of weekly meetings of their representatives. These meetings were

---

[28] William F. Whyte, *Money and Motivation* (New York: Harper and Bros., 1955), pp. 46–49.

informal conferences where members of a staff group had the opportunity to discuss matters of mutual interest with foremen.

Settling formal-informal role-conflict problems is in part a responsibility of the manager in whose jurisdiction the conflict occurs and in part a responsibility of those concerned with company policy. The necessity for treating problems in terms of their concrete reality must be emphasized. Often tensions between the company and informal groups are long standing in tradition. For self-protection these tensions force the group to adopt measures in the form of behavioral norms.

Management cannot expect to minimize role conflict simply by treating symptoms. Output restriction and the pressure to conform to group norms in the situation just discussed are not relieved by pious platitudes. Suspicion of and action against the incentive system probably is a result of a misunderstanding of the nature of the system or a misuse of the system by management. Reduction of role conflict by the manager must be re-enforced by policies coming from top management regarding employee remuneration.

Additionally, a manager in a role-conflict situation has to protect the individual from undue pressure by the informal group. This approach, however, must be balanced by consideration for the structure of the informal organization and the internal harmony of the social system in the manager's unit.

Role Effectiveness. Role effectiveness is something of a counterpart of role conflict. Role effectiveness is a concept which deals with the clarity of the role and the individual's ability to perceive it and play it accurately.[29] Regarding an individual's role perception, Steiner states two propositions:[30]

1. ". . . the more knowledge an individual has concerning the intention, preferences, and beliefs of other persons, the more effectively he can participate in group activity with these persons."
2. ". . . groups composed of individuals with accurate social perceptions will be more efficient than groups composed of members with less accurate social perceptions."

These propositions, according to Steiner, are true only if group members are motivated to cooperate, the social perception of individuals is relevant to the activities of the group, members are free to alter their behavior as a result of their perceptions of others, and behavioral changes result in a more closely knit social organization.[31]

---

[29] For an interesting discussion showing the reaction of individuals in different status levels under varying conditions of role clarity, see Gerard, *op. cit.*, pp. 475–88.

[30] J. D. Steiner, "Interpersonal Behavior as Influenced by Accuracy of Social Perception," *Psychological Review* (62), 1955, p. 268.

[31] *Ibid.*, p. 273.

Steiner feels that achieving these two propositions is rather remote. But they do constitute important benchmarks for management's efforts to achieve both an efficient and an effective organization. Accurate individual role perceptions precede effective performance on a job. Management must clarify the role an individual is to play by communication and training.

A FINAL REMARK

The topics of status and role deal with another facet of behavior explained in this chapter largely in terms of group processes and the interaction of the individual with these processes. The previous chapter, treating aspects of personality, and the subjects in this chapter should not be viewed compartmentally. The material in both chapters is concerned with explaining behavior at work, but from different points of view. Behavior cannot be understood entirely apart from a social context, nor can social processes be explained without considering the influence of individual attitudes and motives upon them.

REVIEW QUESTIONS

1. Distinguish between the objective and the subjective meanings of status. How do they interact in a work situation?

2. What is involved in the process of making "status judgments?"

3. "The status hierarchy is imposed by management." Discuss.

4. Discuss the functions of status symbols in formal organizations.

5. What is meant by a status *system?*

6. Point out the key characteristics of:
   a) the functional status system,
   b) the scalar status system.

7. The concepts of status and role are inseparable. Why?

8. Compare the three usages of the concept of role.

9. What are expectation forces? Give specific examples of these forces in a work situation.

10. Discuss the nature of role conflict.

SUPPLEMENTARY READINGS

BAKKE, E. WIGHT. "Concept of the Social Organization," *Modern Organization Theory* (ed. Mason Haire), pp. 16–75. New York: John Wiley and Sons, 1959.

BARNARD, CHESTER I. *Organization and Management*, pp. 207–44. Cambridge: Harvard University Press, 1949.

BATES, FREDERICK L. "Position, Role, and Status: A Reformulation of Concepts," *Social Forces* (34), 1955–1956, pp. 313–21.

LEVINSON, DANIEL J. "Role, Personality, and Social Structure in the Organizational Setting," *Journal of Abnormal and Social Psychology*, March, 1959, pp. 170–80.

LINTON, RALPH. *The Study of Man*, chap. 8. New York: D. Appleton-Century Co., 1936.

SOUTHALL, AIDAN. "An Operational Theory of Role," *Human Relations* (12) 1959, pp. 17–34.

CHAPTER 7

Organization

CHAPTER 5 treated the cornerstones of individual personality structure, and Chapter 6 dealt with some of the ways the individual interacted with others using status and role ideas as focal points. This chapter and the next shift the analysis from the orientation of the individual proper to a study of groups.

Organization has long been a subject of considerable interest. In the realm of human affairs, some of the first comprehensive treatises on organization are found in military and political literature. Later, and particularly in this century, the study of organization expanded to include business. Now organization and organizing activities are considered essential facets of the business framework and the activities of the executive.

Organization is crucially important in the behavioral sciences. Therefore, it is appropriate to spend a good deal of time in discussing it and pointing out some of the significant implications organization holds for management practice. Modern man is intent on drawing himself into a web of collectivized patterns. He ". . . has learned to accommodate himself to a world increasingly organized. The trend toward ever more explicit and consciously drawn relationships is profound and sweeping; it is marked by depth no less than by extension."[1] This comment by Seidenberg nicely states the pervasive influence of organization in all forms of human activity, including work.

Some of the reasons for the extension and depth of organizational activity are found in the fundamental transitions which revolutionized our society. These transitions have already been discussed in Chapter 1. To repeat, they changed our country from a rural-agricultural civilization to one based on technology, industry, and the city. These changes resulted in the intensification of the collision effect stemming from the proximity and dependency of people on each other. In turn, proximity and dependency, as conditions of social life, harbor the threats of human conflict, capricious antisocial behavior, instability of human relationships,

---

[1] Roderick Seidenberg, *Post-Historic Man* (Boston: Beacon Press, 1951), p. 1.

and uncertainty about the nature of the social structure and its concomitant roles.

Of course, these threats are present to some degree in all societies from the primitive to the modern. But these threats become dangerous when the harmonious functioning of a society rests on the maintenance of a highly intricate, delicately balanced form of human collaboration. The civilization we have created depends on the preservation of a precarious equilibrium. Hence, disrupting forces impinging on this shaky form of collaboration must be minimized or eliminated.

Traditionally, organization is viewed as a vehicle for accomplishing goals and objectives. While this view is probably true enough, it tends to obscure the inner workings and internal purposes of organization itself. For example, the automobile is a form of organization designed to accomplish transportation objectives, and so are trains and airplanes. This bland statement, however, tells nothing of their internal organizational arrangements. And further, it says nothing of the behavioral forms people adopt when riding in a car versus riding in a plane. This analogy can be applied to human organizations. Both the so-called formal and informal organizations are vehicles for accomplishing objectives. But their internal arrangements and purposes are different, and so the behavioral patterns of people in them are often different.

Another and more fruitful way of treating organization is as a mechanism having the ultimate purpose of offsetting those forces which undermine human collaboration. In this sense, an intensification of the organization trend can be thought of as a product of an intensifying collision effect. Organization tends to minimize conflict and to lessen the significance of that individual behavior which deviates from values the organization has established as worthwhile. Further, organization increases stability in human relationships by reducing uncertainty regarding the nature of the system's structure and the human roles inherent in it. As a corollary to this point, organization enhances the predictability of human action because it limits the number of behaviorial alternatives available to an individual. As Presthus points out, "Organization is defined as a system of structural interpersonal relations . . . individuals are differentiated in terms of authority, status, and role with the result that personal interaction is prescribed. . . . Anticipated reactions tend to occur, while ambiguity and spontaneity are decreased."[2]

---

[2] Robert V. Presthus, "Toward a Theory of Organizational Behavior," *Administrative Science Quarterly*, June, 1958, p. 50. Regulation and predictability of human behavior are matters of degree varying with different types of organizations in something of a continuum. At one extreme are bureaucratic-type organizations with tight bonds of regulation. At the other extreme are informal organizations, with relatively loose bonds of regulation.

In addition, organization has built-in safeguards. Besides prescribing acceptable behavior forms for those who elect to submit to it, organization is also able to offset the influence of human action which transcends its established patterns.[3]

Few segments of society have engaged in organizing more intensively than business.[4] The reason is clear. Business depends on what organization offers. Business needs a system of relationships among functions; it needs stability and predictability in terms of the internal and external activities in which it engages. Business also appears to need harmonious relationships among the people and processes which make it up. Put another way, a business organization has to be relatively free from the destructive tendencies that may result from divergent internal interests.

Various theories of organization have been, and are being, evolved to meet these needs. The purpose of organization theory is to provide a grounding for management action. This chapter and Chapter 8 takes up three theories of organization which have considerable influence on management thought and practice. They are the classical, neoclassical, and modern. Each of these theories is fairly distinct, but at the same time they are not unrelated. These theories are on-going, being actively promoted by several schools of management thought.

THE CLASSICAL THEORY

For lack of a better method of identification, the classical theory of organization deals almost exclusively with the *anatomy of the formal organization*. This doctrine can be traced to Frederick W. Taylor's interest in functional foremanship and planning staffs. However, most students of management thought would agree that the first systematic approach to organization in the United States, and the first analytical attempt to find organizational universals, was in 1931 when Mooney and Reiley published *Onward Industry*.[5] Subsequently, numerous books following the classical vein have appeared. Two of the more recent are Brech's *Organization*[6] and Allen's *Management and Organization*.[7]

---

[3] This point has an interesting side light. A bureaucracy with tight controls and a high degree of predictability appears to be unable to distinguish between destructive and creative deviations from established values. Thus, it seems that the only thing safeguarded is the *status quo*.

[4] The monolithic institutions of the military and the government are other cases of organizational preoccupation.

[5] James D. Mooney and Alan C. Reiley, *Onward Industry* (New York: Harper and Bros., 1931). Later published by James D. Mooney under the title *Principles of Organization*.

[6] E. F. L. Brech, *Organization* (London: Longmans' Green and Co., 1957).

[7] Louis A. Allen, *Management and Organization* (New York: McGraw-Hill Book Co., 1958).

Defining the Formal Organization

Finding a definition of the formal organization is not a difficult job. Four elements of a definition reappear consistently in management literature. Briefly explained, they are:

1. *A system of coordinated activities.* This element underscores the fact that all organizations are composed of parts and relationships. The "parts" of the organization refer to activities or functions performed. The formal system appears when these activities are geared into a logical relationship.
2. *A group of people.* Although an organization can be charted on paper it needs people to bring it to life. Personnel are required to implement the activities.
3. *Cooperation toward a goal.* Cooperation is strictly a human phenomenon. In normal behavior cooperation is always purposeful. Therefore, organizations must have objectives to lend purpose to the actions of people performing functions.
4. *Authority and leadership.* Organizations are structured on superior-subordinate relationships. As the result, authority is a universal element in all formal oranizations. Leadership, however, is an executive's personal quality which prompts willing collaborative effort toward a goal.

A comprehensive operative definition is obtained by combining these elements. *A formal organization is a system of coordinated activities of a group of people working cooperatively toward a common goal under authority and leadership.*

A definition, of course, does not explain in a very satisfactory way the rationale underlying organization. Classical organization theory is built about four key pillars. They are the division of labor, the scalar and functional processes, structure, and span of control. Given these pillars just about all of classical organization theory can be derived.

Pillars of the Formal Organization Theory

1. *Division of labor* is without doubt the cornerstone of the four pillars of classical organization theory. Division of labor has been mentioned in previous chapters as constituting one of the technological dynamics underlying the collision effect.

As a human organization grows work must be divided, otherwise one person's job would be so inclusive that its efficient performance would be impossible. So work is broken down, usually along lines as natural as possible, to provide clear areas of specialization. The reason for dividing work is to promote efficiency.

Division of labor, or specialization, is not restricted to production-line jobs but extends to all the functions at the highest levels in the organization. Figure 7–1 illustrates the growth of managerial specialization in a company.

Stage I in this figure represents a one-man operation in which the owner is performing all three organic business functions. As business gets better the boss hires another employee to perform the function of production, as shown in Stage II. Stage III represents a phase in growth where all three organic business functions are performed by specialists,

FIGURE 7–1

THE GROWTH OF MANAGERIAL
SPECIALIZATION

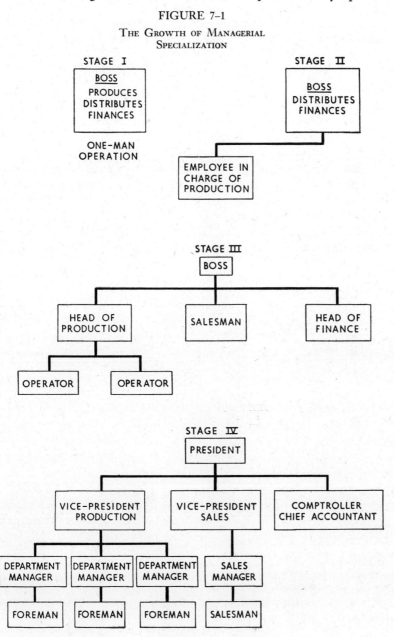

with the boss acting as coordinator. Finally, Stage IV demonstrates a further division of labor within the organic functions themselves.

This demonstration of organizational growth is something of a classical treatment, showing how a business will expand by specializing the organic business functions of creation, distribution, and finance. This approach to the division of labor in classic organization theory is frequently treated under such topical headings as departmentation, or functional evolution and devolution.[8]

The division of labor is so basic to classic organization theory that the other three pillars flow from it as corollaries. For example, vertical and horizontal growth, through the scalar and functional processes, requires specialization and departmentalization of functions. Organization structure is dependent on the direction which specialization of activities travels during company development. Finally, span of control problems results from the number of specialized functions, and specialists, under the jurisdiction of a manager.

2. The *scalar and functional processes* deal with the organization's vertical and horizontal growth respectively.[9] The scalar process refers to the growth of the chain of command which results in levels added to the organizational structure. The scalar process is accomplished through the delegation of authority and responsibility. Figure 7–2 demonstrates this process.

FIGURE 7–2

THE SCALAR PROCESS

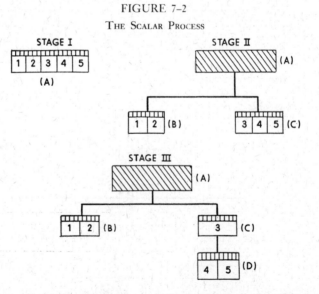

---

[8] For example see Harold Koontz and Cyril O'Donnell, *Principles of Management* (New York: McGraw-Hill Book Co., 1955), chap. 7.

[9] These processes are discussed at length in Ralph Currier Davis, *The Fundamentals of Top Management* (New York: Harper and Bros., 1951), chap. 7.

Assume that "A" starts out with specific job responsibilities 1, 2, 3, 4, and 5 in Stage I. In Stage II, "A" delegates to "B" responsibilities 1 and 2, and to "C" responsibilities 3, 4, and 5. "C" in Stage III delegates to "D" job responsibilities 4 and 5. The shaded areas indicate ultimate authority and responsibility which cannot be delegated. Thus, while at Stages II and III, "A" does not have the *specific* job responsibilities he had formerly, he still is accountable to a higher authority for the performance of those to whom he has delegated these tasks. Through the scalar process, then, the organization has grown vertically from one to three levels.

The functional process is the method by which the organization grows horizontally. This process is illustrated in Figure 7–3.

FIGURE 7–3

THE FUNCTIONAL PROCESS

STAGE I

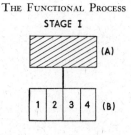

STAGE II

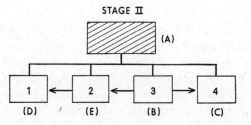

In Stage I, "A" is supervising "B" who has job responsibilities 1, 2, 3, and 4. On the authority of "A" in Stage II, three of the jobs formerly performed by "B" are split off into separate functional jurisdictions *on the same level* under "C," "D," and "E." Thus, the second level in this diagram has moved from one position in Stage I to four positions in Stage II via the division of labor along functional lines.

The basic processes of organizational growth described here are applicable to the line organization as well as to the emergence of the staff functions in a company.

3. *Structure* is a rather inclusive term which is applied to the logical relationships that exist among the various activities performed in an organization. The purpose of structure is to provide an orderly arrangement among functions so that the objectives of the organization can be accomplished efficiently. Structure implies system and pattern.

Classical organization theory usually works with two basic structures: the line and the staff. The line organization refers to the primary chain of command which devolves directly from the organic business functions. The staff organization is frequently treated as advisory and facilitative functions for the line. Also, such activities as committees and liaison functions fall quite readily into the purview of structural considerations. Again, structure is the vehicle for introducing logical and consistent relationships among the diverse functions which comprise the organization.[10]

4. The *span-of-control* concept relates to the number of subordinates a manager can effectively supervise. Graicunas has been credited with first

FIGURE 7–4

SPAN OF CONTROL AND ORGANIZATIONAL STRUCTURE

Tall Structure	*Flat Structure*
X X X X X X X XX XX XX XX	X X X X X X X X X X X
Levels. .4 Span . . .2	Levels. .2 Span . .10

elaborating the point that there are numerical limitations to the subordinates one man can control.[11] In a more recent statement on this subject, Brech points out that "span" refers to ". . . the number of persons, themselves carrying managerial and supervisory responsibilities, for whom the senior manager retains his over-embracing responsibility of direction and planning, co-ordination, motivation and control."[12]

Regardless of interpretation, the span concept directs attention to the

---

[10] For a discussion of structure see William H. Newman, *Administrative Action* (Englewood Cliffs: Prentice-Hall, Inc., 1951), chap. 16.

[11] V. A. Graicunas, "Relationships in Organization," *Papers on the Science of Administration* (New York: Columbia University, 1937).

[12] Brech, *op. cit.*, p. 78. Udy talks of the span of control in terms of the relation of technological processes to formal organization structure. He suggests that size alone does not explain span. Span is related to technological process and the span of attention. Span of attention is equal to the total number of tasks, plus the maximum number of specialized operations ever performed at once, plus a factor "C" which is 1 or 0 depending on whether combined effort is ever present (1) or always absent (0) in the entire process. If the span of attention is greater than any technological process will tend to be performed on three or more levels of authority. If the span of attention is equal to or less than five then technological processes will tend to be performed on fewer than three levels. Stanley H. Udy, Jr., "The Structure of Authority in Non-Industrial Production Organizations," *American Journal of Sociology*, May, 1959, pp. 582–84.

complexity of human and functional interrelationships in an organization. The number of interrelationships among individuals grows at a rapid pace when people are added to a department. Further, span of control has significance also in terms of the shape of the organization that evolves through growth. Wide span yields a flat structure; short span results in a tall structure (see Figure 7–4).

Appraisal of the Classical Doctrine of Organization

March and Simon have two indictments of the classical theory of organization. "First, in general there is a tendency to view the employee as an inert instrument performing the tasks assigned to him. Second, there is a tendency to view personnel as a given rather than as a variable in the system."[13] Because of its focus on the mechanics of organization, the classical school overlooks the significance of the impact of people on the anatomy of the formal structure.

It would not be fair to say that the classical school is unaware of the human problems which affect organization. They simply do not treat in any systematic way the interplay of individual personality, informal groups, intraorganizational conflict, and the decision process in their conception of the formal structure. Additionally, the classical school has failed to incorporate in its theory the contributions of the behavioral sciences as part of a comprehensive explanation of human behavior in the organization.

Classical theory, however, has relevant insights into the nature of organization which should not be discounted. But the value of this theory is limited by its narrow concentration on the formal anatomy of organization.

NEOCLASSICAL THEORY OF ORGANIZATION

The neoclassical theory of organization recognizes and attempts to compensate for some of the deficiencies in classical doctrine. The neoclassical school is commonly identified with the human relations movement. The neoclassical theory of organization has three characteristic features.

Generally the neoclassical approach takes the postulates of the classical school pertaining to the pillars of organization as given. But these postulates are regarded as being modified by people, acting individually or within the context of the informal organization.

The neoclassical school has introduced the behavioral sciences in an interdisciplinary fashion into the theory of organization. Through the

---

[13] James G. March and Herbert A. Simon, *Organizations* (New York: John Wiley and Sons, 1958), p. 29.

use of the behavioral sciences the human relationists demonstrate how the pillars of the classical doctrine are affected by the impact of human actions. Thus, people in organizations are lifted from the class of "givens" to the class of organizational "variables."

Finally, the neoclassical approach includes a systematic treatment of the informal organization, showing its influence on the formal structure and its effect on individuals in the system.

Thus, the neoclassical theory of organization gives evidence of accepting some aspects of the framework of classical doctrine but superimposes on it modifications resulting from individual behavior and the informal group. The inspiration of the neoclassical school was the Hawthorne studies cited in previous chapters. Current examples of neoclassical doctrine are found in such human relations books as Gardner and Moore, *Human Relations in Industry*,[14] and Davis, *Human Relations in Business*.[15]

In this discussion of the neoclassical theory of organization first consideration is given to the modifications of the pillars of classical doctrine. Second, attention is given to a systematic analysis of the neoclassical approach to the informal organization.

Neoclassical Approach to the Pillars of Formal Organization Theory

1. The *division of labor* has been a long-standing subject of comment in the field of human relations. Very early in the history of industrial psychology studies were made of fatigue and monotony caused by the specialization of work.[16] Later, attention shifted to the isolation of the worker and the feeling of anonymity that resulted from an insignificant job which contributed little to the final product.[17]

The division of labor creates a special set of human problems regardless of the level in the organization in which specialization exists. The division of labor intensifies employee interdependency. Each segment of a production line is intimately connected by the functions which come before and after it. Similarly, executives at high levels in an organization are dependent on the activities and decisions of other executives.

The conditions of interdependency generated by the division of labor create strains and tensions. Whyte, in his study *Human Relations in the Restaurant Business*, lucidly describes the stresses which result from the

---

[14] Burleigh B. Gardner and David G. Moore, *Human Relations in Industry* (Homewood: Richard D. Irwin, 1955), esp. chaps. 3, 4, 5, 13.

[15] Keith Davis, *Human Relations in Business* (New York: McGraw-Hill Book Co., 1957), esp. chaps. 4, 5, 6.

[16] Hugo Munsterberg, *Psychology and Industrial Efficiency* (Boston: Houghton Mifflin Co., 1913).

[17] Probably the classic statement is found in Elton Mayo, *The Human Problems of an Industrial Civilization* (Cambridge: Harvard University Press, 1946; first printing, 1933).

interrelations of cooks, countermen, waitresses, and kitchen runners.[18] Nor are these tensions restricted to operative-level employees. The division of labor which results in the emergence of staff organizations creates its own special frictions with the line executives.

Because the division of labor gives rise to many different, and often quite narrow, areas of specialization, the need for managerial coordination becomes paramount. Frequently coordination, or the meshing together of parts, requires a higher order of motivational ability to get people to work cooperatively. This is not a particularly easy assignment. At the operative level, for example, it is extremely difficult to convince an assembly-line worker that his function is contributing significantly to the final product. The routine and boring nature of the job stifles enthusiasm and inhibits any latent desire this employee might have to see "the big picture" and the relation of his job to it.

Specialization breeds a somewhat different problem at executive levels. The division of labor tends to segment the organization into little domains of authority and influence. Often executives come to regard these domains as their own special empires which have first call on their attention and abilities. Efforts to weld areas of executive specialization into a consistent, synchronized part of the over-all organization are frequently resisted by managers as an undue infringement on their jurisdictions. Thus, specialization brings about jealously guarded functional segments in the organization.

These few comments about the effects of the division of labor should be contrasted with the classical idea that the reason for specialization is efficiency. It cannot be doubted that mass-production techniques have brought about a high order of industrial output. But at the same time, the ultimate of efficiency hoped for from the division of labor has been denied because of the human problems this division has created.

In order to overcome these problems, a number of recommendations have been made by the neoclassical school. Participation in the decision-making process has been offered to get the operative employee "involved" in his job and interested in the company. Participation allows the employee to have some say in his destiny in an often all-too-impersonal environment. For the younger executive, bottom-up management, or the establishment of junior boards, is another management device. Bottom-up management gives the junior executive a chance to participate in top-management decisions. This technique allows the younger man to see the company from a top-level perspective and acts as a counterbalance to specialization in one activity.[19]

---

[18] William F. Whyte, *Human Relations in the Restaurant Business* (New York: McGraw-Hill Book Co., 1948).

[19] For further discussion of this subject see William B. Given, *Bottom-Up Management* (New York: Harper and Bros., 1949).

In addition to these specific remedies, development of "human relations training programs" has upsurged. The goal of these programs is to
improve the leadership ability of managers so that they may become better motivators and coordinators of human effort.

2. The delegation of authority and responsibility presents a class of
problems connected with the *scalar and functional processes.* The classical doctrine assumes something of perfection in the delegation and
functionalization processes. The neoclassical school points out that human
problems are caused by imperfections in the way these processes are
discharged.

The first such problem is insufficient delegation of authority. This
means basically that an individual is given a job to do, he is given a
responsibility, but he is not given adequate authority to carry out his
obligation. For example, a sales manager is given the job of improving
sales in his territory, but he has no control over the hiring of salesmen.
This duty may be vested in some other jurisdiction in the company.
Obviously the sales manager will be frustrated in the accomplishment
of his objective if the men who are hired are not up to his standards and
fail to perform.

The next problem stems from gaps in or overlapping of functions.
This problem is illustrated in Figure 7–5. Situation A is a case of gaps in

FIGURE 7–5

GAPS IN AND OVERLAPPING OF JOB RESPONSIBILITIES

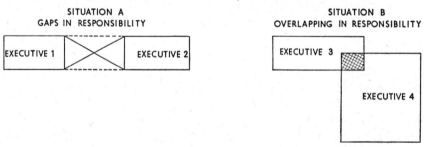

job obligations. The area marked with an x is no-man's land. There is a job
here that has to be done, but neither executive one nor executive two
claims the responsibility for it. When the job does not get done, and the
executives' superior wonders why, both one and two blame each other.
Unclear designation of areas of jurisdiction in this case caused friction.

In situation B, the responsibilities of executives three and four overlap.
That is, both these executives are responsible for part of each other's
area of jurisdiction. Joint responsibility can cause clashes of personality.
Since both executives presumably will be held accountable for the

performance of their mutual responsibility, they may disagree on how the job can be best accomplished. Lack of a clear distinction in delegated jurisdictions in this case makes it difficult for a superior to pinpoint responsibility for failure or to give praise to the right person for success.

The third problem connected with delegation is violation of the unity-of-command principle. This principle states that any individual should have one and only one boss. Considerable frustration can result from being accountable to more that one person for the performance of a job. This is especially true when the two bosses are likely to have different standards by which they judge performance.[20]

3. *Structure* provides endless avenues of analysis for the neoclassical theory of organization. The general theme is that human behavior disrupts the best laid organizational plans and thwarts the cleanness of the logical relationships founded in the structure. The neoclassical analysis of structure centers on frictions which appear internal to the organization among people performing different functions.

Line and staff relations constitute a problem much discussed in this respect. Many companies seem to have difficulty keeping the line and staff working together harmoniously. Line-staff frictions have numerous causes. Dalton, in a study of line-staff relationships, isolated five which he feels to be most important.[21]

First, the basic differences in duties carried on by line and staff executives can be a cause for friction among them. The staff executive usually lives in a technical world and speaks a technical language. The line executive is more of a "generalist;" that is, while he has specific job duties to perform he also is occupied by "human relations" problems of leadership and motivation.

In a very real sense, there is a language barrier thwarting effective communication between the line and the staff. The staff man speaks the language of his technical specialty, which is often misunderstood by the line official. The breakdown in communication resulting from functional differences is a basic cause of line-staff conflict.

Second, Dalton found marked distinctions between the line and the staff executives on the counts of age and education. Overall the staff executive was younger and, as might be expected, better educated than the line executive. A distrust of youth and an anti-intellectual bias on the part of line managers could make for conflict situations. In addition to these differentials, Dalton also found differences between the line and the staff in terms of dress, recreational interests, and social backgrounds.

---

[20] These breakdowns in the scalar and functional processes through faulty delegation practices are adapted from Keith Davis, *op. cit.*, pp. 63–65.

[21] Melville Dalton, "Conflicts between Staff and Line Managerial Officers," *American Sociological Review*, June, 1950, pp. 342–51.

Third, as a matter of attitude, staff personnel constantly felt they had to justify their existence. This sentiment could stem from the insecurity staff might feel in terms of the importance of their jobs relative to the jobs performed by the line.

Fourth, the line executives felt the staff was trying to undermine its authority by expansion into areas thought by line managers to be properly in their jurisdiction.

And fifth, the staff had a feeling it was "under the thumb" of the line organization in the sense that promotion could come only through the approval of influential line managers.

Dalton does not wish to generalize these findings to all industrial situations. However, they certainly contain some universal ingredients of conflict. In many ways the staff executive is not prepared for what he meets in day-to-day company operations. He is trained to enter a world of logical relationships and to carry out precise functions. Instead, his freedom to act logically is limited by the sentiments of the people with whom he must work. It appears the most successful staff men are those who side with the informally powerful line officers.

Further, traditional management thinking points out clear-cut divisions in line and staff roles. Theoretically, line work ends in a finished product or service which is distributed to consumers. Staff work ends in paper. In some companies, however, it is difficult to see a black-and-white distinction between line and staff work. Under such circumstances, a member of a staff organization feels his contribution is an integral part of the finished product. He may be wrong, according to management theory, but it is hard to make him believe otherwise.

Also, it seems that the logic of structure is against the staff man. Typically, the staff organization is a flat type of structure while the line is tall. Some meditation on this point leads inevitably to the conclusion that no matter how good the staff man happens to be there are fewer places for him to be promoted in the staff as compared to the line. The plusher, more lucrative jobs are more plentiful in the tall-type line organization. But, again, the emphasis for line management is balanced more toward administrative, generalist skills rather than technical specialties. This perhaps is a partial explanation for the rather large numbers of engineers, accountants, and the like, who, after taking their first degree in a specialty, are back in graduate school working for an M.B.A. in "management." They found they could progress just so far in their specialty. Advancement, as many of them see it, rests on being equipped to assume broader administrative responsibilities.

4. An executive's *span of control* is largely a function of human determinants; and the reduction of span to a precise, universally applicable ratio is silly, according to the neoclassicists. Writers in the fields of

management and psychology have isolated four factors which determine the span of control:[22]

   a) Individual differences pertaining to a manager's ability.
   b) Effectiveness of organizational communication.
   c) Efficiency of formal control exercised over operations.
   d) The type of job supervised (with everything else equal, the more routine the job, the greater will be the executive's span).

Whenever the span of control is discussed the dilemma of the "tall" versus the "flat" type of organization appears. Which promotes better human relations?

The flat-type structure has the advantage of shorter lines of communication together with "forced delegation" of authority and responsibility. Forced delegation means that a manager has to pass responsibilities and authority on to his subordinates in order for the flat system to work effectively. Dubin notes: "Worthy has suggested that 'flattening' the management structure by reducing the number of levels of managers has had positive consequences for morale among employees of Sears Roebuck and Company."[23] But on the other hand, the flat structure may have the disadvantage of too-impersonal relationships. Also, in some situations the lack of close supervision may result in frustration for subordinates.

Two strong features of the tall-type structure are closer superior-subordinate relationships between adjacent levels and the ability to exercise tighter supervision when and where needed. In terms of human relations losses, the process of "layering" may cause individuals on the lower levels of the organization to feel like "cogs in a machine." Further, the tall organization requires long lines of communication which may result in breakdowns in the communication process.

In the final analysis, the selection of a tall or flat organization is a situational problem. Because of individual and organizational differences both types are found in business. Companies in retailing, such as the J. C. Penney Company; Sears, Roebuck and Company; and Krogers, lean toward the flat structure. Manufacturing, however, is characterized by shorter spans with more levels—in short, the tall structure.

There is a theoretical tendency to favor the flatter form of organization for the reason that tall structures breed autocratic leadership, which is often pointed to as a cause of low morale conditions. Further, as

---

[22] These four factors were drawn from the following sources: John M. Pfiffner, "The 'Third Dimension' of Organization," *Personnel*, March, 1952, pp. 391–99; Waino W. Suojonen, "The Span of Control—Fact or Fable?" *Advanced Management*, November, 1955; and Walter B. Schaffir, "Current Trends in Organization," *Management Review*, March, 1954, pp. 145–46.

[23] Robert Dubin, "Stability of Human Organizations," in Mason Haire (ed.) *Modern Organization Theory* (New York: John Wiley and Sons, 1959), p. 229.

Dubin observes, organizational stability seems to be a function of minimizing the number of links between activities or individuals in organizations.[24] If this is so then the flatter type of organization would tend to be more stable than the taller type, because fewer levels require fewer links.

This concludes the discussion of some of the major contributions made by the neoclassical school to the pillars of the formal organization. One must realize that the human relations movement is far more comprehensive than the organizational aspects just discussed. Such subjects as leadership, participation, counseling, training, wages and incentive systems, and communication could conceivably be shown as further modifications of the classical pillars. However, each of these subjects is so broad in itself that none of them can be included in this chapter.

The informal organization is consistent with the objectives of this chapter, and is treated next.

The Neoclassical View of the Informal Organization

Nothing more than the barest mention of the informal organization is given in even the most recent classical treatises on organization theory.[25] Systematic analysis of this form of organization has been left to the neoclassists. The informal organization refers to people in group associations at work, but these associations are not specified in the "blueprint" of the formal organization. The informal organization is synonomous with natural groupings of people in the work situation.

In a general way the informal organization appears in response to the social motive—the desire of people to associate with others. This explanation, however, is not particularly satisfying for analytical purposes. Research has produced the following, more specific determinants underlying the existence of informal organizations.

Factors Giving Rise to the Informal Organization. The four determinants discussed in this respect are location, occupation, interests, and special issues.

1. The *location* determinant states simply that in order to form into groups of any lasting nature, people have to have frequent day-to-day contact. In the normal course of daily routine, location is an important condition determining who will see whom. Thus, the geography of physical location in a plant or office often is the first elementary consideration in plotting informal organizations.[26] In one mail-order company, for example, two almost identical functions are performed in units located at either end of a building one block long. Although the functions are

---

[24] *Ibid.*, p. 232.

[25] For example: Brech, *op. cit.*, pp. 27–29; and Allen, *op. cit.*, pp. 61–62.

[26] See Leon Festinger, Stanley Schachter, and Kurt Back, *Social Pressures in Informal Groups* (New York: Harper and Bros., 1950), pp. 153–63.

similar, the geographic barrier prevents the employees in these units from forming a lasting informal association.

2. *Occupation* is another key determinant underlying the rise and composition of informal groups. Provided geographic barriers are not insurmountable, there is a tendency for people performing similar jobs to group together.[27] The distinction between factory and office employees provides a convenient example. In addition to a frequent physical separation, a status barrier also divides these occupations.

A case is on record of a girl who previously worked in an office before being transferred to the plant of a company to become secretary to a general foreman. Although the new location was a considerable distance from her old office, the young lady walked it for lunch every day in order to continue her previous associations. She refused to "fraternize" with the girls working on the assembly line in the plant. Our secretary overcame the geographic barrier because her status and occupational attachments to the old group were exceedingly strong.

3. *Interests* are another determinant for informal group formation. Even though people might be performing similar jobs in the same location, differences of interest among them explain why several small informal organizations emerge instead of one large one.

4. *Special issues* often result in the formation of informal groups, but this determinant is set apart from the three previously mentioned. In this case, people who do not necessarily have similar interests, occupations, or locations may join together for a common cause. Issues like layoffs, changes in pay computation, major policy shifts, or relocation of company operations to another part of the country may cause the rise of organizations that transcend the more "natural" boundaries set by the three determinants already mentioned.

Once the issue is resolved the tendency is to revert to the more "natural" informal groupings again. However, there are cases where the existence of an organization is necessary for the continued maintenance of employee interests. When such vigilance is required the previously informal association may crystalize into a formal organization with built-in features to safeguard its continuity. One need only read the history of organized labor to find examples of this phenomenon.

When informal organizations come into being they assume certain characteristics and functions. These are discussed next.

Functions and Characteristics of the Informal Organization. Five characteristics of the informal organization are discussed in this section: the informal organization as an agency of social control; the structure of informal organization; its status and communication systems; its resistance to change; and the informal leader.

---

[27] For an example see W. Fred Cotrell, *The Railroader* (Palo Alto: The Stanford University Press, 1940), chap. 3.

1. Informal organizations act as agencies of *social control*. Like most organizations, the informal organization offers rewards, but it also makes behavioral demands on its members. Each informal organization has a culture that incorporates standards of conduct to which individuals must conform if they expect to derive the advantages of group association.

Schneider lists some of the advantages which flow from informal group membership.[28] They are:

a) Relief from monotony, boredom, and fatigue. This advantage seems largely applicable only to production employees doing routine jobs.

b) Opportunities for status. This factor applies to both production employees and executives. Belonging to prestige groups and associating with influential people in management can result in considerable reflected glory and power for the individual.

c) Increased flow of emotional responses. The group in this case is visualized as providing an emotional outlet for employees, offering an opportunity for self-expression.

d) Increased security. The informal group offers support and reenforcement for the individual in terms of his relationship with the formal structure of organization and also in terms of his social relationships with fellow employees.

Now, obviously, if the individual thinks these advantages are important to him he will be submissive to the demands made by the informal organization in the form of complying to behavioral expectations. These expectations often are innocent enough, involving submitting to rituals of initiation into the group, manners of speech, ways of dress, participating in certain recreational activities, eating at a particular restaurant, and so on. But the informal organization may at times have values which are at odds with those of the formal organization. So an individual may very well find himself in a situation of conflicting expectations. This point has been discussed previously in Chapter 6 under the topic of role conflict.

2. Efforts to chart or plot the relationships of people in the informal organization have revealed their complex nature. Sociometric analysis is used to discover the status relations existing in the informal organization. Figure 7–6 presents one form of a sociometric diagram.

The informal organization depicted in Figure 7–6 shows three status categories: the primary group, a fringe status, and an out status. The primary group is the focal point of the informal organization. It is comprised of a tightly knit group of people who in general agree on the same values. The primary group establishes and maintains the culture of the informal organization. It will also be noticed that the individuals in this group are clustered around a key figure designated "A." This individual is the informal leader.

---

[28] Eugene V. Schneider, *Industrial Sociology* (New York: McGraw-Hill Book Co., 1957), pp. 193–203.

The fringe status position is highly dynamic and is usually occupied by individuals undergoing a ritual of initiation. Ultimately, either they will be accepted by the primary group or they will not be accepted and will move into the out status position.

The people occupying an out status position have neither close ties among themselves nor close ties with others in the organization. They are

FIGURE 7-6

THE STRUCTURE OF AN INFORMAL ORGANIZATION

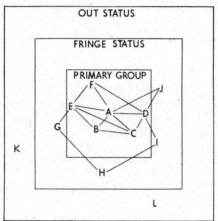

referred to as "isolates." Usually they have this status because of their unwillingness to accept the standards of conduct necessary for admission to the primary group.

It is conceivable, of course, that individuals in the out group in one informal organization might be in the primary group of another. However, the isolate usually chooses nonassociation with any informal organization. He remains to himself by choice, independently holding to his own values.

An out status may or may not be a personal catastrophe, depending on the individual and the nature of the informal organization. If an individual is not interested in ascribing to group values for one reason or another, he may not mind this informal status too much. But if the individual who seeks companionship on the job is not accepted, his ostracism could be a personal disaster.

Sometimes an individual's decision not to accept the norms of the primary group may be interpreted by the primary group as a threat to its existence. For example, a rate-buster is a threat to those practicing output restriction. Group retaliation for the threats posed by the isolate can range from a "cold-shoulder" treatment to a blob of grease in the lunch bucket.

Another use of sociometric technique lies in analysis of the informal working relationships which exist in the formal organization. One method is to show a conventional diagram of the formal organization, and then superimpose on it dotted lines showing informal working relationships. This technique, illustrated in Figure 7–7, depicts work relations among people on the same functional level and up and down the chain of command. The results indicate work patterns considerably different from the rigid structural relations prescribed by the formal organization.[29]

3. Informal organizations have status and communication systems peculiar to themselves and not necessarily derived from the formal organization. The informal status system has been discussed above. The communication arm of the informal organization is the grapevine which is discussed in Chapter 9.

4. Survival of the informal organization requires stable, continuing relationships among the people in it. Thus, it has been observed that the informal organization *resists changes* which appear to be threats to its integrity. Change is often looked on as a challenge to the continued existence of the informal organization. Changes in supervision, rapid turnover of personnel, changes in work methods, and changes in wage payment schemes are all possible sources of resistance.

FIGURE 7–7

THE FORMAL ORGANIZATION AND INFORMAL WORKING RELATIONSHIPS

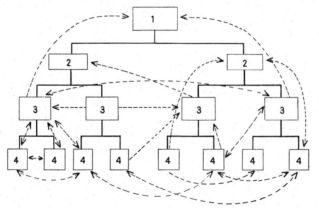

Key:
    1. Plant superintendent.
    2. Department managers.
    3. General foremen.
    4. Foremen.
    – – – – – Informal working relationships.

---

[29] This method is demonstrated by Ralph M. Stogdill, "The Sociometry of Working Relationships in Formal Organizations," *Sociometry*, November, 1949, pp. 276–86.

Probably the classic study of resistance to change was conducted by Coch and French.[30] They found that resistance to change was manifested in several ways. The first overt demonstration was reduction of productivity. But there were also the more subtle reactions of frustration and then aggression toward the supervisor, the time-study man, and higher levels of management. Coch and French found further that resistance to change could be reduced by allowing the employees to participate in the decision-making process before the change was implemented.

5. The last aspect of analysis central to the neoclassical view of the informal organization is the informal leader. The informal leader, unlike the executive, is more or less elected to this position by his associates. It is difficult to say just what criteria are used to determine who the informal leader will be. Work skills, sympathetic personality, age are all possible criteria. However, it appears to be generally true that informal leaders possess two broad characteristics.

a) *Ability to communicate*—the informal leader is both a transmitter and receiver of information. He is a sort of clearing house of information for the informal organization. He is "in on the know." And, probably more important, he is willing to transmit all information to his followers in the informal organization.

b) *Ability to embody the values of the primary group*—this characteristic is somewhat more elusive than the first. The informal leader is a kind of living representation of the things the group stands for. He is able to perceive the values of the group, crystalize them into a coherent ideology, and verbalize them to others outside the group. Perhaps this is what is meant when the informal leader is referred to as the spokesman of the group.

As long as the values of the primary group remain stable, as long as the informal leader continues to embody and communicate these values, and as long as the membership and environment of the primary group remain relatively stable, the informal leader is likely to retain his position. But, as the provisos indicate, stability of values, membership, and environment seem to be critical conditions for his continued leadership. Each provision should be examined in a little more detail.

The composition of group membership and the stability of its values are of course important to the designation of a particular leader. It is interesting to note that a moderate turnover of group membership staggered over a relatively long period of time will not result in a greatly noticeable change in the values of the group. Under circumstances such as these it is likely that a leader will continue in his function. However, a rapid and large turnover of group membership—not including the informal leader himself—may introduce new ideas and values into the

---

[30] Lester Coch and John R. P. French, Jr., "Overcoming Resistance to Change," in Schuyler Dean Hoslett (ed.) *Human Factors in Management* (New York: Harper and Bros., 1951), pp. 242–68.

group which are not adequately represented by the old leader. In this case the old leader may be displaced and his position assumed by an individual selected from the newer employees.

It almost goes without saying that an informal leader will be replaced if he no longer embodies and communicates the values of the group. This provision explains cases where the informal leader no longer acts in a leadership capacity for his old group when he is promoted to a higher level in the formal organization. For example, an informal leader might be promoted to foreman. This change in status requires him to reorient his values. More often than not he is forced to relinquish his former leadership role in the informal organization.

Finally, if the environment changes, the informal leader may also be changed. For example, one individual may serve as informal leader under stable, slowly changing conditions, but if an emergency situation arises a different individual might emerge to take leadership.

The Interaction of the Formal and Informal Organizations.   The discussion of the neoclassical theory has neglected, so far, to treat the way in which the formal and informal organizations interact. A conventional way of looking at the interaction of the two organizations is the "live and let live" approach. As an example, management should recognize that the informal organization exists; nothing can destroy it; and so the executive might just as well work with it. Working with the informal organization involves not threatening its existence unnecessarily, listening to group opinion expressed through the leader, allowing group participation in decision-making situations that will result in change, and controlling dangerous rumors on the grapevine by prompt release of accurate information.

Further, management should recognize that the informal organization is a powerful force which can be a help or hindrance in accomplishing the objectives of the formal organization. Also, the informal leader, if he is won over by an executive, can get the people in the informal organization to perform their jobs quickly and effectively. All in all, if the informal organization and its leaders are treated with respect, if they have confidence in their immediate formal superior, are communicated with, and are allowed to participate in changes, they will respond by facilitating the accomplishment of the formal organization's goals.[31]

As just about everything in human relations, this happy consequence may or may not work out! However, it would not be too unreasonable to expect that an honest and sincere effort of managers to establish a work-

---

[31] For examples of this approach see John D. Stanley, "Group Influence on Technological and Organizational Change," *Advanced Management*, February, 1958, pp. 15–17; John T. Doutt, "Management Must Manage the Informal Groups Too," *Advanced Management*, May, 1959, pp. 26–28; and Robert Saltonstall, *Human Relations in Administration* (New York: McGraw-Hill Book Co., 1959), chap. 13, esp. pp. 330–31.

ing relationship with the informal organization could result in an association where each would contribute tangibly to the accomplishment of
the other's goals. But one danger at all costs should be avoided: "working with the informal organization" should not degenerate into a shallow
disguise for human manipulation.

Some neoclassical writing in organization theory, especially that coming from the management-oriented segment of this school, gives the impression that the formal and informal organizations are distinct, and at
times quite irreconcilable, factors in a company. The interaction which
takes place between the two is something akin to company relationships
with a labor union, or a government agency, or another firm. The interactional arrangements are a hybrid of bargaining, coercion, and diplo-
macy.

The concept of the social system is another approach to the interactional climate between the formal and informal organizations. While this
concept can be properly classified as neoclassical, it borders on the modern theory of organization. As pointed out in Chapter one, the phrase
"social system" means that an organization is a complex of mutually interdependent, but variable, factors. These factors include individuals and
their attitudes and motives, jobs, the physical work setting, the formal
organization, and the informal organizations. These and other factors are
woven into an over-all pattern of interdependency. From this point of
view, the formal and informal organizations lose their distinctiveness
and find their real meaning, in terms of human behavior, in the operation
of the system as a whole. Thus, the study of organization turns away
from description of its component parts to refocus on the system of
interrelationships among the parts. More is said about this approach in
the next chapter.

An Appraisal of Neoclassical Organization Theory

One of the major contributions of the Hawthorne studies was the
integration of Pareto's idea of the social system into a meaningful
method of analysis for the study of behavior in human organizations.
This concept is still vitally important. But unfortunately some work in
the field of human relations has overlooked, or perhaps discounted, the
significance of this consideration.

The fundamental insight regarding the social system, applied to the
industrial scene by the Hawthorne researchers, did not find much extension in subsequent work of the neoclassical school. Indeed, after the
Hawthorne studies the neoclassical school generally seemed content to
engage in descriptive generalizations or particularized empirical research
studies which did not have much meaning outside their own context.

The neoclassical school of organization theory has been called bank-
rupt. Criticisms range from, "human relations is a tool for cynical pup-

peteering of people," to "human relations is nothing more than a trifling body of empirical and descriptive information."

There is a good deal of truth in both criticisms, but another appraisal of the neoclassical school of organization theory is offered here. The neoclassical approach has provided valuable contributions to the lore of organization. But, like the classical theory, the neoclassical doctrine suffers from incompleteness, a shortsighted perspective, and a lack of integration among the many facets of human behavior studied by it. Modern organization theory has made a move to cover the shortcomings of the current body of theoretical knowledge offered by the classical and neoclassical schools. The more recent developments in the theory of organization are taken up in the next chapter.

REVIEW QUESTIONS

1. In what ways does "organization" make human behavior predictable?

2. Are there any advantages in studying the "anatomy" of the formal organization? What are the disadvantages?

3. What are the pillars of formal organization theory according to classical doctrine?

4. Discuss the neoclassical modifications of classical organization theory.

5. What does Dalton consider to be the contributing causes of line-staff conflict? How would you translate this form of conflict into the terms of role theory?

6. Outline the conditions which give rise to informal organizations. What characteristics do informal organizations assume?

7. Why are informal organizations agents of "social control"? What is meant by the culture of the informal organization?

8. What prompts informal organizations to resist change?

9. Who is the informal leader? Why does he arise? What conditions are necessary for him to continue in this role?

10. Describe the relationship between formal and informal organizations in terms of the system concept.

SUPPLEMENTARY READINGS

BRECH, E. F. L. *Organization*. London: Longmans, Green and Co., 1957.

DALTON, MELVILLE. "Conflicts between Staff and Line Managerial Officers," *American Sociological Review*, June, 1950, pp. 342–51.

DAVIS, KEITH. *Human Relations in Business*, chap. 4. New York: McGraw-Hill Book Co., 1957.

MOONEY, JAMES D. *The Principles of Organization*, chap. 1–5. New York: Harper and Bros., 1947.

PRESTHUS, ROBERT V. "Toward a Theory of Organizational Behavior," *Administrative Science Quarterly*, June, 1958, pp. 48–72.

SCHNEIDER, EUGENE V. *Industrial Sociology*, chap. 9. New York: McGraw-Hill Book Co., 1957.

CHAPTER 8

Organization (Continued)

IF A key exists which will unlock the mysteries of human behavior in organizations, it will be in the form of a theory of systems. Lawrence J. Henderson has pointed out that, "The interdependence of the variables in a system is one of the widest inductions from experience that we possess; or we may alternatively regard it as the definition of a system."[1] System and the interdependency of parts are interchangeable ideas. It is really quite impossible to understand individual behavior or the activities of informal organizations apart from the social system in which they interact. A business organization is a social system; the various discrete segments and functions in it do not behave as isolated elements. All parts affect all other parts. Every action has repercussions throughout the organization because all units, human and non-human, are linked.

Henderson has a diagram, shown in Figure 8–1, which by analogy explains the concept of the interdependence of variables in a system. He says, in explanation of this diagram:

> The four rigid bodies A, B, C, and D are fastened to a framework a, b, c, d by the elastic bands 1, 2, 3, 4, and 5. A, B, C, and D are joined one to another by the elastic bands 6, 7, 8, 9, and 10. Here the conditions of statical equilibrium can be worked out mathematically, or determined empirically by introducing spring-balances into the bonds 1, 2, . . . 10, and reading the balances.
>
> Now imagine the point of attachment of 5 on the frame to be moving toward b, all other points of attachment remaining unchanged. What will happen? Consider A. There will be action on A by the path 5, 9, by the path 5, 8, 10, and by the path 5, 8, 7, 6. But in each case these actions do not cease at A, just as they do not previously cease at D. The first, for example, continues along the path 10, 8, and so back to 5. If we try to think of all this as cause and effect we must inevitably reach a state of confusion.[2]

The complicated interdependence problems brought out by Henderson in Figure 8–1 are magnified in a far more complex human system. Human systems contain a huge number of variables which defy the most sophisticated equations to solve. Yet in spite of the complexity of human organizations, studying them as systems provides a fruitful tool of analysis.

---

[1] Lawrence J. Henderson, *Pareto's General Sociology* (Cambridge: Harvard University Press, 1935), p. 86.

[2] *Ibid.*, pp. 13–14.

FIGURE 8–1

THE INTERDEPENDENCE OF PARTS IN A SYSTEM

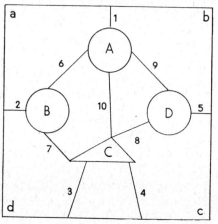

Source: Lawrence J. Henderson, *Pareto's General Sociology* (Cambridge: Harvard University Press, 1935), p. 14. Used with permission.

MODERN ORGANIZATION THEORY

The distinctive qualities of modern organization theory are its conceptual-analytical base, its reliance on empirical research data, and, above all, its synthesizing, integrating nature. These qualities are framed in a philosophy which accepts the premise that the only meaningful way to study organization is as a system.

System analysis has its own peculiar point of view. Modern organization theory accepts system analysis as a starting point. It asks a range of interrelated questions which are not seriously considered by the classical and neoclassical theories of organization. Key among these questions are:

1. What are the strategic parts of the system?
2. What is the nature of their mutual interdependency?
3. What are the main processes in the system which link the parts and facilitate their adjustment to each other?
4. What are the goals sought by the system?

Modern organization theory is in no way a homogeneous body of thought. Each writer and researcher has his special emphasis when he considers the system. Perhaps the most evident unifying strand in modern organization theory is the effort made to look at human systems in their totality. Wolf, for instance, stresses the need to view organization as a "system of causality, which determines an organization's character."[3]

---

[3] William B. Wolf, "Organizational Constructs: An Approach to Understanding Organization," *Journal of the Academy of Management*, April, 1959, p. 7. See also W. W. Haynes, "Toward a General Approach to Organization Theory," *Journal of the Academy of Management*, August, 1959, pp. 75–88.

He emphasizes the necessity of studying organizations as a whole and not just parts of the organization in isolation.

Wolf's position is similar to that of other writers in the area of modern organization theory. Much of the literary output has been in scholarly journals, but two books that are representative in this field are March and Simon's *Organizations*[4] and Haire's anthology *Modern Organization Theory*.[5]

The work in modern organization theory is pioneering—which makes its appraisal difficult and its direction obscure. While its future is not clear, one thing is patently certain. The questions being asked about human behavior within the structure of organizations cannot be adequately answered by classical and neoclassical doctrine. Understanding human organization requires a creative synthesis of massive amounts of empirical data, a high order of deductive reasoning, and an intuitive appreciation of individual and social values. Accomplishing all these objectives and including them in the framework of the concept of the system appears to be the goal of modern organization theory.

The purpose of this chapter is to discuss the ingredients of modern organization theory. This is done in the sections dealing with the parts, the interactions, the processes, and the goals of systems. The last section of this chapter is devoted to some of the implications of organization theory to administrative science.

The Framework of System Analysis

Before discussing the various aspects of modern organization theory, it is useful to present an over-all model of what is involved in system analysis. Figure 8–2 adapts Henderson's frame to the topics of interest here. The large box represents the total system or, if you will, the organization. The circles stand for the parts in the system, keyed as follows:

(A) Individuals.
(B) The formal organization.
(C) The informal organizations.
(D) The structure of status and role-expectancy systems.
(E) The physical environment of the work situation.

The lines both dotted and solid indicate linking processes. The linking processes are:

1. Communication.
2. Balance.
3. Decisions.

The dotted lines simply signify intrapart links—that is, linking individuals to individuals, jobs to jobs within the formal organization, and so on.

---

[4] James G. March and Herbert A. Simon, *Organizations* (New York: John Wiley and Sons, 1958).

[5] Mason Haire (ed.), *Modern Organization Theory* (New York: John Wiley and Sons, 1959).

FIGURE 8–2

THE FRAMEWORK OF SYSTEM ANALYSIS

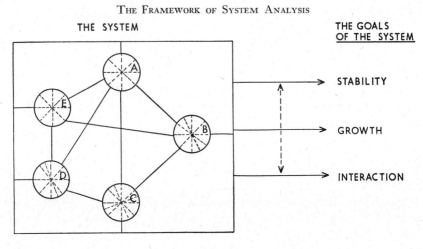

Key:
1. Circles represent parts of the system.
2. Dotted lines represent intrapart interactions, i.e. individuals with other individuals.
3. Solid lines represent interpart interaction.
4. Both the solid and dotted lines are links which tie the parts of the system together.

The solid lines represent interpart links—that is, individuals to the informal organization, the formal organization to the systems of status and roles, and so on.

Finally, the system as a whole strives to achieve certain goals. They are:

1. Stability.
2. Growth.
3. Interaction.

The system can seek any one of these goals, or any combination of them.

With this framework in mind, a discussion of the system's respective parts and processes follows.

The Parts of the System. The first basic part of the system is the individual and the personality structure he brings to the organization. Elementary to an individual's personality, as was shown in Chapter 5, are his motives and attitudes which condition the range of the personal expectancies he hopes to satisfy by participating in the system.

The second part of the system is the formal arrangement of functions, usually called the *formal organization*. The formal organization is an interrelated pattern of jobs which provides the structure for the eco- nomic and efficiency pursuits of the organization.

The third part in the system is the *informal organization*. The nature of this organization has been explained in the previous chapter. The fourth part of the system is the *status and role* arrangements which exist in the organization. It is obvious that in any formal organization, statuses and roles are internally linked by hierarchical ordering. At the same time, there are also informal orderings of statuses and roles in terms of prestige groups and occupations.

The fifth part of the system is the *physical setting* in which the job is performed, plus the technical-engineering-efficiency considerations which link the various jobs together.

1. *Intrapart interactions.* Within each of these parts, interactions exist among the units which comprise them. Obviously individuals interact with individuals, and informal groups with other informal groups; status systems and roles by their relative nature are dependent on each other for meaning, different jobs are interdependent on other jobs for the satisfactory performance of the total organization, and so on.

The fundamental cause for intrapart interactions is the division of labor. Dependency of units within the parts of the system arises from the process of specialization. Now, since the parts are internally interdepend- ent, they have to be bound together by processes. As mentioned before, these processes are communication, balance, and decisions.

2. *Interpart interactions.* Just as the units in the parts of the system have interactional patterns, so also do the parts interact with each other. The individual has expectancies regarding the job he is to perform; and, conversely, the job makes demands (or has expectancies) relating to the performance of the individual. Considerable attention has been given by writers in modern organization theory to incongruencies resulting from the interaction of organizational and individual demands. Argyris, for example, sees a conflict resulting from the demands made by the job and the nature of the normal, mature personality. The formal structure of the job does not meet the demands of the mature individual, hence he is forced to find outlets for his demands in informal organizations.[6]

The interactions which exist between the informal organization and the individual can be conveniently discussed as the mutual modification of expectancies. The informal organization has demands which it makes on members in terms of anticipated forms of behavior, and the individual has expectancies of satisfaction he hopes to derive from association with

---

[6] Chris Argyris, *Personality and Organization* (New York: Harper and Bros., 1957), esp. chaps. 2, 3, 7.

people on the job.[7] Both sets of expectancies interact, resulting in the in-dividual modifying his behavior to accord with the demands of the group, and the group—perhaps—modifying what it expects from an individual because of the impact of his personality on group norms.[8]

In the physical surroundings of work, interactions are present in complex man-machine systems. The human "engineer" cannot approach the problems posed by such interrelationships in a purely technical fashion. As Haire says, these problems are in the domain of the social theorists.[9] Attention must be centered on the human responses stemming from a logically ordered production function. From this standpoint, work cannot be effectively organized unless the psychological, social, and physiological characteristics of people participating in the work environment are considered. Machines and processes should be designed to fit certain generally observed psychological, physiological, and social properties of men, rather than men being hired to fit machines and technical processes.

The interactional pattern among jobs, the informal organization, and the individual have already been discussed in Chapter 6 within the framework of Bakke's fusion process. To repeat, the fusion process is largely concerned with the modification of role expectancies relative to both role demands made by the formal and informal organizations and role perceptions peculiar to the individual. Organizational expectancies and individual perception of the expectancies modify each other. This process is basic to the continuity and stability of the organization.

Let us summarize what has been said so far about systems. First, systems are made up of parts which are interdependent. Additionally, the parts themselves are composed of units which also are interdependent, and the intrapart and interpart interdependencies have been discussed. The parts are woven into a configuration called the organizational system. The processes which link the parts together, which contribute to the maintenance of the configuration, are taken up next.

The Linking Processes.   One can say, with a good deal of glibness, that all the parts mentioned above are interrelated. Although this observation is quite correct it does not mean too much in terms of system theory unless some attempt is made to analyze the processes by which the interaction is achieved. Role theory, discussed at some length in Chapter 6, is

---

[7] Conditions determining whether or not individual expectancies are satisfied is discussed by Alvin Zander, "Group Membership and Individual Security," *Human Relations* (11), 1958, pp. 99–111.

[8] For a larger treatment of modification of expectancies see George C. Homans, *The Human Group* (New York: Harcourt, Brace and Co., 1950), chap. 5.

[9] Mason Haire, "Psychology and the Study of Business: Joint Behavioral Sciences," in *Social Science Research on Business: Product and Potential* (New York: Columbia University Press, 1959), pp. 53–59. See also George F. Weinwurm, "Computer Management Control Systems Through the Looking Glass," *Management Science*, July, 1961, pp. 411–19.

devoted to certain types of interactional processes which link parts of the system together. In addition, modern organization theorists point to three other linking activities that appear to be universal to human systems of organized behavior. These processes are communication, balance, and decision making.[10]

1. *Communication.* Deutsch points out that organizations are composed of parts which communicate with each other, receive messages from the outside world, and store information. Taken together, these communication functions of the parts comprise a configuration representing the total system.[11] It would indeed be possible to speak of the organization as a communication mechanism, because communication is so fundamental to the life of a human system.

Communication may be viewed as the method by which action is evoked from the parts of the system. Communication acts not only as a stimulus for action, but it is also a control and coordination mechanism tying the decision centers in the system into a synchronized whole. From this standpoint, it is useful to think of a system in terms of a communication network. A network is a structure of interlaced lines knotted at intervals. The lines of a communication network are the communication channels and the knots in the structure are the decision centers. Deci-

FIGURE 8–3

A COMMUNICATION NETWORK IN A PRODUCTION ORGANIZATION

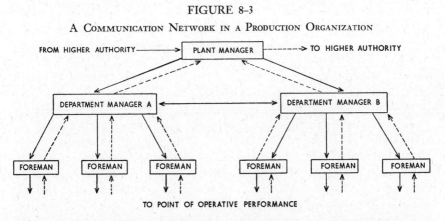

TO POINT OF OPERATIVE PERFORMANCE

sion centers in human organizations are individuals performing functions which require actions either routine or creative in accord with policy and established programs. Figure 8–3 is a simplified example of a communication network.

The communication network in Figure 8–3 is a production or-

---

[10] Chapters 9, 10, and 11 are devoted to communication and balance. Nothing like a complete treatment of these two subjects is attempted here. They are included to lend continuity to the analysis of the system concept.

[11] Karl W. Deutsch, "On Communication Models in the Social Sciences," *Public Opinion Quarterly* (16), 1952, pp. 356–80.

ganization. It has nine decision centers arranged in three levels. The decision centers, of course, correspond to the executives in the organization, ranging from the plant manager, through the department managers, down to the foremen. The connecting lines are communication links which bind the decision centers together. The solid lines represent the downward and lateral passages of information. The downward links carry information of the action-evoking variety such as orders, policies, rules, and the like. The lateral transmissions of information serve as coordinative links.

The dotted lines indicate the upward passage of information. This information pertains to the control function. Control communication originates at the bottom of the organization and passes through channels to the top. The upward, lateral, and downward communication links are essential to the work done by the decision centers. These links synchronize the decision centers, provide them with orders to stimulate action, and transmit control information to them so that performance can be evaluated.

2. *Balance.* The concept of balance as a linking process involves a series of rather complex ideas. Balance refers to an equilibrating mechanism which maintains the various parts of the system in a harmoniously structured relationship.

When speaking of systems the introduction of a balancing idea becomes a logical necessity. It is impossible to conceive of an ordered relationship among the parts of a system without bringing in the concept of a stabilizing, adapting mechanism or process. In Figure 8–1, for instance, the rubber bands and ridged frame are the instruments that maintain an ordered relationship among the parts A, B, C, and D.

Compared to a simple mechanical system, the forces and processes responsible for maintaining balance among the parts of a human system are considerably more difficult to discover and appraise. For purposes of this chapter, balance in human organizations is treated in two forms: (1) a quasi-automatic process and (2) an innovative process. *Both forms act to insure system stability in the face of changing conditions either internal or external to the organization.*

The question which arises now is, under what circumstances will an organizational adjustment to change be quasi-automatic or routine, and under what circumstances will the adjustment be innovative? The answer lies in two interrelated considerations: the nature of the change itself, and the range of programs available to the organization for adjusting to changes. ("A program" means an established plan of action.)

The first circumstance deals with the routine adjustment to change. As shown in Figure 8–4, a change impinges on a system. The system perceives the change and identifies its nature. In this case, the change is identified as one which can be handled by using a program—program 2—

FIGURE 8–4

ROUTINE ADJUSTMENT OF A SYSTEM TO CHANGE

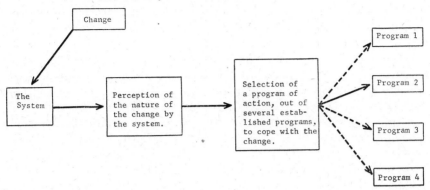

in the system's repertory of programs 1, 2, 3, and 4. Thus, the system's adjustment to change becomes a routine, or quasi-automatic, matter of selecting one out of an established range of programs to cope with change. To summarize, if the change is perceived by the system as coming within the purview of established programs of action the adaptation made by the system to the change generally will be routine, or quasi-automatic.[12]

The second circumstance involves innovative or creative balancing efforts. The need for innovation arises when adaptation to a change is outside the scope of the existing programs that keep the system in balance. The system has to evolve new programs in order to maintain its internal harmony.

New programs are created by trial-and-error search for feasible alternatives of action to cope with a given change. But innovation is subject to two limitations, at least. First, the organization cannot simultaneously adapt all aspects of its structure to change. That is, certain aspects of an organization's structure have to be held stable, while other, more critically affected areas of the system are adjusted. As March and Simon state, ". . . in order for an organization to behave adaptively, it needs some stable regulations and procedures that it can employ for carrying out its adaptive practices."[13] Therefore, the process of innovation presupposes stability in certain segments of the system. By its very nature innovation cannot immediately extend to the total organization.

Second, innovation is limited by the quantity and variety of information present in a system at a particular time. For innovative purposes,

---

[12] March and Simon, *op. cit.*, pp. 139–40.

[13] *Ibid.*, p. 170.

new combinations of alternatives depend on four factors. The first of these is the possible range of output of the system, or the capacity of the system to supply information. Obviously, decision makers (or—perhaps a better phrase—change adjusters) are limited in innovative activity by the capacity of the system to supply data. Alternatives, from which new programs of action are created, arise from the information available in the system. As this information is limited so also are the possibilities for finding appropriate action alternatives.

The second factor limiting innovation is the range of information available in the system's memory. Most human organizations have facilities for storing information, usually in the form of performance records, accounting data, historical information on competition, and the like. Also included in the memory of the system are past solutions to problems of change which appear to be similar but are not identical to the problem at hand. The capacity of the storage centers is not unlimited; therefore, the ability of the system to call on its memory of suitable action alternatives is restricted.

The third factor deals with the operating rules (programs) governing the analysis and flow of information within the system. This limitation on the use of information is similar to the first mentioned above, noted by March and Simon. The use to which information is put for innovative purposes is regulated by the policies of the system. Some action alternatives may be distinct possibilities for change adjustment, but if they fall outside the policies of the firm they will be discarded as unusable.

The fourth factor is the system's ability to "forget" previously learned solutions to problems of change. This interesting limitation means that a system with too good a memory might narrow its behavioral choices to such an extent that innovation is stifled. Previously learned, old programs might be brought into play for an adjustment to change when newly innovated programs are necessary. Often this is what is meant when an organization is termed "inflexible"—it is incapable of learning for purposes of long-range adjustments.[14]

Much of what has been said about communication and balance brings to mind a cybernetic model in which both these processes have vital roles. Cybernetics has to do with feedback and control in all kinds of systems. Its purpose is to maintain system stability in the face of change. Cybernetics cannot be studied without considering communication networks, information flow, and some kind of balancing process aimed at preserving the internal integrity of the system.

---

[14] The four restrictions pertaining to the second limitation on innovative activities are adapted from Mervyn L. Cadwallader, "The Cybernetic Analysis of Change in Complex Social Organizations," *The American Journal of Sociology*, September, 1959, p. 156.

Cybernetics asks several questions regarding the system.

a) How are communication centers connected, and how are they maintained? Corollary to this question: what is the structure of the feedback system; that is, how is control information transmitted from the point of performance to the decision centers?

b) What information is stored in the system and at what points? Corollary: how accessible is this information to the decision-making centers?

c) How conscious is the organization of the operation of its own parts? To what extent do the policy centers receive control information with sufficient frequency and relevancy to create a real awareness of the operation of the segments of the system?

d) What are the learning (innovating) capabilities of the system?[15]

Answers to the questions posed by cybernetics are crucial to understanding both the balancing and communication processes in systems. Although cybernetics has been applied largely to technical-engineering problems of automation, the model of feedback, control, and regulation in all systems has a good deal of generality. Cybernetics is a fruitful area which can synthesize the concepts underlying the balance and communication processes. The next chapter on communication treats some of the problems in the questions noted above.

3. *Decisions.* The decision process is the third linking mechanism. The decision process is closely related to organizational balance, because it is the way by which people adapt to the demands of the system.

March and Simon treat two broad classes of decisions allied to motivated human behavior.[16] The first class is made up of decisions to participate in the organization; the other includes decisions underlying the circumstances of individual productivity.

Decision to participate in an organization is in part a function of the inducements offered to an individual by the organization balanced against the contributions demanded from the individual. Participation is also a function of the ease of movement; that is, the degree to which an individual perceives movement as a feasible alternative to his present situation.

In general, an individual will decide to participate, or continue to participate, in a system if he feels the inducements awarded him are at least equal to the contributions he has to make. If inducements fall below contributions the individual will decide to move, everything else being equal.

---

[15] These questions are adapted from Deutsch, *op. cit.*, pp. 368–70. The growing literature on control of systems displaying cybernetic qualities is attempting to answer these questions. For a recent nontechnical study of this important area see Stafford Beer, *Cybernetics and Management* (New York: John Wiley and Sons, 1959).

[16] Unless noted otherwise this section is based on March and Simon, *op. cit.*, chaps. 3, 4.

The inducement-contribution relationship is connected to job satisfaction. Factors which lessen job satisfaction may throw the relationship out of balance and cause the individual to search for other alternatives. Of course, the ease of movement is conditioned by a number of variables, including economic conditions, and the age, sex, and training of the individual. Ease of movement is also hampered or facilitated by the number of alternatives available to the individual. Naturally, the fewer the alternatives for change perceived by the individual the less likely will he be to move.

"Motivation to produce is a function of the *character of the evoked set* of alternatives . . . *the perceived consequences of evoked alternatives* . . . , and the *individual goals* . . . in terms of which alternatives are evaluated."[17]

The *evoked set of alternatives* means that each individual has frames of reference founded on his personality structure. Stimuli impinge upon the individual, evoking certain reactions. The reactions to production motivations depend on the "set" of psychologically based alternatives called forth by a stimulus.

Along with these alternatives are the systems of expectations and values interpreted by March and Simon as the *perceived consequences* of alternatives which might be selected by the individual as a course of action. Not every alternative will be weighted similarly by the individual. Some alternatives may appear more acceptable than others because of an individual's preconceptions. These preconceptions have strategic importance, however. Human behavior can be influenced (manipulated!) by changing an individual's value system.

Finally, decisions to produce are partially a function of *individual goals*. An individual enters an organization with objectives in ordered arrangement. But these objectives are not immutable. He can be, and is more frequently than not, influenced by the groups, formal and informal, with which he comes in contact. The influence process conducted by the group is, of course, a method by which it preserves its integrity. Thus, when individual goals are modified, an important linking function is accomplished.

Decisions to participate in and produce for an organization are interpreted in terms of a psychological model of adaptive behavior. The general model selected by March and Simon is shown in Figure 8–5.

If an individual is dissatisfied he will search for alternatives to his present situation. The lower his level of satisfaction, the more intensive his search will be. His degree of satisfaction corresponds to the expected value of reward, as does his level of aspiration also. But as the level of aspiration is increased the possibilities for satisfaction decrease.

---

[17] *Ibid.,* p. 53.

Thus, an individual will search for satisfaction as long as he sees that his present situation is not fulfilling his expectations. Satisfaction is dependent on rewards; the greater the anticipated rewards the greater the satisfaction. Satisfaction is also dependent on levels of aspiration. If aspirational levels constantly rise the individual will never be satisfied with his current situation.

March and Simon treat decisions as internal variables oriented around the individual but affected by the social and economic conditions of the

FIGURE 8–5

GENERAL MODEL OF ADAPTIVE MOTIVATED BEHAVIOR

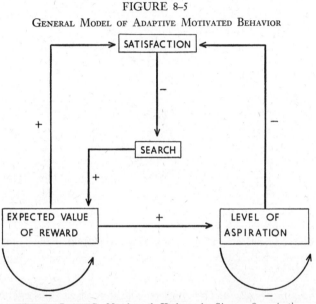

Source: James G. March and Herbert A. Simon, *Organizations* (New York: John Wiley and Sons, 1958), p. 49. Used with permission.

work environment. Decisions looked at in this way can be influenced by management through changing the circumstances around which an individual decides. Marschak[18] sees the decision process as an independent variable upon which the survival of the organization is based. In this case, the organization is thought of as having inherent to its structure the ability to maximize survival needs through its established decision processes.

The Goals of Organization. Organization has three goals which may be either intermeshed, as is usually the case, or independent ends in themselves. The goals are growth, stability, and interaction. The last goal refers to organizations which exist to provide a medium of association for their members with others.

[18] Jacob Marschak, "Efficient and Viable Organizational Forms," in Mason Haire (ed.), *Modern Organization Theory* (New York: John Wiley and Sons, 1959), pp. 307–20.

This statement of organizational goals might strike some as odd, particularly those who have learned their principles of management well. Is it not frequently said that the objectives of organizations are profit, service, social, and personal? From the standpoint of modern organization theory, these traditional objectives are more or less immediate, while the stability, growth, and interaction goals are ultimate.

Interestingly enough, these latter goals seem to exist for all organizations at varying levels of complexity, ranging from simple clockwork mechanisms to social systems. Similarities in organizational purposes have been observed by a number of people, and a field of speculation and research called *general system theory* has emerged dedicated to the task of discovering organizational universals. The dream of general system theory is to create a science of organizational universals—or, if you will, a universal science—using common organizational elements found in all systems as a starting point.

Modern organization theory is on the periphery of general system theory. Both these theories study:[19]

1. The parts (individuals) in aggregates, and the movement of individuals into and out of the system. March and Simon's discussion of individual decision to participate in the organization is one example, just noted above, of this aspect of system theory.

2. The interaction of individuals with the environment of the system. Haire's comments on the interrelation of the individual with the physical surroundings of work is apropos to this facet of system study.

3. The interactions among individuals in the system. Role theory and the theory of the informal organization are two cases of system study applying here.

4. General growth and stability problems of systems. So far, not much has been said specifically about these matters. The appendix to this chapter and the chapter on balance are reserved for these matters.

Modern organization theory and general system theory are similar in that they look at organization as a whole. They differ, however, in terms of their generality. General system theory is concerned with every level of system, whereas modern organization theory focuses primarily on the human organization.

And what, it might be asked, could the science of administration gain by the study of system levels other than the human? Before attempting an answer, note should be made of what these other levels are. Boulding presents a convenient method of classification.[20]

1. The static structure—level of framework, the anatomy of a system.

2. The simple dynamic system—level of clockworks that involve necessary predetermined motions.

---

[19] Kenneth E. Boulding, "General System Theory—The Skeleton of a Science," *Management Science*, April, 1956, pp. 200–202.

[20] *Ibid.*, pp. 202–205.

3. The cybernetic system—level of the thermostat, simple feedback and control circuit designed to enable a system to maintain a given equilibrium.

4. The open system—level of self-maintaining systems that exhibit the ability of rejuvenation, growth, and reproduction. This level moves toward and includes living organisms.

5. The genetic-societal system—level of cell society, characterized by a division of labor among cells.

6. Animal systems—level of mobility, evidence of goal-directed behavior.

7. Human systems—level of symbol interpretation and idea communication.

8. Social system—level of human organization.

9. Transcendental systems—level of ultimates and absolutes that exhibit systematic structures but are unknowable in essence.

By finding universals common to all levels of organization, this approach to the study of systems has intriguing possibilities for the science of administration. For example, a good deal of light could be thrown on social systems if structurally analogous elements could be found in simpler systems. It is usually easier to study the less complex and generalize to the more complex. Cybernetic systems, as a case in point, have characteristics which seem to be similar to the feedback, regulation, and control phenomena in human organizations. Thus certain facets of cybernetic models may be generalized to human organizations.

Considerable danger, however, lies in poorly founded analogies. Superficial similarities between the simpler systems and social systems are apparent everywhere. But instinctually based ant societies, for example, do not yield particularly valuable information for understanding rationally conceived human organizations. Care should be taken that analogies used to bridge system levels are not mere devices for literary enrichment. For systems to be analogous, *they must exhibit inherent structural similarities or implicitly identical operational principles.*[21]

As has been shown, modern organization theory leads almost inevitably into a discussion of general system theory. A science of organization universals has some strong advocates, particularly among biologists.[22] Organization theorists in administration cannot afford to overlook the contributions of general system theory. But the ideas dealt with in the general theory are exceedingly elusive.

For example, equilibrium (or balance) has been singled out as a possible

---

[21] Seidenberg, *op. cit.*, p. 136. The fruitful use of the type of analogies spoken of by Seidenberg is evident in the application of thermodynamic principles, particularly the entropy concept, to communication theory. See Claude E. Shannon and Warren Weaver, *The Mathematical Theory of Communication* (Urbana: The University of Illinois Press, 1949). Additionally, the existence of a complete analogy between the operational behavior of thermodynamic systems, electrical communication systems, and biological systems has been noted by U. S. Touloukian, *The Concept of Entropy in Communication, Living Organisms, and Thermodynamics* (Purdue Engineering Experiment Station, Research Bulletin 130).

[22] For example see Ludwig von Bertalanffy, *Problems of Life* (London: Watts and Co., 1952).

element of universality for all systems. But in speaking of this concept, Easton says, "It [equilibrium] leaves the impression that we have a useful general theory when in fact, lacking measurability, it is a mere pretence for knowledge."[23] The inability to quantify and measure universal organization elements undermines the success of pragmatic tests to which general system theory might be put in administrative science.

This concludes the framework of modern organization theory. The following chapters on communication, and balance and change are extensions of a number of the ideas brought up in the framework. All that remains now is an appraisal of organizational thought covered in this chapter and the former.

Directions and Trends in Organization Theory

Most sciences have a vision of the universe to which the science is applied. This universe is composed of parts. One purpose of the science is to synthesize the parts into an organized conception of its field of study. As a science matures its theorems about the configuration of its universe change. The direction of change in three sciences—physics, economics, and sociology—are noted below for comparison to the development of an administrative view of human organization.

The first comprehensive, and empirically varifiable, outlook of the physical universe was presented by Newton in his *Principia*. Classical physics, founded on the work of Newton, constituted a grand scheme in which a wide range of physical phenomena could be organized and predicted.

Newtonian physics may rightfully be regarded as "macro" in nature because its system of organization was concerned largely with gross events, of which the movement of celestial bodies is an example. For years classical physics was supreme. But as it became applied to smaller and smaller classes of phenomena in the physical universe physics eventually adopted the view that everything in its realm could be discovered simply by subdividing problems. At that point physics had moved into the "micro" order. In the nineteenth century however a revolution took place in physics largely because events in the physical universe were being noted which could not be explained adequately by the analytical equipment supplied by the classical school. The consequences of this revolution are described by Eddington:

> From the point of view of philosophy of science the conception associated with entropy must I think be ranked as the great contribution of the nineteenth century to scientific thought. It marked a reaction from the view that everything to which science need pay attention is discovered by microscopic dissec-

---

[23] David Easton, "Limits of the Equilibrium Model in Social Research," in *Profits and Problems of Homeostatic Models in the Behavioral Sciences* (Chicago Behavioral Sciences Publication 1, 1953), p. 39.

tion of objects. It provided an alternative standpoint in which the centre of interest is shifted from the entities reached by the customary analysis (atoms, electric potentials, etc.) to qualities possessed by the system as a whole, which cannot be split up and located—a little bit here, and a little bit there. . . .

We often think that when we have completed our study of *one* we know all about *two*, because "two" is "one and one." We forget that we have still to make a study of "and." Secondary physics is the study of "and"—that is to say, of organization.[24]

Although modern physics deals in minute quantities and oscillations the conception of the physicist is on the "macro" scale. He is concerned with the "and"—that is, the organization of the world in which the events occur. This does not invalidate the usefulness of classical physics in explaining a certain range of phenomena. But classical physics is no longer the undisputed law of the universe. It is instead a special case.

Early economic theory—and Adam Smith's *Wealth of Nations* comes to mind—examined economic problems in the macro order. Fundamentally, *Wealth of Nations* is concerned with matters of national income and welfare. Later, the economics of the firm, "micro-economics," dominated the theoretical scene in this science. And, finally, with Keynes' *The General Theory of Employment Interest and Money*, a systematic view of the economic universe was reintroduced on the macro level.

The first era of the developing science of sociology was occupied by the great social "system builders." Comte, the so-called father of sociology, had the macro view of society in that his chief works are devoted to social reorganization. Comte was concerned with the interrelationships among social, political, religious, and educational institutions. But as sociology progressed the science of society compressed. Emphasis shifted from the macro approach of the pioneers to detailed, empirical study of small social units. The compression of sociological analysis was accompanied by study of social pathology, or disorganization.

In general, physics, economics, and sociology appear to have two things in common. First, they offered a macro point of view as their initial systematic comprehension of their areas of study. Second, as the science developed, attention fragmented into study of the parts of organization rather than the system as a whole. This is the "micro" phase.

In physics and economics, discontent was evidenced by some scientists at continual atomization of the universe. The reaction to the micro approach was a new theory or theories dealing with the total system on the macro level again. This third phase of scientific development seems to be more evident in physics and economics than in sociology.

The reason for this "macro-micro-macro" order of scientific progress

---

[24] Sir Arthur Eddington, *The Nature of the Physical World* (Ann Arbor: The University of Michigan Press, 1958), pp. 103–104.

lies, perhaps, in the hypothesis that usually the things which strike people first are of great magnitude. The scientist attempts to discover order in the vastness. But after "macro" laws or models of systems are postulated, variations appear which demand analysis, not so much in terms of the entire system but rather in the specific parts which make it up.

Intense study of the microcosm may result in new general laws replacing the old models of organization. Or, the old models and the new may stand together, each explaining a different class of phenomenon. Or, the old and new models of organization may be welded into a creative synthesis. In any event, microcosmic studies appear to be part of a cycle in science which leads to a reformulation of principles on higher levels of generality than had previously existed in the earlier macro phase.

Organization concepts seem to have gone through the same order of development as the three fields just mentioned. It is evident that the classical theory of organization, particularly as expressed in the work of Mooney and Reiley, is concerned with principles common to all organizations. It has a macro organizational view. The classical approach to organization, however, dealt with the gross anatomical parts and processes of the formal organization. Like classical physics, classical theory of organization is a special case. Neither can account for variations from the established framework.

Many variations in the classical administrative model of organization result from human behavior. The only way these variations could be understood was by a microscopic examination of particularized, situational forms of human behavior. The mission of the neoclassical school of organization is "micro" analysis.

Modern organization theory appears to be concerned in large measure with Eddington's "and." This school bases its operational hypotheses on a macro point of view, a study of the organization as a whole. Much of the data and methodology used by modern organization theory is gathered from studies conducted in the micro-order. But these studies are synthesized—creatively, it is hoped—into an over-all view of organizational behavior.

It is questionable just how far modern organization theory can progress as synthesizing effort primarily. Modern organization theory needs tools of analysis and a conceptual framework uniquely its own. It may be that the framework and perhaps some of the tools will come from general system theory. There is also promise of analytical and conceptual tools from relatively new areas of research in decision theory, information theory, and cybernetics. Modern organization theory lies on the frontier of research in the behavioral sciences. Its potential is great, because it offers the opportunity of uniting what is valuable in classical and neoclassical theory into a systematic and integrated conception of human organization.

REVIEW QUESTIONS

1. What is a system? What is its significance in the study of human organizations?

2. Distinguish between the parts, the linking processes, and the goals of systems.

3. In what ways is communication a process which "evokes action"?

4. Differentiate innovative balancing processes from routine balancing processes.

5. How is innovation limited by the information present in a system?

6. What is the cybernetic model as it applies to human organizations?

7. What are the differences between decisions "to participate" and decisions "to produce" in an organization?

8. What is general system theory?

9. What are the various levels of systems? Why is the study of systems at different levels of complexity useful?

10. Discuss Eddington's "and" as it applies to modern organization theory.

SUPPLEMENTARY READINGS

BEER, STAFFORD. *Cybernetics and Management*. New York: John Wiley and Sons, 1959.

BOULDING, KENNETH E. "General System Theory—The Skeleton of a Science," *Management Science*, April, 1956, pp. 197–208.

CADWALLADER, MERVYN L. "The Cybernetic Analysis of Change in Complex Social Organizations," *The American Journal of Sociology*, September, 1959, pp. 154–57.

HAYNES, W. W. "Toward a General Approach to Organization Theory," *The Journal of the Academy of Management*, August, 1959, pp. 75–88.

WOLF, WILLIAM B. "Organizational Constructs: An Approach to Understanding Organization," *The Journal of the Academy of Management*, April, 1959, pp. 7–15.

APPENDIX I*

Organization Growth

MAN lives in a world of dimensions, where the objects frequently encountered have familiar sizes and shapes. This circumstance allows man to determine his relationship to and plan his behavior in his environment. Under ordinary conditions of life, man moves conveniently among the inanimate and living objects which surround him. But other phenomena with which man is associated do not assume the same kind of dimensional characteristics exhibited by things in the physical universe. Human organization is one such phenomenon. Human organization is an abstraction, and it might be argued metaphysically that it has no dimensions whatsoever. What merit there might be to this consideration is not discussed here. *The basic assumption is that organizations do have magnitudes which can be spoken of as shape and size existing in a framework of time.*

It is almost axiomatic in organization theory that the size and shape of an organization is a function of the environment it is in and the problems it must solve to survive in this environment. But a crucial problem in organization theory, which has not yet received an acceptable answer, is the nature of the processes which cause an organization to assume a certain shape and reach a certain size. In short, these are the problems of *growth*.

Biologists have a generalized answer to the matters of size and shape in living organisms. Their view is that adaptation is the mechanism whereby the organism is able to solve the riddle of survival in a hostile environment. Of course, in a vague way, the adaptation principle applies to human organizations also. But the key difference between the organization and the organism is that organizations solve the problem of adaptation by conscious, rational, and volitional processes; the organism does not.

This appendix is a critique of organizational growth theories and the research which has accompanied them. There is no one best way to study organizational size. It has numerous perspectives. A few ways the problem has been approached are listed below.

1. One approach to organization size is the *description of structure* found in various sizes and types of human associations. A segment of

---

* From W. G. Scott, "Organization Size: Some Theoretical Issues," *Management International* (5–6), 1961. Used with permission.

descriptive analysis is concerned with the small, informal group ranging in size from two to around fifteen people. Another segment of descriptive analysis covers medium-size to large formal organizations. Descriptive analysis ends usually with the structure of the giant "super organization" like church groups or political parties which contain a huge heterogeneous aggregate of people.

2. Another approach to organization size is the study of differential patterns of behavior of members and leaders in various sizes and types of organizations.

3. A third way to study size is to analyze organizational "behavior" as it adjusts its size and shape in response to changes in the environment during the process of pursuing goals. This problem is considered here under the subtitle of growth.

4. Next, size may be treated in its relationship to efficiency. Is there an optimum organization size and shape which makes for the most efficient accomplishment of goals? This research question is discussed in this appendix.

5. The last way of studying organization size poses the most elusive problems of all. These problems involve the mechanisms of organizational growth which create the form or shape of an organization as it matures.

Much has been said already in this part of the book about perspectives 1 and 2. Therefore, this appendix concentrates on the perspectives of growth and efficiency—items 3, 4, and 5. However, some analysis from perspectives 1 and 2 is woven throughout.

ORGANIZATION GROWTH

Bertalanffy observes that growth is one of the main problems of biology and is a central mystery of life.[1] Traditionally, biologists are concerned with the study of growth. Organization theorists have come to rely heavily on them for analogies. Currently a good deal of what passes for a *theory* of growth in human organization is based on facets of growth theory drawn from biology. Inherent in these analogies are pitfalls which are misleading unless recognized.

This appendix does not present a theory of organizational growth because the research and speculations which exist do not allow for the development of one. Rather its purpose is to examine some of the work which has been done and to make tentative observations about what might be useful, and what perhaps is detrimental, to the development of an organizational growth theory.

It may be said with assurance that a theory of growth, either in the framework of biology or human organization, deals with three funda-

---

[1] Ludwig von Bertalanffy, *Problems of Life* (London: Watts and Co., 1952), p. 36.

mental variables—*size, shape, and age.*[2] From the standpoint of business organizations, size is often measured in terms of numbers of employees, domination of the market, invested capital, and so on. The age variable is simply measured on a time continuum. The shape of the organization is not so easily measurable. Organization shape is qualitative. It involves the relationship of parts to each other, arranged in such a way as to facilitate the accomplishment of organization goals. Large varieties of shapes are possible because all organizations do not have the same goals. Or, where goals for separate organizations are similar, decision makers perceive their accomplishment differently. In both cases, different arrangements of organizational parts, hence different organizational forms, emerge. Therefore, it is impossible to compare along a single scale the shape of the formal organization with the structural form of a small group. For example, to say the small group tends to be flatter than the production organization of a company makes little sense. Whereas, it is appropriate to say that the formal organization tends to be larger than the informal organization; and that the formal organization tends to persist over a longer period of time than the informal organization. These variables may be looked at another way in which time plays the role of common denominator.[3]

Changes in Size through Time

Most often in research on organization development the starting point of analysis is consideration of changes in size over time. A common procedure is to plot the number of *people employed* against points on a time continuum.[4] For periods in the life history of a firm, times of spurts and declines in the growth rate (employment rate) can be noted. The growth rate of any company at a point in time depends on such matters as the introduction of new technologies, adaptation to change, and external forces of demand and competition. Haire concludes that the general growth rate for a firm seems to fit a growth equation applied to populations in which each member of the population produces 1.5 second-generation offsprings.[5] Limitations on an unrestricted increase in size of the population are imposed by the environment.

---

[2] P. B. Medawar, "Size, Shape, and Age" in W. E. Le Gros Clark and P. B. Medawar, (eds.) *Essays on Growth and Form* (Oxford: Clarendon Press, 1945), p. 158.

[3] In biology, size and shape are functions of time. Time is the independent variable, whereas size and shape are dependent variables. In an organization theory of growth and development, the size and shape of an organization may vary independently of the time factor.

[4] See Mason Haire, "Biological Models and Empirical Histories of the Growth of Organization," in Mason Haire (ed.), *Modern Organization Theory* (New York: John Wiley and Sons, 1959), pp. 277–83.

[5] *Ibid.*, pp. 277, 279.

Historical changes in size are an area of growth research which has been subjected to empirical investigation by behavioral scientists. Biologists also do considerable research in the size-time relationship. Their laws of growth provide the basis for tempting analogies to human organizations. More is said of this later under the topic of "Proverbs of Organization Size."

One point of criticism may be raised now. How satisfactory is the measurement of organization size based on number of employees? Are there not other yardsticks which may be more relevant? The extent of market and amount of invested capital certainly are criteria which cannot be neglected. Under changing technologies it is conceivable that the total number of employees in a firm might be reduced. But is it realistic to say that its size has diminished when by innovation it has increased its invested capital and share of the market? The image of size and growth which a company reflects is composed of a number of factors of which *total employees is only one.*

Changes in Shape through Time

The famous biologist Sir D'Arcy Wentworth Thompson pointed out that ". . . the form of an object is a 'diagram of forces' . . . from it we can judge or deduce the forces that are acting or have acted upon it. . . ."[6] This observation led Haire to state that in business organizations ". . . modification of form as size increases may give us at least a clue to the strength of the force tending to destroy it. . . ."[7] Thus, the shape of the organization is in part a product of the forces which impinge on it from the environment. But the uniqueness in form of human organizations is due to other factors as well.

1. The environment within which organizations operate is not uniform. It would be unlikely therefore that business organizations assume the same forms as religious organizations.

2. Even where the environment is roughly the same, in the case of two comparable firms in an industry, the number of alternative arrangements for the parts of the respective companies is so great that it is highly improbable that precisely the same forms of organization would result for both firms. Their structures may be similar, however.

3. The present form of an organization is partially a result of anticipation of the future. The management of similar companies may make different forecasts of the future. These forecasts would have a differential impact on the present structure of the company. Thus one firm might begin organizing and structuring for automation; the other

---

[6] Sir D'Arcy Wentworth Thompson, *On Growth and Form* (2d ed.; Cambridge: Cambridge University Press, 1942), p. 16.

[7] Mason Haire, *op. cit.,* p. 276.

firm might anticipate no change in its production techniques. The result, however, would be different organizational forms.

Shape refers to structure. And while no two organizations will have identical structures for the reasons noted above, certain classes of organizations have similarities in structure. Formal chain-of-command-type organizations constitute one such class. Some work has been done comparing organizational systems of this type.[8] But this research usually deals with structures at a given point in time and constitutes a static form of analysis.

Considering changes in shape over time is dynamic. The research question is: "Is there any uniformity in the transformation of organization shape along a time continuum?" In other words, as organizations mature, do they undergo predictable changes in shape at identifiable points in their development? As biological organisms develop they predictably change shape at definite stages. Can the same be said for human organizations? An answer to this intriguing question cannot be given one way or the other as far as research currently stands.

Change of form in a biological organism is largely predicated on survival. If the organism lives during the period of its maturation, it will change. Time and life are the important considerations, given a fairly favorable and reasonably constant environment. Time and survival, of course, are basic to change in form of a business organization. But the environmental forces operating on a company from the outside also shape its structure. Under normal circumstances the biological organism finds the sort of environment which is conducive to its survival, and the organism has reasonable assurance of environmental stability which precludes the necessity for numerous drastic adaptations. The business organization frequently is in an environment of intense change where its surroundings oscillate from favorable to unfavorable, from stability to frantic transition. These environmental changes often require changes in organizational shape. From this it can be concluded that to the extent to which changes in the environment of a business are unpredictable, so also are the transformations in its shape unpredictable.[9]

It is not of much value to report changes in organizational shape after the fact, if these data are used to project similar changes for comparable organizations. One must be assured that forces operating externally to the firm will maintain prescribed patterns. There is no proof, however, that this requirement can be fulfilled.

In addition to the external forces, internal forces also shape the struc-

---

[8] See James D. Thompson (ed.), *Comparative Studies in Administration* (Pittsburgh: University of Pittsburgh Press, 1959).

[9] The larger the organization becomes the more capable it is of modifying its environment, whereas the ability of a biological species to control its environment is quite unfeasible. This is not altogether true in the case of man.

ture of the firm. The decision makers in the firm react partially to external forces. They operate also within the internal frameworks of power and influence which change as personalities change. The degree to which power and influence affect structure is unknown in any quantifiable sense. Intuitively, it is felt that power and influence alliances do modify organization structure. Tentatively stated, changes in organization power arrangements will be reflected in structural transformations. But the precise time such changes will occur defies prediction; and so too, structural modifications resulting from these changes are difficult to predict. Thus, internal decisions which affect structure might pose a greater barrier to predicting points of structural transformation than external forces.

All in all, changes in organizational shape over time present extremely abstruse problems for analysis. The surface has hardly been scratched by research in this area. The values of such research are evident, however. Some guidelines formulated for predicting transformations in a firm's structure could facilitate management's planning and controlling functions enormously.

Changes in Size and Shape over Time

Up to this point shape and size are treated as discrete variables. They are not. Both size and shape are interrelated in such a way that a quantitative increase (or decrease) in size over time causes qualitative modifications in structure. And qualitative modifications may result in changes in the growth-rate factor of size. The analytical and conceptual difficulties which have been noted for the variables of size and shape treated independently are compounded when they are viewed as interdependent variables along a time continuum.

Some work of a modest nature has been undertaken on this problem. Writers have observed that as organizations grow (in terms of the number of people employed) a qualitative change in the composition of the work force occurs. From this change certain structural modifications are imputed.

Bendix, discussing bureaucratic indicies, reports that industrial nations since 1900 have exhibited an increase in the numbers of people employed. And further, as more individuals are employed an occupational transition occurs which is reflected in what he calls the A/P ratio.

This ratio compares the growth in numbers of administrative employees to production workers. Over a period of roughly 50 years the numbers of administrative employees increased at a more rapid rate than production workers in five industrial nations. For example, in 1909 there were 750,000 administrative employees and 6,256,000 production workers in the United States, resulting in an A/P ratio of 12 per cent. The ratio in 1947 was 21.6 per cent with 2,578,000 administrative employees compared with 11,916,000 production workers. Upward trends in the A/P ratio hold for all the other industrial nations reported in the Bendix study.[10]

While Bendix discusses the A/P ratio from the standpoint of compositions of *national* work forces, Haire studies work-force compositions in transition for several firms. He reports a growth in both the clerical and staff functions which progresses more rapidly than the growth of the line. Staff and clerical functions are roughly comparable but not identical to Bendix's definition of administrative personnel.

Haire observed that the growth of the staff, relative to the line, occurs at a faster pace in the earlier stages of its introduction into the organization. The growth of the staff tends to level off as the organization matures. The growth of the clerical function for the firms studied was steady, but not runaway over time.

Haire concludes that the increased growth of staff members and clerical employees relative to line employees is caused by external forces and the internal necessity for communication through the passage of years.[11] Thus, changing technology; more complex relationships with other business, the government, and the community; and the imperatives of internal communication, co-ordination, and control have been factors causing administrative staff groups to grow faster than line groups. As organizations get bigger problems of co-ordination and communication appear causing the number of people in organizational units concerned with these activities to increase. Both staff and clerical bodies deal with matters of co-ordination, control, and dissemination of information.

Hence, it is demonstrable that through time the line maintains more or less a "normal" growth rate, while staff organizations and clerical functions increase personnel at a more rapid rate. Growth emphasis shifts from the line to supporting staff and clerical activities.[12] As a result, it is hypothesized that a growing firm changes shape from a symetrical pyramid to a structure with a "bulge in the middle." The bulge encompasses the disproportionately large number of personnel engaging in activities in support of the line. Another modification of structure is the centralization of most administrative staff and clerical functions in support of decentralized production and sales functions. In very large organizations, these latter functions radiate from the "home office" which acts as a centralized co-ordination and communication source. Looking at

---

[10] Reinhard Bendix, *Work and Authority in Industry* (New York: John Wiley and Sons, 1956), pp. 211–26.

[11] Haire, *op. cit.*, pp. 287–302.

[12] Terrien and Mills make the following formulation: "The relationship between the size of an administrative component and the total size of its containing organization is such that the larger the size of the containing organization, the greater will be the proportion given over to its administrative component." See Frederic W. Terrien and Donald L. Mills, "The Effect of Changing Size upon the Internal Structure of Organization," *American Sociological Review*, February, 1955, p. 11.

past records, it is easy to determine that changes like these take place in histories of companies. However, from the "state of the arts" of prediction in the behavioral sciences today, a reliable forecast of when such changes will occur for a given company is impossible. A step in the direction of improved prediction must be the accumulation of huge amounts of research data revealing the crucial points in time when shape transformations take place in organizations. These transformations must then be related to the growth factor of size (using other criteria besides number of employees), plus the strategic changes which occur in the environment that also have an effect on the change of structure.

Proverbs of Organization Growth

Biologists do considerable work on the problems of growth and development in living organisms. Their conclusions have fallen on willing ears among organization theorists. As noted earlier, the behavioral scientists rely heavily on biological axioms for the formulations of their theories. These analogies may or may not be valid.

It seems that much of what is offered by biologists is accepted uncritically by behavioral scientists. The behavioral scientists who too willingly adopt biological analogies have at least one strike against them. Human organizations are not biological organisms. Evidence simply is not sufficient to support the claim that organizational processes correspond to biological processes. In addition to the lack of empirical substantiation, there are logical reasons for believing that biological analogies are on shaky ground. The stage is set for the "proverbs" by discussing next the laws of growth developed by biologists.

Biological Growth "Laws."[13] There is a danger in calling anything a "law," because the best of laws can be disproved by changing the frame of reference. Nevertheless, the following points represent uniformities in observations of growth over time in biological organisms.

1. There is an average optimum size for all living organisms.
2. Organisms increase in size, or at least do not decrease in size, as they grow old.
3. In a constant environment, growth proceeds with uniform velocity. Under actual conditions, there is a progressive dissipation of growth energy. That is, the growth rate decreases as the organism gets older.
4. As a group (species) advances in biologic age, its individuals increase in size, but decrease in fertility. As a result, survival for the species and individuals in the species becomes more difficult.
5. As an organism gets larger it uses up the more favorable parts of its environment, leaving the more hostile parts. Thus, growth is limited.

[13] Most of the points below are adapted from Medawar, *op. cit.* pp. 166–67 and E. R. N. Griggs, "Essay on a Fundamental Law of Life: The Time-Factor (Relativity) in Biological Phenomena," *Human Biology* February, 1956, p. 15.

6. Growth and form are partially controlled by the inexorable workings of the mechanical forces in the organism's environment like gravity, or the surface tension of water, or the buoyant characteristic of water, or air.

Organizational Growth "Laws." The points that follow constitute the proverbs of organizational growth.[14] It is not coincidence that these "laws" parallel some of the biological axioms just outlined.

1. Each organization has an optimum size with an appropriate structure. Attempts to push beyond this optimum result in an organizational breakdown.

2. Size is limited by an increasingly unfavorable internal structure as an organization grows. Limits to growth arise from breakdowns in communication and co-ordination.

3. As an organization grows it uses up the more favorable parts of its environment. Life becomes harsher as the organization's surroundings grow more hostile.

These analogies are tempting. They do, however, involve difficulties. Some problems encountered when these "laws" are looked at critically are discussed next.

A Critique of Organizational Growth Proverbs. The "laws" listed above reveal that constraints on organizational growth are found in the limiting notions of optimum size, unfavorable internal conditions, and unfavorable environmental forces.

1. *The problem of optimum size.* It is commonly observed in nature that each species of plant or animal has an average size. The individuals in the species do not deviate from this average by a very great amount. The first law of organization growth states that there is an optimum size for organizations from which tangible deviations result in lowered organizational effectiveness or complete collapse in extreme cases. How valid is this argument?[15]

Caplow has concluded that size affects organizational character, but that changes in size at certain points on a scale of expansion are more important than other points. He goes on to say that two-person groups have different properties than three-person groups. Doubling a group of

---

[14] In reality these "laws" are not growth laws at all in a dynamic sense. Actually they describe conditions which limit growth. The main source for these laws is Kenneth B. Boulding, *The Organizational Revolution* (New York: Harper and Bros., 1953), pp. 21–23. Other references include Mason Haire, *op. cit.*, and F. Stuart Chapin, "The Optimum Size of Institutions: A Theory of the Large Group," *American Journal of Sociology*, March, 1957, pp. 449–60.

[15] The average size of a species of plant or animal seems to be close to the optimum size for individuals in the species. This does not hold by analogy for firms in the same industry where the average size of firms is not necessarily the optimum for a particular firm.

fifteen is more likely to change patterns of interaction, structure, and activities of members than will doubling a work group of two hundred.[16]

The optimum size of an organization is defined as that size which allows it to accomplish goals more effectively. Therefore, the reason why small groups are small is because they can obtain their objectives most effectively when few people are involved. As Caplow indicates, changes in size of small groups have dramatic consequences on structure and the behavioral patterns of members. Thus, for any small group there appears to be an optimum size whereby the goals can be achieved most satisfactorily. Conversely, upward changes in size, without concomitant changes in goals, is likely to cause reduced group effectiveness or destruction of the group's existing structure.[17]

The same conclusion does not hold for large organizations, which possess the curious property to withstand great fluctuations in size without the need for making extreme modifications in structure. Indeed, not only are large organizations capable of absorbing considerable numbers of people, they also seem to be quite flexible in accepting changes in goals and policies without a great deal of internal restructuring. It may be concluded tentatively that so far as large organizations are concerned there seems to be no upper theoretical limit to their size.[18]

Formal organizations can effectively pursue goals within the framework of the same basic structure even though their membership expands enormously. Size is only important from the standpoint of diminishing returns, which may provide a practical limitation for a particular company at a specific time with a given "state of the arts." However, when favorable changes occur in technology, the market, or the competitive situation, this same firm can increase its number of employees quite conveniently.

The "law" of optimum size is unfortunate because it supposes that generalizations made about one type of organization can be carried over

---

[16] Theodore Caplow, "Organization Size," *Administrative Science Quarterly*, I, (1950–1951), p. 484.

[17] The optimum size for an informal social group might be ten, because at this level the satisfaction of the participants is maximized. The structure of the group would be loose, allowing each member the greatest opportunity for self-expression and interaction with others. Suppose, however, because of a change in goals the group expanded to fifty members. The structure of the group would undoubtedly change also. Given a change in goals with an accompanying increase in size, the informal structure which previously existed might give way to a more formal structure which would be less fluid. Thus by introducing a new set of goals the former structure became obsolete.

[18] Although this point is made now and then in current literature of administration, it is interesting to note that the same observation was made some years ago in John J. Williams, "Is There an Optimum Size of Organization?" *Bulletin of the Taylor Society*, February 1930, p. 22.

to other organizations. Actually, the large organization has means for absorbing membership, adopting to new goals, maintaining stability, and surviving that far surpass the small group.

Again, the question of "optimum size" is only relevant when measured by the organization's effectiveness in achieving goals. Optimum size is an important issue in economic model building of rationalized profit-making machines. Here optimum size is determined by criteria derived from the law of diminishing returns. But when the goals lie outside profit rationality, diminishing returns fade into obscurity as a standard. A militant religious group does not stop recruiting members because someone determines they have already gone beyond the point of efficient utilization of the seats in church.

There are other criticisms of the optimum-size notion. However, they are more conveniently treated in the context of the next topic of "unfavorable internal structure," where additional support is also offered for the idea that there are no upper limits to the size of the large organization.

2. *The problem of increasingly unfavorable internal structure.* As organizations get larger, increasing burdens are placed on communication systems and executive co-ordination. A point of size is reached where the communication network has difficulty in supporting organizational activities. In addition, executive co-ordination is taxed because of an extension of the span of control. Therefore, communication and co-ordination are thought to be effective limiting factors of organization size. First, what can be said about the nature of constraints imposed by communication?

Larger organizations seem to have denser networks of communication than smaller organizations. This is because as organizations grow the need for information increases at a disproportionate rate. There are two ways of handling increased communication bulk. First, the growing bulk can be transmitted more rapidly. Second, more people can be assigned to handle the bulk within the same time span.[19]

This is the same as saying that a given bulk of information can be transmitted in one half the time by doubling the speed of transmission or by doubling the capacity of the channel. With a given state of communication technology, such as the procedures for processing administrative communication, the usual way of handling increased bulk is to increase the *capacity* of the communication network. In practical circumstances this involves hiring more clerks and staff personnel who engage in creating, processing, transmitting, and assimilating information. Even-

---

[19] Drawing from information theory, Haire states the case formally. He says, "If a message takes a channel of x frequencies to travel in y time, one can usually use $2x$ frequencies, and, by simultaneous transmission, achieve $\frac{1}{2}y$ time." See Haire, *op. cit.,* p. 302.

tually this method of handling larger and larger bulks of information becomes quite cumbersome. Under these conditions, there is a point where additions to channel capacity are no longer feasible. This point represents a limit to the growth of the organization. This limit may be stated as follows: communication channels in a network will be added or the capacity of existing channels increased to the point where the incremental *cost* of such additional capacity expansions is equal to the *value* of the incremental addition to the bulk of information carried in the system.[20] When this point is encountered, a limiting factor to the size of the organization is reached.

Business organizations have usually dealt with increasing information bulk by simply expanding capacity; that is, by adding more people. But this is not the only alternative. Greater bulk can be handled by speeding up communication activities. This alternative requires, however, *new technologies* of information handling in business firms. Such technologies are on the horizon with "office automation." The constraints to organization growth created by the extension of capacity are overcome by reducing the time involved in communication dissemination and assimilation. Thus, the unfavorable barrier to further growth resulting from expanded communication needs can be reduced in significance by changing communication technology.[21]

Co-ordination is thought to be the second internal factor limiting organization growth. The proposition is that as organizations grow larger, the executive has greater difficulty timing and synchronizing activities. N. S. Ross sets forth, and then criticizes, a series of propositions which argue that managerial co-ordination is a limiting factor in the size of the firm. The propositions supporting this hypothesis are, according to Ross, the following:[22]

a) Co-ordination must be the act of a single center and, therefore, the division of labor cannot be applied to it.

b) The supply of co-ordinating talent available to the firm cannot be expanded as readily as other productive factors.

c) Co-ordinating centers must have detailed knowledge of problems—so the larger the field of co-ordination the greater the need for more knowledge.

d) Every increase in size must be, beyond a certain point, achieved by an extension of the scalar chain. This results in increasing co-ordinating cost which eventually will offset the economies of the division of labor.

e) The scalar chain cannot be extended indefinitely.

---

[20] On the "cost of information" see Herbert A. Simon, "Theories of Decision Making in Economics and Behavioral Science," *American Economic Review*, June 1959, p. 269–70.

[21] Another attack on the bulk problem is decentralization, by which the organization splits into self-contained administrative units. Decentralization does not constitute a new form of communication technology, however.

[22] N. S. Ross, "Management and the Size of the Firm," *Review of Economic Studies*, 19, (1951–1952), p. 148.

After considerable analysis, Ross offers these conclusions:[23]

a) The job of co-ordination is subject to the division of labor. It is naive to assume that all co-ordinating work is solely the job of a single head.

b) By decentralization and control the firm may expand without increasing costs of co-ordination over a range sufficiently large to cover all possible cases within the limits imposed by scarcity of resources.

c) It is unlikely that the technical optimum size will outgrow the limits of managerial capacity, but there may be technical as distinct from managerial obstacles which place limits to growth.

Taking all his data into account, Ross concludes that ". . . the proposition 'that an optimum firm with an upper limit imposed by difficulties and costs of co-ordination is both a logically satisfactory and a necessary hypothesis to explain facts' is open to doubt."[24]

Fayol cast some light on an interesting aspect of this problem. By making modest assumptions regarding the span of control of executives, Fayol demonstrated that an organization of 12 levels of authority could encompass over 251 million workers, where each superior had 4 subordinates and each foreman had 15 workers under him.[25] Thus, writers who emphasize span of control and length of the scalar chain as limiting factors to size seem to underestimate the magnitude of the unit which can be administered effectively with relatively few authority levels.[26] Considering everything, limiting factors to the size of organizations must be looked for elsewhere; co-ordination alone apparently does not impose insurmountable barriers to the size of organizations within the range of practical experience.

3. *The problem of an increasingly unfavorable external environment.* A biological species would increase in number at an explosive rate if it were not restrained by hostile forces in its environment. The proposition is thought to apply to human organizations as well, in the following sense. The larger the organization gets, the more difficult it becomes to grow more because it has used the favorable parts of its environment for previous growth. The parts of the environment left oppose extension. This might be analogous to a company gobbling up increasing shares of a market. A point is reached, everything else being equal, when the most favorable parts of the market are digested, leaving just lean pickings that

[23] *Ibid.*, p. 154.

[24] *Ibid.*, p. 154.

[25] Henri Fayol, *General and Industrial Management*, trans. Constance Storrs (London: Sir Issac Pitman and Sons, 1949), pp. 55–56.

[26] For example, the Internal Revenue Service employs in excess of 50,000 people, but the basic line organization comprises only 9 levels of authority extending from the commissioner in the national office to the group supervisor in district offices. It might interest the IRS to know that according to Fayol's calculations they can expand by roughly 3,880,160 people without adding more levels of authority.

are not profitable to take over. At this point, further growth is not tenable.

But in a dynamic setting, everything usually is not equal. By changing its marketing strategies, its products, its technology, and by modifying its structure, an organization does not need to be bound to the environment of one market and one industry. Adaptation of human organizations to change is a good deal more convenient and common than mutation of a biological species. Through change, the human organization reorients itself to exploit a new "environment" when the old seems played out. Of course there are limits to such reorientations. But these limitations, since they are imposed by the environment, are in the class of vague ultimates, and even these ultimates will differ from one type of organization to the next. For example, the environmental limits of the United Nations comprise the countries and population of the world.

In conclusion, the hypothesis of the increasingly hostile environment provides little by way of an operational notion of the limits to growth because of the facility of human organizations to redefine their environmental parameters. In terms of markets, products, policies, objectives, size, structure, capitalization, and research, the E. I. du Pont de Nemours & Co. of today is hardly the "same" company it was fifty years ago.

Much more could be said of organizational growth laws. The use of mathematical formulations for the purpose of generating a geometry of growth could be noted in detail.[27] The work in this area, however, is even more tentative than the research and analyses reported previously on growth.

The reader should be aware upon finishing this treatise that there is no "theory" of organizational growth. What pass for a theory are a few questionable proverbs based on biological analogies. It seems, however, that if a theory of growth is to emerge, it must be based on a study of the size, shape, and age variables. Several methodological and research difficulties which should be anticipated in such work have been noted.

---

[27] See Haire, *op. cit.*, pp. 284–87, and Chapin, *op. cit.*, pp. 449–60 for examples. Haire in his research found that organization growth corresponds to the square-cube law, which states a *linear* relationship between mass and surface areas of organisms influenced by the force of gravity. It might be noted parenthetically that if organizations were submerged in water, the law probably would not apply. For his part, Chapin observed in a study of church organizations that the growth configuration approximated a *spiral* which could be expressed in terms of Fibonacci proportions.

CHAPTER 9

Communication

A SK almost any top executive to list five of his most crucial problems; communication will probably occupy a prominent position. Executives deal in symbols—that is, the administrator's world is one in which abstractions have to be placed into acceptable media which will convey thoughts to others for the purpose of accomplishing objectives. Many types of communication vehicles are available, including pictures and actions. But the usual, most convenient, form for symbols is found in language. This leads Roethlisberger and others to observe that the executive's environment is essentially verbal.

To support this observation, a number of studies have shown that most of an executive's time is spent in communication. A British researcher[1] analyzing executive behavior gives a detailed account of the activities of a group of managers. The results show that 80 per cent of their time on the job is spent in conversation. Most of the remaining hours are devoted to reading or writing. In short, communicating is the core of executive activity.

An obvious question at this point is, why this managerial occupation with communication? Answers are many and complex, and it is the purpose of this chapter to delve into some of the reasons. In part, it could be said that organization demands communication. Information is the vital force upon which organization depends. Or it may be posited that a fundamental, distinguishing feature of man is his ability to transmit ideas. Thus, when man communicates he is acting in accordance with his nature.

Communication was treated in the last chapter as a linking process, a process which ties the various parts of a system together. From a managerial standpoint this view of communication is probably the most use-

---

[1] Tom Burns, "The Directions of Activity and Communication in a Departmental Executive Group," *Human Relations*, 1954, pp. 73–97. Burns' study was of "middle managers." A study by Piersol found that supervisors—foremen—spent approximately 50 per cent of their working time in oral communication, either as speakers or listeners. Of this time, 60 per cent was with subordinates, 30 with superiors, and 10 per cent among themselves. See D. T. Piersol, "Communication Practices of Supervisors in a Mid-Western Corporation," *Advanced Management*, February, 1958, pp. 20–21. See also George L. Hinds, "The Communicative Behavior of the Executive," *Journal of Communication*, Spring, 1957, pp. 29–34.

ful. It provides a framework for understanding the process. But the psychological and technical implications of communication should not be ignored. This chapter discusses communication as a social, psychological, and administrative phenomenon.

The first section of the chapter deals with some basic concepts of communication, including, of course, the definitional problem. The remaining sections treat the setting of communication. Four fundamental elements are analyzed:

1. The sender(s)—the encoding process.
2. The channels—the "distribution" system.
3. The symbols—the vehicles or information media.
4. The receiver—the decoding process.

Essentially, this chapter outlines the theoretical base for communication. It does not treat "pathological" conditions which arise in communication practice. The problem of communication breakdown is reserved for the following chapter.

BASIC CONCEPTS IN COMMUNICATION

The term "communication" is fairly common. Most people have a notion of what the word means, associating it usually with communication vehicles such as telephones, radio, television, newspapers, and the like. At slightly higher levels of understanding, the uncritical view of the communication process in organizations assumes the "pipeline concept" to be valid.[2] The pipeline explanation of communication runs as follows: ideas are coded into words; words are sent through pipelines—formal communication channels—and then are decoded by the receiver. Unfortunately for this notion, the plumbing breaks down, leaving the executive at a complete loss. Obviously, the "pipeline" is a gross underestimation of the subtleties and complexities of the communication process. In order to probe the anatomy of the communication process it is first necessary to formulate a definition to establish a common ground of understanding.

Defining Communication

The reader, after some introspection, could probably produce a satisfactory definition of communication by addressing himself to the question: what is involved when I want to express myself to others? To conserve mental energy, the answer is that you want to duplicate the ideas in your mind in the minds of other persons. This elementary consideration prompts Cartier and Harwood to say, "If you analyze any act

---

[2] For a criticism of this idea see Martin Maloney, "Semantics: The Foundation of All Business Communication," *Advanced Management*, July, 1954, p. 26.

of communication, you will always discover this same function: the replication of a memory or a complex of memories. Communications is a process for the replication of memories."[3]

This definition has sufficient generality to apply to communication functions in nonhuman situations as well as in human situations. For example, a simple thermostatic system exhibits the facility of memory and replication. The system "remembers" the information pertaining to the temperature it is to maintain. It then acts to replicate this information by comparing the temperature in the room with the desired temperature. Automatically controlled devices of higher levels of complexity have very intricate internal means of duplicating information stored in their "memories." Thus, even though this chapter is devoted to communication in human systems, the fact should not be overlooked that communication has a considerably broader range of application.

Definitions of communication for management do not differ essentially from the general definition given above. Browne defines communication as ". . . the process of transmitting ideas or thoughts from one person to another, or within a single person, for the purpose of creating understanding in the thinking of the person receiving the communication."[4] Communication, according to Davis, is ". . . the process of passing information and understanding from one person to another."[5]

These definitions have similarities and differences. They stress *understanding* as a necessary facet of the communication process, for example. Hence, communication does not take place unless the receiver understands the nature of the information transmitted. It is Davis' view that communication does not occur unless both a sender and receiver are present, whereas Browne observes that communication can take place "within one." Finally, Davis says understanding is transmitted, while Browne feels understanding is created.

Additional niceties of these definitions cannot be fully discussed here. The "closed loop" of communication and the idea that at least two people are necessary for communication are taken up in the following section. Generally speaking, communication, according to the above definitions, involves ideas (information), some kind of vehicle for transmission, and a receiver who understands what the sender has in mind.

The aspect of understanding found in these definitions requires further thought. Understanding is, of course, a highly relative matter. A rather

---

[3] P. A. Cartier and K. A. Harwood, "On the Definition of Communication," *Journal of Communication*, November, 1953, p. 73. See also Dale D. Drum, "Change Meaning, and Information," *Journal of Communication*, Winter, 1957, p. 162.

[4] C. G. Browne, "Communication Means Understanding," in Keith Davis and William G. Scott (eds.), *Readings in Human Relations* (New York: McGraw-Hill Book Co., 1959), p. 331.

[5] Keith Davis, *Human Relations in Business* (New York: McGraw-Hill Book Co., 1958), p. 228.

low level of understanding generally exists even between people who do not speak the same language. Actions, intonations of the voice, and so on, convey certain impressions which carry meaning. But, obviously, *effective action* based on attempted communication would be severely inhibited by the inability to understand the main vehicle for transmitting ideas—language.

Implicit in most administrative concepts of communication is the need for a high order of understanding. The reason is quite pragmatic. Business depends on human action to accomplish goals. Goal-directed behavior is evoked through communication. So, the greater the degree of understanding present in the communication process, the more likely human action will be to proceed in the direction of accomplishing goals stated by management. Thus, the higher the degree of understanding, the lower the ambiguity on the part of the receiver regarding goals and the appropriate behavior necessary to achieve them. Viewed in this way, communication in business is *utilitarian*. That is, management uses communication in the company in order to accomplish organizational goals.

With these points in mind, an operative definition of communication can be stated. *Administrative communication is a process which involves the transmission and accurate replication of ideas for the purpose of eliciting actions which will accomplish company goals effectively. Since administrative communication largely concerns people, the necessity for a high degree of understanding is implicit in the phrase "accurate replication of ideas."*

Factors in the Communication Process

Five factors are present in any communication situation. Briefly explained, they are:[6]

1. *The Act.* The communication act requires employment of symbols which can be best understood in human interactions. Commonly, language symbols serve the purpose. However, on some occasions signs or symbols other than language are more appropriate.

2. *The Scene.* The scene refers to the environment of communication. The scene determines what is said, what symbols are used, and often the *meaning* of what is said.

3. *The Agent.* Individuals who engage in a communication relationship are said to be the agents of communication. Typically, a sender and receiver are involved, frequently interchanging these roles as the communication situation develops.

4. *The Agency.* The media for communication constitute the agencies. Besides face-to-face oral communication such media as written or-

---

[6] These factors are adapted from C. Merton Babcock, "A Dynamic Theory of Communication," *Journal of Communication*, May, 1952, pp. 65–68.

ders and memos, bulletin boards, telephones, and public-address systems are found in business situations.

5. *Purpose.*   The purpose of communication refers to the objectives sought by engaging in the communication process. Four goals have been noted:[7]

   a) The functional goal. This goal is utilitarian. Information is transmitted so that some organizational objective can be achieved.
   b) The manipulative goal. Communication is used in this case to maneuver people into accepting ideas which may or may not be in conformance to their own attitudes or values. Propaganda is an example of the manipulative use of communication on a mass basis.
   c) The aesthetic goal. The purposes sought by this goal are creative. Communication is employed to enable a person to express his feelings and to interpret his sense of reality.
   d) The confidence goal. This attempts to increase people's confidence in their environment. Scientific research falls in this category. Its purpose is to uncover and communicate findings regarding the nature of the world in which we live.

Business communication includes each of these five factors, although the last factor—purposes of communication—is of particular interest at this point. The utilitarian or functional nature of organizational communication has already been noted several times. It should not be inferred, however, that all communication in an organization is utilitarian. Quite obviously, some organizational communication has manipulative overtones. But on a more noble level, communication in business is for some people both aesthetic and creative.

In any event, the demands made by the organization for functional communication, and the satisfactions an individual gets from engaging in communication, stem from different causes. For example, from the standpoint of the organization communication is utilitarian because it serves as a linking or coupling function. Without communication survival for the organization is impossible. But the utilitarian nature of communication taken from the organization's frame of reference does not restrict individuals in the organization from using communication for personal satisfactions which are not utilitarian.

Company "Machiavellians" utilize communication for manipulating people to achieve their ends of status and power. But the communication process may also be used as an avenue of self-expression and creativity. It must be emphasized that the goals of communication as pursued by the organization and individuals in it are not necessarily inconsistent. An individual may derive creative satisfaction from a communication act, but, at the same time, he may also be serving the utilitarian communication purposes of the organization. This argument has another side, how-

---

[7] Harry A. Grace, "Confidence, Redundancy, and the Purpose of Communication," *Journal of Communication,* Spring, 1956, pp. 16–23.

ever. Communication ends of individuals may differ from the utilitarian objectives of the organization. Unscrupulous use of communication by a person to establish his power and prestige frequently is at odds with the utilitarian needs of the organization.

Further analysis of delicate problems such as these is reserved for the next chapter covering communication failure. The following topic considers the setting of communication in greater depth, beginning with the communication model.

THE SETTING OF COMMUNICATION

The remainder of this chapter is devoted to the conceptual underpinnings of the communication process in human organizations. The major topics covered are the communication model, senders and receivers, the "distribution" system, communication dimensions, communication effectiveness and communication symbols.

The Communication Model

One author says ". . . a model is . . . a structure of symbols and operating rules which is supposed to match a set of relevant points in an existing structure or process."[8] From what has been stated before, in the previous section on definition, an administrative model of communication should contain:

1. Sources to generate information and receivers to assimilate it.
2. Vehicles to convey information—symbols.
3. A channel to distribute information.

In addition to these basic factors, a model also requires some approximation of the activities by which the communication act accomplishes organizational and personal goals. Communication is not homogeneous. Various types of communication activities are used to accomplish different ends in organizations. Using March and Simon's classification, communication activities are said to fall into the following categories.[9]

1. "Communication for nonprogrammed activities." This category includes all individual "talking and listening" not associated with the utilitarian objectives of the organization or the job. The grapevine, gossip, and social conversation fall into this classification.
2. "Communication to initiate and establish programs, including day-to-day adjustment or 'co-ordination' of programs." This type of communication implements routine and innovative balancing processes spoken of in the preceding chapter.

---

[8] Karl W. Deutsch, "On Communication Models in the Social Sciences," *Public Opinion Quarterly*, 16 (1952), p. 357.

[9] James G. March and Herbert A. Simon, *Organizations* (New York: John Wiley and Sons, 1958), p. 161.

3. "Communication to provide data of application of strategies. . . ." Communication of this variety supplies information to decision makers enabling them to activate the programs developed in the second category.

4. "Communication to evoke programs. . . ." In this category, communication is used for motivating people. Commonly, this form of communication is found in superior-subordinate relationships and is the "on-the-job" method of getting work done. It is the communication activity which receives the most emphasis in management human relations literature.

5. "Communication to provide information on the results of activities." This final category refers to communication which feeds back *control* information to decision makers from the point of performance.

Communication provides a utilitarian function for the organization by the activities covered in categories 2, 3, 4, and 5. These activities center in the generation (2) and implementation (3) of programs or plans of action. Category 4 realistically notes the use of communication for motivating people to accomplish the programs; and category 5 reveals the necessity for control to ensure programs are performed according to the standards established by the original plan. Within the complex of these formal (utilitarian) functions of organizational communication is category 1, pertaining to the informal "talk" or nonutilitarian communication which goes on in the organization.

Figure 9–1 illustrates the elements of a communication model. A statement and a diagram of a model, however, hardly do justice to the dynamic

FIGURE 9–1

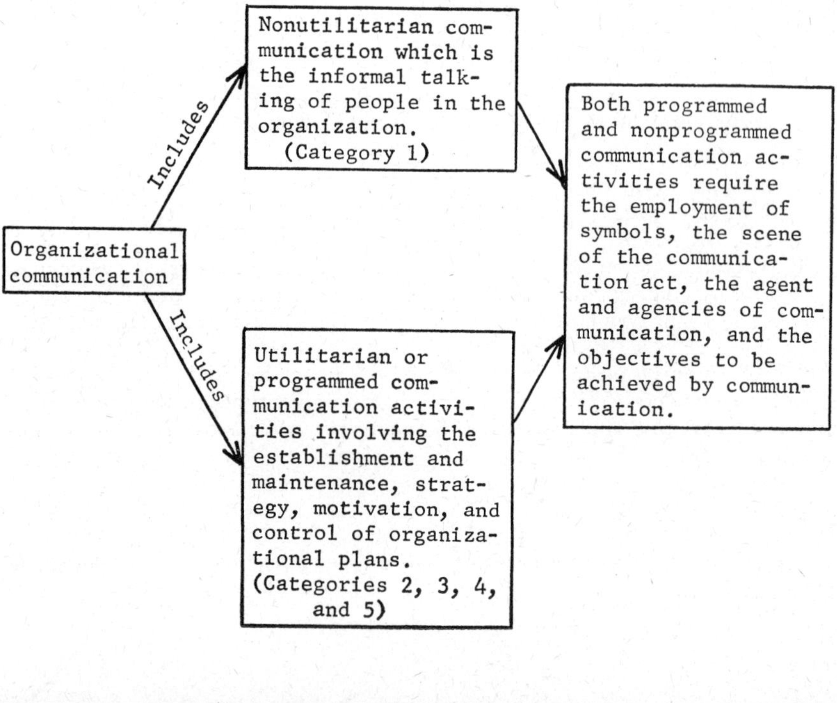

ELEMENTS AND ACTIVITIES FOUND IN AN ADMINISTRATIVE COMMUNICATION MODEL

nature of the process itself. So the following sections consider in detail aspects of the processes and elements contained in the model.

Senders and Receivers: The Psychological Foundations and the "Social Matrix" of Communication

Encoding and Decoding.   A simple approach to communication—which nonetheless has a good deal of merit—is that communication involves a sender who encodes his ideas into symbols and a receiver who who decodes the symbols. The purpose of the process is to reconstruct the ideas of the sender in the mind of the receiver. This statement encompasses the entire notion of human communication. But the fact of its generality obscures much—for example, the psychological basis of communication.

The Psychological Foundations of Communication.   A person who sends information does so with the intention of having his ideas replicated by those who he assumes have need of the type of information offered. The receiver accepts information with the expectation that it will satisfy his needs or demands in the communication situation.

FIGURE 9–2

RESTRUCTURING AN AMBIGUOUS COMMUNICATION SETTING

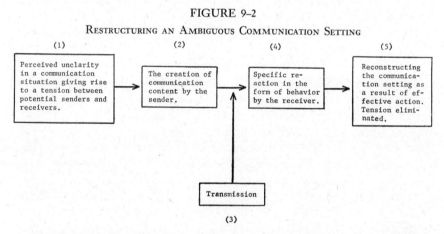

Communicated content is a structured or patterned set of symbols designed to stimulate the sensory organs of the receiver. Content always exists in a communication setting which, according to Fearing, possesses physical, social, and psychological characteristics. These characteristics prompt and determine the behavior of both senders and receivers. The key aspect of the communication setting is that it is often hazy. This lack of clarity about the environment builds up "states of tension" between senders and receivers. Tension, in turn, creates a "need to communicate" and "a need to be communicated to."[10]

Figure 9–2 includes these ideas with some elaboration to demonstrate

[10] Franklin Fearing, "Toward a Psychological Theory of Human Communication," *Journal of Personality,* 22 (1953–1954), pp. 73–76.

the dynamic psychological properties of the communication process. The process is traced as follows:

1. To begin, the parties in a communication situation perceive a lack of clarity and an ambiguity in the setting. Perceptions of this variety cause states of tension that can be resolved only through communication. Communication clarifies and gives definition to the situation.
2. The sender moves to alleviate the tension state by creating communication content. Content is a structured field of symbols which, it is assumed, has meaning for the receiver.
3. The content is transmitted to the receiver via some suitable channel. Administratively, the channels selected are those most readily adaptable to written or verbal language symbols.
4. In accord with the definition of administrative communication, effective action (it is hoped) is forthcoming.
5. If effective action is realized, the tension has been removed from the standpoint of management and the communication setting has been restructured and clarified. An equilibrating function has taken place.

An observation or two must be made about the equilibrating process mentioned in point 5. Effective action as seen by the manager does not necessarily constitute satisfaction of the communication needs of the receiver. Communication needs exist on different levels. At one level, utilitarian communication is necessary for adequate job performance. Supplying this information can resolve states of tension caused by ambiguity in the content of job responsibilities.

At another level are tension states resulting from the individual's need to know the *reason* for his job activities and the over-all role of these activities in the broader scheme of the total organization. The major difference between the levels of specific job knowledge and the purpose of the job is, perhaps, the difference that exists between "how" and "why." An individual's communication needs extend beyond the confines of job activities. Even the most competent sender of utilitarian communication may experience "poor human relations" in his department because he fails to communicate effectively on the subtler, less utilitarian levels associated with human motives for work.

Although deeply rooted in psychological foundations, communication is also a social phenomenon. It is the fundamental basis of social interaaction. The relationship between sender and receiver is not a simple one. The idea that the initial sender has control of the communication situation, with the receiver passively reproducing and responding to what is transmitted to him, is of course erroneous. What the sender sends is often conditioned by what he thinks the receiver will accept. And, further, if what was said in previous chapters about empathy is correct, the sender will constantly modify the content of his messages as the receiver feeds back reactions to him. Thus, communication has social implications. Senders and receivers are affected by and act upon the "social matrix" enmeshing the communication process.

Social Aspects of Communication. Ruesch and Bateson describe some of the dimensions of communication in the social setting.[11] These levels are quite appropriate for a managerial approach to the sociology of communication. There are four levels:

Level I—intrapersonal. This is the process of communicating to one's self. It may appear a little odd that this level constitutes "true" communication, because separate senders and receivers are not present. Nevertheless, a person's physiological processes require communicative activities. So although this level does not fit in the administrative definition of communication, it does constitute a logical and defensible point to begin the presentation of communication levels.

Level II—interpersonal. This level is one of common familiarity in which one person communicates to another, such as a manager discussing a job assignment with a subordinate.

Level III—group-individual communication.

a) The first situation in the category is the "one-to-many" case. In the administrative sense, the obligation of a president of a company to report his activities to the board of directors or stockholders is an example.

b) "Many-to-one" communication is the second situation in this category. Frequently decisions made by a committee are communicated to an individual for final action. The decision is jointly derived but its implementation is referred to an individual in higher authority. An executive committee referring decisions to a company president is an example of many-to-one communication.

Level IV—Group-to-group communication.

a) The first form of this communication is many-to-many, space-binding messages. This type of communication is characterized by messages flowing between organizational segments. The information usually deals with on-going situations and frequently is co-ordinating in nature. Differences in functions performed in an organization may be regarded as separated by space. Communication used for transcending this space and co-ordinating activities is thought of as "space binding."

b) Time-binding messages constitute the second form of "many-to-many" communication. While space-binding messages are concerned with current management activities of co-ordination, time-binding messages link the present with the past. The traditions and policies—in short the image of the company—are a product of the "many" who have gone before the present group of executives.

Figure 9–3 schematically presents the aforementioned levels of communication. Note that each level except the first involves social interaction. Value judgments should not be inferred from the presentation of communication as levels. Level IV is no more important than Level III.

---

[11] This approach to the social aspects of communication is adapted from Jurgen Ruesch and Gregory Bateson, *Communication: The Social Matrix of Psychiatry* (New York: W. W. Norton and Co., 1951), chap. 2.

FIGURE 9–3

LEVELS OF COMMUNICATION ACTIVITIES IN THE SOCIAL MATRIX

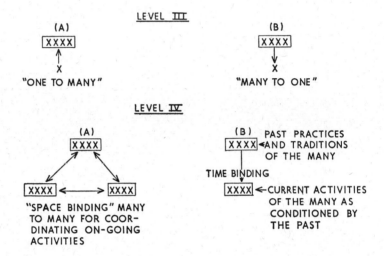

If anything, the levels are ordered in terms of the complexity of the social interactions portrayed.

Each level, however, has social implications peculiar to it. Level II provides for close, personalized communication. This level offers the greatest opportunity for senders and receivers to modify their messages as the communication situation develops. Reactions to communication information on Level II are relatively more rapid than on the other levels.

Two social situations prevail at Level III. In the "one-to-many" case, the individual—say, a president of a company—may be communicating to a rather heterogeneous aggregate of people such as stockholders, or he may be communicating to a small, homogeneous group such as a board of directors. These two cases require distinctly different communication approaches.

The first case is often quite impersonal. Communication with stock-holders is accomplished at annual meetings or through annual reports. The opportunity for feedback from the stockholders to the president is relatively low. Votes of confidence or no confidence in the form of proxies are the delayed reaction to company policy.

The second case—the president's communication with the board of directors—is considerably different. Here a more immediate reaction to communication is achieved in the intimate surroundings of meetings. Also, since this group is fairly homogeneous technical terminology is feasible for explanations of the operations of the business and the formulation of policy. The heterogeneous, detached nature of the stockholder group, then, requires general, impersonal, and nontechnical forms of communication from which feedback is infrequent. In contrast, the homogeneity and smaller size of the board allows the president to communicate in technical and specific terms with every expectation that the feedback from the group will be immediate and direct.

The second situation in Level III is "many-to-one" communication. A number of companies use formally constituted committees to generate policy and to thrash out problems. The results of these joint deliberations are relayed to individuals for action. The receiving individual can be either a member of the committee itself or a nonmember. He, further, can be situated above the committee in formal authority, at the same level, or below the committee.

Reactions by individuals to committee decisions are quite varied. A decision by a group is difficult for an individual to resist at best, even if his better judgment tells him to. In any event, a strong man in a status position above committee members is strategically placed to derive the greatest advantage from the committee's "combined mind." He can offset the weight of the committee by not yielding to schemes which he thinks are poorly conceived. Individuals at the same status level or below the committee in status may not be so fortunate.

Committees are the product of large complex organizations. They serve useful purposes from the standpoint of advice and co-ordination. But there are many dangers in their use, and not the least of these is the difficulty of pinpointing responsibility for decision. As Ernst Pawel observes:

> A committee is not just a group of men. A group of men, once they constitute a committee, form a mythical, mystic, mysterious, inaccessible entity whose decisions have the same force and effect as an Act of God and are equally beyond appeal.[12]

Of course, communication by the many to the one does not have to occur in the context of formally established committees. Informal pressures for conformity and acceptance of values exist throughout organizations. The result, however, is much the same as noted above. Mass opinion tends to lend authoritativeness to communication, regardless of whether in fact the judgment of the group is sound. Some people will form personal judgments that are inaccurate as long as they are told others are making the same judgments.[13]

---

[12] Ernst Pawel, *From the Dark Tower* (New York: Macmillan Co., 1957), p. 68.

[13] The problem of conflict between the individual's view of reality and social pressures is discussed by S. E. Asch, "Effects of Group Pressure Upon the Modification and Distortion of Judgment," in H. Guetzkow (ed.), *Groups, Leadership, and Men* (Pittsburgh: Carnegie Press, 1951), pp. 177–90; and, T. D. Tuddenham, "The Influence of a Distorted Group Norm Upon Individual Judgment," *Journal of Psychology*, 46 (1958), pp. 227–41.

At Level IV in situation *a*, the space-binding functions of communication serve co-ordinative purposes. This type of communication (called horizontal, at times) ties together diverse activities of the business. Space-binding communication exists in a company's line organization among departments in all the organic business functions. It also binds the staff organization to the line.

The concepts involved with situation *b* at this level are rather elusive but are nonetheless real. Through time-binding communication, the past "speaks" to the present in the form of history, established policies, and the company "image." These heritages of past management provide either cherished traditions or burdensome problems for incumbent management. The past does indeed send messages to the present which have to be nurtured or lived down.

Communication Distribution Systems

Now that some of the social and psychological foundations of communication have been discussed, and a definition of administrative communication has been established, thought must be given to the way information is distributed in organizations. Again, models have to be relied on for generalizations. Two basic models are offered here as conceptualizations of organizational communication systems. They are the "circuit model" and the "net model."

The Circuit Communication Model. The simpliest way to visualize an organizational communication system is the circuit illustrated in Figure 9–4.

FIGURE 9–4

THE COMMUNICATION CIRCUIT

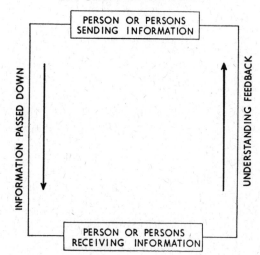

This model fits quite nicely into the definitions of administrative communication quoted from Davis and Browne earlier in this chapter. The model clearly shows that for communication to exist both a sender and a receiver are necessary. Additionally, communication in this model relies on a *closed* circuit, requiring both the elements of downward passage of information and understanding feedback to be present. As a first approximation, this model adequately represents the basic ingredients necessary for effective communication. It should be hastily added that the model is indeed a first approximation.

The circuit model is quadratic, symmetrical, and continuous. It is quadratic in that four elements are basic to it; it is symmetrical because information emitted by the sender (ideally) is balanced by understanding evidenced by the receiver; and it is continuous because it portrays communication as an undisrupted interchange between the sender and receiver.

Newman advances the interesting idea that "although communication is . . . a circular process, circular should not be construed as continuous. . . . There need not be an unbroken, continuous relation among the sender, the signal, and the receiver . . . communication may be said to exist wherever there is a relationship effected between any two of the three factors involved, even though the third may be in abeyance."[14]

A diagram (Figure 9–5) is useful to explain Newman's point.

FIGURE 9–5

A DYADIC COMMUNICATION MODEL

Brackets *A* and *B* identify communication dyads. These dyads may eventually link up to form a completed communication circuit. But their linking is neither direct nor continuous as the model in Figure 9–4 suggests.[15] Instead the two dyads may couple at different times and for different reasons in the organization.

The dyadic aspects of communication do not fundamentally change the circuit model. They modify it to accord more with the realities of communication in complex organizations. Certainly not all organizational communication is the personal, direct, and circular interchange which the

---

[14] John B. Newman, "Communication: A Dyadic Postulation," *Journal of Communication*, June, 1959, p. 53. Grace also holds that communication occurs when a message is emitted regardless of whether it is immediately received and prompts action. Grace, *op. cit.*, p. 17.

[15] While the circuit model uses four elements, two of these elements—information and understanding feedback—are carried by the vehicle of a signal to link the sender to the receiver. So, in principle the same elements exist both in Newman's model and the circuit model.

simple circuit model implies. Administrative communication is frequently impersonal and is disconnected both in space and time from intended receivers.

It is important to appreciate how the communication process operates in the continuous, circular, face-to-face relationship. But it is equally essential to know the circumstances under which dyads link up to form systems in more complex communication situations. For this reason, the topic of the net model follows.

Communication Networks. Communication networks have been mentioned in the preceding chapter on organization theory. Feedback also is closely related to communication networks. These matters are expanded in this section.

The subject of communication networks inevitably brings the analysis back to organization, and clearly focuses on communication as a linking process—for as Rothstein says, "Organization presupposes the existence of parts, which, considered in their totality, constitute organization. The parts must interact. Were there no communication between them, there would be no organization for we should merely have a collection of individual elements isolated from each other."[16] Similarly, Dorsey points out that administration can be viewed as a configuration of communication patterns relating individuals and groups.[17]

A network is best visualized as a system of decision centers interconnected by communication channels. A network always has feedback features; that is, *control* of the system is accomplished by a retroactive mechanism. Feedback, through a communication network, allows for self-regulation of the system. By sampling the output, the system automatically regulates the input in such a way as to maintain stability in the face of change. Feedback is a basic property of cybernetic systems. And the business organization is an example of one of the most complex of all such systems.[18]

Now, the circular model incorporates all the features of a network. In reality this model *is* a highly simplified network because it contains decision centers, information, and a feedback property. However, the network model is far more complex, containing numerous intermeshed loops which do not necessarily behave in a continuous, direct pattern. Further, because of its complexity the network possesses greater capabilities for variety. It is able to assimilate a wider range of inputs, to operate on these inputs in diverse ways, and to produce a larger number of outputs. For

---

[16] Jerome Rothstein, *Communication, Organization and Science* (Indian Hills, Colorado: Falcon's Wing Press, 1958), p. 34.

[17] John T. Dorsey, "A Communication Model for Administration," *Administrative Science Quarterly*, December, 1957, p. 310.

[18] For an excellent discussion of feedback see Stafford Beer, *Cybernetics and Management* (New York: John Wiley and Sons, 1959), chap. 4.

example, compare the intricate communication network shown in Figure 9–6 with the circuit model illustrated in Figure 9–4.

There is no need for a detailed explanation of Figure 9–6, but two points relative to this discussion should be mentioned.

1. Note that this production communication net is a highly complex system, containing all the communication elements discussed before. There are decision centers, indicated by the boxes or cells on the chart; information is present in the system in the form of various messages such as blueprints, records, and reports. Communication channels are shown by lines with arrows noting the flow. And finally, control or feedback information is present as customer complaints, tool receipts, system change recommendations, inventory balances, and so on.

2. Within the network some simple circuits are found. For example, order-dispatching requests for blueprints and the blueprint department's direct channel for returning completed prints constitute a simple circuit. But the communication relationship between order dispatching and the operating department is far less direct and continuous. The system corresponds more conveniently to the dyadic modifications introduced into the circuit model. Thus, order dispatching sends messages directly to the operating department, but the response from operating is far from continuous. Operating feedback to dispatching is routed through many different channels and departments which can be easily followed in Figure 9–6. Hence, the communication activities set in motion by a message from dispatching to operating cause events to occur which are separated from dispatching by both space and time. Results of such initiating messages are neither immediately nor directly available to the sending department.

In summary, the network exists to accomplish *goals* set by decision makers. Movement toward these objectives implies the need for control information relative to the progress of the system in achieving its objectives. *Control functions operate through the feedback of information from strategic points of performance to the decision centers.* Therefore, as stated before, a network is the nervous system of an organization which, in turn, is an elaborate cybernetic mechanism. Again, cybernetics is not the exclusive property of engineers; rather, "cybernetics is about all manner of control, all kinds of structure, all sorts of systems."[19]

Finally, control via the feedback mechanism is the distinguishing feature of a true communication network. Decision centers utilize information feedback to appraise the results of the organization's performance and to make any adjustments to insure the accomplishment of the purposes of the organization. Additionally, feedback is crucially important for maintaining balance among the parts of the system. Feedback cues executives as to when changes are to be instituted.

Administrative Communication Dimensions

Communication models supply information necessary for understanding organizational communication patterns. The dimensions of communi-

---

[19] Stafford Beer, "The Irrelevance of Automation," *Cybernetics,* 1 (1958), p. 295.

FIGURE 9–6

COMMUNICATION IN INTERMITTENT PRODUCTION

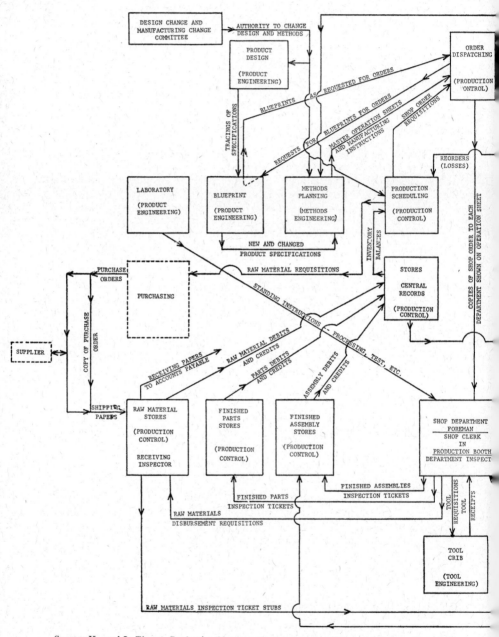

Source: Howard L. Timms, *Production Management* (Bloomington: Bureau of Business Research, Indiana University, 1958), p. 43. Reprinted with permission from Indiana Readings in Business, No. 22.

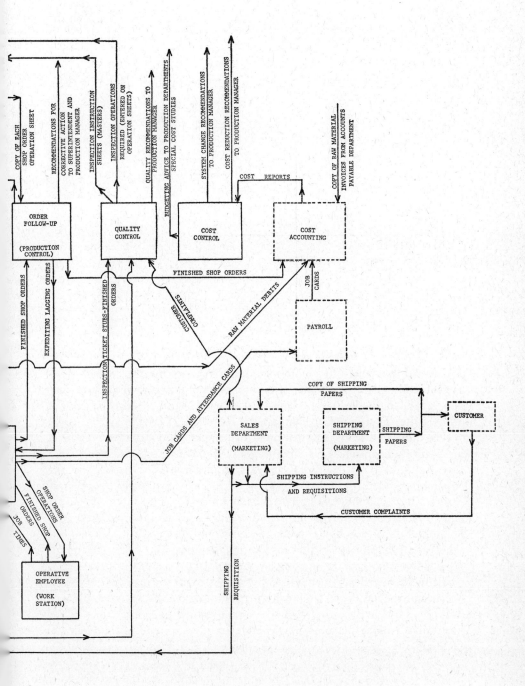

cation from the point of view of the executive will be considered now. Formally, communication moves vertically and horizontally within an organization;[20] plus moving outside the organization. In business, external or extraorganizational communication takes place with other companies, the union, government agencies, and even with the informal organization. The dimensions of organizational communication are shown in Figure 9–7.

FIGURE 9–7

FORMAL COMMUNICATION DIMENSIONS

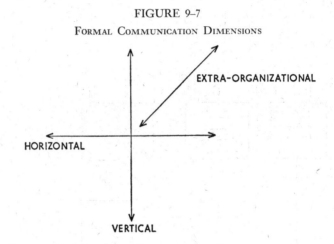

The Vertical Dimension. Most businessmen are well aware of the downward movement of communication. It carries memos, orders, policies, objectives, and programs of action. Formal downward communication is related to the scalar chain-of-command status system, because it follows the superior-subordinate status structure.

The upward flow of information is the other aspect of the vertical communication dimension. This direction is related to the scalar status system also. But instead of authority, upward communication stresses the accountability side of superior-subordinate relationships. *Upward communication is the instrument of management control.*

The Horizontal Dimension. Sending and receiving information on the horizontal dimension corresponds to communication among various positions on a functional status level. The major purpose of horizontal communication is co-ordinating company activities. Co-ordination is achieved partially by interdepartmental transfer of written information. However, because of the impersonality of this method it often fails to accomplish its purpose. Thus, written messages are supplemented by conferences in the hope that a more personal interchange of ideas among executives will facilitate the co-ordinative process.

---

[20] For an extensive analysis of these two communication dimensions see Charles E. Redfield, *Communication in Management* (Chicago: University of Chicago Press, 1953).

Henri Fayol first developed the logic behind horizontal communication in postulating his classic "bridge."[21] The bridge was the result of his studies, as an industrial engineer, of the hidebound traditions of communication in the French civil service. A diagram in Figure 9–8 illustrates the bridge.

FIGURE 9–8

FAYOL'S BRIDGE

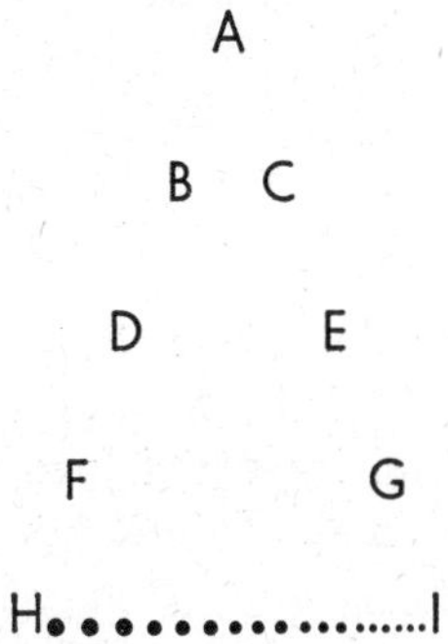

A

B   C

D   E

F   G

H•••••••••••••••....I

Typically, in Fayol's time, if "H" wanted to communicate with "I" he would have to go up the various levels through "A," and down again until he finally reached "I." Fayol observed that this method of communication was inefficient and time consuming. He therefore postulated the idea of lateral communication between persons performing functions on similar levels (in Figure 9–8, from "H" to "I").[22]

The Extraorganizational Dimension. This communication dimension does not have a counterpart to organizational status systems as did the previous two. The inclusion of this dimension adds depth to the communicative activities of the company. It recognizes that an organization does not exist in a vacuum but is constantly talking to the outside as well as to other organizations present in the formal structure. Information fed into the organization from the outside is instrumental in causing the company's decision makers to undertake internal adjustments in its structure, programs, and behavior.

The Relationship between Communication Dimensions and Organization Programs. Earlier in this chapter, four types of programs and their

[21] Henri Fayol, *General and Industrial Management*, trans. Constance Storrs (New York: Pitman Publishing Co., 1949), pp. 34–36. The original work appeared in 1916.

[22] Davis mentions two conditions necessary for horizontal communication: (1) permission for such communication must be obtained from each communicator's direct supervisor in advance or laid down in a general policy; and (2) the communicator's supervisor must be informed of any significant results of such communication. Keith Davis, *Human Relation in Business* (New York: McGraw-Hill Book Co., 1958), p. 247.

associated communication activities were discussed.[23] Referring again to categories 2, 3, 4, and 5, it is seen that they are related to the communication dimensions in the following ways:

1. Vertical communication moving downward in the organization carries programs of the type found in categories 2 and 4—that is, communication to initiate programs, and communication to motivate people to accomplish programs. The upward transmission of information along the vertical dimension relays messages of the type found in category 5, pertaining to control data.

2. The horizontal dimension utilizes communication of the kind peculiar to category 3. Staff and line organizations feed technical data to decision centers so that strategies can be planned and programs put into action. This dimension also makes use of communication activities relating to category 2, to the extent that programs established in this classification are communicated for the purpose of internal co-ordination of functions.

The Informal Communication Dimension. While formal communication exists to meet the utilitarian needs of the organization, informal communication is the method by which people carry on social, "non-programmed" activities within the formal boundaries of the system. Informal communication channels, commonly called the *grapevine*, are not always occupied with information oriented toward organizational goals.[24] Rather, the grapevine is a vehicle for achieving satisfaction of employees' personal objectives. Since personal and organizational goals are either consistent or inconsistent with each other, information on the grapevine reenforces or undermines an organization's objectives.

Simon points out that the grapevine generally performs a positive service to the organization.[25] For one thing, it provides an outlet for expression, thus satisfying a "need to communicate." Additionally, for the executive who can "tune in," the grapevine is a pulse of employee sentiment. Further, it offers a channel for disseminating information that cannot conveniently be sent through formal channels.

Irresponsibility is probably the most mischievous feature of the grapevine. Since the origin and direction of the flow of information on the grapevine is hard to pinpoint, it is difficult to assign responsibility for false information or morale-lowering rumors.[26] The speed at which the

---

[23] *Supra.*, pp. 175–76.

[24] For a detailed account of the functioning of the grapevine, see Keith Davis, "Management Communication and the Grapevine," *Harvard Business Review*, September–October, 1953, pp. 43–49.

[25] Herbert A. Simon, *Administrative Behavior* (New York: The Macmillan Co., 1945), pp. 160–61.

[26] Festinger points out that rumors arise and persist because of ignorance or uncertainty about events which directly affect people. He develops three principles of rumors: (1) rumors begin in situations people find highly relevant to their own affairs; but these situations lie outside their control; (2) rumors always contain a central theme; and (3) when people accept the rumor's general content or theme, they will distort future happenings to conform with the theme. Leon Festinger (and others), "A Study of a Rumor: Its Origin and Spread," *Human Relations*, August, 1948, pp. 483–85.

grapevine is capable of transmitting information makes control of invalid messages extremely troublesome.

Grim as some executives picture the grapevine, it need not be considered a dangerous nuisance. The grapevine is a natural phenomenon; it cannot be destroyed. Fact can usually end rumors, and when principal communicators on the grapevine are identified they can provide a direct and personal channel of information to employees. Also, the information they feed back to the manager enables him to gauge the attitudes of employees.

Another aspect of informal communication is the *by-passing* of formal communication channels in the normal course of job performance. Figure 7–7 depicted a relationship of this kind. Some have said that if the usual channels of formal communication were not by-passed in the routine of the day-to-day work situation very little would get done, and *it* would take a long time.

Formal communication involves a good deal of regimentation. Superceding formal channels often expedites the accomplishment of plans. Although formal channels are by-passed, the methods of going around them are usually quite well specified by custom and protocol. For example, two executives may communicate outside the formal channels, but the occasion for the communication is well defined.

Some of the elements which define when executives can by-pass are:

1. The nature of the information as it pertains to a job situation. Some information is routed through a by-pass; some is sent along the formal channels.
2. How well the by-pass is established in tradition. Some by-passes are so well established they become quasi-formal channels of communication.
3. The recognition of the need for a by-pass by higher level executives. Tacit approval for by-passing formal channels should be a matter of "unwritten" policy.

Communication Effectiveness

Up to this point definitions, the setting, models, and dimensions of communication have been discussed. It is appropriate now that a word or two is offered regarding communication effectiveness. There are at least two general criteria for evaluating the effectiveness of a communication system. The first is how well the system performs to meet the utilitarian demands of the organization. The second is the extent to which the non-utilitarian motives of employees are satisfied by the communication system.

1. It is fairly well substantiated by the theory of linkages that the fewer the number of links between decision centers the more effective organization communication will be. Dubin, for example, argues that a minimization of communication links results in greater organizational stability.[27]

---

[27] Robert Dubin, "Stability of Human Organizations," in Mason Haire (ed.), *Modern Organization Theory* (New York: John Wiley and Sons, 1959), pp. 225–31.

Following Dubin, three basic types of linkages may be identified: the serial, the radial, and the circular. Figure 9–9 illustrates each.

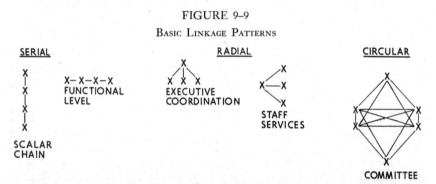

FIGURE 9–9

BASIC LINKAGE PATTERNS

Source: Robert Dubin, "Stability in Human Organizations," in Mason Haire (ed.), *Modern Organization Theory* (New York: John Wiley and Sons, 1959), p. 223. Used with permission.

Numerous hybrid arrangements may be derived from these basic patterns. Two typical combinations in business organizations are shown in Figure 9–10.

FIGURE 9–10

HYBRID LINKAGE PATTERNS

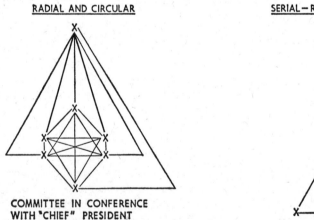

Source: Robert Dubin, "Stability in Human Organizations," in Mason Haire (ed.), *Modern Organization Theory* (New York: John Wiley and Sons, 1959), p. 223. Used with permission.

Figure 9–10 indicates that both linkage patterns have the same number of decision units. But 21 links are required to tie the radial-circular system together, while only 8 are needed in the serial-radial-serial system. So from the standpoint of organization structure the typical line organization comes out on top when communication effectiveness is measured in terms of minimum linkages.

2. The relative efficiencies of linkage patterns do not tell the whole story, however. A considerable amount of research has demonstrated that the authoritarian line structure undermines employee satisfaction. Stated another way, minimization of the number of links in a structure may provide for higher efficiency in communication for utilitarian organizational purposes but it does not necessarily produce nonutilitarian satisfactions for employee communication motives. Indeed, it has been found that the circular (committee or participation) pattern contributes far more to human satisfaction on the job *and* it increases productivity.

Thus, management is faced with a dilemma resulting from conflicting data. Which is the most appropriate system to serve both the needs of the organization and the people in it?[28] The claims made for the circular pattern seem to tilt the balance in its direction. However, the amplification of committee activity has lethal consequences—both for people and for organizations. People may be happy "participating" because they are relieved from their primary obligations of production. Or even worse, production demands may remain while time is consumed by the compulsive sociality of the committee.

Yet, the research on the effectiveness of participation and group decision making is too formidable to be denied entirely.[29] Some circumstances may require a committee-participative form of decision or joint consultation on problems. These conditions include highly involved technical problems or the co-ordination of complex organizations. Participation is also useful when it can be shown to improve both morale and efficiency. However, group decision making or participation is not defensible as a pure "morale booster" if it interferes with efficient operation of the simple serial-radial-serial communication pattern.

Communication Symbols

Communication symbols are, in a sense, an extension of the subject of communication effectiveness. In the final analysis, communication is effective if it *conveys meaning and evokes action*. This subject, treating the vehicles used for the expression of ideas, is so fundamental that it could have appeared at the start of the chapter. However, because symbols go hand-in-hand with meaning, it is useful to apply this topic as a transition to the next chapter. The first part of the following chapter is devoted to problems of communication breakdowns involving meaning.

---

[28] For a further discussion of communication patterns and their relationship to morale and efficiency see Alex Bavelas and Dermot Barrett, "An Experimental Approach to Organizational Communication," *Personnel*, March 1951, pp. 366–71.

[29] Some research is finding participation of questionable value, however. See for example Donald W. Taylor, Paul C. Berry, and Clifford H. Block, "Does Group Participation when Using Brainstorming Facilitate or Inhibit Creative Thinking?" *Administrative Science Quarterly*, June 1958, pp. 23–47.

Language or words, pictures, and actions are the forms communication symbols assume. Of the three, words through common language are probably the most important symbols used in the world of management. Roethlisberger[30] notes that language serves three purposes:

1. *Logico-experimental function.* This function expresses logical attitudes of the kind discussed in Chapter 5. Usually, technical ideas involving the jargon of the trade are transmitted by this type of language. The main characteristic of this function is its objectivity, referring to matters "outside the skin" of the senders and receivers. The subjects discussed are capable of verification to a greater or lesser degree by an informed, impartial third party. Much less time than might be supposed is spent by management in this form of language.

2. *The emotive function.* Most of an individual's communicative time is devoted to emotive language. This form expresses *nonlogical* attitudes and thereby provides a vehicle for the statement of feelings. Verification or criticism of another's feelings is not as simple as an objective evaluation of logical expression.

3. *Daydreaming function.* Daydreaming is the last form of language. It involves a "within-one," intrapersonal kind of communication. Daydreaming is a means of expression and satisfaction for many needs.

Pictures and actions are also symbols which communicate meaning. Pictures may be used to replace words; they may also be used to convey specialized types of information, in the sense that slaps on the back, smiles, frowns, gestures, and the like convey meaning.

When symbols are transmitted some act by another usually is expected. When a manager gives an order he anticipates the job will be done in a certain way at a certain time. He has an idea about an objective to be accomplished. He places this idea in symbolic form and transmits it with the hope that the idea he has symbolized means the same thing to the receiver. Unfortunately, it frequently does not. Part of the reason is associated with the technical difficulties of language itself. Language is a relatively inefficient, imprecise way of sending ideas.

When ineffective action takes place because of poor communication despite the best intentions of senders and receivers, the fault often is attributable to language. A science called *semantics* has developed to treat systematically the relationship between word symbols and meaning. The next chapter, in discussing the subject of understanding, will consider the problem of meaning in greater detail.

SUMMARY

This chapter dealt with the major aspects of communication theory. These are the considerations underlying a definition of communication, the ingredients of organizational communication, the factors necessary for an administrative framework of communication, the social and psy-

---

[30] F. J. Roethlisberger, *Management and Morale* (Cambridge: Harvard University Press, 1941), pp. 89–91.

chological foundations of communication, the distribution system, the dimensions of communication, communication effectiveness, and finally communication symbols. Little attention was given to the causes of communication failure. The next chapter is devoted to these problems.

REVIEW QUESTIONS

1. What is the fundamental purpose of any communication act?

2. Discuss the role of "understanding" as it applies to administrative communication.

3. Outline the basic factors in the communication process.

4. Relate the various forms of communication activities noted by March and Simon to the dimensions of communication in formal organizations.

5. Why does the "tension of an ambiguous communication setting" create a need to communicate? Discuss the psychological processes.

6. Compare the circuit model of communication to the network model.

7. What is a communication dyad? Why is it a "realistic" explanation of organizational communication?

8. Discuss the roles of feedback and control in communication networks.

9. How are the communication dimensions related to organizational status systems?

10. Discuss the functions and characteristics of the grapevine.

11. Discuss the implications of the criteria for communication effectiveness.

SUPPLEMENTARY READINGS

BABCOCK, C. MORTON. "A Dynamic Theory of Communication," *Journal of Communication*, May, 1952, pp. 64–68.

CARTIER, F. A. AND HARWOOD, K. A. "On the Definition of Communication," *Journal of Communication*, November, 1953, pp. 71–75.

DAVIS, KEITH. "Management Communication and the Grapevine," *Harvard Business Review*, September–October, 1953, pp. 43–49.

DORSEY, JOHN T. "A Communication Model for Administration," *Administrative Science Quarterly*, December, 1957, pp. 307–24.

HINDS, GEORGE L. "The Communicative Behavior of the Executive," *Journal of Communication*, Spring, 1957, pp. 29–34.

CHAPTER 10

Communication
(Continued)

AFTER covering the theoretical foundations of communication, some thought may now be given to operating problems that appear in management practice. The first part of this chapter dwells on reasons for communication failure and suggests approaches for overcoming it. The appendix to this chapter considers information theory in organizational communication.

COMMUNICATION FAILURE AND REMEDIES

Communication has many pathological states which beset executives. In general, communication difficulties arise from one or a combination of the following five causes:

1. The nature and functions of language.
2. Deliberate misrepresentation.
3. Organization size and complexity.
4. Lack of acceptance.
5. Failure to understand.

Almost all communication breakdowns can be traced to these five causes. The first set of communication problems analyzed is *distortion and filtering*. Probably the severest and most frequent communication breakdowns result from these diseases of the communication system. Technically, distortion is caused by the nature of language while filtering is produced by deliberate misrepresentation. Filtering and distortion occur both in the vertical and horizontal communication dimensions.

Distortion

Distortion is largely a semantic problem. The amount of distortion contained in any communication act is a function of three variables—the relative efficiency of language, the type of language employed, and the degree of incongruency in the frames of reference of the sender and receiver.

Distortion occurs because of the inadequacy of language to carry precisely the ideas of the sender, and because of the inadequacy of the sender to frame his ideas in correct language. Not much can be done to improve the efficiency of language commonly used in ordinary written or oral communication; but a great deal can be done by improving the sender's facility to work with what he has. In short, the human use of language can be bettered although the basic structure of language itself is not susceptible to rapid change.

Messages sent up and down in an organization have to be *translated* to suit the levels at which they are received. Top policy makers in business tend "to speak a different language" than those on levels below them. But general policies have to be implemented down the line, so a translation process occurs in order to relay policies from top to bottom.

However, something is usually lost in the translation, to say the least. The very nature of language does not allow precise translation of ideas from one level to the next. This inability to bridge organizational levels by precise translations cannot be entirely overcome. However, the distortion resulting from the inefficiency of language can be minimized. One way is for the executive to get a feedback from receivers to check whether they have truly understood the content of a message. (The role of "listening" as it relates to understanding is discussed later.) Redundancy is another technique the sender can use to reduce the distortion in message content. A technical treatment of redundancy is found in the appendix on information theory.

Distortion also occurs because of differing frames of reference. People in various functions in business often perceive problems differently. Sales people tend to view business problems from the marketing standpoint, the plant manager from the manufacturing standpoint, and so on. The technical staff presents a magnification of this situation.

Apart from the differences in jargon of various specialists in business there also is a difference in the "thinking apparatus" of one organizational group compared with another. The confusion which results from the clash of different frames of reference is apparent in the day-to-day communication of the line with the staff.[1] The staff has been trained to think in terms of the logic of its speciality. For example, establishing or adjusting job standards is a matter of logical procedure. The staff expert feels he can set, by scientific measurement, fair standards on the job. It is, however, not his responsibility to sell the standards to the men; this is the foreman's job. So the foreman and the staff man may often clash on standards. Both try to communicate their feelings to the other. Neither succeeds, because they are talking on two different planes—two different frames of reference. The staff man speaks the logico-experimental language of

---

[1] For an example see Melville Dalton, "Managing the Managers," *Human Organization*, 3 (1956), pp. 4–10.

work measurement; the foreman uses the emotive language of operative supervision.

Analogous to the communication barriers erected by differences in technical frames are the social barriers which result in distortion up and down the scalar chain. Social barriers come from what sociologists call *social distance*. For reasons of specialization, the staff man does not think the same as the line executive. For social reasons, the superior does not think the same as his subordinate. The boss has a different frame of reference than the people working for him. One research study[2] shows that between the boss and subordinate most communication breakdowns occur because:

1. The two do not rank job responsibilities similarly in order of importance.
2. There is little agreement on relative priorities of job requirements.
3. There is little agreement on future changes in the job content of subordinates. Subordinates see fewer possibilities for change than the boss.
4. There is a great lack of agreement on obstacles and problems the subordinate faces. The boss seldom knows the problems which are of the most concern to his subordinate.

Another study[3] found that people on different levels in the organization have dissimilar criteria for making status evaluations of others. For example, upper management based its evaluation on class distinctions and background. Lower management felt power was important as a status criterion. And operative employees looked for reliability and authority as bases for making status judgments.

In any event, social distinctions created by authority levels in the organization separate communication groups. This forces each group, and the individuals in it, to adopt a particular frame of reference in forming and interpreting communication. Obviously, the greater the similarity of frames of reference the less likely will be distortion stemming from social distance. Empathy is one method by which social distance is overcome. The ability to project one's self into the other's frame allows the sender to formulate his message so it will be understood by the receiver.[4]

For the reasons just mentioned, distortion is found in the horizontal and vertical communication dimensions. Filtering, because of its peculiar nature, is more apt to appear in the upward flow of communication.

---

[2] Norman R. F. Maier, "Breakdowns in Boss-Subordinate Communication," *Communication in Organization: Some New Research Findings* (Ann Arbor: Foundation for Research on Human Behavior, 1959), p. 22.

[3] Harry C. Triandis, "Similarity in Thought Processes and Boss-Employee Communication," *Communication in Organization: Some New Research Findings* (Ann Arbor: Foundation for Research on Human Behavior, 1959), p. 29.

[4] Lester T. Arnopol, "Attitudes Block Communication," *Personnel Journal,* February, 1959, pp. 325–28.

Filtering

Filtering is the conscious manipulation of "facts" to color events in a way favorable to the sender. It is interesting to note that "coloring" takes place primarily in upward communication, because this direction of flow carries managerial control information. Management evaluates performance as a result of what it hears via the upward channel. The motivation, then, to misrepresent the true situation is strong—stronger, of course, than in downward or horizontal communication where the motives for altering messages seem less imperative from a personal standpoint.

No one likes to appear incompetent in the eyes of his boss. Subordinates study their superiors with great care to find out what they approve or disapprove, what they want to hear, and what their interests are. Then they tend to filter their upward reporting and send their superiors the material most likely to be acceptable. Filtering involves sins of omission as well as commission.

Upward communication carries more than filtered and unfiltered control information. Planty and Machaver[5] note that the upward information flow also contains:

1. Problems on which subordinates need help.
2. Suggestions for operating improvements.
3. Subordinates' opinions about jobs, associates, and the company.

This list may be summarized by saying that much of the content of upward communication is nonlogical. Upward communication is peculiarly susceptible to opinions, gripes, and complaints. It is a channel of emotional expression for people down the line in the company.

This channel has been formalized to some extent by grievance machinery in unionized firms. Systems of this sort operate for the benefit of operative employees. Management, however, "contaminates" upward communication channels just as frequently as do operative employees. No amount of formalization can eliminate emotive language and misrepresented information from upward communication.

Of course, there are many ways management can attempt to separate fact from fiction and logico-experimental language from emotive. Tighter formal controls over the sender of control information can reduce deliberate misstatements of facts. However, the degree to which checking on subordinates can be carried is obviously limited. The simple notion of "span of control" is an example of an important limitation.

Numerous suggestions have been made for unclogging formal upward communication channels by reducing the amount of emotive language

[5] E. Planty and W. Machaver, "Why Doesn't Somebody Tell Me These Things?" *Supervisory Management*, October, 1958, pp. 5–6.

found in them. Likert feels filtering can be cut down by building confidence and sources of expression through teamwork.[6] In much the same vein, Planty and Machaver observe that "unless superiors are particularly receptive, subordinates may prefer to withhold or temper bad news, unfavorable opinions, and reports of mistakes or failures."[7]

The recommendations for reducing filtering include:

1. Tighter controls to ensure that upward communication contains a realistic estimate of the actual situation.
2. Building confidence by teamwork so subordinates see how their reports fit into the over-all picture of company operations.
3. Developing receptivity on the part of superiors to alleviate subordinates' fear of failure.
4. Improving the sensitivity of management to the problems, opinions, and feelings of subordinates so another method of expression is available to them besides the formal channel.

Communication failures caused by filtering and distortion are connected to the nature and function of language and the problem of conscious misrepresentation of facts. The next three classes of problems—overload, timing, and short-circuiting—are largely related to organization size and complexity.

Communication Overload

It is common in business that an executive is literally buried in administrative communication. Communication at times becomes so heavy that an executive is saturated. He cannot absorb or adequately respond to all the messages impinging on him. This problem brings up the *principle of sufficiency*.

Sufficiency pertains to the regulation of communication to insure an optimum flow of information to executives. Communication, thus, should be regulated in terms of both quality and quantity. Sufficiency is implemented by what Dubin calls the "monitoring effect."[8] The monitoring unit acts as a valve which both clears information in order of priority and condenses all messages so that only the relevant information is channeled to executives up the line. In a sense, middle management is a monitor of information between the point of operation and top management.

Weil illustrates the sufficiency principle by drawing his example from reporting by engineers and scientists to higher levels of line management. Figure 10–1 reproduces his model. Note that a monitoring of information

---

[6] Rensis Likert, "A Motivation Approach to a Modified Theory of Organization and Management," in Mason Haire (ed.), *Modern Organization Theory* (New York: John Wiley and Sons, 1959), pp. 195–200.

[7] Planty and Machaver, *op. cit.*, p. 5.

[8] Robert Dubin, "Stability of Human Organizations," in Mason Haire (ed.), *Modern Organization Theory* (New York: John Wiley and Sons, 1959), pp. 247–248.

occurs at each level of transmission in this process. The reports marked
with asterisks are prepared by a service group which performs both specialized work in the development of the report and a monitoring function.

The principle of sufficiency is supported by the hoary management
"exception principle" applied to the field of communication. The excep-

FIGURE 10–1

THE PRINCIPLE OF SUFFICIENCY AND PROGRESS REPORTING OF THE
SCIENTIFIC STAFF ORGANIZATION

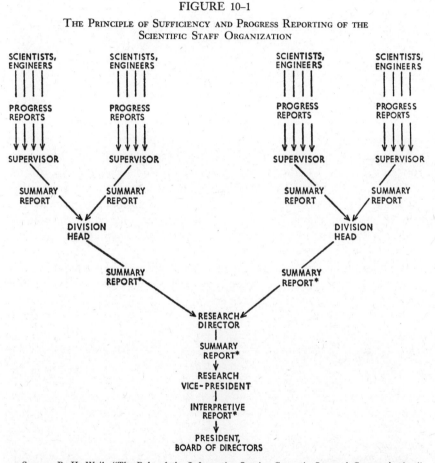

Source: B. H. Weil, "The Role of the Information-Service Group in Internal Communication,"
in T. E. R. Singer, *Information and Communication Practice* (London: Chapman and Hall, Ltd.,
1958), p. 57. Used with permission.

tion principle states that only significant deviations from standards, procedures, and policies should be brought to the attention of the superior.
Put another way, subsidiary units or subordinate individuals should handle
all matters coming in the scope of their jurisdiction. Thus, the superior
should be communicated with only on matters of exception and not of
standard practice. This principle is implicit in business organizations
founded on the military line structure.

Timing

When asked what his greatest communication problem is one executive answered, insuring that all people who are affected receive a message at the same time. Timing involves two major considerations: the strategic release of information, and the simultaneous, or—as the case may be—correct sequential, receipt of information by individuals or company units.

The Strategic Release of Information. Communication sets in motion the machinery for accomplishing objectives. The timing of information release is part of the strategy of decision making. Messages are received and reacted to in various ways at different times by the same people. Politicians are very aware of the timing factor when they try to pick the most opportune moment to release their message. The time selected should have the greatest possible psychological impact. The executive must be conscious not only of the psychological consequences of communication timing but also of the adverse effect poorly timed information has on the company.

Co-ordination of the Release of Information. Business communication is such that receivers must get information either simultaneously or in a sequential order. The interdependency of the parts of a company requires established patterns to maintain the receipt of information.

In addition to the technical operating matters associated with communication co-ordination are the status problems. If five individuals of equal rank are supposed to receive information simultaneously, status difficulties may occur when one receives information before the others. Although it may not be intended, the four could interpret this act as lowering their status positions.

Short Circuiting

A company may apply all the known theories of communication with little effectiveness if consideration is not given to the routing of messages. *Who* is to be communicated with is as important as what, when, and how the message is stated. Frequently, "who" will determine the content and route of a message.

Short circuiting is a common failure of the routing mechanism. Short circuiting means someone has been left out of the communication chain who normally should be included. Figure 10–2 is an example of this problem. Assume the department manager informs a staff representative of an impending layoff without telling the foreman. The staff man "leaks" the information to the operative employees. The foreman, being short circuited, is in no position to answer his employees' questions about the situation. Although the foreman was informally rather than formally short circuited the results are equally unfortunate for him. The foreman's status is lowered because he does not have information on matters of importance to his subordinates.[9]

As a company grows the problems associated with communication overload, timing, and routing increase at more rapid rate. Organizational growth generates both communication and the amount of paper with which an executive must deal. Growth also results in complexity of the timing and channeling of information in the system. Recently, a number of companies have used electronic data-processing equipment to alleviate some of the difficulties of communication flow.

FIGURE 10–2

SHORT-CIRCUITED COMMUNICATION

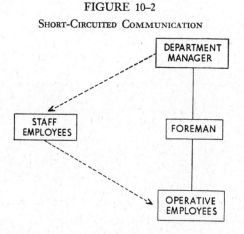

Acceptance

Administrative communication fails not only because of language problems, misrepresentation, or difficulties of size. Two additional causes—lack of acceptance and lack of understanding—also contribute to failure. This section and the next are devoted to these topics.

Receipt of information does not guarantee acceptance. Acceptance is a psychological phenomenon based on, among other things, the needs, motives, experience, and education of the receiver, plus the environment in which he finds himself. Escher comments that, "Since unconscious selection [of information] is closely allied to our psychological needs and desires, it may be said quite aptly that we hear what we want to hear and reject what we don't want to hear."[10]

Assuming that the content of a message is understood, acceptance of

---

[9] The quasi-formal system of communication by-passes, discussed in the preceding chapter, is a form of short circuiting. But the by-pass, as it was established, facilitates the operation of the organization. Short circuiting in the present context assumes that the individual left out of the communication flow needs the information for operating and morale purposes.

[10] Albert J. Escher, "But I Thought . . . ," *Supervision*, July, 1959, p. 24.

the message's statement is a desirable—but not a necessary—prerequisite of effective action. From the standpoint of "good human relations" and "democratic leadership," acceptance carries the force of a value; that is, people will be happier doing things they accept. Nonacceptance, however, does not preclude effective action. People do many things quite efficiently even though they neither agree nor accept the rightness of their act. A manager may not "accept" a sales policy, but he operates under it because of loyalty, or fear of the loss of his job, or the transient nature of the undesirable policy.

Several factors condition human acceptance of communication. They are:[11]

1. *Reality*. This very important factor refers to the individual's appraisal of the situation in which he finds himself. Reality is a person's definition of his environment. Reality for one may not be reality for another. But the relevant reality in this case is the one which the *receiver* defines for purposes of his acceptance or nonacceptance of the contents of a message.

2. *Ambiguity*. All communication is susceptible to varying interpretations. The receiver may not have a clear idea of his "reality," or the content of the communication may be unclear in itself. In any event, lack of clarity results in ambiguity. And the more ambiguous a communication situation the less likely the receiver will be to accept a message.

3. *Credibility*. A good deal of communication is accepted as a "matter of faith" in the sender. The trustworthiness of the source of information is an important variable promoting or hindering acceptance.

4. *Congruency*. The congruency factor applies to the relevancy of the communication to the needs, motives, and values of the receiver. Acceptance in this case depends on whether the information in a message conflicts with or re-enforces the receiver's values and his social, psychological, and economic needs. Obviously, conflict between the contents of the message and the receiver's value-need system lowers the probability of acceptance.

These factors are clearly interrelated. A person's view of reality defines what information is ambiguous, who is credible, and what communication is congruent with his needs and values. So it seems that the manager who wants acceptance of his communication should work first on his subordinates' definitions of reality. If these definitions can be changed to conform with the manager's (or organization's) view of reality, then higher levels of communication acceptance are reasonably assured.

This statement, however, only points out the strategic factor for the executive to work on. It says nothing about accomplishing changes in reality definitions. A variety of techniques is available, ranging from private informal discussions to brainwashing, with participation, training, and "group dynamics" in between.

---

[11] These factors are adapted from Franklin Fearing, "Toward a Psychological Theory of Human Communication," *Journal of Personality*, 22 (1953–1954), pp. 81–84; and Robert Zajone, "Distortion at the Receiving End," *Communication in Organizations: Some New Research Findings* (Ann Arbor: Foundation for Research on Human Behavior, 1959), p. 6.

Changing people's perceptions of reality is an extremely delicate practice; its implications extend far beyond the topic of communication. On the surface, nothing is particularly wrong in tampering with another's view of reality. Indeed, changing the perspective of an individual's outlook on the world is the main function of education. In business, a manager has the obligation to his company, to himself, and to his employees to educate them in the affairs of the company. And the employee has the reciprocal obligation to change his views. This is all part of maturing in business.

Yet, there are boundaries beyond which the manager and the organization must not trespass. Loosely, these limits are the views held by a person regarding his private life. The fundamental integrity of the individual rests upon keeping his organization life and his personal life separated as much as possible. Political ideals, religious principles, cultural pursuits, and family life are private matters which must not be forced into some preconceived mold to suit the whims of the boss or the policies of the company.

As noted before, numerous tools are available for changing individual perceptions of reality and gaining acceptance of a newly defined situation. These tools are simply means to an end. The ends sought are defined by an executive, or by company policy, or by both interacting. The ends may be good or bad, noble or ignoble. If the ends are questionable, the application of the tools is questionable. If the ends are good, but the tools are used to manipulate people into accepting ideas which do not normally accord with their principles, the use of the tools is still ethically questionable. Ends do not justify means.

Teamwork has often been cited as an effective device for changing an individual's perception of reality, and achieving acceptance as the result. A rather lengthy quote from Likert serves as a starting point for showing a problem or two connected with the use of human relation tools.

The fact that an effectively functioning group presses for solutions which are in the best interest of *all* of the members and will not accept solutions which unduly favor a particular member or segment of the group, is an important force in the group pattern of organization. . . . It provides the president, or the superior at any level in an organization, with a powerful managerial tool. This tool is very effective in dealing with the problem of how to handle special requests or favors from subordinates, including requests which the subordinate may feel are legitimate but are not in the best interest of the organization. In the man-to-man operation, the typical line organization, . . . the chief sometimes finds it difficult to turn down such a special request from a subordinate. Sometimes he may be virtually blackmailed into approving it. With the group pattern of operation, however, the superior can readily handle such requests, by merely telling the subordinate to submit his proposal to the group at the next staff meeting. This usually will kill requests for unreasonable favors or treatment.[12]

----

[12] Likert, *op. cit.*, p. 197. Quoted with permission. Italics mine.

All this is nothing new. Using group pressure to force individual non-conformists back into line is well-known. The process Likert describes goes something like this in practice. The manager gains the confidence and acceptance of the group. He sets goals and spells out proper forms of behavior to reach the goals. Then the "well-developed team" takes over, pressuring the individual into conformity with its standards, which in Likert's case are also the standards of the manager.

Of course, Likert recognizes the imperative of preserving individual integrity. But the fact is that executives who set goals are not infallible. The executive working through a "well-developed team" can secure acceptance of his errors in judgment by individuals who under other circumstances might dispute them. Thus, the "well-developed team" cuts both ways. On the one hand, it can relieve the executive of a lot of petty annoyances. On the other hand, it can stifle initiative and preserve an untenable *status quo*.

In general, "human relations tools" applied intelligently by a responsible, mature executive are useful in promoting human satisfaction and accomplishing company objectives. But they are also effective for covering mistakes or paving the road to power for an unscrupulous manipulator.

The Problem of Understanding

Communication takes place through symbols which activate the senses. However, administrative communication most commonly refers to symbols that stimulate the higher senses of sight and hearing. Communication symbols, therefore, are classified as words, pictures, and actions. One of the main reasons for communication failure is a receiver's lack of understanding the symbols.

Understanding is a subjective mental function. A good example of understanding breakdown is a story from World War II. An aerial-gunnery student was taking a ride in a plane for the first time. Although the pilot was enjoying the trip, the student was terrified. While in the air, the pilot pointed over the side of the plane to an object below. The student interpreted the action as the realization of his worst fears—something was wrong with the plane and he should jump for his life. This he did.[13]

Lack of understanding is caused—as in the example of the gunnery student—by differences in meaning assigned to communication symbols by a sender and a receiver. Naturally, achieving uniformity in the interpretation of symbols is a major problem for managers who are trying to transmit ideas to others. As noted already, language communication symbols are relatively imperfect media for conveying ideas. No receiver is able to translate symbols into the precise meaning a sender intends.

---

[13] Mason Haire, *Psychology in Management* (New York: McGraw-Hill Book Co., 1956), pp. 76–78.

However, the margin of difference between the sender and receiver can be minimized.

An executive cannot force understanding but he can frame the communication situation in ways that establish a "climate for understanding." To do this, he must first know what he wants to say. The manager should *plan* for communication. Next, the manager should tailor information to fit the receiver's language and frame of reference. Information should be meaningful, in the sense that it is rendered in terms with which the receiver is familiar.[14]

Finally, the manager must nourish the feedback of information by *listening* to what the receiver has to say. In face-to-face communication a receiver's mind may wander because it is possible to listen at a rate three times faster than a sender is able to speak. Thus, the executive should continuously check for understanding. Guides for improved understanding through listening are outlined in Table 10–1.

TABLE 10–1

GUIDES FOR IMPROVING UNDERSTANDING THROUGH LISTENING

Responsibilities of the Sender	*Listening Obligations of the Receiver*
1. He considers his status position in relation to the receiver.	1. He thinks ahead of the sender, trying to anticipate where the discussion is leading and what conclusions will be drawn.
2. He considers the receiver's opinion of him.	2. He weighs and evaluates the evidence the speaker is presenting.
3. He considers the background of the receiver.	3. He reviews and summarizes the points as they are covered in the discussion.
4. He considers both his and the receiver's attitudes toward the message by empathizing.	4. He listens between the lines, concentrating on meaning and not just the words.
5. He considers the language the receiver will understand.	5. He appraises the message in terms of his and the sender's attitudes toward it.
6. He is constantly aware of the impact of his words on the receiver.	

Source: Points adapted from Harold P. Zelko, "An Outline of the Role of Listening in Communication," *Journal of Communication*, Fall, 1954, pp. 72–75; and Ralph C. Nichols and Leonard A. Stevens, "Listening to People," *Harvard Business Review*, September, 1957, pp. 87–88.

Interviewing is closely allied with listening, although they have different objectives and methods. Listening is a generic term associated with

---

[14] Some information is not susceptible to reduction to simplified language. Remember that the receiver also has the obligation to understand, and must make every effort to master ideas framed in complex language.

every communication act.[15] Interviewing is more formal. It is both a technique to achieve understanding and a therapeutic method to solve personal problems.

Interviewing is defined as a planned discussion between persons.[16] However, the actual process of interviewing is more complicated. Interviewing programs are either directive or nondirective. The directive interview, sometimes called a structured interview, has a list of questions to ask. This sort of interview is used to gather specific information rapidly.

The nondirective interview has a different intent and method. The nondirective interview gathers information regarding the feelings and attitudes of the interviewee. It can be used to produce information of value to the company, such as morale data derived from depth interviews, or it can be used as a therapeutic device, enabling the interviewee to identify and solve his own problems. In either case, the interviewer acts merely as a sounding board, asking no leading questions and giving no hints regarding the directions the interview could take. In fact, the interviewer should have no specific direction in mind.

The nondirective interview usually generates considerable information regarding the attitudes, interests, suggestions, needs, complaints, and personal goals of people. Also, interviewing of the nondirective variety has value in helping employees with their personal problems. However, one major danger of this form of interview, is that of turning inward an employee's legitimate complaint against the company, so that he views his inability to "accept or adjust" as a personal shortcoming. Organizations and the executives running them are not perfect, and the burden for failure should not be forced upon unsuspecting employees by the perversion of a human relations tool.

This part of the chapter has pointed out some basic communication difficulties which occur in practice. Some of the causes for them have been identified and remedies suggested. Also, certain ethical pitfalls associated with, but extending beyond, the communication process have been noted. The appendix to this chapter departs from the tone of the immediately foregoing material to cover an important development in communication—information theory.

REVIEW QUESTIONS

1. Distinguish between filtering and distortion.
2. Discuss the various causes of distortion.
3. Why is filtering peculiar to upward communication?

---

[15] In the usual sense, listening is applied to face-to-face oral communication. But the rules for listening, given in Table 10–1, are easily adapted to written communication.

[16] Harold P. Zelko and Harold J. O'Brien, *Management-Employee: Communication in Action* (Cleveland: Howard Allen, 1957), p. 93.

4. What is the principle of sufficiency? How is it associated with communication overload?

5. Differentiate communication by-passing from communication short circuiting.

6. Outline the determinants of communication acceptance.

7. What are the implications of a manager's efforts to "change a person's perception of reality?"

8. Discuss the role of understanding in communication.

9. What is the "listening" process in communication?

10. Distinguish between the directive and nondirective interview.

SUPPLEMENTARY READINGS

ARNOPOL, LESTER T. "Attitudes Block Communication," *Personnel Journal,* February, 1959, pp. 325–28.

MAIER, NORMAN R. F. "Breakdowns in Boss-Subordinate Communication," *Communication in Organization: Some New Research Findings.* Ann Arbor: Foundation for Research on Human Behavior, 1959.

PLANTY, E., AND MACHAVER, W. "Why Doesn't Somebody Tell Me These Things?" *Supervisory Management,* October, 1958, pp. 2–9.

TRIANDIS, HARRY C. "Similarity in Thought Processes and Boss-Employee Communication," *Communication in Organization: Some New Research Findings.* Ann Arbor: Foundation for Research on Human Behavior, 1959.

ZELKO, HAROLD P. "An Outline of the Role of Listening in Communication," *Journal of Communication,* Fall, 1954, pp. 71–75.

APPENDIX I

Information Theory

WEAVER[1] categorizes the subject of communication as a series of problems on three levels:

Level A—How accurately can the symbols of communication be transmitted? (The technical problem.)

Level B—How precisely do the transmitted symbols convey the desired meaning? (The semantic problem.)

Level C How effectively does the received meaning affect conduct in the desired way? (The effectiveness problem.)

After persevering through these chapters on communication, the reader should be aware that much of the content has dealt with the last two levels of communication problems—the semantic level and the effectiveness level, or the problem of evoking action. The one level that has not been touched is the technical level (Level A), and it is treated by information theory.

Now it might well be asked, why complicate the subject of communication further by bringing up a theory outside the realm of human behavior? In the first place, there is no neat division between where the technical problems leave off and the other problems on Levels B and C begin. So although information theory has its most precise application in the domain of the communication engineer, some of its insights seem to be relevant to human communication problems. In the second place, some recent pioneering research efforts are being made to extend information theory into theories of communication in human organizations, into semantics, and into psychology.[2] Therefore, since information theory is

---

[1] Claude E. Shannon and Warren Weaver, *The Mathematical Theory of Communication* (Urbana: University of Illinois Press, 1949), p. 96.

[2] For a sampling of some of this work see Anatol Rapoport, "A Logical Task as a Research Tool in Organization Theory," in Mason Haire (ed.), *Modern Organization Theory* (New York: John Wiley and Sons, 1959), pp. 99–117. For the use of the concepts in semantics see Dale D. Drum, "Change, Meaning, and Information," *Journal of Communication*, Winter, 1957, pp. 161–70. In the area of psychology see George A. Miller, "What is Information Measurement?" *American Psychologist*, January, 1953, pp. 3–11. For an excellent managerial analysis of the relationships among information theory, system theory, and cybernetics see Stafford Beer, *Cybernetics and Management* (New York: John Wiley and Sons, 1959).

making inroads into both the behavioral and managerial sciences some aspects of it must be examined here.[3]

The labels attached to the basic concepts of information theory are among its most misleading features. For example, "noise," "redundancy," "channel," and "capacity" are fairly common words. Yet their most usual connotations do not apply to information theory. The communication engineer has a precise meaning for these terms.

Take the name of the field itself: "information theory." Normally, the word *information* conveys the idea that a given message contains *meaning* for the sender and the receiver. Whereas, in the field of information theory "information" has nothing to do with meaning.

These semantic difficulties should warn that "things are not as they seem" in information theory. But in both practical and theoretical circumstances the elements of information theory are:

1. Defined with precision.
2. Frequently observable and quantifiable phenomena.
3. Subject to experimentation with outcomes that can be predicted empirically and mathematically.
4. Available for concrete application in telephone communication systems, electronic computing apparatus, and control devices for automated equipment.

However, when it comes to applying information theory concepts to human behavior in human systems, precision breaks down, the phenomenon defies quantification, predictability becomes far more tenuous, and the regions for fruitful concrete applications rapidly diminish. To a great extent, bridging the gaps between *Level A* and *Levels B* and *C* is accomplished by analogy. And analogies, as pointed out previously, may hide basic dissimilarities while revealing superficial similarities in seemingly parallel phenomena.

In spite of the dangers of carrying over concepts from the natural to the social sciences, some of the major contributors to the field of information theory feel this process can render useful insights into the problems of human organization and behavior. Both Norbert Wiener[4] and Warren Weaver,[5] for example, attest to the fact that information theory, cybernetics, and other associated areas possess sufficient generality to warrant their extension into most every facet of the animate universe.

What Is Information?

Perhaps it would be better to ask, what is the technical meaning of information? Information is a quantitative measure of the amount of order

---

[3] For a recent nontechnical treatment of information theory see J. R. Pierce, *Symbols, Signals and Noise* (New York: Harper and Bros., 1961).

[4] Norbert Wiener, *The Human Use of Human Beings* (New York: Doubleday Anchor Books, 1954).

[5] Weaver, *op. cit.,* pp. 114–17.

(or disorder) in a system. Since order and certainty are positively related, information theory yields a yardstick of the degree of certainty or uncertainty in a given system. The more uncertain a system the greater is its potential for varieties of behavior. Information introduces organization into the system—killing variety—thus making the system more predictable.

Information theory tells how much one needs to know in order to proceed from a state of uncertainty to a state of certainty about the organization of a system. As Miller puts it:

> A well-organized system is predictable—you know almost what it is going to do before it happens. You don't acquire much information from a well-organized system. A perfectly organized system provides no information at all. The more disorganized a system the more you can learn by watching it. Information, organization, and predictability are all related.[6]

This leads to the conclusion that the price paid for greater degrees of organization is the cost of the information necessary to introduce more order or certainty into the system.

The next step in understanding the nature of information is to note its statistical character. It has been pointed out that the amount of information in a system is related to what you *can* say about the system, rather than what you *do* say.[7] Therefore, the more disorganized a system is the more you can say about it. Again, if a system is perfectly organized it is perfectly predictable. It has no variety. One does not have a *freedom of choice* in selecting messages from it because a perfectly organized system produces just one message.

Now, freedom of choice is related to the statistical nature of information. In a situation where one selects alternative *A* from possible messages *A* and *B*, the amount of information derived is arbitrarily called one bit.[8] Realize, however, that message *A* itself does not yield one bit of information. Rather, it is the combination of alternative messages *A* and *B* that is capable of producing this amount of information. The measurement of information is, therefore, based on the *total* communication situation, not on specific messages or alternatives. Several examples are offered next to clarify this point.

Assume one wishes to move from uncertainty to certainty about a system which produces 128 equally probable messages. How much in-

---

[6] Miller, *op. cit.*, p. 3.

[7] Weaver, *op. cit.*, p. 100.

[8] A "bit" stands for *binary digit*, which is a unit of information measurement. While the ordinary method of counting is based on 10, the binary system uses the base of 2. The two digits, namely 0 and 1, can be used to correspond to yes-no, all-nothing alternatives. Technically, the measurement of information is the logarithm of the number of choices computed to the base 2. The amount of information in the systems with the following number of equally probable messages is: 32 messages—$\log_2 32$ or 5 bits; 16 messages—$\log_2 16$ or 4 bits; and so on.

formation, in bits, is required? The answer is shown in Figure 10–3. Seven bits are needed ($\log_2 128 = 7$). Also it is observed in this figure that one bit of information halves the number of alternative messages. Or, one bit of information is gained when the number of messages is halved.

The next example is more complex. Suppose a person is waiting on a floor for an elevator and there is no indicator showing the position of the cars. The bank in the building contains six elevators. The probability of any one arriving is one-sixth. The average amount of information gained by knowing which elevator will appear first is 2.58 bits.

FIGURE 10–3

RELATIONSHIP BETWEEN NUMBER OF ALTERNATIVE MESSAGES AND NUMBER OF BITS NEEDED TO MOVE FROM UNCERTAINTY TO CERTAINTY

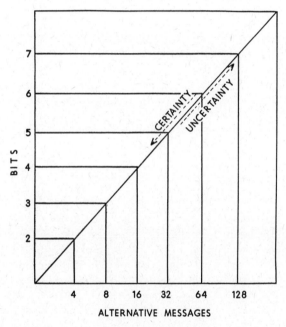

Now imagine that the superintendent tells the waiting individual that two elevators are out of order. The number of alternatives is reduced to four and the system is able to produce just two bits of information. Thus, moving from six to four alternatives reduces the amount of information needed for certainty by .58 bits.

So far the elevator example assigned equal probabilities to the alternatives. Imagine that the situation changes so that the alternatives are not equally likely, exhibiting an array of probabilities as follows:

A	B	C	D	E	F
.1	.2	.2	.125	.125	.25

The average information in this example is computed by the formula:

$$H = -(p_1 \log p_1 + p_2 \log p_2 + \cdots p_n \log p_n).$$

Plugging the probability data in, $H = 2.497$ bits of information needed to produce certainty about the system. Note that this figure is slightly below the number of bits computed for six equally probable events. The reason is because alternative F weights the unequal system of probabilities a little more toward certainty. This phenomenon can be demonstrated more dramatically if these possibilities are used:

A	B	C	D	E	F
.001	.001	.001	.001	.001	.995

The average information needed for certainty in this case is only .057 bits. The F alternative makes the system almost perfectly predictable. Very little information, therefore, is necessary to order it further.

Thus, the more disorganized a system is the more information it is capable of producing. Rapoport summarizes these points by saying:

> . . . [The] 'amount of information' can be equated to the 'amount of disorder.' That is not to say the information is a carrier of disorder. On the contrary, information is the carrier of order. What is meant by the equivalent is that the more disordered a portion of the world is, the more information is required to describe it completely, that is, make it known. Thus, the process of obtaining knowledge is quantitatively equated to the process of ordering portions of the world.[9]

The Concept of Entropy

That information is a measure of disorder, and that disorder in a system is measured in terms of probabilities, lead to the second law of thermodynamics and entropy. One of the most interesting features of information theory is its parallel to the concept of entropy in physics. The formula used to calculate the amount of information in a system, $H = \Sigma P_i \log P_i$, is structurally similar to the equation used to solve entropy problems in thermodynamics.

Entropy expresses the tendency for the organization of any closed system to deteriorate, to become more shuffled, more chaotic. Entropy describes, in relative before-after terms, the inevitable movement of a physical system toward greater degrees of randomness (often called the point of highest probability). This can be demonstrated by a simple example.

Visualize a tank of water divided by a removable partition. On one side of the divider the water is colored with blue ink, the other side with red ink. If the partition separating the different colors of water is raised, the colors merge into an over-all purple hue. The entropy of the system has increased. Before the removal of the partition, a form of order existed with

---

[9] Anatol Rapoport, "What is Information?" *ETC: A Review of General Semantics*, Summer, 1953, p. 260.

the red-ink molecules separated from the blue. But after the change, the molecules distributed themselves evenly throughout the tank, resulting in a single color.

It is quite natural to expect this experiment should end this way. Finding that the colored waters remained in their respective positions, retaining their identity after the removal of the divider, would be exceedingly unusual. Generalizing, systems tend to approach their highest probability, which is greater randomness as opposed to greater organization.

The implications of this law are enormous. Life itself is an improbable form of existence, death being statistically a more "natural" condition. Entropy has only one direction and it is the inevitable movement toward chaos. Wiener views the universe as caught in the inexorable current of entropic disaster, while life, in the broadest sense, is locally swimming upstream.[10]

The vast generality of the "second law" encompasses information theory. Where a system is highly organized the entropy—and hence the information—is low. A small entropy figure represents a system capable of little variety. As randomness increases, so also does the amount of information needed to restructure the system.

In the process of communication, messages are transmitted with a certain entropy value at their origin. When the messages are received it is found that the entropy value is higher, indicating that somewhere in the transmission process random interference of noise has been introduced. In a sense, it can be said that information has been lost, and further that the organization of the original message has deteriorated.

Entropy, from the standpoint of the receiver of a message, is related to the amount of information gained. Information is equal to initial ignorance less final ignorance.[11] So if the entropy value of the received message reflects a large increase relative to the entropy value at its source, the difference between initial ignorance and final ignorance is not great and little information has been gained. All this means is that one major problem of the communication engineer is to combat the "natural decay" of information, so that the difference between initial and final ignorance is maximized.

Wiener has a valuable observation as a summarization of this section on entropy:

The commands through which we exercise our control over our environment are a kind of information which we impart to it. Like any form of information, these commands are subject to disorganization in transit. They generally come through in less coherent fashion and certainly not more co-

---

[10] Wiener, *op. cit.*, chaps. 1, 2.

[11] Y. S. Touloukian, *The Concept of Entropy in Communication, Living Organisms, and Thermodynamics* (Purdue Engineering Experiment Station, Research Bulletin 130), p. 16.

herently than they were sent. In control and communication we are always fighting nature's tendency to degrade the organized and to destroy the meaningful. . . .[12]

Noise and Communication Channels

The "natural decay" or increasing entropy of information is due largely to noise. Noise is the introduction of undesirable uncertainties somewhere in the transmission process—static on a radio is an example. Noise or equivocation refers to "lost" information. Coding messages in various forms can reduce the ill effects of noise, but noise can never be eliminated entirely. There will always be some uncertainty about the message at the receiving end.

Noise can be combated by repeating. However, repeating means adding to the bulk of signals the communication channel must handle. Compensating for noise by repeating reduces the efficiency of a channel because greater capacity must be added to carry a larger bulk of signals. Repeating, therefore, cuts down the rate of information flow. This poses a problem of compromise to the communication engineer. He must balance the system in terms of bulk and excessive sensitivity to noise.[13]

Redundancy

The fact that noise cannot be eliminated or entirely compensated for by a code brings up the function of redundancy or repeating. As Miller states, "Redundancy is an insurance against mistakes."[14]

All codes have a certain amount of redundancy, because they have structure. Since structure implies a departure from chance, it follows that all codes must repeat. Redundancy is the opposite of randomness. It is anything that makes a code system predictable. Language is a code itself, so the remarks that follow pertain to language.

The English language is roughly 50 per cent redundant, which means that books and lectures are about twice as long as they would be if the language was 100 per cent efficient. However, the brain is constructed such that it could not handle the information flow from a language much less redundant than 50 per cent.

Drum mentions two sources of redundancy in English:[15]

1. *The general level of redundancy.* At this level redundancy is attributed to the statistical nature of language—"A" 's occur more frequently than "Z" 's, "I" 's more often than "R" 's, and so on. It is certain

---

[12] Wiener, *op. cit.*, p. 17.

[13] Brockway McMillan, "Mathematical Aspects of Information Theory," in *Current Trends in Information Theory* (Pittsburgh: University of Pittsburgh Press, 1953), p. 6.

[14] Miller, *op. cit.*, p. 9.

[15] Drum, *op. cit.*, pp. 167–69. He also mentions two other sources—the semantic and the pragmatic—which are not discussed here.

that each "q" will be followed by a "u." If hundreds of letters of the alphabet were put in a bowl according to their frequency of appearance in the language, and then randomly withdrawn, a gibberish looking something like English would appear. The reason is, of course, the statistical structure of the language.

2. *The syntactical level.*

a) Formal syntax or grammar limits freedom of choice, introduces structure, and hence makes language more predictable. For example, "the men are going;" not, "the men is going." The plural form of the main verb can be predicted from the grammatical structure of the language.

b) Many words can be used with grammatical correctness, but in terms of context only a few make sense. This is known as the contextual level of redundancy. For example, "the snow is falling;" not, "the snow is running."

Thus a certain degree of redundancy is imposed by the structural limitations of language, or of any code for that matter. This accounts for the fact that even though a radio program is intermittently interrupted by static the listener is able to construct the sense of the message being transmitted. The same principle holds for all codes in a variety of communication systems.

Information Theory and Administrative Communication

The social sciences have a propensity for borrowing concepts from the natural sciences, regardless of whether the connections are real or imaginary. The temptation is great, indeed, to apply the concept of entropy to information as it flows through organizational communication channels.[16] It seems rather useful to think of naturally increasing randomness of administrative communication during transmission as an explanation of communication failure. But how is the physical concept of increasing entropy in administrative communication to be distinguished from failures caused by filtering, distortion, semantic differences, misrepresentation, short circuiting, and dozens of other afflictions of the communication system? In the generalized notion of entropy such distinctions are not necessary because increasing entropy of information is a result of human and non-human interferences. In the practical, operational sense, however, it is still quite fruitful to think of communication breakdowns in a more specific way. For example, if misrepresentation of information is a problem it should be recognized as such and treated by the executive in a straightforward way.

Consider, next, the problem of channel capacity and communication overload. An executive may experience communication overload because

---

[16] In fact, management could be considered as source of "negentropy." That is, management is constantly combating the natural tendency of systems to become more disorganized. Management tries to reverse the direction of entropy in a company.

of his limited abilities and not because the channels are jammed with messages. How, then, is the technical capacity of a system to be distinguished from individual differences? For that matter, how is the capacity of an administrative communication channel to be expressed quantitatively in the first place?

What can be said about noise? The technical meaning of noise has no real counterpart in administrative communication. Unwanted additions to administrative communication are probably analogous to noise. But how useful is this analogy? Cannot the same phenomenon be understood as conveniently with the more conventional theory of filtering?

These objections and more are summarized nicely by McMillan who says ". . . one must be careful to distinguish between proved relationships among precisely defined concepts on the one hand, and speculative relationships suggested by the names of these concepts on the other."[17] Confusing the technical meanings of information theory with administrative processes is a pitfall that should be recognized and avoided.

Yet, after all this has been said, language and communication are at the core of administrative practice. Information theory is intimately bound up with the concept of organization itself. Information plays a crucial role in the notion of cybernetics which was shown in Chapter 8 to be basic to human organizations. Thus, information theory supplies a powerful conceptual tool for management plus being useful in attacking specific problems of human communication—provided the range of these problems is carefully delineated.[18] Finally, there is a feeling that information theory is the theoretical linkage between various systems which exhibit feedback characteristics. If such is the case, and progress is made in determining the precise application of these ideas to administrative communication, then revolutionary insights into the management process itself will evolve.

---

[17] McMillan, *op. cit.*, p. 14.

[18] See, for example, Anatol Rapoport, "A Logical Task as a Research Tool in Organization Theory," in *Modern Organization Theory*, op. cit., pp. 91–114.

CHAPTER 11

Balance and Change

BALANCE, like communication, is a linking process in organizations. This subject has been met in previous chapters, but this chapter treats balance in greater depth, integrating it with the notion of change.

BALANCE

The *black box* is an interesting idea found in the literature of physics and, more recently, in cybernetics.[1] The black box is a device for converting inputs into outputs. But the operations it employs to transform inputs are quite obscure. Indeed, the black box is never fully knowable! Its inscrutable nature is produced by two important properties:

1. The internal structure of the black box is highly complex. Elementary cause-effect relationships are impossible to find. The mind simply cannot comprehend the multitude of interconnections and interdependencies which exist among its parts through its linkage system.

2. The black box defies investigation of its innards because if it is tampered with it will change its internal properties. The significance of this statement should not be underestimated. It implies that experimentation with the black box could be futile, since the experimenter is not entirely certain his results are properly relevant to what he wished to study in the first place.

Thus, about all that can be known about the way the box functions is to observe what is put in and see how it comes out. From the changes occurring in the input, inferences can be drawn about the processes within the box which actually wrought the changes. As a consequence, incomplete knowledge of the box is obtained indirectly.

In spite of all this, the black box is not as stubborn as it seems. The black box is a system. And all systems have structures which lend them a certain degree of predictability. Therefore, the black box is not altogether capricious in its behavior. It can be ascertained that in response to certain inputs the black box will produce specified outputs. How this is accomplished is not completely describable; in fact, for practical purposes it is not really necessary to know much about the internal operations

---

[1] An excellent description of the black box is found in Stafford Beer, *Cybernetics and Management* (New York: John Wiley and Sons, 1959), esp. chap. 6.

of the box. Desired outputs can be had by *controlling* strategic inputs.

Business organizations are quite similar to the black box because: (1) they convert inputs of productive factors into outputs of goods and services; (2) they are often highly complex; and (3) they tend to rearrange their structure as a response to the introduction of foreign influences.

To elaborate point three: assume an organization is being observed by a detached, objective viewer who is making inferences about its operations. Now, suppose an experiment is undertaken to check the accuracy and validity of the conclusions arrived at through the observations. No matter how careful the experimenters are they inject a new element into the organization by their presence. In so doing, they rearrange the interactional patterns in such a way that they cannot be positive they are experimenting with the "same" organization previously observed.

FIGURE 11–1

THE BALANCING PROCESS AS IT APPEARS TO THE OUTSIDE OBSERVER

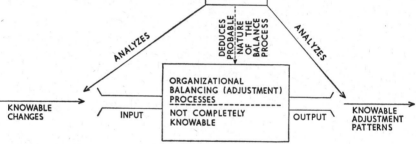

Thinking in terms of the subject of this chapter, imagine that a change occurs in an organization. The change is arbitrarily called an input, although some may prefer the word "stimulus." The organization reacts, and an adjustment to the change follows. The adjustment is the output. Figure 11–1 shows that the outside observer can make some deductions regarding the balancing process by knowing the nature of the change (input) and by dissecting the adjustment (output). Complete understanding of the process, however, is hidden from the observer.

Next the observer decides to include himself as part of the organization to test the validity of his deductions by experiment and to gain a greater insight into the process of balance itself. He cannot, however, be assured that the adjustment process is the same after he has joined the organization. The best which can be said is that if the inputs and outputs are the same under both the conditions of observation and those of experiment, the investigator may be fairly confident that his presence has not affected the balancing process. He feels he has the right to say he understands the balancing process. The investigator's confidence is reinforced because his experiments support his observed deductions, *and* he has, in fact, been observing and experimenting with identical situations.

What does all this mean for the job of management? Is it true that the efforts of management to facilitate adjustment to change are futile, because organizational reactions to change are complex and unknowable? The answer to this question fortunately is no. Management can obtain desired reactions to change (output), by controlling the changes (inputs) themselves. Thus management regulates the nature and administration of changes so that the adjustments accord with the objectives of the organization and satisfy the needs of the people in it.

From an analytical standpoint, balance is an elusive concept. But as a result of observation, deduction, experimentation, intuition, and analogy some things can be said about the black-box process of balance. Generally, balance is considered as a process which reconciles and maintains structural interrelationships among the many forces and elements that make up the organization. Balance has been defined as ". . . a condition in a company where there is accord among the objectives of individuals, the informal organization, jobs, and the formal organization." It is a process which acts ". . . to insure system stability in face of changing conditions which are either internal or external to the organization." The first definition treats balance in a management context specifically. The second definition has greater generality and is found frequently in the literature of the behavioral sciences. In essence the two definitions refer to the same process.

Concepts Related to Balance

Equilibrium and, more recently, homeostasis are terms often encountered in the behavioral sciences. They pertain to concepts which are fundamentally the same as balance. Balance, equilibrium, and homeostasis are *almost* interchangeable; they do, however, have some subtle differences. A little closer attention to the latter two ideas casts some light on balance and its administrative applications.

Equilibrium. Equilibrium refers to a state of adjustment between opposing forces. It also describes a tendency of a system to move toward a condition where the forces or influences in it are resolved. Two kinds of equilibrium are applied to social phenomena—static and dynamic.[2]

Static or stationary equilibrium is a situation where the environment of the system is held constant over a period of time. Dynamic equilibrium

---

[2] For a discussion of various types of equilibrium see David Easton, "Limits of the Equilibrium Model in Social Research," *Profits and Problems of Homeostatic Models in the Behavioral Sciences* (Chicago Behavioral Sciences Publications #1), 1953, pp. 26–40.

implies change and the ability of the system to preserve its internal structure of relationships despite a changing environment. Neither of these two forms of equilibrium carries the meaning that activities internal to the organization cease.

The equilibrium concept was borrowed from physics and has had a long tradition of application to economics. Somewhat more recently equilibrium has been used to describe processes in psychological and sociological research and theory. Pareto noted the usefulness of the idea in application to social systems, observing that systems have the tendency to return to a state of equilibrium if their original adjustment is disturbed.

Homeostasis. This formidable word is derived from the Greek and means "steady state." It has been borrowed from biology and refers to a process by which a system regulates itself around a stable state. But as Penrose observes, "Strictly speaking, the basic principle [self-regulation] is not a biological one at all in spite of the name given it. It is a general principle of organization, examples of which may be found in biology, in mechanics and in social organization. . . ."[3]

FIGURE 11–2
The General Principle of Feedback

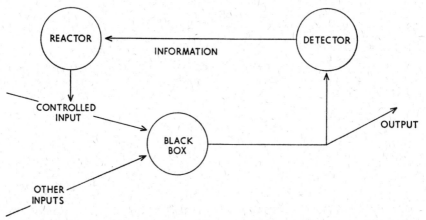

Source: Adapted from Pierre de Latil, *Thinking by Machine* (Boston: Houghton Mifflin Co., 1957), p. 50.

Self-regulation requires feedback and control, both operating in such a way as to minimize the adverse effects of change on a system. On the surface, it appears that equilibrium and homeostasis are quite similar. However, all equilibrium states do not involve homeostasis. *Constancy does not imply feedback.* Davis[4] cites an example of a system moving through several states as follows: 10, 9, 8, 7, 6, 5, 4, 3, 2, 1 . . . . . ! If

---

[3] Edith Tilton Penrose, "Biological Analogies in the Theory of the Firm," *American Economic Review*, December, 1952, pp. 804–19.

[4] R. C. Davis, "The Domain of Homeostasis," *Psychological Review*, Vol. 6, 1958, p. 10.

these states are not dependent on each other, and are equally probable, it is predictable that the next state is 0. The stability or equilibrium of this system is not dependent on a feedback mechanism.

Following Davis, homeostasis has feedback as its basic feature. That is, some energy must be taken from a latter part of the system and introduced in an earlier part so as to oppose the change produced there by the original input. In human systems information is analogous to energy and is a major part of feedback. Data pertaining to the status of a given result in terms of objective accomplishment are fed back so that modification of action can be made if necessary.

Thus, feedback is a process of retroaction whereby activities are modified in terms of what has been accomplished and what still needs to be done in order to reach a goal. Figure 11–2 illustrates the general principle of feedback.

The operational sequence of the feedback system in Figure 11–2 is as follows:

1. The *detector* is sensitive to variations in the output generated by the black box; information regarding the output is transmitted by the detector to the *reactor*.
2. The reactor is sensitive to the reception of this information and is capable of altering the nature of the *controlled* input.
3. The controlled input is modified (if necessary) thus changing the performance of the black box.

To summarize what has been said so far, equilibrium has inherent to it the notion of the resolution of opposing forces. Homeostasis also incorporates this idea, but adds to it the matter of self-regulation. Both these concepts offer a useful way of viewing the interdependency of parts of a system. They are, however, not complete in themselves. They describe ends—constancy or stability under changing conditions. They do not specify particularized means whereby these ends are achieved.

Stability in the Simple System

Mills offers the adjustment process of an uncomplicated system as a first approximation explaining the means used by organization to preserve stability. He points out that at least three conditions are necessary for stability.[5]

First, all possibilities of behavior can be controlled. That is, all relevant behavioral alternatives which may emerge in reaction to change fall within the spectrum of the established control machinery. Control can assume numerous forms, including formal regulation through policies, standards, and rules. The informal organization exercises control over behavior by the group through norms, values, and sanctions of conduct.

Second, the system is able to allow for constructive change even though

---

[5] Adapted from Theodore M. Mills, "Equilibrium and the Processes of Deviance and Control," *American Sociological Review*, October, 1959, pp. 673–74.

such a change may deviate from established norms. A discriminating ability between constructive and destructive changes is necessary because stability in a system does not imply stagnation. Indeed, stability may be dependent in some cases on the facility with which an organization is able to adapt to change. Adaptation requires the modification of organizational relationships.

Third, the system has a feedback mechanism. Once a change from standards is sensed evaluative action is initiated, and if necessary offsetting strategies are introduced.

Under these circumstances, the simple system would operate something like this:

$$A \hspace{8cm} B$$
$$1 \quad 2 \quad 1 \quad 2 \quad 1 \quad 2\text{—change—control—}1 \quad 2 \quad 1 \quad 2 \quad 1 \quad 2$$

Starting with the pattern A a change is introduced. The control system is activated offsetting the change and preserving the structure of the system as indicated by pattern B.

Obviously, this is an oversimplification. But the example does at least point up some essential features of the stability process. All organizations have internal controls designed to maintain a harmonious relationship among the parts. Any change or deviant form of behavior will be interpreted in terms of the threat it poses to the stability and continuity of the system. If the organization interprets the change as a menace to its integrity actions will be set in motion to counterbalance the change.

The performance of the simple system is limited by at least four conditions.[6]

First, the effectiveness of the stability process is restricted by lack of information regarding the change. Because of this limitation, change-combating strategies may be totally ineffective for the preservation of stability.

Second, each system, like a business organization, is composed of subsystems which may be pressed into an unwanted readjustment because of the power exerted by one subsystem relative to the other. For example, an informal organization could be forced into a realignment of its values, status positions, and standards of conduct because technological change is forced on it by the formal organization. The informal group may resist and strive to maintain its established structure. But the power exerted by the formal organization is too strong to withstand. The informal organization capitulates grudgingly. A tenuous truce emerges.

Third, the individual seeking personal ends can undermine stability. Individual goals are not necessarily integrated with organizational goals. The amount and the way in which personal objectives deviate from those of the system determine the extent to which stability is reduced.

---

[6] Adapted from *ibid.*, p. 677.

Fourth, the system buys stability at a price. Feedback and control cost, if not in dollars then in some other value. The value of stability is weighed against the cost of control. If the cost is too high for the value derived, then some stability is sacrificed.

Balance is closely related to equilibrium and homeostasis. Balance is concerned with the resolution of numerous influences in an open (self-regulating) system. The nature of balance is discussed next.

The Nature of Balance

Balance is a management concept. It has specific reference to the business organization and the major components which make it up. Particular note is made in Chapter 3 of the four basic elements which comprise the business organization. It is useful to repeat them here.

1. The *individuals* in the organization, including their attitudes and motives.
2. The *jobs*, including the status hierarchy and roles, the formal job processes, and the equipment used to do the job.
3. The *informal* organization, including its status and role systems.
4. The *formal* organization, the over-all structure of the company including policy, decision making, and the specific relationships which exist among jobs, departments, divisions, and so on.

These elements are interwoven and can be viewed by a manager from a number of frames of reference: he can think of these factors in terms of their interaction in the entire company, in a division, or within his own department. A convenient way of looking at balance is through the patterns-of-balance diagram.

FIGURE 11–3

PATTERNS OF BALANCE

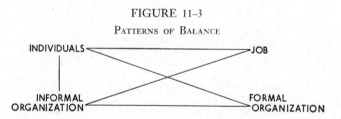

The purpose of this diagram is to show that there are ten areas of conflict or harmony of *objectives* among the factors on the chart. Each element on the chart has objectives which may or may not be in accord with the objectives of the other elements.[7] The objectives of any one element—

---

[7] Except in the case of "job" and "formal organization" where it is assumed for the sake of simplicity that jobs which are no longer useful will be eliminated. Job elimination and consolidation are largely technical problems. However, even this relationship has human relations overtones. Jobs may not be dropped, or redundant functions may be added, because of the personal power of individuals in the organization. Empire building is an example of this situation. An individual may expand his activities to enhance prestige. The jobs which are created do not serve to meet the objectives of the organization. Rather, they may indeed be in conflict with objectives of the company.

say, individuals—can conflict or be in balance with the objectives of the other elements. As a result, the objectives of one element in the diagram may be in conflict with one other element, two other elements, or all the other elements. But, for that matter, an element can also be in balance with all the other elements.

The patterns of balance is not an automatic, problem-solving device. It is merely a way of thought to guide management in identifying the real cause contributing to conflict in an organization. This device is a tool like situational analysis. Even the manager with the best intentions can go astray in handling human relations problems by not recognizing the true parties or elements in conflict. The patterns of balance, therefore, is a method of diagnosis.

Achieving and maintaining organizational balance is a responsibility of management. In human systems, particularly business organizations, harmony of objectives is accomplished through conscious management effort. The primary obligation for balance rests with the line organization, not the staff. Many companies claiming to have "human relations programs" are just attaching this name to traditional personnel functions. When the desired "balance" is not forthcoming from these programs, employees are branded as ingrates.

As long as human nature is as it is, perfect balance is impossible. However, for most organizations accord among the objectives of the above elements is more the rule rather than the exception. Anarchy is incompatible with the system concept.

Through the concept of balance, it is evident that management is the human instrumentality which acts to resolve conflicting influences. While equilibrium and homeostasis are useful for conceptual purposes, they smack of impersonality. The processes which maintain body temperature at a fairly constant level are homeostatic. But the operation of the sweat glands is hardly similar to the administration or "self-regulation" of the business organization. It cannot be stressed too strongly that self-regulation of business is a product of conscious effort. It is not automatic.

The Role of Conflict

Balance carries a value connotation. That is, harmony of objectives is good; conflict of objectives is bad. It is near treason in some circles to assert that a happily adjusted organization is not ideal. Conflict, however, serves as a positive stabilizing force in some instances. Too much harmony can be as dangerous as constant destructive conflict.

Conflict is far from being homogeneous in nature. Conflicts differ in form as well as effect with varying types of group relationships. Table 11–1 classifies some types of conflict and some of their associated effects.[8]

---

[8] Conflict can be classified in many ways. The approach followed here is adopted from Lewis A. Coser, *The Functions of Social Conflict* (Glencoe: The Free Press, 1956). For other views see James G. March and Herbert A. Simon, *Organization*

TABLE 11–1
CONFLICT: TYPES AND EFFECTS

INTERNAL

Type	*Effect*
1. Conflict among individuals in a group centering on subordinate or minor goals, but not questioning the basic values of the organization.	1. Serves a positively useful function of re-evaluating established norms of behavior and facilitating movement of individuals in the status system of the organization.
2. Conflict where parties no longer endorse basic values of the organization.	2. Tends to destroy the fabric of the organization.
3. Conflict in a closely knit organization.	3. Generates greater intensity, thus tending to be destructive.
4. Conflict in a relatively loosely established organization.	4. Tends not to be destructive since it is not as intense as the previous situation, because people are less personally committed to the organization.
5. Conflict in flexible organizations.	5. Tends to have relatively minor, localized conflicts, obviating rifts which may split the organization into antagonistic camps.

EXTERNAL

Type	*Effect*
1. Groups continually in conflict with outside organizations.	1. Demands greater conformity of members —tends to reduce internal conflict so as to focus all organizational energy on the antagonist.
2. Organization not involved in continual external struggles.	2. Makes fewer demands on members.
3. Conflict of a rigid organization with outside organizations.	3. Tends to suppress internal adaptation to the conflict, refuses to change to cope more adequately with a dynamic environment.
4. Conflict of the flexible, more loosely structured organization with outside organizations.	4. Modifies its internal relationships to meet the exigencies of external conflict.
5. External conflict in general.	5. Tends to vitalize organizational values and makes members of the organization interested in the activities of the opponent.

While by no means inclusive, the types of conflicts and their consequences shown in Table 11–1 do point up some patterns. First, internal conflict is beneficial to the extent that it promotes:

(New York: John Wiley and Sons, 1958), chap. 5; Ross A. Stagner, *The Psychology of Industrial Conflict* (New York: Arthur Wiley and Sons, 1956); and Arthur Kornhauser, Robert Dubin, and Arthur M. Ross (eds.), *Industrial Conflict* (New York: McGraw-Hill Book Co., 1954).

a) *The circulation of leadership.* The advancement of new, vital leaders who are better equipped to reflect the values of the organization and to serve its purposes.

b) *The modification of old goals.* The modification of previously held values to facilitate organizational adjustment in the face of change.[9]

c) *The institutionalization of conflict.* The organization to establish outlets so that people can "blow off steam" without damaging the structure of the organization.

Second, the benefits of internal conflict accrue more to the loosely structured rather than the rigid organization. Rigid organizations demand greater personal involvement of the individuals in them. By so doing, conflicts, even minor conflicts, become more intense and increase the likelihood of dangerous factional splits. Further, rigid organizations tend to suppress instead of institutionalizing conflict. Smothering conflict can be costly, and as tension builds even the most elaborate method of control may not be able to contain expression of pent-up feelings.

Third, conflict with outside organizations serves four purposes by:

a) Promoting closer bonds of unity among individuals within the organization.

b) Building new life into organizational objectives and values.

c) Making organizational members aware of the strategy and tactics of the antagonist.

d) Acting as an agency of social control. Conflict in this case results in a contervailing power relationship in which organizations will tend not to transcend limits of propriety because if they do they will be set back by another equally powerful organization.

Fourth, the effect of external conflict on internal organizational structure is not clear-cut. External conflict builds *esprit de corps*, but continual conflict requires the organization to make greater conformity demands on members, reducing internal conflict. This reaction may or may not result in rigidity in the structure. Military organizations are extremely rigid relative to advertising agencies. But both organizations are geared to a continual conflict type of situation. In general, internally rigid organizations seem less able to adapt to a changing conflict environment while flexible organizations can more readily make adjustments. Thus, conflict serves the flexible, loosely structured organization better than the rigid.

Dynamic Balance

An open system like a business organization either changes or it fails to survive. The only way to exist in a changing environment is for the organization to change its structure. Dynamic balance pertains to manage-

---

[9] Torrance notes that task-oriented disagreements serve beneficial purposes by increasing the range of judgments, by reducing chances for misunderstanding because each person's position is expressed, and by increasing willingness to take calculated risks because each person knows where others stand on issues. See E. Paul Torrance, "Group Decision-Making and Disagreement," *Social Forces* 35 (1957), pp. 314–18.

ment's ability to adjust the structure of the organization in face of constantly shifting technological, economic, and social conditions.

Obviously, the caliber of management is a key variable associated with adjustment to change. But even the best management is limited to the extent it can accomplish such adjustment. Limitations are inherent in the system itself. These limitations are very similar to those noted previously in Chapter 8 as limits to innovation. Additionally, it can be said that the rate management is able to adjust to change is, in part, dependent on the way in which the company has organized its method of solving problems. Ideally, the organization should be such that it encompasses the widest range of possible changes which might arise. However, something less than the optimum must be accepted because of limitations of both company resources and human ability to foresee the future.

Management looks upon a dynamically balanced company as one which:

1. Exhibits continuity with its past. The past serves the company in the form of tradition and lends it some identity.
2. Affords control over the present direction and amount of change in the organization's policies, structure, personnel, and physical facilities.
3. Offers a workable degree of predictability for the future.[10]

Thus, dynamic balance involves the past, the present, and the future. It requires future organizational integrity and continuity in the face of uncertainty. But the future direction of the company is partially charted by present conditions and the traditions of the past.

CHANGE

The foregoing comments on change have centered largely on organizational adaptation to change. This section treats the effects of change on the individual and the implications for management.

The modern world—actually quite unlike the world of even 100 years ago—is characterized by constant change. That which is called progress is predicated on change. Schumpeter has characterized the dynamic quality of our society as a "perennial gale of creative destruction."[11] The old is destroyed and is incessantly replaced by the new. This process of change is responsible for our way of life and the standard of living presently enjoyed.

But because change usually involves elements of uncertainty people are wary of it. Much research has been done in the field of human relations on the problems of change. Generally, it has been shown that people

---

[10] Suggested by Robert Dubin, "Constructive Aspects of Industrial Conflict," in Kornhauser, Dubin, and Ross, *op. cit.*, p. 41.

[11] Joseph A. Schumpeter, *Capitalism, Socialism, and Democracy* (New York: Harper and Bros., 1947), chap. 7.

accept some changes while resisting others. Although this is not a particularly profound statement, it is necessary to point out early in this discussion that resistance to change is not a monotonously uniform human trait. Indeed, just the opposite seems to be true. People accept change. If this is not the case, humanity would still live in caves and paint itself blue. But changes are not always accepted without question. In business, management has to sell many changes. Gaining acceptance of change is a crucial point upon which successful or unsuccessful administration rests

Change Defined

Change can be defined easily. *It is any alteration in an established way of doing things.* This definition applies equally to personal routines as it does to patterns of formal and informal organizational performance. Changes may be resisted because they threaten to disrupt behavioral patterns of individuals or organizations.

The definition of change must be qualified however. Change is not homogeneous but has three phases—the threat, the impact, and the after-effects.[12] These phases are important to management and must be analyzed further.

Frequently management is so concerned with the implementation of change that it fails to see the significance of the threat change poses to people. If people believe a change will be made it is of little consequence whether it is true in fact. Those who think they are to be affected may feel under stress and respond adversely toward their job and company. Therefore, job behavior, in some cases, can be explained by people's reaction to the threat of change.[13]

The impact is the phase of change which comes under most popular consideration. Human reaction to the impact can range from complete acceptance, through active resistance, to stunned immobility. Change can dislocate the social system and individual adjustment to the work environment. Slow, small changes seem more likely to be assimilated, but large, rapid change impacts can upset established patterns of behavior. This observation appears elementary. But the speed and size of change and their effects on organizational balance and personal adjustment cannot be overemphasized.[14]

Oftentimes situations arise where the impact of change has no adverse reaction to it. But when people have lived with the change for a while,

---

[12] This point is brought out by Irving L. Janis, "Problems of Theory in the Analysis of Stress Behavior," *The Journal of Social Issues*, Summer, 1954, pp. 12–25.

[13] Alvin Zander, "Resistance to Change—Its Analysis and Prevention," *Advanced Management*, January, 1950, pp. 9–11.

[14] For the relation of the impact of change to balance see Alex Bavelas, "Some Problems of Organizational Change," *Journal of Social Issues*, Summer, 1948, pp. 48–52.

favorable or unfavorable response sets in. This is the third phase of change—the aftereffect.

Management may feel once it is past the initial impact of a change the battle to win acceptance is over. This is not necessarily true. The aftereffect of change indicates the need for follow-up. If a "delayed action" resistance develops management should know the cause so proper measures can be taken to remedy the situation.

The Principles of Change

Researchers working in the field of group dynamics have developed much data concerning change. From this work several principles can be derived for management use.[15] First, most important of these is management recognition of the cohesiveness of group behavior. When a change occurs it is not isolated to one subpart of a group but extends to the entire organization. When a change is instituted management cannot expect its influence to be contained in a single part of the company. The effects of change spread throughout the organization.

Second, change is more effectively accomplished among people who have a strong attachment to the group, as long as the change does not run contrary to the fundamental standards of the group. Thus, if management is to be successful in gaining acceptance of change through the group it must consciously develop a sense of attachment of the members to the company or the job, or both.

Third, the greater the prestige of a group member the more influence he can exert over the people he contacts in the group. This principle emphasizes the functions of the informal leader and his role in aiding management to gain acceptance of change.

From all of this, seven conclusions regarding change are forthcoming.

1. Change is a management problem. Management is directly responsible for instituting and gaining acceptance of change.
2. Resistance to change is a human relations problem. Resistance either collectively or individually results from an imaginary or real threat to a group or to a person's security.
3. The threat of change can be as disrupting as the impact.
4. Change is not isolated to a subpart of a group or to a unit in a company. Change is felt throughout the social system.
5. People are just as likely to accept change as to resist it. Change is a positive as well as a negative force.
6. The informal leader plays an important role for management in the administration of change.
7. The speed and size of change is a determinant of whether it will be assimilated or not.

---

[15] These principles are adapted from Dorwin Cartwright, "Achieving Change in People: Some Applications of Group Dynamics Theory," *Human Relations*, November, 1951, pp. 381–92.

Factors Underlying Acceptance or Rejection of Change

Ultimately, acceptance or rejection of change depends on people's attitudes toward it. Janis,[16] describes six determinants which condition attitudes toward change.

1. *Preconceived notions.* These prejudices are developed over a long period of time. Suppose a person's (or group's) experience with change had been bad in the past. It is likely he would feel that future changes would also affect him adversely.

2. *Expectations.* These are objectives concerning what a person or group wants out of a particular situation. Changes which give evidence of fulfilling expectations are likely to be accepted.

3. *Opinions of self.* This includes personal self-evaluation of strong and weak points.

4. *Connection with primary group.* A person's position in the informal organization has much to do with the way he will react toward change. A person in the primary group may feel completely different about a change compared with a person in the out group.

5. *Status.* The rank of a person in the formal status system will condition his reaction toward change.

6. *Training.* Preparation for change through training and education goes far in determining attitudes of acceptance or rejection of change.

These six determinants underlie whether people will accept, reject, or be doubtful about change. Usually, people will favorably consider a change which includes improved status, more money, or better working conditions. Rejection factors for people may involve breaking up informal groups, losing security, or a major change in location.

In most cases the acceptance and rejection factors are not too difficult to identify. The doubtful factors present a harder problem because they involve uncertainty. An individual facing change asks himself: if this happens what will be its net effect on me? It is important to recognize that doubtful factors eventually become rejection or acceptance factors after the change has been experienced. But by this time it is too late for the manager to do anything about facilitating adjustment to change.

It is up to a manager to ensure that the people involved in a change see it initially in its true perspective. Stressing the bright side of a change and distorting the dark side may be asking for trouble in terms of the after-effect in the future. Effort should be made to remove the doubtful factors as much as possible. Fear of change is caused mainly by uncertainty. If the manager is skillful many doubtful factors can be cleared up and placed on the acceptance side of the ledger.

*   *   *   *   *

---

16 Janis, *op. cit.*, p. 21.

The analytical material covered in this part concerns the individual and the organization viewed from the perspective of the behavioral sciences. A large number of topics are considered ranging from individual motivation and morale to stability, change, and conflict in human organizations. In spite of the diversity of material it must be appreciated that the forms of behavior and processes investigated are found together in unique configurations in every human organization.

The chapters just completed certainly are not a comprehensive survey of the behavioral sciences. Instead, they are an effort to extract from these sciences that which is relevant for management. In this respect, attention is given to the research, analysis, and concepts which are most appropriate in a business context.

At times it may appear that the connection with what is said to be the "real" world of business is vague. While this may be, it is true that the nature of the "real" world is not altogether evident. It is a fact, however, that in business man works in surroundings having social, economic, psychological, and political characteristics. Being a social institution, in the broadest conceivable sense, business organizations are in some ways microcosms of the prevailing cultural values of American society.

For years behavioral scientists have studied social and psychological phenomena outside the business context. Their findings, generalized to conceptual principles, undoubtedly have application to business settings. Tests of the validity of such applications to business have been and are being made. Also it is encouraging that the interest of behavioral scientists in business organizations and men at work is increasing in intensity. The consequence of this can be nothing but deeper scientific probing into the nature of man and organization.

The next part of this book moves away to some extent from the "theory" of the behavioral sciences toward a treatment of issues of importance to management. But before the reader sighs, "Thank heavens this is the end of theory," he should be warned that perhaps the next part is actually the beginning.

The issues included in Part III are there precisely because they can be analyzed in terms of the analytical and conceptual positions stated in the foregoing chapters. Thus, the reader should study the next chapters with the purpose of discovering the implicit and explicit applications of the analytical and conceptual frameworks already developed.

REVIEW QUESTIONS

1. Analyze the characteristics of the black box. Why does the black box defy experimentation?

2. How does an observer make inferences as to the nature of the processes going on in the black box?

3. Compare the concepts of equilibrium and homeostasis. What are their major differences?

4. Discuss the feedback principle.

5. Analyze the concept of balance "as an administrative process." How does it differ from equilibrium and homeostasis? What does it have in common with these concepts?

6. Review the positive aspects of organizational conflict.

7. What is meant by the institutionalization of conflict?

8. Discuss the three phases of change.

9. What determinants underlie an individual's "readiness" to accept change?

SUPPLEMENTARY READINGS

CARTWRIGHT, DORWIN. "Achieving Change in People: Some Applications of Group Dynamics Theory," *Human Relations*, November, 1951, pp. 381–92.

COSER, LEWIS A. *The Functions of Social Conflict*. Glencoe: The Free Press, 1956.

MILLS, THEODORE M. "Equilibrium and the Processes of Deviance and Control," *American Sociological Review*, October, 1959, pp. 671–79.

TORRANCE, E. PAUL. "Group Decision-Making and Disagreement," *Social Forces* (35), 1957, pp. 314–18.

ZANDER, ALVIN. "Resistance to Change—Its Analysis and Prevention," *Advanced Management*, January, 1958, pp. 9–11.

PART III

Issues

CHAPTER 12

Bureaucracy

BEFORE launching into the issues selected for attention, it is wise to give thought to the purposes and structure of this part of the book. The title "Issues" for Part III is appropriate because the subjects considered here are matters over which "reasonable men can disagree." The purpose of the following chapters is to bring into the light of discussion topics which are of major consequence to management in the realm of interpersonal relations in business organizations. The reader should compel himself to study the issues not only in terms of what is said on the remaining pages but also in terms of what he feels can be derived from preceding chapters in application to these problems. This suggests, therefore, that both the analytical and ethical considerations dwelt upon in Parts I and II are key conceptual foundations to this part.

The connections between chapters in this part are more loosely drawn compared to the previous chapters. There is one common theme, however. It is implicit thoughout these chapters that the type of business organization providing the framework for the problems and issues is medium to large in size. This is particularly evident in the discussion of executive incentives and constraints in Chapter 17. The subtitle of this chapter might well be "in the *large* corporation." A predisposition of this sort might be validly challenged. But the trends toward large centralized institutions are evident in business, government, labor, and voluntary nonprofit associations. This commends the orientation of this part to issues as they appear, generally but not exclusively, in the perspective of the sizeable business organization.

With this in mind, the bulk of this chapter is devoted to the subject of bureaucracy in order to establish the groundwork for the rest of the chapters. Chapters 13 and 14 are aimed primarily at issues involving operative employees. Chapter 13 treats the nature of work and incentives. While the first few pages of this chapter deal with matters that are sufficiently general to encompass all employees at every level of a business organization, it is dedicated in content and spirit to the operative level. Chapter 14, on the union, also is devoted in part to worker problems from another point of view; a point of view which assumes the union to be an organization which like the company demands worker productivity, loyalty, and support.

Chapter 15 moves from the operative level to consideration of the first level of supervision, where the problems of foremanship are treated. Chapters 16 and 17 go up the executive hierarchy dealing with matters of issue in higher levels of management. Thus, Chapters 13 through 17 take up problems and issues at various levels of the organizational hierarchy starting with operative employees and ending with top management.

Chapters 18 and 19 treat leadership and training in the behavioral sciences, respectively. These chapters constitute a logical grouping because the need of leadership in management and supervision has often been viewed as satisfied by some form of training in the behavioral sciences and human relations.

BUREAUCRATIC ORGANIZATION

The term "bureaucracy" can be taken to apply to all sizes and types of formal organizations. Thus, bureaucracy is part of the general extension of organized activities into most facets of life in our society. The study of bureaucracy consists of the analysis of formal organizational structures, of human behavior within these structures, and of power and influence.

The words "bureaucracy" and "bureaucrat" are emotionally charged. They conjour up a gigantic governmental organization of monumental inefficiency peopled with lazy, narrow-minded functionaries. This stereotype centers on shortcomings. Actually, bureaucracy is a characteristic possessed to a greater or lesser extent by most formal organizations. In this discussion, therefore, it seems to be far more fruitful to speak of a degree of bureaucratization rather than of bureaucracy or nonbureaucracy in an absolute sense.

Bureaucracies neither have to be large nor do the people in them have to display a uniform type of behavior which is supposedly repugnant to "nonbureaucratic" behavior. Bureaucracies have only two elementary characteristics—rules which prescribe and govern functional relationships; and rules which prescribe and govern behavioral patterns and desirable habits of members of the organization. It can be seen readily, therefore, that the concepts of bureaucracy extend to just about every formal organization in an ordinary person's experience.

The analysis of bureaucracy has fallen largely within the province of sociologists and political scientists. In certain respects, however, the framework of the treatment of bureaucracy closely parallels the work on the formal organization found in management literature. At the same time it is surprising how little cross reference exists between work on bureaucracy by the behavioral scientists and work on the formal organization by the students of management.

Since some of the concepts of bureaucracy are similar to those of the formal organization treated in an earlier chapter, is there any value in picking up these ideas again? To the contrary, this section does not restate in sociological jargon what has been said in Chapter 7. New ground is covered for the purpose of bringing to light some of the insights of sociologists and political scientists in the sphere of organization.

It is valuable for the student of management to be aware of contributions to the theory of the formal organization by scientists outside the area of business organization. Additionally, bureaucracy poses issues in organization, human behavior, and ethical values which can hardly be ignored in a book of this type.

The Scope of the Study of Bureaucracy

The study of bureaucracy has proceeded along two lines.[1] First, the traditional approach is the study of bureaucracy as an administrative tool. This view is attributed to Max Weber.[2] The bureaucratic organization is seen in this respect as a mechanism for the achievement of goals. To Weber, the bureaucracy is the epitome of rationality. No other form of organization, to him, could grind out goal accomplishment better. The second and a somewhat more recent view is concerned with bureaucracy as an instrument of power and influence. Within the context of this view are a number of subtopics including the effect of human behavior on the so-called rational organization instrument, the modification and stagnation of bureaucratic goals, the internal power-plays of bureaucratic functionaries, and the relationship of bureaucracies to society as a whole. In short, the study of bureaucracy in this sense looks at the *process* and *implications* of bureaucratization rather than the static characteristics of the machine itself.

Why Do Bureaucracies Develop?

A civilization must reach a certain degree of maturity before bureaucracies emerge to exert a significant influence on the life patterns of people in a society. Some features of maturity which foster the growth of bureaucracies follow.[3]

The institutions in society must be differentiated in terms of the role they play. Differentiation takes place along functional lines; for example, the separation of the economic functions from the family. In this case, the family is no longer the locus of the production of goods and services. Instead, such activities are centralized in specialized institutions.

Once differentiation occurs the selection of individuals to perform

---

[1] See S. N. Eisenstadt, "Bureaucracy, Bureaucratization, and Debureaucratization," *Administrative Science Quarterly* 4, (1959–1960), p. 303.

[2] See Max Weber, "The Essentials of Bureaucratic Organization: An Ideal-Type Construction," in Robert K. Merton *et al.* (ed.), *A Reader in Bureaucracy* (Glencoe: The Free Press, 1952), pp. 18–27.

[3] See Eisenstadt, *op. cit.*, pp. 305–8; and Peter Blau, *Bureaucracy in Modern Society* (New York: Random House, 1956), pp. 27–44.

tasks in bureaucracies is based on possession of the necessary qualifications for adequate dispatch of the duties. In other words, bureaucracies require that individuals, to "qualify" for their roles in differentiated organizations, possess specialized forms of training and education.

The society as a whole must be in a position to supply the resources for support of bureaucratic organizations. As such, society is expected to underwrite bureaucratic activities. Theoretically, therefore, the bureaucracy has to pursue socially acceptable goals.

Implicitly, a society which is ripe for bureaucratization is highly complex, exhibiting considerable interdependence among its parts. Under these circumstances social needs can best be met by marshaling and administering resources in centralized bureaucratic organizations. Some social demands requiring centralization are imposed from the outside, like war. Other demands are internal, such as where solving agricultural, employment, or tax problems are thought more efficiently achieved through centralization of authorities.

Many bureaucracies exist in a modern society: governmental bureaucracies, military bureaucracies, labor bureaucracies, and business bureaucracies, to name a few. Within these institutional segments are discrete bureaucratic organizations which represent aggregations of power in competition with other bureaucracies for resources which supposedly will be channeled to meet some social need. However, with proliferation bureaucracies are propelled into a power situation. The bureaucracy in a mature society must engage in activities which enhance its power and its ability to compete with other bureaucracies for a favorable allocation of resources. Thus, the accumulation of power and the wielding of influence are adjuncts of bureaucracies in mature societies regardless of whether these societies are totalitarian or democratic.

The Characteristics of the "Ideal" Bureaucratic Instrument

As stated earlier, one method of studying bureaucracy is as a tool of administration. In this respect, the framework of analysis differs little from that applied to conventional formal-organization theory. However, there are several points stemming from bureaucratic analysis worth mentioning here.

Weber, in his treatment of bureaucracy, emphasizes its superiority over other organizational types. The source of this superiority is based in rationalization and the utilization of technical knowledge. As a result, the bureaucracy is able to achieve the highest degree of efficiency for accomplishing objectives. The ideal bureaucracy has, in the Weberian sense, the following characteristics.[4]

1. A clear division of labor is found in which regular tasks are distributed in a fixed way and legitimatized by recognition as official duties.

[4] As cited in Blau, *op. cit.*, pp. 28–32.

2. Functions are arranged hierarchically, resulting in a chain of command—the scalar principle.

3. All activities in the bureaucracy are governed by abstract rules which are applied uniformly in particular cases.

4. Officials of the bureaucracy act impersonally in the application of rules to the internal affairs of the organization and to contacts outside the organization.

5. The selection criteria for employment applicants are based on the qualifications of the applicant relative to objective standards for the job set by the officials of the bureaucracy.

Weber implies that any deviation from the ideal bureaucratic framework reduces the efficiency with which the organization operates. Yet it is difficult to consider these standards meaningfully if they are taken in an absolute sense. It is more plausible to talk of the degree of bureaucratization in formal organizations. In this regard, Carl Friedrich presents six criteria which are useful as tests of the extent of bureaucratic development.[5] They are:

1. *The degree of functional differentiation:* How far has the division of labor gone in an organization?

2. *The degree of centralization of control and supervision:*

   a) How complex are the organizational problems of coordination and communication? The greater these problems are the more bureaucratic the organization has become.

   b) How many levels are there in the scalar chain? The larger the number of degrees of subordination the more bureaucratic the organization.

3. *The degree of qualification for office:* To what extent have the requirements for employment in specific tasks been spelled out according to objective standards?

4. *The degree of objectivity:* How much pride do employees of the bureaucracy derive from recognition of their technical competence by fellow bureaucrats? (Technical competence in this sense means mastery and application of bureaucratic rules and procedures.)

5. *The degree of precision and continuity:* How much do employees adhere to precedents and routines essential to the preservation of complex administrative machinery?

6. *The degree of discretion:* To what extent do employees exercise judgment in making known or withholding information of a special character to the public at large? Presumably a bureaucratic organization of a high degree restricts information to a greater extent than a bureaucratic organization of a lesser degree.[6]

---

[5] Carl Joachim Friedrich, *Constitutional Government and Politics* (New York: Harper and Bros., 1937), pp. 32–40.

[6] Merton says, "Bureaucracy is administration which almost completely avoids public discussion of its techniques, although there may occur public discussion of its policies." Robert K. Merton, "Bureaucratic Structure and Personality," in Robert K. Merton *et al.* (ed.), *Reader in Bureaucracy* (Glencoe: The Free Press, 1952), p. 363. For example, the public was fully aware of Ford's plan to bring out a new car—the Edsel—but such matters as cost data, production processes, and the like were kept secret.

On the basis of these six standards some degree of bureaucratization is evident in formal organizations of many different sizes. However—although this cannot be taken as a general rule—the larger the organization becomes the more bureaucratic it becomes. Sometimes this statement is assumed to be a self-evident truth, but it is interesting to investigate possible reasons underlying it. Clues might be found in the notion that larger organizations are more stable than smaller organizations. Caplow offers several points in support of this idea.[7]

1. Large organizations afford more chance for greater vesting of interests than small organizations.

2. Large organizations tend to support each other. Society generally will not tolerate the collapse of a large organization.

3. Large organizations frequently have a wide range of activities so that disaster to one activity does not jeopardize the entire organization.

4. Large organizations apparently devote a greater proportion of their resources to the maintenance of their internal operations such as communication, control, and co-ordination. Through making these allocations the large organization has greater control over its continuity and ultimate survival than the small organization.

Caplow's stabilizing influences add up to these conclusions about bureaucratic tendencies in large organizations.

1. Vested interests make the crystalization and perpetuation of rules governing functional relationships, procedures, and behavioral patterns more convenient.

2. Society preserves the large organization because it cannot stand the consequences if the organization should be lost. Thus, society at the same time supports implicitly the intensification of bureaucratic practices which grow as the organization grows in protected surroundings.

3. Through multiplication of activities and objectives the bureaucracy enhances its survival prospects. Diversification enhances stability. For example, the March of Dimes organization continued even after the discovery of the Salk vaccine because it changed the objectives of its program.

4. By having command over considerable resources the large organization can take steps to insure its integrity over time. It can structure and run its internal operations more effectively and it can exercise more power and influence in society than can the small organization.

In summary, size acts to insure stability. And in its turn stability allows for the intensification of bureaucratic practices.

This entire discussion so far is predicated, following Weber, on the assumption that the ideal bureaucratic mechanism offers the most effective vehicle for the accomplishment of goals. Further, this argument takes the people in the organization as givens rather than variables whose behavior

---

[7] Theodore Caplow, "Organization Size," *Administrative Science Quarterly* 1 (1950–1951), pp. 501–2.

influences the process of bureaucratization. The next topic considers deviations from the "ideal" bureaucratic model.

Some Facets of Bureaucratic Performance

The perfect bureaucratic machine does not exist; even if it did it probably would not work. Were it not for deviations from rigid prescriptions of bureaucracy, the organization would be immobilized. Modifications of Weber's ideal model, therefore, are either positive or negative from the standpoints of organizational efficiency and goal accomplishment. Three sources of bureaucratic modifications are discussed next: selection of employees, structural paradoxes, and the power relationships of suborganizations within the bureaucracy.

Selection, Recruitment, and Training. One of the criteria of bureaucracy is the selection of employees by objective standards that stipulate the skills, education, and experience necessary for entry into a bureaucratic position. This is the "qualification for office" characteristic.

This criterion presumably assures the organization of employees equipped with sufficient technical information to discharge the job efficiently. However, carried to an extreme, highly specialized employees may be a liability rather than an asset in the event of change. Very often, as Page notes, a rigid selection criterion results in "trained incapacity" of the official.[8] He observes that the peacetime naval bureaucrat frequently is not up to handling the rigorous demands of a rapidly changing organization under the strain of war conditions. As a result, actual leadership reverts to others in the organization. Consequently, people carefully selected for one type of job often are not able to cope with jobs emerging under stress conditions.

There is another facet to the selection problem. Early forms of bureaucracy were very selective in the sense of recruiting members from special segments of society. Thus, the military, the church, the government tended to draw recruits from certain social strata to the exclusion of others. This situation is dangerous in a democratic sense. The selective bureaucracy appeals to a segment of society which Smith says to be "atypical"[9] since the values of the segment may not represent the values of the whole society. Thus society's values are subjugated to rule by a group whose standards and goals are not representative. All in all, the more selective bureaucratic recruitment is the greater the chance that socially beneficial ends are jeopardized.

The alternative of selective recruitment is saturative. Through satura-

---

[8] Charles Hunt Page, "Bureaucracy's Other Face," *Social Forces*, October, 1946, pp. 88–94.

[9] Edmund Arthur Smith, "Bureaucratic Organization: Selective or Saturative," *Administrative Science Quarterly* 2 (1957–1958), pp. 361–75.

tive recruitment the bureaucracy draws employees from a wider social cross section. This does not mean, however, that the bureaucracy has become less concerned about the "qualification for office" standard. It simply has offered the opportunity to compete for positions to more people from many layers of the social structure.

In order to compete, aspirants for jobs must have access to the education or training necessary for meeting the qualification requirements. There is some evidence that bureaucracies are drawing employees from a broader base. Formal education has been a force in making this transition possible.[10] Access to education, then, is the first step toward saturative bureaucracy. Ideally, the more saturative the bureaucracies in our society are the more likely they will be to administer their affairs in the public interest rather than for a restricted clique.

Problems of Structure. The emphasis bureaucracy places on structural maintenance leads to sanctification of procedure and to domineering attitudes of officials. Although apparently quite unlike, these two structural pathologies have one thing in common: the frequent failure of the bureaucratic functionary to separate means from ends. Procedures which are means become ends for the functionary who is imbued with the sanctity of impersonal application of abstract rules.

Restricted to the domain of his function, resulting from the division of labor, the bureaucratic official often becomes domineering when dealing with the public. While acting within his own province he gives the impression that he actually speaks for and represents the character of the entire organization. Such behavior is self-defeating for a bureaucracy which ultimately relies on public support for its existence. It is interesting in this respect to note the care which large protected utilities exercise when instructing employees in "proper" behavior in customer relations.

Problems of Subordinate Groups. Just as the total bureaucratic organization is a center of power so also are suborganizations within the structure power centers. Subordinate power centers can arise as typical informal organizations or they can appear as power groups by virtue of their position in the formal organization. In either event, the power adhering to these subgroups may be sufficient to detract the bureaucracy from its major purposes, by displacing resources into the accomplishment of the subgoals of special-interest cliques.

Selznick describes the process underlying goal displacement.[11] He observes that the division of labor requires the delegation of authority to minor officials. Such delegations set the stage for a division of interest

---

[10] Joseph R. Gusfield, "Equalitarianism and Bureaucratic Recruitment," *Administrative Science Quarterly* 2 (1957–1958), pp. 521–41.

[11] Philip Selznick, "An Approach to a Theory of Bureaucracy," *American Sociological Review*, February, 1943, pp. 51–52.

between those who initiate action (the top authorities) and those who carry out action (the intermediate authorities).[12]

The initiator most often is prompted in policy formulation to pursue ultimate organization goals. Whereas the intermediary, having another social position and role, is sometimes prompted to seek goals which are different from those set on top. As a consequence a struggle ensues between these groups for control over the organizational mechanisms which will enable each group to solve the problems of their own special interest.

Because the intermediaries possess skills, technical qualifications, and proximity to the machinery of implementation in the organization, they are in a strategic position to dominate in the power struggle. If this occurs, the intermediate group is able to establish the goals for the entire organization, leaving higher officials to rubber-stamp lower-level decisions.

Thus the organization moves away from its original purpose toward aims which are internally generated by lower-level executives. There is no doubt that this situation is pathological from the standpoint of organizational effectiveness and social relevance. It is representative of a case where the *actual* center of power does not correspond to the formal center of power; that is, the individuals occupying the top positions in the structure are not the people who make decisions regarding the purposes and directions to be assumed by the organization.

This situation usually does not arise where top management is able to retain the right of review and control, plus sufficient proximity to intermediate organizational levels for effective appraisal of performance in the light of policy. A situation of this sort is more probable when top management *abdicates* control or becomes so *distant* from the point of policy implementation that adequate appraisal is nearly impossible. Both these conditions go hand-in-hand. The implication is that the larger the organization grows the more likely it is for the center of power to devolve on the intermediate levels, in which case the organization tends to depart from its original purposes. Hence, the bureaucratic machine becomes the instrument for the satisfaction of special interests rather than an efficient device for achieving social goals.

One Fundamental Issue—Goal Displacement or Goal Succession?

It must be clear by now that bureaucracy is a tool by which people solve problems. As such its life is predicated on the accomplishment of socially acceptable ends. But as an organization endures and grows it,

---

[12] A distinction is made between a division of interest and a division of interpretation. The former involves a conflict in objectives between two groups; the latter pertains to a breakdown in communication between two groups. See David M. Levitan, "The Responsibility of Administrative Officials in a Democratic Society," *Political Science Quarterly* 61 (1946), p. 568.

at times, remains merely figuratively associated with the purpose it was originally constituted to achieve. New goals emerge. This transition of objectives is what is meant by the displacement or succession of goals. On the one hand, succession of goals refers to the healthy adaptation of the organization to meet changing needs. The accomplishment of past goals becomes the foundation supporting new and socially relevant objectives. On the other hand, goal displacement pertains to a switch from the pursuit of social ideals to a conservative policy which values the preservation of the organization for the sake of preservation.[13]

Many years ago Robert Michels wrote a significant book called *Political Parties* in which he proposed the "iron law of oligarchy." His thesis is that bureaucracy is fundamentally opposed to democratic ideals. Further, he says there is an inevitable tendency as organizations get larger to become more tyrannical and stagnant with the final cost borne by society. The organization comes to exist for itself; bureaucratic preservation emerges as an end of the first priority. With such a displacement of goals, Michels concludes that, "That which IS oppresses THAT WHICH OUGHT TO BE."[14]

At the heart of the issue of goal displacement or succession is the matter of responsibility. A bureaucracy is not responsible if it exists for itself only nominally serving the public which supports it. The responsible bureaucracy is one which is able to adapt its ends to meet changing social needs. The basic question is: where are the sources of pressures in society for responsibility?

Some look to the impersonal free market as the source of pressure for organizations operating in the economic segment of society. Others find the electorate as the source of pressure forcing responsible behavior on government bureaucracies. And still others look to the membership of unions as the source of pressure on labor leaders.

Where the public fails to exert pressure for responsible performance a vacuum is created allowing for the exercise of irresponsible power by administrators. Rapoport has observed that, "There is hope only if the players of the power game are to some extent receptive to public pressure."[15] It must be added, however, that the motives to exert pressure for responsibility in administrative leadership have to be stirred first. As Blau notes, in our complex civilization innovation and progress may be obtainable in the future largely through the bureaucratic mechanism. The challenge to the public is to maintain sufficient vigilance to ensure

---

[13] For a discussion of goal succession and displacement see Blau, *op. cit.*, p. 95.

[14] Robert Michels, *Political Parties* (Glencoe: Free Press, 1958; first published 1915), p. 418.

[15] Anatol Rapoport, *Fights, Games, and Debates* (Ann Arbor: University of Michigan Press, 1960), p. 308.

that bureaucracies move in the direction of socially valuable goal succession rather than socially futile goal displacement.

REVIEW QUESTIONS

1. In what respects does the term "bureaucracy" apply to all formal organizations regardless of size?

2. Why must a culture be "ripe" before bureaucracies emerge?

3. The study of bureaucracy necessitates the study of power and influence as well. Discuss.

4. Outline the characteristics of the "ideal" bureaucratic mechanism.

5. Why is it more useful to talk of the degree of bureaucratization than of bureaucracy in an absolute sense?

6. What support may be offered for the common observation that the larger an organization becomes the more bureaucratic it gets?

7. Distinguish between "selective" and "saturative" policies of bureaucratic recruitment. Which policy has the greatest social value? Why?

8. What is meant by "subgroup" determination of organizational policy? Why are those who implement policy in a strategic position to influence the basic objectives of an organization?

9. Discuss goal displacement and goal succession.

10. Why is public pressure at the heart of the issue of goal displacement and goal succession?

SUPPLEMENTARY READINGS

BLAU, PETER. *Bureaucracy in Modern Society*. New York: Random House, 1956.

EISENSTADT, S. N. "Bureaucracy, Bureaucratization, and Debureaucratization," *Administrative Science Quarterly* 4 (1959–1960), pp. 302–20.

MERTON, ROBERT K. "Bureaucratic Structure and Personality," *A Reader in Bureaucracy* (eds. Robert K. Merton *et al.*), pp. 361–71. Glencoe: The Free Press, 1952.

SELZNICK, PHILIP. "An Approach to a Theory of Bureaucracy," *American Sociological Review*, February, 1943, pp. 47–54.

SMITH, EDMUND ARTHUR. "Bureaucratic Organization: Selective or Saturative," *Administrative Science Quarterly* 2 (1957–1958), pp. 361–75.

WEBER, MAX. "The Essentials of Bureaucratic Organization: An Ideal-Type Construction," *A Reader in Bureaucracy* (eds. Robert K. Merton *et al.*), pp. 18–27. Glencoe: The Free Press, 1952.

CHAPTER 13

Work and Incentives[1]

M OTIVATED primarily by the survival drive, but also by social and psy-chological needs, man "rents" his muscles and his brain. He enters into an agreement, usually with the highest bidder, to exchange his physical and intellectual assets for money. The process whereby he fulfills his part of this agreement is work. Formally defined, ". . . work is the totality of prescribed and discretionary activities that a person does in discharging the responsibilities he has contracted to undertake in order to earn his living."[2]

In our society, man has won the struggle for pure existence. The "affluent society" has obscured work as the elemental activity of simple survival. Instead, social and psychological needs and derived work motives have interposed themselves between survival and man. In short, work now means more to man, and it offers him a richer variety of satisfactions. The essence and purpose of work have not changed, but the social and psychological content of work has assumed different meanings for man.

A man is judged by the work he does, and invariably his status is linked to the functions he performs in an "employee society."[3] Not only is this true in a free society like ours but it is evident in communist societies as well. Work determines the individual's position in the social hierarchy.

A "normally" motivated person wishes to climb as high as possible on the social ladder, and money is the most convenient way of doing it. Money has not lost its significance as the medium for moving up in the world. As such it is a basic incentive. But money is sought not just for pure survival; it is a resource to buy the symbols of social status which are appropriate to an individual's role and function in society.

For years it has been an accepted axiom in economics that money is paid for the creation and distribution of goods and services. And, in some

---

[1] I am in debt to Mr. Marion V. Podlusky, Dipl-Ing, MBA, project engineer at Motorola, Chicago Center Military Electronics Division, for his contributions to this chapter.

[2] Elliott Jaques, *Measurement of Responsibility* (Cambridge: Harvard University Press, 1956), p. 85.

[3] See Peter Drucker, "The Employee Society," *American Journal of Sociology*, January, 1953, pp. 358–63.

vague way, the amount of money which an individual receives for his efforts is related to the value of his contributions to the affairs of an organization.

While it is impossible to deny this hypothesis completely, some writers feel that this concept of wages is incomplete. Some look on money as a "bribe" to overcome the unpleasant factors in the work environment. Another writer's view is that, "The amount of money an individual . . . may earn is dictated by the amount of loss he is expected to avoid by the use of his discretion, rather than by the amount of value he creates."[4]

These and other approaches to a wage rationale range over a span of concepts starting with the conservative motto, "A fair day's pay for a fair day's work," to the revolutionary position, "Abolition of the wage system and emancipation of the working class."

The many theories and solutions offered for the wage issue are a sign that work and wages are interrelated, complex matters with explosive content. While it is admitted that "man does not live by bread alone," the disputes which arise over the means by which man earns money to buy bread (and much else) are substantially in the forefront of contemporary labor-management relations.

This chapter is concerned mainly with issues, problems, and solutions which arise in the area of financial work incentives as they are applied to operative employees. Problems of executive incentives are treated in greater detail in Chapter 17.

THE NATURE OF INCENTIVES

An *incentive* is a stimulus which incites action. In its broad usage "incentive" is applicable to any inducement, material or nonmaterial, which impels, encourages, or forces a person to perform a task to accomplish a goal. *A psychological reaction is the primary effect of an incentive. Its secondary effect is behavior.*

As learned in Chapter 5, each individual responds uniquely to stimuli. His sentiments regarding an event are determined by elements of heredity and experiences old and new. Thus, each individual looks on an incentive in light of his attitudes.

But between sentiments and behavior are motives. Motives are unsatisfied needs which prompt an individual toward the accomplishment of specifiable goals. Motives determine a line of action; incentives (rewards) are the forces which induce the individual to pursue an objective to fruition.

It is useful—although perhaps an oversimplification—to think of a motive as an inner force and an incentive as an outer force operating on

---

[4] Jaques, *op. cit.*, p. 112.

an individual. Motives and those forces which are perceived by the individual as incentives are interwoven in a personality configuration. The matching of appropriate incentives to motives will result in behavior by an individual.

Man in a work situation is motivated in part by a class of needs called economic. For the performance of tasks he is offered economic incentives which are scaled both to the type of work done and to the quantity and quality of the work. The economic incentives provided "outside" the individual are supposed to satisfy the "inner" motives based upon economic needs.

The relationship between economic motives and financial incentives is hardly one-to-one. If it were, then the axiom, "A fair day's pay for a fair day's work" would constitute more than an emotional appeal. But as it is, the measurement of work and pay defies precise calculation. However, even if such precision were possible, and even if on the basis of accurate measurement management was assured of what constitutes a day's work and the individual a day's pay, the appropriate adjustment of wages and human effort still would not be forthcoming. Intertwined with the work-wage relationship are economic-political forces of power and market domination on the parts of labor and management which make "fair" adjustments in wages and effort utopian.

Reduced to its basic ingredients, however, money incentives are inducements which constitute effective means for evoking action. For centuries money has been the common denominator expressing the relationship between the effort expended by the individual and the value derived therefrom by the employer. Consequently, the wage issue in "human relations" is far older than the science of management; scientific management, however, had its roots in the wage problem. Chapter 2 discussed this linkage. Some further considerations on the development of wage incentive plans are brought out next.

Directions in the Evolution of Wage Incentives

The industrial revolution along with the closing of the frontier shattered the ideal of individualism in America in the late nineteenth century. Modern technology, mass production, mass employment, and huge investments placed considerable pressure on the owners and managers of industrial enterprises to improve profitability. Methods were sought to boost output per unit of capital and per unit of labor.

Technological improvements, standardization, and revolutions in transportation and communication increased the efficiency of industrial processes. These developments alone were not adequate, however, because human inefficiency partly neutralized the gains resulting from engineering advancements.

It was entirely reasonable, therefore, that the embryonic school of scientific management turned upon the "human factor" of production as the next logical step in improving the efficiency of the industrial undertaking. Operating under the notion that human behavior responded predictably to inexorable economic laws,[5] the scientific management pioneers developed several incentive systems to tie productivity of the individual worker to his paycheck. Taylor, the Gilbreths, Gantt, and Emerson are associated with wage incentive plans and with the development of scientific measurements upon which such plans could be based. Others followed in the paths charted by these people.

Frederick W. Taylor, of course, stands off from the other pioneers as the founder of the scientific management movement. It is not surprising that one of his most important contributions to the "mechanisms" of this movement was the differential system for piecework payment. But regardless of the type of time or piecework incentive plan, all systems are based on the fundamental notions that man is motivated by money and there is a direct relationship between how much a person is paid (or allowed to earn) and how hard he will work.

The "human factor of production" could scarcely remain relegated to a theoretical economic limbo no matter how sophisticated or complex the evolution of incentive plans. More than any one other piece of research, the Hawthorne studies drove home to management that man is a basic modifier of plans, directives, and policies. In the same vein, the human element could not be considered as without influence on wage and incentive systems.

The impetus provided by the Hawthorne studies prompted behavioral scientists to study human response to wage incentives in terms of broad organizational contexts. Profiting by this work, personnel administrators and wage specialists have modified, to some extent, their orthodox approaches to wage incentives by introducing new concepts or rediscovering old ones, like profit participation plans.

The inadequacies of monetary incentives have led management to seek new ways to motivate employees. These efforts have combined to produce "families" of financial and nonfinancial incentive programs in many companies.

No matter how well conceived a program of incentives is, the troublesome fact persists that all such programs create unanticipated adverse reactions by individuals and groups in the work environment. But in spite of their shortcomings, a multitude of incentive plans are in operation. The rest of this chapter is devoted to the consideration of their essential features and the human problems they create.

---

[5] Mutuality of economic interests based on productivity, intelligent self-interest, and "the economic man."

CLASSIFICATION OF INCENTIVES

The financial incentive is, and will remain, one of the most important motivators of men at work. As such it constitutes one major class of incentives. Nonfinancial incentives is the other.

Financial Incentives

Straight daywork is the oldest system of wage payment, closely followed by straight piecework. In contrast to daywork, all *time-based* incentive plans are constructed to vary earnings directly with output according to a predetermined formula. Three possibilities for time-based plans are shown in Figure 13–1.

FIGURE 13–1

GENERALIZED FEATURES OF TIME-BASED INCENTIVE SYSTEMS

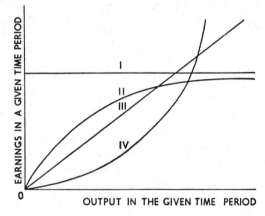

Source: Michael J. Jucius, *Personnel Management* (3d ed.; Homewood, Ill.: Richard D. Irwin, Inc., 1955), p. 370. Used with permission.

Line I shows the characteristics of a straight piecework system having strict proportionality between output and earnings. Curve II represents systems giving workers high earnings at low output levels but relatively lower earnings at high output levels. Curve IV illustrates those systems which recognize the fact that it is more difficult to increase already high output and therefore allow the worker to earn proportionately more at higher output levels. Line III shows direct proportionality between output and earnings found in straight piecework systems.

There are numerous variations and modifications of these themes but all time-based systems follow these basic patterns. Time-based plans apply both to individual and group incentive systems.

While time-based plans tie individual or group remuneration directly to output, other forms of financial incentives are not so closely related to productivity. These incentive plans are revenue participation systems and wage stabilization systems.

Nonfinancial Incentives

Nonfinancial incentives supplement monetary rewards by providing job satisfaction in other forms. The number of nonfinancial incentives is large because each individual perceives differently what would make him happy in the work situation. However, management's programs of nonfinancial incentives are framed in terms of what it feels the majority of workers want, consistent of course with company policy. Certain patterns of nonfinancial incentives often appear in employee-attitude surveys. These incentives are:

1. Job security.
2. Company concern of the individual.
3. Opportunity for advancement.
4. Good working conditions.
5. Prompt and equitable handling of complaints.
6. Good supervision.
7. Liberal vacation policy.

The various types of financial incentives are classified in Table 13–1. Many companies combine these, along with nonfinancial incentives, in a package program.

TABLE 13–1

CLASSIFICATION OF FINANCIAL INCENTIVE SYSTEMS

Time-Based Systems		Revenue Participation Systems	Wage Stabilization Systems
Individual Plans	*Group Plans*		
Piecework	Piecework	Profit sharing	Voluntary (i.e.: Hormel)
Measured daywork	Scanlon	Stock ownership	Negotiated (i.e.: automotive industry)
Taylor	Lincoln	Co-operative ownership	motive industry)
Halsey			Governmental
Gantt			
Emerson			
Bedaux			
Rowan			

HUMAN PROBLEMS OF INCENTIVE SYSTEMS

An enterprise is made up of interrelated but independent variables which function best in a state of balance with each other. Disturbances to a balanced system are often generated within the system itself. A factory is an example of this sort of system; an incentive program, and the industrial engineers who administer it, may well be the sources of disturbing influences which upset the equilibrium of the shop system.

A financial incentive system, particularly one that is time based, is a logical economic program which management uses to achieve higher productivity at lower unit cost. It is also a system which if fairly administered results in higher earnings for the "average" to "better-than-average" employees.

Workers, however, do not necessarily react logically to incentive plans. Their attitudes toward these programs are colored by nonlogical sentiments, particularly in time-based systems where the pace of work and the pay are geared to standard times established by rate setters. The operative employee is concerned with the effects of these programs on him, not only financially but also in terms of his status in the organization.[6] Some problems generated by the individual time-based systems, revenue participation systems, and wage stabilization plans are considered in this section.

The Time Determination Problem

In such incentive systems as the Taylor, Emerson, and Gantt plans, and in other plans which are modifications of these three, discontinuities are present in wage payment curves at certain standard output levels. This means that above the standard output level the worker has the opportunity to increase his earnings substantially by added increments of productivity. The use of discontinuities as an incentive to higher levels of achievement is contrasted with straight piecework plans where additional increments of pay are simply a linear function of output.

This point is brought out to emphasize the need for accurate time and rate determination by the industrial engineer. If the rate is "loose" the "average" worker can reach the high pay segment of the curve with comparative ease. The result is increased production costs and lower efficiency. When the rate is too "tight" workers have difficulty in reaching high incentive earning, causing morale problems due to frustration with the "system."

The "rate setter" is a crucial figure not only because of the technical need for adequate standard determinations but also because of his effects on the human "equilibrium" in the shop. In the eyes of operative employees, the rate setter (or time-study man) is an individual to be feared, hated, avoided, or fooled, depending on the situation. The foreman also reacts to the visits by representatives of the industrial engineering department with a certain trepidation. He knows that *he* must sell his workers on rate changes instituted by the engineering department.

The industrial engineer and his corps of rate experts and time-study men create difficulties not only for those who are working on the shop

---

[6] For an excellent discussion of incentives and their effect on the social system see William F. Whyte, *Money and Motivation* (New York: Harper and Bros., 1955), Part 4.

floor. The job content of the industrial engineer is itself problematical and is often viewed critically by industrial management writers.[7] The main criticism stems from the fact that the methods used currently for the measurement of human application have not eliminated subjective elements in the determination of rates.

Time-study men employ techniques to develop standard times for jobs. But none of the procedures, regardless of their complexity, are free from subjective judgments of the rate setter. Human judgments, and therefore human error, are often involved in rate calculations.

As equally significant as the technical faults in time determination is the interaction of the rate setter with workers and foremen on the production floor. The foremen in particular consider "visitors" from the industrial engineering department as intruders—an attitude which fuels the fire of line-staff conflict.

For his part, the worker may be unnerved by the rate setter or time-study man at his side. Although the employee studied is supposed to represent an "average" worker operating at "normal" speed, it is likely that the worker will not maintain a normal production pace but will slow down instead.

This behavior results from conscious intent or subconscious apprehensions caused by a mixture of attitudes including:

1. Fear of the unknown.
2. A desire to maintain an established financial and status position.
3. Resentment of being studied.[8]

When a staff man from industrial engineering appears the worker is immediately on his guard. He does not fully understand what is going on during the rate-setting process, but he is aware of shop lore which convinces him that this person "is up to no good." Regardless of how much reassurance is given to the workers by management that time determinations are for their own welfare, the general reaction is "who's kidding whom?" This worker cynicism toward the rate-setting process is re-enforced by the industrial engineer and his staff. They are highly specialized, technical people who often sincerely believe in the infallibility of their slide rules, stop watches, equalization factors, fatigue coefficients, and so on. They pay little heed to the human "guinea pig" under their scrutiny.

---

[7] See for example, R. Blackwell, "The Impact of Work Study on the Operative," *Time and Motion Study*, July, 1956, pp. 12–14; and William F. Whyte, *op. cit.*, chap. 3.

[8] It is difficult for a worker to appreciate the impersonality of the time-study-rate-setting process. The industrial engineer is interested in the job, not the person who happens to be performing it at the time. This fact, however, has not been adequately communicated because a worker inevitably feels it is *he* who is being observed and resents it.

It is amazing that the methods used for time determination—which are inherently inaccurate and create many human problems when applied —have been so widely accepted in industry. They may be better than nothing, but their shortcomings are embarrassingly highlighted by the ingenuity of the worker in beating the system.[9]

The strong negative feeling of workers toward time-based incentive plans has a long history. It cannot be doubted that Taylor, Gantt, the Gilbreths, and others who developed systems of this nature were motivated by the desire to improve efficiency and to pay workers adequately for their efforts. But the other side of the picture involves the cases of abuse where the techniques of time determination and rate setting were used to speed up operations and cut pay unjustly. It was in the 1920's when the term "efficiency expert" received the onerous connotation of one who rigged jobs by mysterious time determination techniques to squeeze the last ounce of energy out of the workers.

Problems of Time-Based Systems: Individual Plans

Although not a time-based system, daywork is a logical starting point for the considerations of this section. Daywork is the oldest and still most commonly used method of compensation. However, it does not provide much incentive for higher efficiency or greater output. A worker receives the same pay, per day or per hour, no matter how fast and accurately he works.

This situation may frustrate ambitious individuals because paywise they are classed with slow, disinterested employees. This problem points to management's failure to appraise jobs correctly and to establish standards which relate individual competence to wages.[10]

Daywork is used most often because it is impossible to apply piecework or time-based methods of incentive rewards to certain types of jobs. These are jobs requiring "brainwork" and "judgment," or other elements which are not conveniently reduceable to "objective" measurement.

Inequities in daywork and hourly methods of pay are well known, and the flagrant abuses of these systems have prompted wage and hour legislation. But the law has not completely eliminated the chances for unfair practices on the part of management; and it certainly has not overcome worker unfairness to management through "soldiering" on the job.

Piecework. Straight piecework is widely used because it is simple to administer and so uncomplicated that it is easily grasped by the least intelligent worker. The worker can compute his paycheck in advance

---

[9] See Whyte, *op. cit.*, chaps. 5, 6.

[10] Elmore Peterson and E. Grosvenor Plowman, *Business Organization and Management* (3d ed.; Homewood: Richard D. Irwin, Inc., 1953), p. 483.

since he knows his output and the value of each piece he has produced. Further, the relationship between production and earnings is unequivocal. Each piece produced reflects a constant pay increment.

Though this plan is simple enough it is not without human problems. In some circumstances workers are paid for actual output even if production stoppages are outside his control. The combination of union efforts and minimum wage legislation has reduced this problem by guaranteeing workers a specified hourly amount regardless of the work flow. Such provisions require management to reduce "downtime" to a minimum.

When piecework rates are based on standards coming from time studies, the shortcomings inherent in time-measurement practices appear. The problems of loose and tight rates have been discussed already. Tight rates, or rates *perceived* as tight, generally produce dissatisfaction on the workers affected. Serious conflicts also arise when management tries to change established rates from loose to normal levels. Such attempts are interpreted by employees as attacks on their paycheck and status.

Further, the tightening of loose rates affects the morale structure severely. Even employees who are not immediately involved in the change are fearful that their own jobs will eventually be studied and re-rated. All this conjures up old slogans of speed up and sweat shop. Thus, adjustments of loose rates pose a real problem for management in communicating to employees the reasons for changes which may lie in improvements in the production processes or technological advancements.

Generally it is comparatively easy for a worker to reach the "average" level of output under a piecework system. However, to go beyond this point is difficult and not particularly desirable from the employee's standpoint because he is compensated at the same rate per piece. Thus simple piecework does not provide a strong incentive to reach a plateau of output above standard. This feature of straight piecework is not encouraging to workers capable of producing more than average.

The worker shies off from high output levels for another reason which is put well by a German saying, *"Akkord ist mord,"* or "Piecework is murder." This warning, taken to heart by many workers, admonishes not to overdo efforts to make money because of the strain that the system places on the physical and mental health of the individual.

The Taylor Differential Piecework Plan. Taylor realized the shortcomings of straight piecework many years ago. His classic paper, "A Piece-Rate System," offered the differential plan to overcome these difficulties.[11] Taylor's method provides additional incentives to reach higher output levels by employing two piece rates—one high and one low. The

---

[11] Frederick W. Taylor, "A Piece-Rate System," American Society of Mechanical Engineers *Transactions*, Volume 16 (1895), pp. 856–903.

incentive value of producing on the high scale is sufficiently strong to entice a worker to this level.[12]

The dangers in this plan were recognized at the time of its inception. The plan forces workers to speed up. Beginners are penalized without justification and no provision is made for pay equalization. In practice, the break point between the two incentive scales was set so high that the average worker might never, or only under hardship, collect the bonus rate. Actually, it was the unenlightened application of the Taylor plan and its modifications that was responsible for negative worker attitudes toward incentive plans in general.

The Halsey Plan. This plan, and the "100 per cent time-saving plan" which is similar to it, are based on time saved doing a particular job. In earlier plans the amount of time to do a job was determined by past records of performance. Later, job times were predetermined by motion and time studies. In both cases, a standard time for a job was established. If the worker, or the work team, finished the job faster than the standard, a bonus was paid. The bonus was computed on the savings realized by the reduction of labor costs.

Psychologically the effects of these plans are good in that they condition employees to the attitude of gaining through saving.[13] However, when the Halsey plan was introduced the worker did not participate fully in the savings. On any job, his share of the savings amounted to one third to one half. There were two reasons for this policy:

1. The method for determining standard times was crude and management wanted plenty of latitude in case of error.

2. Halsey felt that good supervision and technical improvements in a job contributed to time savings as well as worker diligence. Therefore, management was entitled to a slice of the benefits.

The 100 per cent time-saving plan was introduced when time standards could be determined more precisely. Although this plan paid workers the full amount of the time saved, it did not necessarily produce higher earnings because standards might be tightened as a result of more accurate methods of calculating time.

The Gantt Task-Bonus System. Henry L. Gantt, a student and close associate of Taylor, realized the hardships of the differential piecework system. He developed his own plan, which has some improvements in it from the worker's standpoint.

---

[12] "Assuming that the low and high rates on a job were $0.02 and $0.03, respectively, and the breaking point 25 units, an operator's earnings would be:

24	$0.02	$0.48

if he produced below the breaking point and

25	$0.03	$0.75

if he produced above the breaking point." Jucius, *op. cit.,* p. 377.

[13] *Ibid.,* p. 379.

Gantt replaced the low piece rate characteristic of Taylor's plan with a guaranteed straight time wage. He retained the high bonus rate at *standard or average* output and introduced a "super" incentive rate for production above the standard.

Accurate time determination is critical in this plan for management and for the worker. Small errors in either direction create serious problems for both parties. The Gantt plan also accentuates status problems. It seems to establish two groups of people—those before reaching standard and those after reaching it. A natural conflict situation can develop out of this dichotomy. The substandard group may press for looser rates and the above-standard group is anxious to protect its position from encroachments from below.

There are many other plans. The Emerson efficiency plan, the Merrick multiple wage plan, the Bedaux plan, the Baum plan, and the Rowan plan are modifications of the basic time-based systems already mentioned. They are more complicated than the earlier plans; nevertheless the fundamental problems of subjective time studies and rate determination are not solved by them.

The fact that time-based plans have had spotty success as incentives is attested to by experimentation with other systems using a different rationale for applying financial incentives. Revenue participation plans form another category of financial incentives.

Rationale of Revenue Participation

The objective of revenue participation plans is to allow the employee more diversified opportunities for sharing in the progress and profitability of his company. The philosophy is derived from a desire by management and owners to make an "equitable" distribution of the net income of a business enterprise. Part of the rationale is that all members of an organization contribute to its success. Profit, as a measure of success, is also a measure of the ability of those who aid in producing it at all levels of the organization.

Thus, from the principle of distributive justice it follows that some of the profits should be returned to the employees in one form or another. The fulfillment of this "obligation" currently takes shape under programs of stock ownership, profit sharing, and bonus plans. The main characteristic of these plans, and all plans that come under the general title of revenue participation, is the absence of a *direct* connection between the effort the individual expends on his job and the amount of money he receives from his company's program. Of course, revenue participation plans are found in firms side-by-side with other financial incentive systems.

Revenue participation plans have a strong psychological impact on workers provided they are carefully selected and well administered.

They relieve the worker, at least partially, from his antagonism of the stop watch and the rate setter as the leading symbols of management philosophy. Further, they may lift the employee more subtly to a higher level of motivation. To receive official information from top management about the progress of the business and to be complimented for contributing to its success is a stimulus for an individual which is not translatable into economic terms.

From another point of view, revenue participation plans can be discussed as a manifestation of the social ethic. In the atmosphere created by the collision effect, it is not surprising that people have sought and are still seeking forms of remuneration which are consistent with the main feature of modern industrial society—mutual dependency.

Pioneers have introduced wage systems which reflect the fact of human interdependency in the task of making profits. Plans such as the Scanlon plan encourage active participation in the business and place an official mark of recognition on mutual dependency, making *it* the basis of an industrial wage plan.

Thus, it can be assumed that management in some instances has perceived the ideological shifts in our society and has been inspired to try out new wage plans more consistent with the contemporary social tenor. Of course, management's motives for introducing revenue participation plans are not simple. They probably are composed of a mixture of motives, with individualistic self-interest and social consciousness predominating.

So far the discussion has turned on generalities pertaining to revenue participation plans taken as a whole. Lest the reader be misled that the millennium is at hand, he should be conscious of the difficulties encountered by specific plans in practice.

Profit Sharing.   Profit sharing is not one particular system. It is a descriptive name for a number of plans, "Under which an employer pays to all employees, in addition to good rates of regular pay, special current or deferred sums . . . based on the prosperity of the business as a whole."[14]

In practice, accounting procedures clarify the meaning of profit sharing further. A true profit-sharing plan is not a cost chargeable to operations. Its revenues are part of a business' income which normally would be distributed to owners or retained in the firm.

Management uses profit sharing, as it uses other types of revenue participation plans, to create an atmosphere of a stable integration of interests between the employer and the employee. If these incentive forms prompt a feeling of real involvement by workers in the affairs of the company, then a step is made toward a reconciliation of opposed

---

[14] "Profit Sharing," *Proceedings of the Council of Profits Sharing Industries,* 1953, p. 3.

interests. Hence the reconciliation of the interests of management and labor is the *raison d'être* of profit sharing. Thompson calls it a form of "democratic capitalism" and considers it to be a combination of "ethical idealism and hard practicality."[15]

Profit sharing has pitfalls in spite of the eulogizing by many about its merits. Not all firms are in a position to undertake such a program. When a company feels it is ready it must select *the plan* which fits its objectives. Before introducing a profit-sharing program thorough investigation has to be made to determine as far as possible the future prospects of the firm and its profitability. Profit sharing is based on the assumption of sufficient future earnings to assure an adequate return to the owners on investment, funds for reinvestment into the company, and, of course, a distribution to the employees.

The role of employees in profit-sharing programs is unique. They are in one way elevated to the status of owners.[16] The question which often arises in this respect is whether or not employees should have the right to determine the distribution of profits. As it stands, the final decision rests with management even though companies may have "advisory employee committees" to discuss profit-sharing matters.

One reason why organized labor has been cool to profit sharing is the lack of a real employee voice in *the* major profit-sharing decision—how the pie is to be cut. Management is obviously not willing to divulge accounting information to employees as a basis in making the decision. If demands for this prerogative are pressed management could wipe out the program, or insist that employees accept their share of the losses when they occur.

The value of profit sharing as a stimulus for achieving the customary aims of financial incentive systems[17] is comparatively low. There is no direct relationship between individual effort and the cash or deferred payments received from the plan. Unless a company constantly reminds employees of the benefits and the obligations of the plan, workers are apt to forget that profits follow from performance.

As a morale builder, profit sharing is effective only when there is a record of continuous distribution. One year without profits can damage the program. Because of the uncertainty of earnings, profit sharing is only moderately effective as a device to enhance an employee's feeling of security.

In many profit-sharing plans employees do not receive any current remuneration. Payments are deferred until retirement or until the em-

---

[15] K. M. Thompson, *Profit Sharing—Democratic Capitalism in America* (New York: Harper and Bros., 1949), p. 16.

[16] They have a claim on income. But they are not penalized for loses nor are they able to sue the company for mismanagement.

[17] Higher productivity, lower waste, improved quality.

ployee leaves the company, provided his tenure is long enough to ac-
quire vesting privileges in the plan. However, there are short-term cash-
bonus plans. This form of profit sharing has an interesting psychological
effect. The worker, who receives a profit-sharing bonus at regular intervals, comes to feel that it is part of his wages and adjusts his standard of
living to it. When the profit situation comes under pressure and payments
are reduced or withheld, adverse effects on performance and morale may
appear.

The administration of a profit-sharing program requires trust and a
well-developed channel of communication between management and
workers. The pitfalls of profit sharing are numerous, and with a few exceptions profit sharing has not been especially successful when applied to
operative employees. Without much detailed information of the current
affairs of the company it is hard for them to appreciate the factors
working in any particular time period which determine profit levels.

Plans for Stock Ownership. The corporation is the predominant form
of legal and financial organization in American business. Some corporations use the purchase of stock at a special rate, or stock distribution in
lieu of cash payments, as financial incentives. This approach has found
considerable acceptance in industry in the form of executive stock-
option programs. It has also been made famous in the Sears, Roebuck
plan in which profit sharing and stock ownership are combined.

Although stock ownership programs may increase the operative employee's loyalty to the company and produce a positive morale effect,
human problems also arise.

The direct incentive effect of stock ownership on individual effort is
low just as it is in profit-sharing plans. Further, the behavior of the stock
market, in which the possibility of losses in a declining market is always
present, may have a negative influence on morale which ultimately would
be manifested in productivity. In the extreme case, the incentive value of
a stock ownership plan may become a function of the daily quotation.
At the opposite extreme are workers who are less informed about the
functioning of stock exchanges. They may not feel any incentive at all,
and may even accuse management of giving them a piece of paper for
their work.

Co-operative Ownership. Beyond the basic revenue participation plans
of profit sharing and stock ownership is co-operative ownership. Under
these systems employees participate in both the ownership of the firm
and its management. This approach is quite different from other incentives already mentioned.

Co-operative ownership is rather foreign to American business experience so it is difficult to give a competent answer to the question of
whether or not it constitutes a higher form of incentive than other systems currently in use. There are arguments to the effect that it does. But

in practice it is difficult to visualize how employees could have any more voice in running a large organization than do the existing nonemployee owners. Management has to remain centralized regardless of the locus of ownership. Accepting this premise, then co-operative ownership is merely an extension of prevailing stock ownership plans.

Wage Stabilization Systems. For people who rely on their jobs as their only source of economic security, a stable employment situation is of primary importance. At various times in the past, and probably with increased frequency in the future, organized labor has and will press for some type of wage stabilization plan.

Wage stabilization plans may be voluntary (initiated unilaterally by a company) or they may be negotiated with a union. Typical of the voluntary wage stabilization plans are those pioneered by Hormel, Proctor and Gamble, and Nunn-Bush. These plans are popularly called the Guaranteed Annual Wage and Guaranteed Employment. The GAW, of course, implies a minimum of guaranteed employment because it is impossible to guarantee a yearly salary without productive employment during the period.[18]

In practice the period of guarantee is limited. Sometimes participants are selected on the basis of seniority, occupation, or job classification. Short-tenure employees usually have less protection under these plans.

Management faces basic socioeconomic problems in wage stabilization plans. The key issue is how much to guarantee for how long without putting the company in a difficult financial position. From the administrative standpoint, the guaranteed annual wage does not eliminate supervisory pressures for efficient work. On the contrary, supervision may become tighter to counteract laxity. However, on the positive side, workers tend to reduce output-restriction practices because group-inspired "work rules" are not threatened by layoffs.[19]

Group Incentive Plans

Most of the discussion so far has centered on individual incentive plans. Incentives, including time-based plans, are also applied to work groups. According to Lovejoy, the group approach is recommended when:[20]

---

[18] The Supplementary Unemployment Benefit plan in the automobile industry is an example of a negotiated wage stabilization program. It is tied to state unemployment compensation programs with the objective of providing laid-off workers with roughly 65 per cent of their weekly salaries while they are eligible. Unlike voluntary plans, SUB favors the short-tenure employee. While the employer contributes to the plan for all employees, the short-service employee is most likely to experience a higher layoff incidence.

[19] Emerson P. Schmidt, "The Economics of Guaranteed Wages," *Practical Approaches to Labor Relations Problems* (American Management Association Personnel Series Number 91), 1945, pp. 26–27.

[20] Lawrence C. Lovejoy, *Wage and Salary Administration* (New York: The Ronald Press, 1959), p. 343.

1. Work is performed by a team.
2. Individual measurements are too difficult to make.
3. The nature of the job changes often.

Lytle refers to group plans as ". . . an incentive applied collectively to employees whose operations are definitely interdependent or related, and who are equally suited to their various duties. Such a group will have a community of interests and mutual respect of individual members."[21]

Lytle's definition explicitly states three conditions necessary to the success of a group plan:

1. Workers should be equally suited to the job.
2. They should have a community of interests.
3. They should have respect for the individual interests of members.

The first condition requires an adequate appraisal of human qualities in order to establish groups that are homogeneous in respect to the capabilities of members to perform the job. While personnel managers expend much effort to assure that jobs are manned according to specification they can hardly guarantee that all employees in a work group will be motivated by the same incentive factors. Work-group homogeneity is difficult to achieve as far as individual motivation is concerned.

Because of different work motives, it is unlikely that a community of interests among individuals in the group will exist over long durations. The industrial processes causing change and employee turnover undermine the conditions which make for a stable community of interests.

By ordinary group processes, some workers gain positions of power and influence over others in the group. Hence it is hard to imagine a group so democratic that all members' interests are equally respected.

These objections to group incentives are mentioned to show that such plans do not have an answer for the basic ills of incentive systems. The larger the group covered by a time-based incentive plan the more management may expect to encounter problems in its administration. The long-run expectancy of group performance is average output. This should not be surprising, because of the lack of individual incentives in these systems. Some workers, regardless of group pressure (if indeed any is applied), will just coast along on the productivity of others. Individual efforts above average are not rewarded by any special provisions.

Group plans generally are installed for the technical reasons stated by Lovejoy; they are not instituted because management feels they conform to the social and psychological climate of small-group behavior on the job. Exceptions to this observation are discussed next.

The Scanlon Plan.   The Scanlon plan represents an approach to the total mobilization of co-operative forces of all employees from top manage-

---

[21] Charles Walter Lytle, *Wage Incentive Methods* (New York: The Ronald Press, 1942), p. 312.

ment down to the lowest level of workers for the purpose of reaching organizational goals.[22] It is at once a group incentive plan and a revenue participation system coupled with a suggestion system. The plan includes a wage-bonus formula and a method for processing suggestions and implementing them.

The wage-bonus formula is adjustable to suit each company adopting the Scanlon plan. Basically, the formula makes wages a sliding function of productivity. It is arranged in such a way so that the gains of increased productivity are distributed proportionally among all employees concerned.

The suggestion system under the Scanlon plan does not have individual payoffs. The *production committee*, made up of union officials and foremen, meet to pass on the merits of individual suggestions. Suggestions not accepted by them are turned over to a plantwide *screening committee* on which members of top management and the union serve. Suggestions do not necessarily come from individuals. A structure is established, including the production committee, which taps group inventiveness for the development and presentation of suggestions.

The interactional patterns involving management, the union, and the employees, though complex, are essential. Also essential is the communication patterns which vitalize the suggestion system. Communication through suggestions is actually a feedback device which gives employees a measure of the success of co-operation among the parties in the organizational system. Viewed this way, the suggestion system facilitates the balancing process by allowing for the expression of attitudes by employees. This intricate mechanism requires a communication system of the "highest fidelity" in a company.

The Lincoln Plan. The Lincoln plan has been in operation for many years at the Lincoln Electric Company.[23] It has been successful in showing notable improvements in business operations and by generating so much interest in the company that it has long lists of people waiting for employment.

The Lincoln plan has modified the conventional piecework system so that its disadvantages practically do not exist. For example, cutting piece rates is not tolerated. This suggests that standards of performance are set fairly and accurately the first time. An advisory board of employees and an extensive suggestion system underscore the group participative nature of the plan.

That Lincoln is a down-to-earth practitioner in addition to an idealist

---

[22] For a discussion of the Scanlon plan see George Strauss and Leonard Sayles, "The Scanlon Plan: Some Organizational Problems," *Human Organization*, Fall, 1957, pp. 15–22.

[23] See James F. Lincoln, *Incentive Management* (Cleveland: Lincoln Electric Co., 1951).

is observable in his writings. This union is demonstrated by the economic and nonfinancial incentives built into his plan—a plan which among other items includes a substantial revenue participation program. Above all, however, he has succeeded in developing an attitude of employee trust in the integrity and honesty of management. This is an ingredient without which the best-conceived plans will fail to achieve their objectives.

INCENTIVES AND THE SOCIAL SYSTEM

The routine of introducing a new employee to his co-workers triggers an interesting set of group reactions. It is assumed that before entering the work situation the new employee is oriented by his foreman to the workings of the incentive system, especially if it is a time-based plan. Once the individual is on the job he is taken in hand by members of his work group and instructed in how the plan "really" works.

At the start, the new employee is treated by his foreman as an economically motivated, passive man who "obviously" wants to earn as much as he can on the job. Later, under the tutelage of his fellow workers, he sees the incentive plan's social and psychological aspects.

To the older employees, the newcomer represents a change, a potential source of disturbance to their social system. They are willing to accept him in their ranks if he is inclined to subscribe to their rules of behavior.

Research has shown that the phenomenon of output restriction is a form of group behavior.[24] It is not a random practice of disgruntled individuals in its significant manifestations. Therefore, if group norms demand restriction of output in order "to belong," the individual faced with these demands is also confronted by several dilemmas:

1. Loyalty to management or acceptance by the group.
2. Desire to earn more money or the desire to derive nonmonetary satisfactions from group membership.
3. Protection and companionship of the group or the loneliness of "going it on his own."

Reporting on a study of individual reactions to incentive systems, Whyte observes that the *majority* of individuals in a work group do not make a commitment to either extreme—the small number of "rate busters" on the one hand and the output restricters on the other.[25] The ma-

---

[24] Groups practice output restriction for several reasons:
1. They restrict output so as not to kill a "gravy job"; that is, a job in which workers can make and exceed standard output with comparative ease. The logic is that if workers consistently earn high-level bonuses, the job will be restudied and the loose rates tightened.
2. Workers goldbrick on "stinker" jobs, jobs with tight rates, where standard output is difficult to achieve. They know they will earn a guaranteed minimum regardless of how much they produce. Their restriction of output is a form of protest against the tight rates. For an elaboration of these points see Whyte, *op. cit.*, pp. 20–27.

[25] See *ibid.*, pp. 46–48.

jority are "men in the middle," as he calls them, oscillating between conformance with the rules of the incentive system and conformance with the norms of the restricters.

No general solutions seem possible in these cases, given the "ground rules" of incentive systems based on measured output. An individual's response to money as an incentive is learned and naturally he will react strongly toward it. But this response cannot be easily separated from other learned responses to other incentives like group support and protection, group pressure, and so on. Conflicting incentives such as these are often the cause of tension and frustration in the industrial environment.

Facilitating the Acceptance and Administration of an Incentive System

While it is doubtful that output restriction and negative worker attitudes toward time-based incentive plans can be eliminated entirely, management is able to take steps which will ease their assimilation into the social systems of the factories. A successful wage incentive plan depends on so many factors that it is impossible to recommend a generalized program. However, several specific points should be considered by management.

1. The objectives of the incentive plan must be clear. Usually, time-based plans have the following goals:

    a) To pay workers on the basis of productivity to raise output.

    b) To increase the wage level of the plant.

    c) To reduce costs.[26]

2. After deciding on the objectives, the details of a specific program are worked out. From a technical standpoint, the plan should be as understandable to the operative employee as possible. A simple relationship between productivity and wages helps the acceptance, administration, and maintenance of the system.

3. The active participation of supervisors and employee representatives during the planning stages of an incentive program is essential. They are key figures in gaining acceptance of the system at the operative levels. If they are thoroughly familiarized with the plan during its development phase and have had a hand in its formulation they will be in a better position to sell the plan to the employees. They should not only know the technical details but they should also be "sold" themselves on the worth of the system.

4. The standards of output, on which incentive earnings are based, must be carefully determined inasmuch as the welfare of the company and its employees depends on the accuracy of these measurements. Once set, standards tend to become entrenched and subject to change only by complex and disrupting procedures.

To promote employee trust in the system, job standards should be guaranteed. This, however, should not be construed to mean that standards take on a permanent and absolute character. Change in work standards may be required by technological advancement. But as far as possible workers should be assured that standards on their jobs will not be changed capriciously.

---

[26] For a critique of this objective see R. H. Roy, "Do Wage Incentives Reduce Costs?" *Industrial and Labor Relations Review,* January, 1952, pp. 195–208.

5. Once set, the hourly base rate for each job under an incentive plan should become a guaranteed rate as a matter of company policy. If both day-work and piecework payment systems are used side-by-side in a plant, it should be arranged that the lower skill jobs on the incentive system do not receive more pay than the higher skills covered by daywork.

6. All aspects of the incentive plan must be adequately maintained if worker trust in the integrity of the system is to be preserved.

7. The communication of the plan to employees should be directed to them, as individuals, by their foremen, backed up with general policy statements by management. If the support of foremen and employee representatives is gathered at the start of an incentive program their "selling job" to operative workers is facilitated at the time of implementation.

The incentive system must have information feedback built into it, in order for the program to be successful over an extended period of time. The installation of an incentive plan is simply the beginning of a bigger project. The system is not self-correcting. Even if it is introduced in the manner prescribed by the previous seven specifications, the social system will act on the plan continuously while in operation. Some modifications of it are inevitable. Knowledge of the precise nature of these modifications caused by both human and technological dynamics is essential for management. Various channels of feedback are available for information and should be fully developed. These include the reports of line foremen and the staff charged with the administration of the plan, plus information originating in a suggestion system and from union representatives.

CONCLUDING OBSERVATIONS

Deeply rooted in the philosophy of all incentive systems is the aim of integrating the interests of management and the workers. The lowest common denominator of these interests is productivity. From it, wages are derived for employees and profit for management. The point has already been made that there is more to motivation than money. If "economic man" is not dead he is at least resting in a dormant state. Money is still an important motivator but it is far from being the only force for promoting the cause of mutuality of interests.

The concept of mutuality of interests is something of a myth which management has endorsed at least from the time Charles Babbage put it into print. By digging deeply enough, one is able to find a bit of truth in most myths. It is man's economic needs which have provided the fragment of truth that has dominated management's attitude toward and understanding of human motivation for years.

To the extent that man is motivated by money there is a possibility that a mutuality of interests does exist on an economic level and that an integration of interests can be accomplished through financial incentives. But a harmony of interests is illusory if rewards from the work situation are framed in terms of money alone. The social and psychological planes of human motivation, which are entwined with economic motivations, need to be considered in any far-reaching program of worker incentives. The absence of such considerations has been the curse of conventional piecework and time-based incentive programs. Though widely used, they seem to have the propensity to disrupt, rather than to weld, the interests of various human segments of a business organization.

Group programs like the Scanlon and Lincoln plans are promising, but they are quite unique in their planning and execution. They achieve the goal of total participation of employees, giving them the opportunity for the self-expression necessary for fuller satisfactions. Because of the complex features of these systems, it is questionable whether they are suitable as the preferred plans of the future.

Wage stabilization plans are tempting. As in the past, so also in the future they will be used as a tactical weapon in labor-management contract negotiations. The tendency for these types of programs to gravitate to the realm of the power struggle between unions and companies diminishes their psychological impact on workers.

Profit sharing and other types of revenue participation plans are by far most promising vehicle for a wide range of business enterprises, provided they are properly administered and supported. They have the potential of creating in the participants the feeling of belonging to a common endeavor.

The development of the social ethic has led, if not to a socialistic world in the customary sense, then to an "ethically collectivistic" form of a mutually dependent society. In this society all segments, including management and labor, must curb their self-interests in return for peace and social justice. Revenue participation plans are a logical step consistent with the social ethic in the industrial order.

REVIEW QUESTIONS

1. "Work now means more to man and it offers him a richer variety of satisfactions." Discuss.

2. What are incentives? What are the primary and secondary effects of incentives? How are incentives related to attitudes and motives?

3. Why was it "reasonable" that the scientific management pioneers turned their attention to the "human factor" in the production process?

4. Outline a classification system for various forms of incentives.

5. Discuss the basic shortcomings of time determination. What problems does the time-study man encounter when he enters the "social system" on the production floor?

6. How is the rationale of revenue participation plans related to "interdependency in an industrial society?"

7. Discuss the advantages and disadvantages of profit-sharing systems.

8. Group incentive plans generally do not overcome the shortcomings of individual time-based systems. Why?

9. "Output restriction is a form of group behavior." Discuss.

10. To what extent are financial incentive plans capable of achieving a mutuality of interests?

SUPPLEMENTARY READINGS

BLACKWELL, R. "The Impact of Work Study on the Operative," *Time and Motion Study*, July, 1956, pp. 12–14.

LINCOLN, JAMES F. *Incentive Management*. Cleveland: Lincoln Electric Co., 1951.

STRAUSS, GEORGE AND SAYLES, LEONARD. "The Scanlon Plan: Some Organizational Problems," *Human Organization*, Fall, 1957, pp. 15–22.

WHYTE, WILLIAM F. *Money and Motivation*, chaps. 16–19. New York: Harper and Bros., 1955.

CHAPTER 14

Contemporary Unionism

THE current membership of all labor unions runs to over eighteen million. All major manufacturing industries are organized, although some companies within these industries have withstood organizational efforts. The combined assets of labor unions reach into the hundreds of millions of dollars. Because of favorable legislation, organized labor enjoys stability an institutional security of a sort which the early leaders of American labor movements never dreamed possible. The voice of labor is heard on all political fronts from the federal government down to municipalities. And finally, labor-management relations seem to have shown evidence of improvement, admitting some lapses, in the years following World War II.

Thus, unions have become established, if not fully accepted, members of American society. The days are passed in which the injunction, conspiracy trials, and militant antiunionism made the survival of unions problematical. The fighting union leader and his followers have largely given way to people at all levels of a union organization engaged in the business of running a stable operation and conducting affairs with management.

In the last twenty-five years, unions have emerged from adolescence with its insecurity and belligerence, to adulthood with its maturity and conservatism. And although modern unions are more comfortably situated today, maturity has brought difficulties requiring reorientation of the principles and practices which were formulated and were more suitable to the earlier era of union development.

Among the many problems are the following.

1. Unions have reached the limits of "organizable" workers.[1] Most workers in manufacturing and the trades who could be organized, are.

2. Unions have reached the limits of collective bargaining.[2] Further gains must be based on productivity.

---

[1] This problem is accentuated by automation and its elimination of jobs. These conditions are especially apparent in the steel and automotive industries. As a consequence of technological change, particularly in mass-production industries, unions face the possibility of smaller membership relative to the total work force, if not even a declining membership in absolute numbers.

[2] Some have cited the bargaining tactics at General Electric as an example of this development. For a discussion of bargaining at G.E. a là Boulwarism see William F. Whyte, *Men at Work* (Homewood: The Dorsey Press, 1961), pp. 367–71.

3. Although unions may be considered as mature because of age and size, recent racketeering reports leave the responsibility of certain unions and their leaders open to doubt.

4. The matter of size alone has presented modern unions with a variety of problems involving undemocratic practices and public criticism of economic and political power.

5. The grass-roots union member stands accused of an apathetic attitude toward his interest and participation in union affairs.

6. Maturity has forced upon some unions a reorientation of goals. Emphasis on the single purpose of bread-and-butter unionism has evolved into a concern for multiple goals in the sphere of social welfare.

These are some of the major issues facing modern unions and their leadership. It is not the purpose of this chapter to treat all of these matters in depth. But for reasons of perspective, the discussion which follows begins with an analysis of the trends affecting modern labor organizations—particularly the large unions which organize in manufacturing industries. Next attention is turned to union structure and the determinants of control. Then union leadership is considered, followed by the issue of union democracy and its relevance to various levels of union organization. Flowing directly from the subject of union democracy is the issue of membership participation in the local union.

CHANGES IN AMERICAN UNIONISM

The aggressive, militant union which gained support of the unemployed in the 1930's has largely disappeared. The crusading atmosphere in which the unions affiliated with the CIO grew has diminished so that little remains of it but the songs and slogans of old. The personality of American unions has changed. Their new character is a result of several trends outlined below.[3]

1. *The new middle class.* The improved standard of living of American labor makes the symbol of the economically depressed, industrial proletariate hollow compared to the 1930's. The harsh economic conditions which caused great suffering for large numbers of American workers have lost meaning for the new generation. The modern industrial worker is relatively better off economically and more conservative politically. The availability of credit, goods, and improved transportation to and from suburban communities has transformed potential proletarians into members of the middle class. As such, industrial workers in this status subscribe willingly to a conservative middle-class ideology rather than to a philosophy advocating fundamental changes in the economic system.

---

[3] Unless otherwise indicated the following is based on Harry Seligson, "The Paradox and Challenge of Unionism Today," *Labor Law Journal*, March, 1959, pp. 182–84.

2. *Power and bigness.* Rapid growth has made unions targets for criticism. Oddly enough, effective public relations activities since World War II have caused the American people to look upon business and government as sources of social change and keepers of the public conscience. Unions which had previously made claims to a higher morality find their thunder stolen and instead are viewed as irresponsible and self-centered in their demands.[4]

3. *Conservatism.* Obtaining respectability is important to many unions and their leaders. Their search for status is ". . . motivated by a desire to achieve the recognition accorded the businessman. . . ."[5] But this quest is frustrated by a supposed necessity of keeping members "keyed up" by the use of old fighting slogans which are generally antagonistic to the conservative elements in our society.

In spite of militant utterances in union conventions, the feeling is strong that most American labor unions have grown conservative. Essentially this conservatism takes the form of dedication to and support of the existing social and economic order. In reference to German labor unions, Michels pointed many years ago to the "natural tendency" for organizations, as they become larger and more secure, to assume a conservative posture.[6] His observations seem appropriate to American labor today. The great principles around which labor rallied in the 1930's are now tired slogans.

4. *Inertia.* Closely allied to size and conservatism is the inevitability of inertia in institutions which achieve security and stability. Leadership and membership alike become content with the *status quo.* The role of the union shifts from that of a protest group acting as a socially useful countervailing force, to an interest group seeking to maintain itself internally while gathering a stabilized share of the economic pie for its membership.

5. *Leadership.* Militant antiunionism forced a negative strategy on union leadership in the 1930's. With the reduction and in some cases the abandoning of antiunion tactics on the part of employers a new world was created for union leaders. To a certain extent the flow of members and revenue is actually underwritten by the employer.

A number of influences have been at work to cause these changes. Among them are the National Labor Relations Act, favorable decisions of the National Labor Relations Board, and continued prosperity since the end of the second World War.[7]

---

[4] Unions have argued that their objectives are on a higher plane than those of business and have as a consequence conditioned the public to expect high-minded attitudes and altruistic behavior.

[5] Seligson, *op. cit.,* p. 183; see also Dick Bruner, "Has Success Spoiled the Unions?" *Harvard Business Review,* May–June, 1960, pp. 73–78.

[6] Robert Michels, *Political Parties* (Glencoe: The Free Press, 1958; first published 1915).

[7] George W. Brooks, "Observations on the Changing Nature of American Unions," *Monthly Labor Review,* February, 1957, p. 151.

The improved industrial relations climate after World War II forced a change on labor leaders, requiring a re-evaluation of their strategy and tactics. These demands on union leadership are examined in another section of this chapter. For now, suffice it to say that the modern union leader is becoming increasingly more a managerial "type" similar to his rivals in companies with whom he carries on collective bargaining.

6. *Environmental impasses.* The supply of "organizable workers" has come close to reaching its upper limits of availability.[8] Most of those workers who were "fair game" for organizing have now been enrolled in unions. Workers in other occupational groupings, such as white-collar and service employees, present a potential for union expansion—but one that will be difficult to realize. The philosophy of the people who are filling the expanding ranks of salaried employees does not fit prevailing union values closely. Unionism is not very appealing to this group of women and young men seeking executive jobs by route of low-level white-collar posts.

In addition to the membership impasse is the bargaining impasse noted by some writers. Bell observes that unions have reached the limits of collective bargaining.[9] He argues that there is a growing awareness among labor leaders that unions in the future can get wage and welfare increases equal only to increases in productivity. In other words, the cream of the "unearned surplus" has been skimmed off.

7. *Shifting goals.* Samuel Gompers felt that unions had a single purpose: the improvement of the economic status of their membership. Bread-and-butter unionism as an operational philosophy has served labor well for years. Without doubt, this philosophy is still the foundation of the American union movement. However, unions progressively have been shifting away from this single purposeness to embrace objectives in the realm of social welfarism. Thus, from an economic movement unionism is turning into a social movement.

Most of the trends discussed above are traceable to the following influences:

External influences:
a) Favorable legislation and administration of the law.
b) Prosperous economic conditions after World War II.
c) Increasing stability in bargaining relationships accompanied by a less-aggressive antiunion attitude of employers.
d) Narrowing potentials in the organizational and bargaining spheres.

---

[8] The rapid growth in numbers of administrative employees relative to production employees is an unfavorable development from the standpoint of future union membership.

[9] Daniel Bell, "The Capitalism of the Proletariate? American Trade Unionism Today," in Jack Barbash (ed.), *Unions and Union Leadership* (New York: Harper and Bros., 1959), pp. 42–43.

Internal influences:
a) The aging and conservatism of leadership.
b) The low turnover of key figures in union leadership roles.
c) Shift in power from membership to leaders.
d) Centralization of power in the international union organization accompanied by a decline in local union autonomy.

UNION CONTROL STRUCTURE: SOME DETERMINANTS

Voluntarism is one of the cornerstones of trade union philosophy. The concept of voluntarism rests on the principle of self-determination of rank and file union members in the decision-making process. It also involves the source of power in a union organization.[10] According to the principle of voluntarism, power should be granted by mandate from the bottom up. However, frequently the grass-roots sources of power atrophy as power becomes centralized in the upper echelons of the international union hierarchy. In cases like these power is delegated from the top down, increasing the degree of control of the international over the local. The consequence of this is the dilution of the local's opportunity for self-determination.

Voluntarism applied to union organization in the Gompersian scheme of things meant that the federation (like the American Federation of Labor) should be composed of international unions loosely tied to it. The amount of control exercised by the federation over the internationals was slight. In turn, the international union (like the International Brotherhood of Electrical Workers) was made up of local union affiliates. The international had more control over its component locals, but they enjoyed considerable autonomy in making decisions relating to their affairs.

The AFL–CIO, which is the current federated labor organization, does not exercise much control over its member international unions. Presently the major issue is the control of the international union over local affiliates. The degree of control at this level varies considerably from one international organization to the next. In general, it can be said that craft locals organizing in the construction industry are freer from international control than locals of industrial unions (like the United Steelworkers) organizing in manufacturing companies.

The problem of the structure of control is important because it bears directly on the leadership, democracy, and participation topics taken up in the following sections. The tendency in American unionism has been for the locus of control to shift from subsidiary units of the union organization—the locals—to centralization in the international union.

It is difficult to isolate simple causes of this trend. However, four factors

[10] See Gerald Popiel, "Bureaucracy in the Mass Industrial Union," *American Journal of Economics and Sociology*, October, 1955, pp. 51–52.

are considered as underlying determinants of the control structure prevailing in international-local relationships.

1. *Environment as a determinant of structure.* Blumer states the environmental determinant of centralization in the following quotation:

> We should note, first, that the large union and the large management are steadily forced in their relations with each other to act as single entities. This creates in each the need for effective organization, effective inner control, and expert direction. The hierarchic structure readily allows, in its case, for meeting these needs. For its part the union in meeting these needs is increasingly forced to lodge the making of policies and of decisions in a top leadership and thus to strip away autonomy from the rank and file member and from the local union. The effort to achieve unitary direction on the part of a heterogeneous composition introduces an inner power process into the union—a condition which, in itself, is met in time by a concentration of control in a directing leadership.[11]

Hence, in terms of the bargaining environment where the union faces a powerful centralized management, it of necessity is forced to meet management on its own terms with a concentration of the tools of economic warfare in the international hierarchy.

2. *Objectives as determinants of structure.* It is a long-standing doctrine in organization theory that structure is determined by the goals of the organization. According to Hoxie, the union represents a common interpretation of values and beliefs.[12] Therefore, revolutionary unionism, uplift unionism, and business unionism reflect the values and objectives which the memberships of these various unions think worthwhile.

Pursuit of these ends, coupled with the bargaining environment, requires an assortment of control structures running from relatively decentralized control of local unions by the international union for organizations oriented toward bread and butterism to centralized control of unions endorsing the ends of revolution. Between these extremes are a number of goals and combinations of goals admitting different degrees of control intensity of the international union over locals.

3. *Functions as determinants of structure.* Given certain objectives, functional differentiation occurs so these can be accomplished. As the complexity of the union's environment increases, the more likely will be the concentration of control in centralized hierarchies. Union leadership in these situations relies on expert advice for guidance and thus union staff organizations emerge.

It is almost axiomatic that the staff is bred out of complexity. But the

---

[11] Herbert Blumer, "Social Structure and Power Conflict," in Arthur Kornhauser, Robert Dubin, and Arthur M. Ross (eds.), *Industrial Conflict* (New York: McGraw-Hill Book Co., 1954), p. 238. Quoted with permission.

[12] See John T. Dunlop, "The Development of Labor Organizations: A Theoretical Framework," in Richard A. Lester and Joseph Shister (eds.), *Insights into Labor Issues* (New York: Macmillan Co., 1948), pp. 168–69.

staff can operate effectively only when activities are centralized. Thus staff organizations are found most frequently in the large international and far less often in the local. By equipping the top union officials with technical information, staff activities are a method of developing and retaining control.[13]

4. *Means used to achieve ends as determinants of structure.* The most obvious example of this determinant is the use of the strike as a means to achieve economic objectives. Tannenbaum suggests that the frequency of conflicts—strikes—leads to a restriction rather than an expansion of freedom *within* a local union.[14] It might also be hypothesized that frequency of conflict leads to greater centralization of power within the international union over the local. This is particularly true of industries in which pattern bargaining prevails—the steel and the automotive industries, for example.

It is evident that no one of these four determinants alone provides the entire explanation of the control structure existing between the international union and its local affiliates. Probably all of them in concert act to produce the tendency for greater control centralization in the international union with the local losing more of its opportunity for self-determination. With a situation like this, it is natural therefore to look at the leadership on the international level.

UNION LEADERSHIP

Modern unions are led by men whose background, experiences, and training exclude them from the usual career ladders dominated by business and professional people. Phelps gives a thumbnail profile of the "typical" labor leader. His characteristics include:

1. Being born and brought up on the "wrong side of the tracks."
2. Receiving little formal education.
3. Identifying with union and with manual wage workers.
4. Rising rapidly through the union and assuming a good deal of responsibility while quite young.
5. Being a Democrat.
6. Being highly skeptical of businessmen.[15]

---

[13] Brooks observes that the rise of staff organization has had exactly the opposite effect of the one intended. "It has been largely a matter of turning over to the experts significant aspects of the collective bargaining or internal union processes. In its worst form, the officer or representative of the union abandons his role as spokesman for the union and contents himself with vouching for the qualification of the expert who then performs independently of the union, the decision-making function." Brooks, *op. cit.*, p. 153.

[14] Arnold S. Tannenbaum, "Control Structure and Union Functions," *American Journal of Sociology*, May, 1956, pp. 542–45.

[15] Orne W. Phelps, "Community Recognition of Labor Leaders," *Industrial and Labor Relations Review*, April, 1954, p. 420.

By the standards of our society labor leaders are not highly paid when their income is cast against their authority and responsibilities. They seldom accumulate wealth; and they do not possess sufficient status to gain recognition in social registers. American labor leaders, according to Phelps, are under-represented in *Who's Who*. Further, labor leaders do not seem to be recognized by other forms of prestige associations and honors such as representation on Boards of Trustees of colleges and universities, foundation trusteeships, corporation directorships, honorary degrees, and membership in service clubs.

Phelps concludes that about the only form of recognition comes from the status of union leadership itself. This isolation from the affairs of the social and business community leads Phelps to observe: "If the segregation they now experience is continued it may be expected that as a group they will develop their own ideas of a proper social order, the desirable extent and intensity of regulation of industry, and the correct management of community affairs."[16]

It is not entirely apparent that it is desirable for union leaders to take the steps necessary, even if they are so disposed, to gain community recognition of the forms outlined by Phelps. If the union leader is to be accepted and awarded the symbols of community status he will have to change his attitudes and behavior to accord with the standards our society uses in offering recognition, since it is doubtful that the community will change its standards to fit those of the labor leaders. This means that union leaders would have to adopt the ideology of the business society, because it is on these terms that success is measured and status is bestowed. Trends in this direction, however, would appear to neutralize the union as an effective countervailing force that acts as an offset of business power in certain spheres of economic and political activities.

One of the major issues facing union leadership is its ability to retain independence of business ideology so as to function as a balance against business power. But C. Wright Mills feels that union leadership is working toward an integration with the corporate system rather than toward producing a more effective mechanism of social protest and counterbalance. He says:

As procapitalist, hardheaded, pressure-group captains and as members or would be members of the national elite, in so far as labor men talk seriously of programs, they will invariably conceive of them as realizable alongside the present corporations and within the present state framework. . . . These unions are less levers for change of that general framework than they are instruments for more advantageous integration with it. . . . They seek greater integration at the upper levels of the corporate economy rather than greater power at the lower levels of the work hierarchy, for, in brief, it is the unexpressed desire of American labor leaders to join with owners and managers

---

[16] *Ibid.*, p. 433.

in running the corporate enterprise system and influencing decisively the political economy as a whole.[17]

Union leaders can gain access to the ranks of the elite by means of power—political power and economic power—for they are neither born nor educated to the role of the national power elite, which is supposedly occupied by high corporate officials and by top-level politicians and military personnel. Many of the labor leaders who are now in office rose during the time unions were fighting for recognition. They have had to make the transition from militant unionism to bargaining unionism. Consequently not all the old leaders have worn down the rough edges or recovered from the bruises of past fights sufficiently to feel comfortable in the rarified atmosphere of the elite. But the old generation of leaders is passing. It is being replaced by new men who are better educated and smoother in the new order of labor-management relationships. These men are the cadre of the labor managers of the future.

Union Leaders as Managers

Labor-management relations, being in the bargaining stage of development, place the top officials of international unions in a peculiar position. They must appear as dynamic fighting leaders to the membership as well as acting as managers in the contexts of collective bargaining and internal administration of the union.

Union officials have three orientations which complicate their role.[18]

1. *Toward the rank and file* they symbolize the homely virtues of unionism. As such, they must construct an administrative machine which de-emphasizes the "cult of personality" within the union. They have to convince the membership that the union is truly democratic.
2. *Toward the outside* they have to adopt attitudes of rationality and reasonableness, searching for ways to blend the interest of unions and management.
3. *Toward the internal formal union structure* they must search for ways of stabilizing top leadership positions, insuring their continuity in office by careful manipulation of the formal relationships within the union.

In many instances the negotiator from the international union finds the main obstacle to acceptance of a collective bargaining agreement in the local union, not in the company. The role of the international representative changes in such cases to become a mediator. He must convince the membership of the local that the offer of management is fair or "all that could be gotten." This is managerial statesmanship. ". . . The first requirement," of labor leaders, comments Brooks, "is that they are able to

---

[17] C. Wright Mills, "The Labor Leaders and the Power Elite," in Kornhauser, Dubin, and Ross (eds.), *op. cit.*, pp. 151–52. Quoted with permission.

[18] Popiel, *op. cit.*, pp. 57–58.

get along with management. It is not nearly so necessary that they be able to capture and retain the 'loyalty' of workers."[19]

Numerous pressures on modern union officials force them to behave more as responsible administrators and less as fighting emotional leaders. These pressures are derived from several sources.

In the first place, the tenor of collective bargaining and the attitude of the principals who have an interest in the bargaining process stress stability in the work relationship. From the standpoint of the individual worker stability means continuous employment and relative freedom from the economic hazards associated with a strike. From the standpoint of management stability means labor peace with its attendant cost and competitive advantages. From the standpoint of the public stability means freedom from the inconvenience of shortages and from the crippling of essential services. Thus, the demands of union membership, management, and the public force upon union officials the necessity for "reasonableness" and sincere effort in settling differences by the accepted methods of bargaining. All of this requires of the union leader rationality, the desire to compromise, and a mature insight into the implications of the positions he assumes.

Secondly, the size of modern labor organizations with their complex administrative and financial problems forces the labor official to develop a managerial outlook. Unions literally are big business and pressures from the public and to some extent from the membership require the leaders to run them according to rational management principles.

Third, the protection of unions as a matter of public policy insures continuity of the union in the form of institutional security. Security gives unions reasonable assurances of membership and revenues. With their existence no longer jeopardized the leaders can attend to administrative matters with a vigor not allowed when their major concern was with rallying support for the union cause and battling management.

The new and evolving unionism will develop along with it a new breed of union leader. The functions he performs will parallel those of the executives in the company with which he negotiates. Whether associated with the union or with the company, representatives of both sides will be engaged in the management processes of planning, organizing, motivating, and controlling. But it must be remembered that the use of management processes is merely as a means to an end. Unions are organizations too, and their leaders perform management functions to obtain goals. The real danger to union membership, and indeed to society as a whole, is if the ends sought by unions and corporations do not differ. So the real test of union leaders in the future is to become better managers in the sense of

---

[19] Brooks, *op. cit.*, p. 153.

mastery of management process but to hold their goals separate and distinct from corporate ends.

This will be no easy task because union leaders qua leaders progressively will find more in common with corporate leadership than with their own membership. Not only will they be "brothers under the skin" in the sense of a common participation in and understanding of the administrative process, but they also will be more and more concerned with forming a symbiotic relationship between corporation and union to ensure the continuity and prosperity of both institutions. The ultimate effect of such an arrangement naturally will be the securing of the positions and the enhancement of power of the top officials of both organizations. At this point, union membership may be reduced to the disenfranchised powerless estate in which the stockholders of large corporations find themselves. A turn of events of this sort is by no means inevitable. But the integrity of the union will require leaders of principle, dedication, and vision more in the future than at any other time in union history.

UNION DEMOCRACY

Underlying the issue of union democracy is the question: "Is democracy in subsidiary units of American society necessary for the preservation of democracy in the state as a whole?" Without much reflection, the inclination is to answer with an unequivocal "yes." But on second thought, this requirement is met in very few so-called democratic states. Business is essentially autocratic; and by their nature most private voluntary associations are undemocratic.[20] There is hardly a unity of opinion among writers on this subject. Some take the approach that democratic unions are required to maintain a democratic state.[21] Others feel that democracy is possible in the state without the necessity of democratic practices in its subsidiary organizations.[22]

This issue is hardly one which is resolvable here if, indeed, it can be resolved at all. However, the major arguments for and against union democracy are stated so the reader may determine some of the dimensions of the issue.

[20] Since voluntary organizations strive for homogeneity in the character and attitudes of their memberships, the isolated and irregular factional opposition which does occur against the incumbent leadership does not provide the basis for a party struggle. "Lacking differences of principle and interest, the voluntary organization will be abandoned to the iron law of oligarchy." See Lloyd H. Fisher and Grant McConnell, "Internal Conflict and Labor-Union Solidarity," in Kornhauser, Dubin, and Ross, *op. cit.*, p. 135.

[21] Clyde Summers, "Growth of Social Consciousness in Internal Union Affairs," *Monthly Labor Review*, January, 1960, pp. 22–25.

[22] C. Peter Magrath, "Democracy in Overalls: The Futile Quest for Union Democracy," *Industrial and Labor Relations Review*, July, 1959, pp. 503–25.

The arguments for union democracy:

1. If democracy is a superior form of government, it should be practiced wherever possible.
2. Workers enjoy a more effective voice in union affairs and derive a greater sense of satisfaction from participation.
3. If leadership breaks contact with the workers, they will lose responsiveness to the interests of the union membership.
4. Whenever power is present, as it is in labor unions, it should be controlled by democratic processes.

But against these arguments are the following points:

1. Unions have not had sufficient experience with systems of checks and balances in defining and protecting membership rights.
2. Unions are autocratic, at least on the international level, because the matters they attend to can be best handled by a centralized authority.
3. The union functions most efficiently when removed from the pressures of democratic life.
4. The need for organizational unity in the face of external conflict does not admit democratic practice.
5. Union leaders in their desire for internal organizational cohesion and for the solidification of their own positions have sacrificed democracy for membership discipline.[23]

Concepts of Union Democracy

It is appropriate to inquire at this point as to what criteria are available to judge the level of democracy in unions? According to Magrath, the concept of democracy in western political thought includes these elements:[24]

1. Broad policy objectives consistent with membership objectives.
2. Responsibility and accountability of rulers to the ruled.
3. The legitimacy of continual opposition to incumbent parties.
4. The guarantee of certain rights as fundamental to the functioning of democratic processes, such as the right to vote and the right to criticize leadership.

While these principles are found piecemeal in union practices, they are not altogether appropriate standards to judge union democracy. The reason is that the state, to which these standards are most frequently applied, is a far different creature than the union. On the one hand the state is a public organization made up of a heterogeneous population. The state is a multipurpose institution which exists to satisfy a wide variety of its citizens' expectations. The union on the other hand is a private voluntary organization with a fair degree of homogeneity in its membership. It is a

---

[23] The pros and cons above are taken from Clark Kerr, *Unions and Union Leaders of Their Own Choosing* (Santa Barbara: The Fund for the Republic, 1957), pp. 10–11; and Joel Seidman, "Some Requirements for Union Democracy," *American Economic Review*, May, 1958, pp. 36–37.

[24] Magrath, *op. cit.*, pp. 504–5.

limited-purpose organization largely devoted to the single aim of satisfying the economic expectations of its membership.[25] Further, the state has been able to institutionalize conflict arising from opposition parties, a feat unions—with but one exception—have not been able to accomplish. Consequently, if union democracy is judged by the standards developed for the political state, labor's showing is likely to be disappointing.[26]

If political principles of democracy are not fair standards to apply to unions what other criteria are there? Seidman offers other measures of democracy such as the determination of policy by rank and file union members. The application of this criterion would make the union democratic at the local level but autocratic at the international level, because delegates to the national convention have little to do but endorse with cheering ovation the policies already settled. He also suggests that the responsiveness of union leaders to membership needs and membership approval of policy and performance at the national level are other democratic criteria. Application of these criteria generally makes the national organization appear quite democratic.[27]

Segal, in his turn, applies some procedural tests to determine the extent of union democracy.[28] He asks the following questions:

1. Is there constitutional machinery for delegating authority to elected representatives?
2. Does the machinery work?
3. Do the representatives have the will and power to make decisions?
4. Do all members have equal opportunity to run for office without fear of reprisal from incumbents?
5. Do members have rights of appeal against unjust actions of officers?
6. Can an opposition party develop?
7. Can membership control irresponsible expenditure of union funds?
8. Do officers make an accounting of financial conditions?
9. Can racial or religious minorities gain access to the union?

The issue of union democracy is not a simple one. But in spite of its complexity it reduces to the notion of how much freedom and opportunity the individual has for self-determination as a union member. Freedom means the absence of restraint. But because unions impose obligations on members some loss of freedom is inevitable. Kerr says, "The challenge is that the price not be higher than necessary."[29]

---

[25] See Grant McConnell, "Factionalism and Union Demorcacy," *Labor Law Review*, September, 1958, pp. 637–38.

[26] Actually there is but one union which comes close to fulfilling these principles in form as well as in spirit. It is the International Typographical Union. And the ITU is considered by some to be atypical.

[27] Seidman, *op. cit.*, p. 35.

[28] Ben D. Segal, "Some Efforts at Democratic Union Participation," *American Economic Review*, May, 1958, p. 54.

[29] Kerr, *op. cit.*, p. 9.

Anti-Democratic Tendencies

Union constitutions are often pointed to as evidence of the inherent democratic character of labor organizations. But these documents are trappings of democratic procedure which may disguise whether in fact the union is actually democratic.

In the summary of a penetrating analysis of union constitutions, Bromwich cites six areas that harbor potential antidemocratic tendencies and the denial of membership rights. A rather lengthy extract from this summary clearly outlines the problem areas.

1. *Admissions:* Apprenticeship rules may be a bar to a person seeking membership in the union and sometimes provide an informal means for racial or political discrimination ("fraternal" approval of the applicant by the membership has the same effect).

2. *Concentration of power:* Generally speaking, most American unions reveal a concentration of power in the hands of the international president and grant only a limited effectiveness to the executive board in its task of overseeing all policy decisions.

3. *The convention:* All the unions in the sample designate the convention as the supreme body of the organization, but here again the president's power to appoint convention committees in some cases, and to preside over the convention in others, strengthens the tendency toward a concentration of executive power.

4. *Discipline:* In unions like the ITU and UAW, and the Upholsterers, there is a sensitivity to procedural rights in disciplinary cases, but in many of the unions in the sample the disciplinary board is staffed by the local executive committee or the local president—a dangerous situation because accused members are usually in opposition to the local administration.

5. *Union press:* In almost all of the unions, the press is under the control of the incumbent administration, so that the official newspaper tends to be monopolized by a few people at the top of the union hierarchy and excludes vigorous controversy or opposition to prevailing administration policies.

6. *Procedures:* There is a democratic design and intent in the constitutions of the American unions, but there are serious structural deficiencies which *can* act to the detriment of the democratic rights of the membership.[30]

In addition to these problems, other compelling reasons exist for tendencies toward centralization and autocracy in unions. First, it is rather difficult for organized opposition to develop in a labor union, particularly on the international level. A two-party system is precluded not only by the fact that the means of communication are dominated by the incumbent power but also because of the nature of voluntary associations. The history of labor has amply demonstrated that when ideological or even policy differences occur, it is far more likely for the union to split than for it to resolve difficulties by the ballot in which the losing side will accept the de-

---

[30] Leo Bromwich, *Union Constitutions* (A Report to the Fund for the Republic, 1959), pp. 38–39.

cision of the majority but remain with the union as the "loyal opposition."

Second, there is little doubt that incumbent union leaders have vested interests in their positions and are loathe to see their powers usurped by their opponents. But the incumbent union official is usually an "odds-on" favorite for re-election anyway, because he can carry out his re-election campaign at union expense; in addition to the services of the union press the national officer also has a number of patronage positions around which he can build a political machine.[31]

In all-out combat with challengers at periods of re-election the incumbent officer has three strategies he employs to win support of the membership and discredit the opponent. These strategies are noted by Coleman:[32]

1. *"All-out-for-welfare:"* allowing membership participation in peripheral union activities on the assumption that one form of participation is as good as another in giving the membership the illusion of a voice in union affairs.

2. *"You-never-had-it-so-good:"* assuming the role of the benevolent dictator identifying with a tangible list of gains.

3. *"Here-come-the-saboteurs:"* attempting to forge a link between the opposition group and the work of the devil; or even worse, pro-communist or pro-company associations.

Third, the apathetic attitude of rank and file union members toward the activities of the union may be itself a cause of antidemocratic tendencies. This possibility is probed in the next section.

MEMBERSHIP PARTICIPATION IN THE LOCAL UNION

The local union is a bastion of democracy in the trend toward union centralism. The local, its leadership, and its membership are the foundations of the labor movement organizationally and spiritually. The local provides a basic source of policy for officers at the international level and it gives rank and file membership about their only opportunity for participation in union affairs.

However, the fact that most union members do not take advantage of this opportunity is a matter of much concern to many commentators on the current union scene. They see lack of participation as a danger leading to disengagement of international officers from the needs of their constituents in the plant, centralization of power without restraints, and irresponsible leadership at all levels of union organization. A number of considerations bear on the topic of participation and it seems appropriate to start the discussion with local union leadership.

---

[31] Seidman, *op. cit.*, pp. 38–39.

[32] John R. Coleman, "The Compulsive Pressures of Democracy in Unionism," *American Journal of Sociology*, May, 1956, p. 626.

Local Union Leadership

The organizational structure of the local union is a mirror of the international in many ways. The local elects officials to serve as president, vice-presidents, secretary, and treasurer. In addition to these positions local members function in various shop committees such as the grievance committee, the bargaining committee, and the safety committee. Finally, the mainstay of the local's life in the shop is the steward who is also elected; among other duties he represents individual members in grievance hearings as the first step in the grievance procedure.

The elected officers of the local differ from their counterparts in the international in one important formal matter: they generally receive no pay from the union for the efforts they expend on it. Their source of income, like the rank and file, is from the company.

Miller and Stockton outline the character of the work undertaken by local union officers.[33] The findings of their study show that union work requires about eight hours a week. The officers' functions encompass administration, finance, secretarial work, grievance handling, and contract negotiation. Most of the decisions made by the officers require membership approval, particularly policy decisions relating to collective bargaining negotiations. Also, the local officers attend a good many meetings at the local, city, state, and international levels of union organization.

The local officers in the Miller and Stockton study are significantly above the average of the rank and file in education. Further, the officers are joiners, actively participating in other organizations outside the union.

Local officials listed the following reasons for accepting and continuing in office.

1. Officers see in the union an opportunity for improving the lot of the workers and the policies of the union, and for following a deep interest in the labor movement.
2. Incumbent officers feel there is a lack of replacements for them.
3. Officers feel that part of their remuneration for doing the job is greater prestige.
4. Officers feel that a union position offers the chance for higher community status and recognition.
5. Officers feel a conflict of interest exists between workers and management and that the union keeps management in line.[34]

One main activity of the local official is to preside at meetings. As a manifestation of union activism and solidarity the meeting itself warrants some attention.

---

[33] Glenn W. Miller and Edward J. Stockton, "Local Union Officer—His Background, Activities, and Attitudes," *Labor Law Journal*, January, 1959, p. 31.

[34] *Ibid.*, p. 35.

The Local Union Meeting

The meeting serves three purposes. First, it is a symbol of common aim. Through its ceremony, the membership demonstrates solidarity in the cause of their local and adherence to the principles of organized labor. Second, the meeting allows communication upward, so the membership may express opinions and state grips and criticisms of the conduct of union affairs. Third, the meeting facilitates downward communication by which officers relay information to the membership, motivate the membership to support union policies, and communicate the results gained by policies.[35]

Decisions are rarely reached at local meetings, with the exception of small locals. Usually it is necessary for the executive board of the local to structure alternatives and present them to the membership for a vote. The matters submitted to the floor resolve to five—ratification of the collective bargaining agreement; appeals from the grievance procedure; approval of extraordinary expenses; constitutional changes; and election of officers.[36]

Despite its significance in the life of the local, the meeting has a number of discouraging features which reduce attendance figures. Strauss and Sayles note that inconveniences in time and place of the meeting are shortcomings since meetings are held after working hours and are frequently located in halls which are not too close to the homes of members.

Also, the meeting often runs too long and the content is boring. The chairman may be conscientious but not well trained for the job. The meeting may be stalemated over parliamentary procedure with little of value being accomplished. Finally, not much opportunity is allowed for the expression of needs and complaints by members from the floor. The difficulties some have in expressing themselves, the lack of parliamentary sophistication, and the hostility of being excluded reduce the effectiveness of upward communication.[37]

For these reasons—and others which will be mentioned later—the union meeting is not an especially attractive event. The consequence is low attendance.

Union Participation

It is not unusual for average attendance at local union meetings to range between 2 and 8 per cent of total membership, although certain meetings dealing with contract negotiations or the election of officers generally draw larger numbers. But numbers alone do not tell the story of union participation.

---

[35] George Strauss and Leonard R. Sayles, "The Local Union Meeting," *Industrial and Labor Relations Review*, January, 1953, pp. 213–15.

[36] *Ibid.*, pp. 215–18.

[37] *Ibid.*, pp. 207–8, 213–14.

Patterns of Participation—Group.[38]   Although participation at union meetings is low, this is neither new nor is it peculiar to the union. Voluntary associations of all varieties find it difficult to attract members to business meetings. Stockholders' meetings also are notorious for low attendance.

Union participation cannot be measured entirely by attendance at meetings. It includes participation in many union affairs both inside and outside the shop. Turning to the union is an act of expediency for some groups. These groups are concerned with their own interests; they look on union activity as a protection against management and from competing groups within the union. Economic dissatisfaction or fear of technological displacement may drive others to take part in union affairs. In any event the persisting pattern of participation is a function of the extent to which union members perceive that the union is satisfying their needs.

Union participants and nonparticipants do not seem to be strewn homogeneously throughout the departments and occupational groups found in a plant. Indeed, Strauss and Sayles observed meetings where 50 per cent of those present came from a single department in the shop.

That some groups are likely to participate more actively than others is conditioned by four factors.

1. *Homogeneity of the group.*   A closely knit group seeking satisfactions through union activity has considerable influence on individuals to participate. The majority of rank and file members need personal motivation and group pressure to get them to engage in union affairs. Homogeneity and solidarity in a group are caused by locational proximity of members working under the same supervisor. Also, occupational similarity, belonging to the same ethnic group, and coming from the same neighborhood combine to create group cohesiveness.

2. *Job status.*   Participation is more likely among those who are better paid and who have higher-prestige jobs.

3. *Strategic technological position.*   Key groups in a production process are in a more favorable bargaining position with management. Their participation in the union is encouraged because of the influence they can exert with management.

4. *Nature of the work.*   Some jobs make fewer demands than others, allowing the employees time and energy for union activities.

Patterns of Participation—Individual.   One point is fairly clear about individual participation in union activities. Individuals who take an interest and become involved in the union are not necessarily those who are dissatisfied and discontented. Indeed, union involvement is associated

---

[38] This section is based on George Strauss and Leonard Sayles, "Patterns of Participation in Local Unions," *Industrial and Labor Relations Review*, October, 1952, pp. 31–43.

more with those in higher-status jobs, as measured by pay and prestige. Thus, craft locals generally show higher participation rates than industrial locals. And with few exceptions the burden of activity in industrial locals themselves is carried by workers in higher pay- and job-status positions.[39]

Form and Dansereau point to two other determinants of individual union participation.[40] First, the greater the individual's orientation toward union goals and policies the greater will be the extent of his participation. And second, the degree of union participation is positively related to the degree to which the individual is socially integrated in the plant, neighborhood, and community life.

Form and Dansereau's study bears out their hypothesis that the most active members are those who view the union's main function as that of providing a *social* world for the participants. Those who have economic and political conceptions of the union's function follow after the socially oriented as to the degree of their participation. As might be expected, individuals who are apathetic or hostile toward the union show the lowest participation rates.

However, the typical union member does not look at the union as providing him a social world. Consequently, it is not surprising to find union participation rates low, if indeed the major load of union affairs is assumed by those who are socially oriented in terms of the satisfactions they expect to derive from union work. As Spinrod indicates:

Theories about trade unions are generally concerned with the function of the union as an organization—in the collective bargaining process, in the plant organization, in the community, and so on. The members are in fact usually viewed as consumers, satisfied, or occasionally resentful, of the manner in which the leader-entrepreneurs are achieving basic union goals of fulfilling economic demands and checking management authority. Unquestionably, this is the predominant orientation of a large proportion of those who belong to most American unions. In this case, they view their union as a service. The unions become a protective agency to which dues are paid regularly. Therefore personal involvement is minimal.[41]

Unlike European workers who have a class identification which is made tangible by union membership, the American workers cease to be such when the bell rings to end the day. Their social satisfactions are derived from associations outside the plant and outside the union.

---

[39] William Spinrod, "Correlates of Trade Union Participation: A Summary of the Literature," *American Sociological Review*, April, 1960, p. 239.

[40] William H. Form and H. Kirk Dansereau, "Union Member Orientations and Patterns of Social Interaction," *Industrial and Labor Relations Review*, October, 1957, pp. 4–9.

[41] Spinrod, *op. cit.*, pp. 243–44. Quoted with permission.

Union Participation: an Alternative Hypothesis

Regardless of the reasons for low participation, many despair of good and responsible union government at the local level because of the lack of membership interest. The feeling is that low participation opens the door for persistently poor leadership, a detachment of union goals from membership needs, a breakdown of union solidarity, and a show of weakness to management. Racketeering and communist takeover of locals are pointed out as examples of what can happen when the rank and file is indifferent to the union.

There can be no denial that widespread interest and participation in the local are forces for responsible unionism. Thus external evidence of union solidarity like attendance at meetings and committee work should not be minimized. However, Kovner and Lahne bring to light a concept of "informal representation" which may offset, in part, the negative effects of low formal participation. These authors state that:

> Our observations suggest that participation in formal union activity . . . is not the full measure of awareness and interest on the part of the membership; that on the contrary, these formal activities, although carried on by only a few members, are outward manifestations of an interest and awareness of union affairs of most of the shop society.[42]

Through shop talk and personal interactions among union members, representatives, and leaders, the workers are able through the activists who attend meetings and participate in other union matters to bring their wishes and needs to the attention of union officials. Accordingly, Kovner and Lahne feel that there is too much emphasis on the formal character of union activities. The people who do not show up for meetings are likely to be represented by those who do.

Karsh makes much the same point when he observes that local union vitality and power do not turn on the *number* present at meetings but upon *who* is present. The values of participation are achieved if the interests of all are represented. The "solid core" of participants often does represent the interests of the membership as devised in the shop.[43]

CONCLUDING OBSERVATIONS

People join unions to satisfy needs. The major form of satisfaction sought by American workers from the union is economic. The union has obtained this satisfaction for its membership not only in terms of direct wages but also through job security and fringe benefits. In addition to

---

[42] Joseph Kovner and Herbert J. Lahne, "Shop Society and the Union," *Industrial and Labor Relations Review*, October, 1953, p. 4.

[43] Bernard Karsh, "Union Traditions and Membership Apathy," *Labor Law Journal*, September, 1958, p. 644.

economic satisfactions there is also the opportunity to find social and psychological satisfactions through union activity. As a matter of fact, both employment with a company and membership in a union offer the individual rewards on the economic, social, and psychological planes. The individual participates in these two formal organizations with the expectation that rewards of this type will be forthcoming from both.

In some cases the company and the union may make equal and parallel contributions to the satisfaction of an individual's needs. But more frequently, perhaps, the rewards from one organization supplement the shortcomings in the reward structure of the other. If this is a valid statement, then it is possible to make a strong case for the concept of dual allegiance, which according to Father Purcell is ". . . an [individual's] attitude of favorability towards the company or the union as institutions, or general approval of their overall policies."[44]

The workers who perceive *both* the company and the union as sources for the satisfaction of needs are likely to feel allegiance simultaneously to these organizations even though their objectives and policies conflict, and even though this conflict may lead, at times, to outright economic warfare.

But the concept of dual allegiance has another side. While the individual has an allegiance to the company and the union, he may view his association with these organizations as a client who participates in them as long as the rewards they offer balance the sacrifices he has to make for the privilege of membership. The typical worker probably does not internalize the basic ideologies of the company or the union except to the extent that the value systems bear directly on his own self-interest.[45]

With the growing size and increasing impersonality of business and labor organizations it is hard to visualize a worker having much involvement in the organizations to which he must belong to make a living. There are too many other associations outside the union and the company from which he may derive a deeper sense of self-fulfillment.

Dual apathy may more fittingly describe the attitude of workers toward unions and companies. The individual enmeshed in collectivized patterns of the company and the union can do little to modify either. All he can hope is that his personal interests are not violated. He travels along in a stream of events decided by bureaucracies with which he has little direct contact. Is it any wonder, therefore, that the individual hardly bothers himself about the reasons for being of companies and unions? Rather, he is concerned with the concrete activities of shop administration and far less with the abstract principles of labor and management.

[44] Theodore V. Purcell, "Dual Allegiance to Company and Union-Packinghouse Workers: A Swift-UPWA Study in Crisis Situations, 1949–1952," *Personnel Psychology*, Spring, 1954, p. 48.

[45] Karsh, *op. cit.*, p. 646.

There are certainly work situations in which the small size of shop and union provides the intimacy necessary for a feeling of individual involvement and worth. However, the modern emphasis is on mass—mass production and mass unionism. This emphasis, accompanied by centralization of union and management authority, deprives the individual as an employee and as a union member of the privilege of self-determination which is crucial to real participation in organizational affairs. Consequently, it is not unreasonable to expect that the worker will seek the opportunity of involvement and self-expression outside the organizational contexts of the work situation.

These points may provide partial explanations for the lack of participation in the union, and reasons why the democratic challenge of the union is going unanswered by the membership. Perhaps the union member does not care. But someone must, and without doubt those who will carry the load of membership apathy will be the leaders. It will be no easy task for them to face indifference on one hand and fight for union integrity on the other. Yet this is the fate of all leaders in a mass society based on democratic principles.

REVIEW QUESTIONS

1. Describe the key changes which have transformed the character of American unionism in the last thirty years.

2. Discuss the four factors pointed to as determinants of union control structure. What are the reasons usually given for the trend toward centralization of union power?

3. "One of the major issues facing union leadership is its ability to retain independence of business ideology." Discuss.

4. In what ways are union leaders managers? From what directions comes pressure for responsibility?

5. Discuss the pros and cons of the argument for union democracy.

6. Why are incumbent union leaders "odds-on" favorites for re-election?

7. Outline the dimensions of the local union membership participation problem.

8. Why are some groups more likely than others to participate in union affairs?

9. Evaluate the concept of "informal representation" as an alternative hypothesis of union participation.

10. Compare and evaluate the notions of "dual allegiance" and "dual apathy."

SUPPLEMENTARY READINGS

BELL, DANIEL. "The Capitalism of the Proletariate? American Trade Unionism Today," *Unions and Union Leadership* (ed. JACK BARBASH), pp. 40–46. New York: Harper and Bros., 1959.

BROMWICH, LEO. *Union Constitutions*. A Report to the Fund for the Republic, 1959.

BRUNER, DICK. "Has Success Spoiled the Unions?" *Harvard Business Review*, May–June, 1960, pp. 73–78.

MAGRATH, C. PETER. "Democracy in Overalls: The Futile Quest for Union Democracy," *Industrial and Labor Relations Review*, July, 1959, pp. 503–25.

SELIGSON, HARRY. "The Paradox and Challenge of Unionism Today," *Labor Law Journal*, March, 1959, pp. 180–87.

SPINROD, WILLIAM. "Correlates of Trade Union Participation: A Summary of the Literature," *American Sociological Review*, April, 1960, pp. 237–44.

CHAPTER 15

The Status of the Foreman

LIKE the lady who protesteth too much, management constantly feels compelled to reassure itself and the foreman that he is still part of management. Fifty or sixty years ago such protestations would not have made much sense. They are understandable today because the status of the foreman has changed.

Around the turn of the century the foreman knew where he stood; he was part of management. There was no doubt in anyone's mind about it. However, industrial philosophy, organization, and technology have undergone vast transitions since the time the foreman was master of the shop. As a result, the foreman, like many other occupational categories, has ended up in an historical backwash to the main stream of industrial change.

Since the end of World War II many people have concerned themselves with the plight of the foreman. Businessmen and academicians have combined to commiserate with him and to reaffirm that, indeed, he is still the keystone of management. But in spite of what company presidents say at annual foremen banquets, the status of the foreman has declined. And the factors which have produced this decline are as complex as the industrial evolution which caused it.

Merely saying the foreman is part of management avoids the issues. The foreman's status is complicated by a number of events which are considered in this chapter. Whether or not the foreman is a segment of management is in part a matter of definition, in part a matter of personal identification by the foreman with management, in part a matter of legal mandate, and in part a matter of acceptance of the foreman by higher levels of management. These problems and others are dealt with in detail in this chapter.

For many foremen, the debate about their managerial status has only remote interest. The declining status of the foreman relative to the rest of management is, more or less, an academic issue. But one problem is of practical concern to the foreman; it is that his status is not clear. As a matter of practical, day-to-day significance, the foreman is aware and concerned that he operates in an ambiguous setting. He knows, for example, that his daily activities bring him into contact with others who have diverse expectations of what might be called desirable foreman behavior. Chief among these groups and individuals are the union, members of the staff, his boss, and his subordinates. These expectations play upon the foreman's position from many directions, making his role difficult to discharge effectively.

The current problems of foreman status are attributable to three basic causes.

1. The declining skill level of the operative employees supervised.
2. The usurption of functions by the staff.
3. Indifference of higher executives.

It is evident that these causes have not had equal impact in all industrial segments. Consequently, the foreman's role appears to be affected differentially from industry to industry, or for that matter, from company to company. Ample evidence is available to demonstrate that the "problem foremen" are largely concentrated in one particular part of the American business complex. So, before going any farther, it is important to indicate what foremen are being considered and why other first-line supervisors are left out of the discussion.

DEFINITION OF FIRST-LINE SUPERVISION

The foreman's position may be defined descriptively and functionally. From a descriptive point of view, it is said that the foreman:[1]

1. Is a head of a department or section in touch with rank and file workers.
2. Receives policies and directives from higher management and is responsible in varying degrees for their execution.
3. Gives orders and direction.
4. Does little or no work of a manual variety since such work is usually handled by subordinates.
5. Receives compensation usually higher than subordinates.

Descriptively, the main point of distinction between the foreman and higher levels of management is the supervision of operative personnel. In the line organization, *the foreman is the only person who does not supervise other managers.*[2]

---

[1] *The Development of Foremen in Management* (New York: American Management Association, Research Report Number 7, 1945), p. 14.

[2] This is not entirely accurate. In Chapter 6, "Status and Role," mention was made of the working supervisor and the unique role he has enjoyed in manufacturing. It was noted in this chapter that the working supervisor possesses some limited managerial prerogatives such as training, making work assignments, and acting as lead man on the production line. The working supervisor, however, does manual operations. Further the scope of his supervisory authority is so restricted that he is eligible for union membership and is not included in an exempt status for purposes of the Wage and Hour Law.

Functionally, the foreman performs the activities of planning, organizing, motivating, and controlling, as do all other personnel having executive responsibility in a business organization. But the foreman's position is the lowest level in the management hierarchy where the performance of the basic functions of management can be clearly identified. Thus, the foreman represents the first line of management to rank and file employees at the point of physical production of goods and services.

Manufacturing Classifications

Now that the organizational position of the foreman has been established, it is possible to reintroduce an idea raised earlier. The status of first-line supervision is not universally the same across American business. Indeed, the locus of foreman status problems is seated in one particular part of American industry. It is convenient to follow Howard L. Timms[3] in establishing which foremen are most affected by a declining status situation, and why. Timms' breakdown of manufacturing into three types is useful for pinpointing the problem segment. The three manufacturing classifications are: continuous, job order, and intermittent.

Continuous Manufacturing. Companies falling in this category are commonly in the process industries. Included are petroleum refineries and the producers of chemicals. The makers of highly standardized goods like tennis balls, flashlight batteries, and some electronic components frequently are also part of this over-all category.

Typical of continuous manufacturers is production in anticipation of demand rather than in direct response to customer order. Paralleling anticipatory production is making goods to inventory so that production can be maintained at a fairly constant level over a period of time. The product itself is made uniformly to a standard. The length of the production run is relatively long and the lot sizes manufactured are relatively large.

Continuous manufacturing lends itself quite readily to a high degree of mechanization or, in some cases, automation. The activities involved in the production process are repetitive, and the flow of product through the production cycle is continuous from one stage to the next.

Job-Order Manufacturing. In the broadest sense, job-order manufacturing requires customizing a product for a buyer. The characteristics of this type of manufacturing are almost exactly the opposite of continuous manufacturing. The products are heterogeneous, varying according to different customer specifications. Production is undertaken only as a result of demand—specifically, the receipt of an order. Products are not manufactured to stock. Production runs are relatively short and the lot

---

[3] Howard L. Timms, *Production Management* (Bloomington: Bureau of Research, Indiana Readings in Business, Number 22, 1958), pp. 1–3.

sizes are small. The nature of the production process is largely nonrepetitive.

Some examples of companies in job-order manufacturing may be found in the machine-tool industry, the construction industry, and in the electronic industry where a firm might be making, say, miniaturized parts for missiles.

Intermittent Manufacturing. This type of production is a hybrid of job order and continuous. It is the type most common in American industry. Contrary to popular opinion, mass-production assembly industries, like the automotive industry, are the intermittent rather than the continuous variety.

In this form of manufacturing the components of a particular product are made for inventory, although the final product can be made to reflect different component combinations specified by the customer. For example, an automobile dealer can request the colors, body styles, and equipment he needs to meet customer demand. Each dealer order accompanies the car through the assembly process. Thus, the car is "made to order" by putting together a certain combination of components selected from a wide variety of standardized parts and equipment.

Therefore, in intermittent manufacturing parts are usually produced on a continuous, or repetitive, basis to stock. The finished product is not produced to inventory. Typically, then, intermittent production is in part in response to customer demand and in part in anticipation of demand. The finished product is heterogeneous, but it is heterogeneous within a range of standardized variations established by the manufacturer.

All in all, the intermittent manufacturer has quite complex problems to solve, including scheduling, forecasting demand, co-ordinating production activities, and balancing inventories. Within the intermittent category fall automobile manufacturers, aircraft manufacturers, and radio and television producers.

Manufacturing Types and Foreman Status

The foreman discussed in this chapter is generally not found in continuous or job-order manufacturing. There are several reasons why this is so.

First, purely continuous manufacturing is something of a rarity. The number of foremen employed in process industries is relatively few compared to the total.

Second, in those few cases of continuous manufacturing where the foreman is found, his role often is quite different from the stereotype. Those individuals who might be defined as first-line supervisors are frequently in charge of crews of highly specialized and skilled maintenance workers. This hardly conforms to the common picture of the foreman heading up a gang of semiskilled assembly workers. The status and nature of supervision in continuous manufacturing is not typical for the bulk of American foremen.

Third, the pure job-order shop, while not as rare as the continuous manufacturer, still does not employ foremen on a mass scale. The job-order manufacturer is often small. The foremen on the payroll must be highly qualified and capable of handling the variety of technical problems which often occur with the production of a customer's order. Since each order usually presents a different problem, the foreman must be skilled and flexible enough to meet each effectively.

Fourth, because of the small size of the job-order shop, the technical staff usually is not large. In these cases, of course, the staff has not usurped the foreman's prerogatives. Consequently, the functions of planning, organizing, and controlling still devolve on the foreman to a great extent. Thus, because of the need for considerable skill and the retention of traditional management functions, the foreman's status in job-order manufacturing has remained relatively high.

In summary, the foremen in continuous and job-order manufacturing have managed to maintain their status position while the foremen in intermittent manufacturing have suffered a declining status. In large part, the relatively higher status of the foremen in continuous and job-order manufacturing is attributed to the fact that the skill level of the people they supervise is high. Other factors are at work here, of course, but the level of skill of those supervised appears to be the crucial determinant of the foremen's status in industry. Hence, the higher the skill level supervised the higher will be the foreman's status.

The Foreman in Intermittent Manufacturing. Intermittent manufacturing is by far the most important type in American industry by any measure one wishes to apply, be it the number of people employed or the value added to gross national product. Intermittent manufacturing is found in most of the major industrial classifications, ranging across the automotive, appliance, steel, electronic, farm equipment, and garment industries. Therefore, the foremen in intermittent manufacturing are the main focus of this chapter.

In the sphere of intermittent manufacturing, the determinants which have lowered the foreman's status can be singled out easily. Manufacturers in this category have been diligently engaged in rationalization, which in part involves the specialization of labor. For production jobs specialization means constant simplification, leading to a decrease in the skill level required of operative employees. Lowering operative skill levels naturally affects the amount of skill needed by the foreman. At present the foreman in intermittent manufacturing supervises only a fragment of the total production process and heads a department employing semiskilled or unskilled workers.

As noted before, the problems of intermittent manufacturers tend to be very complex. Where companies are large enough and can afford it, a technical staff is usually introduced. Bringing in staffs to facilitate the planning, organizing, and control functions can have just one result from the standpoint of the foreman. It is the dilution of his job. Technical staffs in planning, production control, cost control, quality control,

FIGURE 15–1

EVENTS IN INTERMITTENT MANUFACTURING WHICH HAVE CONTRIBUTED TO THE DECLINE IN FOREMAN STATUS

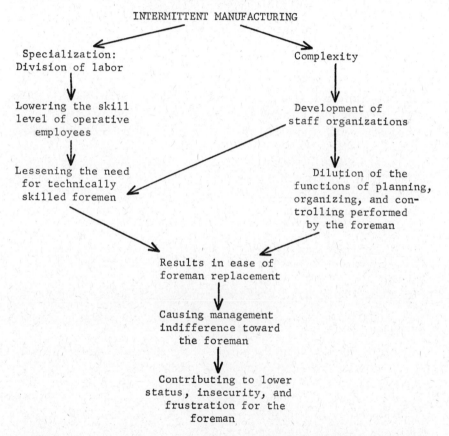

product and process development, and industrial management have all combined to machine tool many decisions that the foreman made previously.

The lowering of skill requirements of foremen and the usurptions of their functions by the staff has had this effect—*any particular foreman, like any particular production worker, is easily replaceable.* This fact of industrial life of course has its impact on higher management's thinking. Managerial attitudes toward the foreman have been characterized by indifference in many instances. The foremen's response to indifference has shown up in attitude surveys as feelings of insecurity; in large part, insecurity played a major role as the motive behind the union organization movement of the foremen in the 1940's.

Figure 15–1 summarizes the factors in intermittent manufacturing which have had direct bearing on the lowering of the foreman's status. The dilemma of the foreman in intermittent manufacturing today is the product of industrial evolution. It could be said that the modern foreman represents an historical anachronism in the process of being phased out. In any event, it is useful to gain a perspective of current foreman problems from the standpoint of history.

HISTORICAL BACKGROUND

In 1920 Sanford E. Thompson related a conclusion he reached when he was a young man. He said that the nineteenth- and early twentieth-century foreman could not be effective unless he possessed a completely sulphurous vocabulary.[4] Another writer observed that the early foreman ". . . was picked . . . for two reasons, he knew his job technically and mechanically better than the others and he was aggressive; he would not spare himself and he could be depended upon that no one of his men lay down on the job."[5] In a description of the early foreman's job, Jones writes:

> The foreman is commonly the sole administrative agency of the shop. He is expected to look after tools and machines, find material and supplies for his men, instruct them in the manner of doing work, arrange tasks so that every one is kept busy, enforce a proper pace, write up the job cards and other records, preserve order, make orders and reports as requested concerning the progress of individual jobs, and give an opinion on which to base promotions and discharges.[6]

The early foreman filled the picture of the autocratic stereotype well. He disciplined and fired with impunity and he was arbitrary in the distribution of favors. The unchallenged authority of the foreman in the shop led John Golden of the United Textile Workers to remark that next to wages, the biggest problem of organized labor was "the autocracy of minor officials, including the foreman."[7]

The composite which emerges from this indicates that the early fore-

---

[4] Sanford E. Thompson, "The Foreman," *Bulletin of the Taylor Society,* February, 1920, p. 43.

[5] Charles W. Clark, "Field of the Foreman in Industry," *Industrial Management,* January, 1920, p. 18.

[6] Edward D. Jones, *The Administration of Industrial Enterprises* (New York: Longmans, Green and Co., 1926), p. 268.

[7] Quoted in Jones, see *ibid.,* p. 295.

man had uncommon responsibilities of both a technical and human nature. He was required to be a technical specialist, a shop administrator, and an enforcer of harsh labor policy. In respect to the latter responsibility, Sumner H. Slichter notes that the foundation of management's labor policy rested in crudity and the drive system. He points out further that labor policies were designed to overawe the worker with power, and that the foreman was the main instrumentality for accomplishing this end.[8]

But the foreman did not retain his pivotal position long after the turn of the century. It was evident to many writers in the 1920's, including Jones, Clark, and Thompson cited above, that a new type of foreman was emerging as a product of a number of industrial changes which undermined the foreman's power. Key among these were:

1. Management's labor relations philosophy.
2. Functional foremanship.
3. Growth of human relations idealism.

Management's Labor Relations Philosophy

Immediately following World War I, the "American Plan" was introduced. The purpose of this plan was to combat the union movement which had grown extensively during the war. As already stated in Chapter 2, the plan's strategy was to give the workers wage, hour, and "fringe" concessions directly which the unions hoped to achieve indirectly through organizing and collective bargaining.

A staff position introduced in industry shortly before 1920 came to act as the administrative agency for the American Plan. This position was best known under the title of "employment manager." It is interesting to note that the first major intrusion by a staff organization on foreman activities was in the area of personnel. Another quotation from Jones shows some of the results that this change was expected to have.

. . . the foreman is relieved of the importunities to hire the friends of the employees of his department. . . . He can no longer sell jobs, nor hold his favorites in soft assignments. He is deprived of the easy device of covering his own incompetence by firing a man.[9]

The outcomes of the employment manager's efforts were mixed, because so much depended on the effectiveness of the man in the job and the management philosophy under which he had to operate. A well-administered personnel program could beneficially eliminate a good deal of foreman arbitrariness. It must be remembered, however, that one of the chief motivating forces behind the establishment of the employ-

---

[8] Sumner H. Slichter, "The Management of Labor," *Journal of Political Economy*, December, 1919, pp. 814–16.

[9] Jones, *op. cit.*, p. 392.

ment manager was to offset the gains of organized labor and, for that matter, to destroy the union movement itself.[10] Alone, the American Plan did not constitute a fundamental change in management's attitude toward workers. It was a "soft sell" to convince workers they had nothing to gain by joining unions.

Management's labor relations philosophy is not the primary concern of this chapter. The main point is that the personnel function was the first major foreman activity to be diluted on a large scale by the growth of the staff.[11] Clark nicely characterized the impact of the change on the "old-fashioned" foreman when he said:

> This type of man [the autocratic foreman] is the man who at the present time is rubbing his eyes to find out where he stands. . . . He has hired men and fired them at will. The employer now organizes a new department called the "Personnel Department" and the men under the foreman's direction are hired and discharged according to a new-fangled scheme he does not understand.[12]

Functional Foremanship

Frederick W. Taylor introduced functional foremanship for the purpose of making intensive use of foreman specialization to render him a more valuable person to the company. The ironic consequence of functional foremanship was the undercutting of the position of the foreman in an unanticipated way.

Taylor observed that many foremen had abilities and specialties which were not used to their fullest extent. His solution to this waste of supervisory talent was to employ the foreman as overseer of those who were working in his area of specialty as well as overseer of those who fell within the administrative scope of his department. Thus, under functional foremanship the foreman would have dual responsibilities. He had functional responsibility for a certain specialized activity of operatives in another department; and he had general administrative responsibility for all the operatives in his own department regardless of the specialized jobs they performed.

---

[10] Of course, other important factors led to the creation of the personnel staff. The press of World War I focused attention on the ineffective use of human resources. Sources of all labor were drying up. Old wastes could not be tolerated as they were under the prevailing inadequacies of foremanship. Specialists in the form of employment managers were brought in to develop a science of work-force administration. See Paul H. Douglas, "Plant Administration of Labor," *Journal of Political Economy*, July, 1919, pp. 544–60. Another influence which cannot be overlooked is the scientific management movement. The application of scientific management principles to personnel administration was felt, especially by the Gilbreths, to be quite appropriate. These principles could be best applied if their execution was delegated to a specialist in personnel.

[11] See Henry Eilbirt, "The Development of Personnel Management in the United States," *Business History Review*, Autumn, 1959, pp. 359–64.

[12] Charles W. Clark, *op. cit.*, p. 18.

This obviously cumbersome arrangement was not accepted by industry in the form Taylor recommended. But functional foremanship was the genesis of the concept of *functional staff authority*. With this plan, a technical staff organization is delegated functional authority within a limited area of jurisdiction over a specialized area of line operations. For example, the foreman must be concerned with quality. However, in order to ensure the maintenance of quality many manufacturers established quality-control staff departments with authority over this functional area. In a very real sense the staff can exercise line authority over the foreman to guarantee his department is run in conformity to the quality standards the staff sets up and administers. The example of the quality-control staff applies equally well to other technical staff jurisdictions in a large manufacturing company.

The rising significance of the staff and the parallel decline of foreman status cannot, of course, be attributed to a plot of power-mad technocrats. One might conclude that the growth of the staff was inevitable, given the evolution of industry to higher forms of technology and greater degrees of complexity. The typical foreman simply was not equipped to cope adequately with specialized problems of control and engineering.

Industry was forced to accelerate its demands for more effective controls over quality, quantity, and cost. Additionally, manufacturers needed advanced planning and organizing efforts in the areas of product research and development, process engineering, work simplification and work standards. Faced with these needs, it is not surprising that the staff emerged in force, displacing the foreman from many of his traditional activities and imposing new imperatives which the foreman did not understand nor appreciate.

Growth of Human Relations Idealism

Much is made of the point today that the foreman, above and beyond everything else, *must be a leader of men*. The emphasis on leadership and the human relations responsibilities of the foreman is nothing new. Clark in 1920 said, "The former most important qualifications for foremanship . . . are eclipsed by the modern requirement that a foreman must know how to handle men."[13]

With his other functions reduced or denied him, it is obvious that the foreman is left with only the function of motivating. This is not to obscure the significance of the motivating activity. The foreman, as a competent leader, can go far to create the conditions necessary for an efficient and quality-conscious department. Also, by establishing a satisfactory "work climate" the foreman may be able to reduce labor turnover, gain the confidence of employees in the management of the company, sell

---

[13] Charles W. Clark, *op. cit.*, p. 18.

them on the value and legitimacy of their work, and reduce gripes, complaints, and grievances. In short, the foreman has a human relations laboratory to which he goes every day. The way he exercises his human skills can contribute immeasurably in the structuring of a co-operative system within the limits of his own department.

At first, management was slow to realize the true value of the human relations approach in dealing with operative employees. More than anything else, the Hawthorne studies brought home to management the importance of centering leadership on the satisfaction of human needs as a prerequisite for accomplishing organization goals without sacrifice of an individual's dignity.

After the initial impact of the Hawthorne studies, the human relations movement spread rapidly. First-line supervision was most affected, because it was felt that here the greatest gains could be made by the practice of "good human relations." This can be attested to by the number of human relations training programs for foremen undertaken with the blessing of higher levels of management. The outcomes of these programs have not been uniformly satisfactory. However, this is not the place for a discussion of human relations training. Let it suffice to say that the foreman's leadership role based on the principles of human relations loomed very large and management recognized the significance of this role by intensifying training for it.

It is evident that the foreman's job entails daily face-to-face contact with his subordinates. It is possible that the foreman has on the average more contacts with more subordinates than any other person in the management hierarchy. Thus, a certain expertness in interpersonal relationships is essential to his job. Further, this ability or "specialization" in leadership is something which cannot be delegated to a staff to perform. Motivation or leadership of subordinates on a face-to-face basis is most likely to remain a function uniquely associated with foremanship.

Yet, from the standpoint of the foreman leadership does not pay off. Precisely what does this mean? First, promotion is not based entirely on leadership potential. The "best" operative employees do not always make good leaders at the foreman level. Selection criteria for promotion purposes rest largely on technical qualifications. Hence, the foreman's position often is not filled by one who represents the best leadership risk. Second, the ability to lead and to motivate as a function relative to the functions of planning, organizing, and controlling, is not sufficiently recognized so that the status of the foreman can be elevated by it alone.

Consequently, while human relations idealism has not actually contributed to the deterioration of the foreman's status, neither has it raised it. The shifting of emphasis to motivation and leadership has not proven to be a substitute in compensating foremanship, statuswise, for its reduced scope in the other spheres of management activities.

Foreman Unionism

This section on historical background would not be complete without some words on the foreman's efforts to organize in the 1940's. It is not unusual to find foremen as card-carrying union members in the construction trades and in the maritime, printing, and railroad industries. In these cases, the foreman belongs to the rank and file union. Up until 1941, a union exclusively for foremen was a rarity.[14] In 1941, the foremen at Ford Motor Company decided to have a go at unionism and organized the Foreman's Association of America. Once established, this union made modest gains in the organization of foremen in other companies.

Several factors operating at this time made the emergence of a foreman's union understandable. First, it is interesting to note that the foreman's union began in the most intermittent of the intermittent manufacturers—the automotive industry. One major reason for the rise of the union can be attributed to the foreman's declining status and insecurity in intermittent manufacturing. The union movement of foremen was very likely their response to their frustrating position.[15]

Second, foremen were included within the scope of the labor law of this period. This meant that under the Wagner Act foremen could join unions and seek recourse for unfair labor practices in the event that employers interfered with their efforts to organize and bargain collectively.[16] This protection, of course, was an encouragement to organization. The employer could not legally thwart his foremen's efforts at collective self-determination.

And third, rank and file production workers were extensively organized in the late 1930's and early 1940's. Rather large gains accrued to them as a result of organization, particularly in seniority and wages.[17] Wage

---

[14] In 1939, the CIO chartered a foreman's union called the United Foremen and Supervisory Local Industrial Union #918 at Chrysler Corporation. This local was disbanded by an action of Philip Murray to overcome a bargaining impasse which developed between the UAW and Chrysler management.

[15] Robert C. Scigliano, "Trade Unionism and the Industrial Foreman," *Journal of Business*, October, 1954, pp. 297–98.

[16] The National Labor Relations Board vacillated on whether or not to include foremen within the scope of the act. Foremen were included up to 1942, but in 1943 the board excluded them. Then another shift in policy was made, returning the foremen to the provisions of the act. Finally, in the Packard case in 1947 the Supreme Court put its stamp of approval on this policy. But by this time the issue was quite academic, because the Taft-Hartley Act specifically excluded the foremen from the definition of "employee." "Thus while foremen remained free to organize and form unions, their employers were equally free to crush any such attempts by any of the retaliatory practices they were forbidden to use against ordinary unit workers." Charles O. Gregory, *Labor and the Law* (New York: W. W. Norton and Co., 1958), p. 348.

[17] Philomena Marquardt, "Foreman's Association of America," *Monthly Labor Review*, February, 1946, p. 241.

increases for production workers narrowed the pay differentials between them and the foreman. The results were demoralizing for the foremen, because often the production worker with overtime earned more in a week than his boss.

These general reasons set the stage for foreman unionism. Now, it might be asked why the FAA started at Ford Motor Company. The reasons can only be inferred. According to Smith, Ford had a policy of aggressive antiunionism until 1941. The foremen were carefully trained to fight organization efforts at the shop level. But in June 1941, Ford signed a union shop agreement with the UAW quite suddenly without advance notice to the foremen. As a result, foremen were caught between the antagonism of labor and the indifference of management.[18]

The foremen responded three months later, in September, 1941, by establishing their own union. They had 350 foremen to begin, and by the end of 1941 the FAA claimed 4,020 members, all at Ford. Ford granted the FAA recognition and bargained with it for over five years. The FAA struck at Ford in 1947, right at the time Congress was considering the Taft-Hartley Act. The foremen were utterly defeated. After the Taft-Hartley Act was passed the FAA lost one half its membership.[19]

The FAA was never a sparkling success. It had only two significant contracts, one with Ford and the other with Kaiser-Frazer. Even at its peak, the FAA organized only a fraction of the total foremen in America, with its strength concentrated in the Detroit area.

A number of reasons lie behind the failure of foreman unionism. First, and probably most significant, is that in general foremen are not union minded and the FAA had little appeal to them. Second, even during the time foremen were covered by the law employers bitterly opposed their unionization. The employers felt that a third party in the form of a union interfered with managerial prerogatives at the first level of supervision. As John S. Bugas, vice-president–industrial relations at Ford, noted: "The notion is false that supervisors can be dependent upon a union and still retain a primary loyalty to the job of supervising men and operations."[20]

The third, and very telling point, is also made by Bugas: "Supervisors cannot strike effectively without the support and cooperation of the rank-and-file union. And rank-and-file unions, fully conscious of the advantages to them in applying pressures on supervisors, are not likely to ignore the potential for reciprocal favors inherent in this situation."[21] Thus, without rank and file support FAA efforts to achieve goals would be severely impaired.

---

[18] Charles Copeland Smith, *The Foreman's Place in Management* (New York: Harper and Bros., 1946), pp. 49–50.

[19] Scigliano, *op. cit.*, p. 294.

[20] John S. Bugas, "Statement before the Senate Labor and Public Welfare Committee," April 15, 1953 (typed manuscript), p. 9.

[21] *Ibid.*, p. 7.

The passage of the Taft-Hartley Act was the last factor contributing to the failure of the FAA. The Taft-Hartley Act once and for all excluded foremen from the scope of the law. The legal tide against the foreman turned in 1947.

This brief history points out how the foreman's job was transformed over the years. It is a history with few bright spots. In large companies in the assembly industry, the machine paces the work, technical problems are solved by the staff, and the skill level of operative employees is low. Therefore, the foreman no longer sets the standards of performance for the group; he no longer does significant planning, organizing, or controlling in his department; and he no longer is able to protect his position by developing a high degree of competency in a specialized technical field.

The foreman is actually a policeman. He administers the work force and the job according to well-defined standards and policies emanating from the line and staff. He sees that the necessary paper work is completed. He acts as the first step in the settlement of worker grievances. Above all, the foreman's role, according to the experts, requires a good deal of human relations ability to maintain harmony in the department.

In summary, history has made the foreman expendable. That is, any particular foreman is easily replaceable, although a first line of supervision cannot be eliminated. More than anything else for the individual this ease of replaceability has been the most demoralizing consequence to result from the declining status of the foreman.

With the historical background and the current status of the foreman in mind, the next section discusses how the foreman of today sees himself and his job.

THE FOREMAN LOOKS AT HIMSELF AND HIS JOB

The foreman has been the object of a number of research studies. Consequently, considerable data are available on which to base this section concerning foremen attitudes, problems, and self-perceptions.

Foremen's Self-Perceptions Reflect Their Unique Position in the Manufacturing Process

Certain rigidities or role stereotypes are readily apparent in a manufacturing organization of some size. Roethlisberger[22] has summarized these rigidities as follows:

1. *Production workers* are supposed *to conform* to standards and changes that they do not originate.
2. *Foremen* are supposed *to uphold* or enforce standards of performance determined by other groups.

---

[22] Fritz J. Roethlisberger, "The Foreman's Dilemma," *Planning Supervisory Development* (American Management Association, Personnel Series #96, 1945), p. 7.

3. *Technical experts*, usually staff, are supposed *to originate* better ways of doing things.

4. *Top management* is supposed *to formulate* policies.

To Roethlisberger, these rigidities have the effect of insulating people into groups according to the role they play. This process of exclusion causes the individuals in a particular group to develop a common perspective regarding their own function, plus a warped view of the functions performed by other groups.

This conclusion is supported by a good deal of research. In a recent study, Porter pointed out that the foreman's self-perception is distinct from upper management and the line operative employee. The self-perceptions of the foremen are those of a different group compared with groups above and below them in the organizational hierarchy. Porter concludes that his study ". . . tends to show that the self-perception of the supervisors reflects their unique position in the structure of the organization. Their self-descriptions show certain differences from those of men they direct, but they also show somewhat the same differences from those of men who direct them."[23]

One feature of the foreman's position is the conflicting role expectations which impinge on him from many directions, in particular from those he supervises and from those who supervise him. As a result of these differing expectations, the foreman is forced to tread a fine line. He cannot completely satisfy one set of demands without forsaking another set. The only feasible course of action *is* compromise.[24]

Porter's study shows, quite in line with these observations, that the foreman's self-perceptions reveal him to be an individual acting with restraint and caution. The game he plays requires keeping peace among groups with different opinions of what constitutes effective foreman behavior. The foreman is usually aware of these conflicting expectations and he takes the only acceptable course of action. He compromises.

There are other dimensions to the foreman's unique position. As already noted, the foreman is the only individual in an organization with supervisory responsibility who does not supervise other managers. That the functions of foremanship provide the connecting link between policy levels of management and operative employees at the point of production is, indeed, quite unique. Whether or not this position is a "keystone" is debatable. However, it is certain that effective performance at this level of the organization is a major contribution to a company's success.

It is fair to say that foremen have an awareness of their peculiar role in

[23] Lyman W. Porter, "Self-Perceptions of First-Level Supervisors Compared with Upper-Management Personnel and with Operative Line Workers," *Journal of Applied Psychology*, June, 1959, p. 186.

[24] William S. Toddie, "When Foremen Feel 'Sacrificed'," *Personnel Journal,* October, 1957, pp. 170–73.

the organization. Stemming from this role are a number of conditions found by foremen to undermine their morale and effective performance.

Conditions Which Undermine Foreman Performance and Morale

Although not exhaustive, five major deficiencies in management policy and practice are cited by foremen as reducing their effectiveness and morale. These are: poor communication, little participation in management, disagreement regarding job responsibilities, compensation, and using foremanship as a training ground.

Communication. Probably the biggest foreman complaint, next to pay perhaps, is poor communication. Communication pertaining to policy matters seems to be weakest at the foreman level. Obviously, all policy considerations should not be transmitted to foremen. The foreman, however, ought to be appraised fully of policies which affect his job directly, and policies which stimulate him to identify with management.

In the first case, careful indoctrination in labor policy is a matter of crucial importance. The second case is more difficult. A foreman would find it hard to feel associated with management if he were not informed, at least in a general way, of top-level deliberations regarding the future directions of the company and the effect of such directions on supervision. It is unpleasant to work in the dark and not see the significance of one's activities as they relate to the over-all goals of the company.

The failure of the foremen's immediate supervisor to keep them appraised of their job performance is another communication deficiency frequently mentioned. Foremen complain they receive little praise for a well-done job; and they do not hear soon enough about their weak points.[25]

Little Voice in Policy Decisions. The second group of foreman complaints is in the area of participation in policy making. According to Mullen's findings, foremen feel they are given infrequent opportunity to voice their sentiments in labor negotiations.[26] If true, this is indeed a blind spot in management practice.[27] Because the foreman is in a strategic position in the administration of the labor agreement, it seems reasonable

---

[25] Some steps taken by management to overcome communication difficulties are reported by Wilmar F. Bernthal, "Foremanship: Business' Achilles' Heel?" *Business Horizons,* Spring, 1958, pp. 115–19.

[26] James H. Mullen, "The Supervisor Assesses His Job in Management: Highlights of a Nationwide Survey," *Personnel,* September, 1954, pp. 101–4.

[27] Contrary to Mullen's findings, a *Management Record* report indicates nearly all the firms in their survey solicited information from foremen relative to contract negotiations. Sixty-one of 213 firms allowed foremen to sit in on negotiations. Other firms obtained information in a variety of ways through conferences, questionnaires, and interviews. The conclusions indicated that foremen opinion was especially useful in seniority, wage, and discipline matters. See James J. Bambrick, Jr. and Marie P. Dorbandt, "Role of Foremen in Collective Bargaining," *Management Record,* January, 1957, pp. 2–5.

that he be provided with channels through which he can express his opinions about the content of the agreement.

In addition to the problem of nonparticipation in labor policy, the foreman would like to extend his authority and increase his voice in decisions relating to the over-all administrative aspects of his job. But there appears to be some discrepancy between what the foreman visualizes as the content of his job and what his boss sees as his responsibilities.

Disagreement Regarding Job Responsibilities. In large part the foreman's problems relating to job responsibilities are a matter of role definition. Herbert H. Meyer's study of this issue reveals a fairly high level of disagreement between the foreman's and his boss' conception of the foreman's job responsibility.[28] Interestingly enough, even the most effective foremen in the study disagreed with their general foreman on the content of their job as often as the least effective. Apparently, the level of foreman achievement, as appraised by the general foreman, was not a factor conditioning the degree of disagreement. The best foremen were as much at odds over the content of their jobs with their boss as the worst foremen.

Meyer concludes that:

Some of the disagreement between foremen and general foremen may very well be due to the nature of the foreman's job itself. . . . In almost every area of his job he shares responsibility with functional specialists. "When" jobs are to be performed is often dictated in part by production planning specialists, the "how" is taken care of by methods specialists, to what standards the work is done is determined by quality control specialists, and in the personnel area many of the foreman's responsibilities are shared with employee relations specialists.[29]

Thus, the scope of foremen authority and responsibility is complicated by functional staff groups. Where there is a large number of staff bodies the ambiguity of job definition is so great that the boss himself probably is not clear where his foremen's authority begins and ends. The real issue is not so much *what* the foreman is supposed to do but to what *degree* he possesses authority in a given area.

This issue is raised specifically in another study.[30] The question is: what authority does a foreman have over people who visit his department—for instance, maintenance men or quality-control inspectors. Does he have control over them? Is he responsible for their work? Almost three quarters of the bosses and supervisors in this report feel that the activities of

---

[28] Herbert H. Meyer, "A Comparison of Foreman and General Foreman Conceptions of the Foreman's Job Responsibility," *Personnel Psychology*, Autumn, 1959, pp. 445–52.

[29] *Ibid.*, p. 451.

[30] Lee E. Stern, "The Foreman's Job: What are the Boundaries?" *Supervisory Management*, July, 1958, pp. 15–23.

outsiders do fall in the scope of the foreman's jurisdiction. They are, however, uncertain as to the degree of this jurisdiction. For example, can the foreman assign work to the outsider? There seems to be no clear-cut answer to the whole problem of the extent of the foreman's authority over the staff.

The leadership characteristics which make a foreman effective constitute another area of disagreement pertaining to job responsibilities. Kay[31] conducted a study at a company of 600 employees and asked the foremen, their subordinates, and higher management what characteristics in their opinions made the most effective foreman. All three groups agreed on the following characteristics:

1. Ability to develop subordinates.
2. Practice of tact and discretion.
3. Ability to plan.
4. "Proper" behavior.
5. Willingness to assume responsibility.

The differences among the three groups are interesting. In addition to the above, higher management added:

1. Ability to think for himself.
2. Attention to detail.
3. Adherence to company policy.

The foremen added:

1. Ability to communicate.
2. Concern for worker welfare.
3. Ability to distinguish between important and unimportant work.
4. Concern for safety.

The subordinates added:

1. Communication with them.
2. Willingness to support them.
3. Respectful treatment.
4. No show of favoritism.

Kay's results, although different in detail, conform closely to the findings of other studies of "appropriate" foreman behavior. These common elements emerge:

1. The foremen, their subordinates, and executives above the foremen agree that "human skills" are essential for foreman effectiveness.

2. Higher management wants the foremen to police organization policy; in addition, as other studies show, they want the foreman schedule-production oriented.[32] This is especially true for foremen in assembly-type operations.

---

[31] Brian R. Kay, "What Makes an Effective Foreman?" *Supervisory Management*, May, 1959, pp. 2–12.

[32] See, for example, Edwin R. Fleishman, "Leadership Climate, Human Relations Training, and Supervisory Behavior," *Personnel Psychology*, Summer, 1953, pp. 205–23.

That there is perhaps a discrepancy between the human relations approach and the policing–production-orientation approach is evident here.

3. Subordinates are most attached to foremen who are considerate of them, respect and support them, and communicate with them.

Thus, the foreman and his subordinates see his job as requiring a good deal of expertness in human relations. The foreman's boss does too, but he adds what may be at times the contradictory requirement of schedule and output mindedness. The demands for consideration and production efficiency create a leadership dilemma for the foreman which in the final analysis often is solved by compromise.

Foreman Compensation. One notable deficiency undermines foreman effectiveness and even prevents foreman identification[33] with higher levels of management. That is the problem of compensation. The issue of narrowing pay differentials between first-line supervision and operative employees is keenly felt by foremen.

The problem of wage differentials is complex. There has been an over-all national trend for many years to narrow differentials among various skill levels of operative employees. This trend has also been observed between operative employees as a whole and the first line of supervision. Added to this historical trend is the problem of overtime pay. Foremen are exempt from the provisions of the wage and hour law whereas operatives are subject to it. This means that employers must pay operatives overtime while there is no such requirement for foremen.[34] Finally, the gains of organized labor have done much to reduce the pay gap between operative employees and foremen. In addition to achieving higher wage levels for production workers, many economic fringe benefits have been won by unions and introduced into the wage package. These gains include shift premiums, premiums for holidays, and pension and insurance plans.

Several recommendations[35] followed by a number of companies have

---

[33] Mullen makes the point that positive foreman attitudes toward his job and identification with management correlate more highly with level of earnings than with other variables like age, seniority, or education. See Mullen, *op. cit.*, p. 107.

[34] Many employers voluntarily pay foremen overtime. One survey showed that of 345 companies, 201 paid overtime. The reasons given for paying overtime were to maintain differential, to apply overtime policy equally, and to preserve the ability of the company to attract and hold qualified supervisors. Nicholas L. A. Martucci, "Overtime Pay Practices for Exempt Supervisors," *Management Record*, April, 1959, pp. 110–13, 134–38.

[35] Robinson makes the comment that the emphasis on salary differential is misplaced. He says attention is focused on foreman-subordinate differentials, not on foreman-management differentials. Further, he observes, "This type of sustained emphasis and attention to the problem of proper differentials orients the foreman-compensation thinking toward the hourly-rated workers, rather than toward other management personnel. It confuses the foreman's own thinking as to his true status in the organization." See Carl W. Robinson, "A Critical Look at Foreman Compensation," in

been offered to attack the wage differential problem. They fall into five categories.

1. Use a higher base rate, with a built-in adjustment factor to compensate for upward movements in the base rates of production employees.
2. Pay overtime.
3. Allow foreman participation in executive compensation plans such as profit sharing, bonuses, and the like.
4. Relate foreman fringe benefits to an executive scale rather than the scale used for production workers.
5. All-in-all management should be concerned with maintaining adequate foreman-operative differentials on a gross annual earnings basis. Week-to-week fluctuations in differentials are not too important.

Foremanship as a Training Ground. The practice of using the foreman's job as a step in executive development can be extremely galling to old-line supervision. Historically, the job of the foreman, despite its frustrations and shortcomings, was looked upon by ambitious production workers as a career opportunity. Once achieved, the individual settled into it without anticipation of further promotion, much like a master sergeant in the Army or a chief petty officer in the Navy.

The glow of achievement in obtaining this position has been dampened by the practice in some companies of using the supervisory job as a training ground for management recruits. Side by side with foremen who "came up the hard way" are youngsters just out of college enjoying their first "real" job. This fact alone is enough to take the edge off a career foreman's ardor. Certainly the significance of his accomplishment is reduced. To him, management apparently considers his job such that anyone—regardless of tangible experience—can fill it. Added to this, management trainees are a transient lot. They move about to different departments; they move up the promotion ladder; or they quit or are fired. In any event the whole business is rather demoralizing to one who sees his career objective tampered with in such a cavalier fashion.

* * *

Several points have been established in this section. The foreman is in a unique position in the organization; he perceives it as such; and his behavior reflects his perception. The foreman's position generates problems peculiar to the role he has to play. Inherent in these problems are the conditions just discussed which undermine the foreman's performance

---

Building Up the Supervisor's Job (American Management Association, Manufacturing Series #213, 1953), pp. 19–26.

Whatever merits Robinson's argument might have, it obscures one important fact. *The foreman knows what his subordinates make;* he probably has only a foggy idea of what his boss makes; and he probably has no idea of what "other management personnel" makes. So if the foreman is going to engage in invidious comparisons on the matter of pay they will be between himself and his subordinates where he has data to compare.

and morale. These conditions are largely a result of deficiencies in management policy and practice. Actually, however, the problem fore-manship faces is deeper than the deficiencies described above; they are just symptomatic of the declining status of the foreman. Many companies are conscientiously treating these symptoms in an effort to improve the attitudes and performance of supervision. However, the fundamental cause remains. The status of the foreman will not improve until he is able to make a greater economic contribution to the firm. And this can be accomplished only by supervising individuals of a higher skill level.

THE FOREMAN—A MARGINAL MAN

The decline of the foreman's status, his singular role in the organiza-tional hierarchy, and his perception of the problems associated with this role combine to give the picture of a "marginal man," as Donald Wray dubbed him a number of years ago. This appelation has remained as-sociated with first-line supervision ever since.[36]

Marginality in the case of the foreman means that he is on the periphery of the main stream of industrial events. He is by-passed. Marginal roles in society are common, but they are nonetheless un-comfortable to fill. The foreman is neither fish nor fowl in terms of his industrial status. He is not a worker nor has he had much success with the trappings of unionism so effective for the status of production workers. He is told he is part of management but he has little tangible evidence in the form of acceptance accompanied by the symbols of executive status. It is reasonable to say that the foreman is in a group unto itself, isolated from the technical staff, the higher line executives, and the production workers. It is a group which:

1. Does not enjoy the high status the *staff* derives from technical specializa-tions.
2. Does not participate in the high status of *line executives* based on au-thority positions in the scalar chain.
3. Does not have the security of *production workers* based on the collec-tive strength of organized labor.

Thus, the gains which any of these groups accomplish in the industrial world stem from their own peculiar characteristics of organizational power and influence and do not necessarily accrue to the foremen. Such is marginality!

Implications of Being Marginal

Gains and losses are associated with the individual's decision to partici-pate in any organization. The losses to marginal groups seem to be dis-proportionately large. Some of these losses are brought out next.

---

[36] Donald E. Wray, "Marginal Men of Industry: The Foremen," *American Journal of Sociology*, January, 1949, pp. 298–301.

Trait Differentials among Organization Personnel. Ghiselli's study of traits found among individuals at various organization levels shows some interesting differentiating characteristics.[37] Ghiselli divided the organization structure into four categories—top management, middle management, lower (supervisory) management, and production workers. These groups were compared by measuring the traits of intelligence, supervisory ability, initiative, self-assurance, and occupational level. The last trait involved measuring the accuracy of role perception of individuals in the four groups.

Ghiselli found that:

1. Top and middle management score much higher than lower management and production workers and are, therefore, quite distinct from them on the basis of the above traits.

2. The differences in trait-measurement scores between lower management and production workers are negligible.

The findings of this study show that the foremen were quite similar to the people they supervised but quite different from higher management levels, from the standpoint of the traits measured. It is questionable therefore that any differentiation between foremen and production workers can be made on the basis of traits. The major distinguishing feature between these two groups is found in the amount of authority and responsibility accruing to them from their position in the formal organization. This distinction is sufficient in itself to insulate the foremen from production workers.

As expected, the trait differences between higher management and foremen are dramatic. The foremen are insulated, therefore, from middle and top management not only by differences in degrees of formal authority but also by great differences in intelligence, initiative, supervisory ability, and so on.

Although not conclusive, these thoughts at least suggest that the foreman's personality and motives are more closely akin to production workers than to the executives above him. Foremen are, however, separated from production workers by the rigors of the formal structure of authority in organizations. Hence, foremen constitute a separate group founded on personality traits and formal authority. As such, the foreman is prevented from participating with real effectiveness in the affairs of either higher management or production workers. Now, what can be said regarding the uniqueness of the work of the foreman?

The Boundaries of Foremanship. Reducing the foreman's job to a planning, organizing, motivating, and controlling form of analysis is useful for an insight into the nature of his work. Figure 15–2 shows the management functions with specific foremen activities peculiar to them.

---

[37] Edwin E. Ghiselli, "Traits Differentiating Management Personnel," *Personnel Psychology*, Winter, 1959, pp. 535–44.

FIGURE 15–2

FOREMAN ACTIVITIES WITHIN THE SCOPE OF MANAGEMENT

FUNCTIONAL AREAS

Planning Organizing	Motivating	Controlling
1. Personnel requirements, manpower allocations, work assignments. ←———→	1. Induction and orientation. 2. Training.	1. Quality. 2. Cost. 3. Production.
2. Materials, tools, and equipment needed for current operations, replacements, and program changes. ←———→	3. Rating and classification. 4. Settling gripes, complaints, and grievances.	4. Man hours. 5. Expenditures of materials, tools, and equipment.
3. Methods improvement. ←———→	5. Safety. 6. Leadership of subordinates to goal accomplishment.	

Listing activities, as in Figure 15–2, is useful but tends to hide the qualitative and quantitative aspects of the foreman's job. It does bring out one point, however. The foreman still performs work in all management functions, in spite of the limitations placed on planning, organizing, and controlling activities. The foreman's work in these latter areas is dominated by routine and detail with most of it involving policing programs and plans passed on to him by staff groups or higher line executives for performance at the operative level.

Figure 15–2 also brings out another point. It is difficult to distinguish between the planning and the organizing functions performed by the foreman. His activities, shown in Figure 15–2, overlap these functions. The nature of foreman planning is short range. The futurity of his considerations seldom extends further than a month ahead and is largely involved with daily and weekly adjustments to meet changing production situations. The quantities of manpower, tools, and equipment that the foreman plans for are intimately associated with the organization of work in his department. Hence, when a foreman thinks ahead about his personnel needs it is difficult to say whether he is engaging in a planning activity or an organizing activity. A "pure" foreman planning activity which constitutes a regular part of his job is difficult to conjure up.

The function of control is the area which involves the foreman in much administrative detail. Control in the various spheres of cost, manpower, quality, and so on requires the foreman to relay quantitative data on performance to functional staff groups as well as his own boss. A good deal of the foreman's time is used in filling out records and reports for interested groups that have established performance standards. While the foreman is required to maintain control systems and to feed back control information, he has very little to say about setting the standards against which his effectiveness is measured. The job of the foreman as a policeman is never more evident than in the control function.

The motivating function contains the significant features of the foreman's job. He is paid mainly to be a "handler" of men. As a motivator his activities range from such generalities as stimulating his men to accomplish objectives to specifics as on-the-job training and settling grievances. So it seems that beyond all else the foreman must be a human relations expert.

On Being a Human Relations Expert. One conclusion seems to emerge from the tortured body of leadership theory. *Leadership is situational.* There is no single criterion to recommend to foremen upon which they can base their leadership perspectives.

Likert calls effective supervision "an adaptive and relative process."[38] When leading, the foreman should realize that subordinates' reaction to a supervisory act is dependent on the *meaning* of the act to the subordinate and not the objective nature of the act itself. Foremen should also be aware that the effectiveness of their leadership depends on their awareness and sensitivity to subordinates' needs, values, and interpersonal relationships. So to be a good leader the foreman must sense and react positively to the individual differences of each subordinate.

These observations are probably quite valid. Plenty of evidence is available to support the hypothesis that subordinates respond most favorably to considerate foremen. But there is also evidence to support the view that the foreman's boss judges effectiveness on departmental output as well as on the harmony and happiness of the foreman's work group.[39] This leads Lachman to comment that the foreman is right in the middle. He is accused of poor human relations if people are happy but the job does not get done. And he is accused of poor human relations if an individual or two in his group is unhappy but the job does get done.[40]

Foreman Morale. It is easy enough to state glibly that the foreman's morale is low. Certainly, the factor of marginality plus the deficiencies observed in management policy and practice would make such a universal statement tempting. Morale, however, is an individual's state of mind; it is not an attribute of a group as amorphous as "the foremen."

---

[38] Rensis Likert, "Effective Supervision: An Adaptive and Relative Process," *Personnel Psychology*, Autumn, 1958, pp. 317–32.

[39] Robert O. Besco and C. H. Lawshe, "Foreman Leadership as Perceived by Superiors and Subordinates," *Personnel Psychology*, Winter, 1959, pp. 573–82.

[40] M. S. Lachman, "The Supervisor Hasn't a Chance," *Advanced Management*, November, 1958, pp. 17–18.

The morale level of foremen is at once a question of relativity and a question of individual reactions to his role. In the first instance, if the foreman's morale is high or low, to what other individual or group of individuals is he being compared? It is of scant encouragement to find that foremen's morale on the "average" is higher in a company than the morale of the operative employees. This is particularly true when the same company finds that the morale of the foremen is lower than other levels of management, on the "average." A discovery of this type simply reinforces the case of foreman insulation from management and reduces the possibility of foreman identification with higher-level executives.

In the second instance, no two individuals react exactly the same to the demands of their role. Certain generalized behavioral patterns may indeed develop, but the proof of the relationship between morale and foreman performance must be tested in each and every department. One of the consequences of generalizing about foreman morale is the hasty introduction of poorly conceived paneceas. Foreman training in human relations is an example of such a faddish cure-all.

At one time, wide-scale human relations training for foremen was thought to be a solution which would cause the foremen to identify more with management and to improve their human skills simultaneously. The success of foreman training in accomplishing these objectives is questionable. The morale of the foreman probably would be improved universally by more money (perhaps a prorata share of the cost of the training program) and a clarification of the scope of his job.

All in all, it is not surprising to hear talk of low foreman morale. But at the same time, for the practical purposes of a company it is useful to locate both specific morale trouble spots and specific cases of high foreman morale. In both situations it is more than necessary to find tangible reasons for the level of morale.

Foreman Identification with Management

There is no doubt that the foreman is part of management, at least from the standpoint of the logic of formal organizational theory. The issue is whether or not the foreman "feels" he is part of management. A direct or easy analysis of this issue is impossible.[41] The evidence offered in this chapter points to the conclusion that if the foreman identifies at all, it is with his own group.

Being a distinct group *between* other groups is not abnormal in itself. The foreman's role has its dual aspects. He must lead production workers and empathize with their problems. He must also support management policies and pursue goals set by higher executives. As Walker and

---

[41] See M. J. Balma, J. C. Maloney, and C. H. Lawshe, "The Role of the Foreman In Modern Industry: III; Some Correlates of Foreman Identification with Management," *Personnel Psychology*, Winter, 1958, pp. 535–44.

his associates point out, the danger is that the foreman does not appre-ciate this duality. He may "overidentify" with production workers or management.[42] Overidentification in either direction could reduce fore-man effectiveness as leader of the operative group on the one hand, or as a member of management charged with managerial responsibilities on the other.

Those who insist on unequivocal foreman identification with manage-ment do not realize what a paradoxical situation this creates. It asks the foreman to identify with a group which appears to have personality char-acteristics quite dissimilar from his own. It asks the foreman to go against the nature of the role he plays as intermediary of two very diverse groups. And it asks the foreman to overlook all those conditions of mar-ginality and deficiencies in practice which have separated him from other executives.

Perhaps, when all is said, it would be better to look on foremen as a distinct group, one of a number of such groups created by industrial change. If the uniqueness of the foreman group is accepted, then it is pos-sible to treat with greater effectiveness the problems of status, communi-cation, authority, compensation, and the leadership and technical needs that are peculiar to this group.

So much for the current issues. What now can be said for the future of foremanship?

THE FUTURE OF FOREMANSHIP

Massive upward shifts of operative skill levels in intermittent manufac-turing are essential to a general upgrading of foreman status. This conclu-sion has been stated before. Management may treat symptoms of low, meager status, or management can redefine the foreman's job,[43] but the only lasting cure for the status problems of the foreman is to provide conditions in which he has the opportunity to make a greater economic contribution to the firm.

Automation is one of the products of changing technology. The ef-fect of automation on upgrading skill levels is not altogether clear. James R. Bright questions the proposal that automation will result in a significant upgrading of the labor force.[44] One consequence of automation will be to displace large quantities of direct labor. The direct labor that does remain in a company after automation is not likely to be any more

---

[42] Charles R. Walker, Robert H. Guest, and Arthur N. Turner, *The Foreman on the Assembly Line* (Cambridge: Harvard University Press, 1956), pp. 135–38.

[43] See "'Upgrading' Foremen with an Ax," *Business Week*, February 11, 1961, pp. 110, 112.

[44] James R. Bright, "Does Automation Raise Skill Requirements?" *Harvard Business Review*, July–August, 1958, pp. 85–98.

skilled than the assembly workers who have gone before them. So supervisors of direct labor in an automated factory probably will not enjoy any higher status than the production-line foreman does today; but their number will be reduced substantially.

The hope of higher status for foremanship lies in the supervision of certain categories of *indirect* labor required by automation. It is well to quote Bright on the specific nature of these labor classes.

1. New types of setup work may require extraordinary education-skill increases as in computer or numerically controlled machine tool programming work.

2. Machine design and building skills required are increased significantly.

3. Some classes of maintenance work show severe increases in skill requirement. . . . There is evidence of need for a new kind of "over-all machine repairman" who understands *all* the control technologies and has superior ability at "trouble-shooting."[45]

Obviously the type of foremen who supervise labor in these skill categories needs high technical competence indeed. Foremanship in the future under automation will be different than what is known of it today. The future foreman may be the analogue of his earlier predecessor—the skilled craftsman who was head of the shop. Ironically, just as it was innovation which displaced the foreman who was the master craftsman, so is it also innovation which may restore the status of the foreman by demanding higher degrees of technical competence.

Technological change causes shifts in employment patterns. It should not be anticipated that the foremen now supervising assembly operations will be upgraded, *as individuals*, into higher-status jobs. The function of first-line supervision will remain in automated plants but the activities of this function will be discharged by different people possessing the requisite skills. Therefore, the future of the typical modern foreman in intermittent manufacturing is not bright. The probability is high that he will be displaced because his job is eliminated. At the same time, he will find difficulty relocating because he does not have the skill necessary to supervise technical indirect labor.

The advent of the new foreman will be just as fast as industrial transition permits. The modern assembly foreman will probably be phased out slowly, but perhaps never completely. However, it may be stated plausibly that as industry introduces new technologies in production the foreman of today will become less common. The problem of modern foreman status may never be solved; it may just cease to exist.

REVIEW QUESTIONS

1. Why is the foreman in intermittent manufacturing singled out for special treatment?

[45] James R. Bright, *Automation and Management* (Boston: Graduate School of Business Administration, Harvard University, 1958), p. 187.

2. Discuss the major factors which have contributed to the decline of the foreman's status.

3. Contrast the earlier foreman's role with that of the modern foreman.

4. In what indirect way did Taylor's concept of functional foremanship contribute to the deterioration of foreman status?

5. Outline the developments which led to foreman unionism.

6. "One feature of the foreman's role is the conflicting role expectations which impinge on him from many directions." Discuss.

7. Discuss the deficiencies in management policy and practice which undermine foreman performance and morale.

8. What is meant by the statement that the foreman is a marginal man?

9. Discuss the implications of trait differentials found among organizational personnel. To what extent do these differentials support the argument that foremen are a separate group from operative employees and higher management levels?

10. Discuss the effects automation may have on foreman status.

SUPPLEMENTARY READINGS

BERNTHAL, WILMAR F. "Foremanship: Business' Achilles' Heel?" *Business Horizons*, Spring, 1958, pp. 111–19.

GHISELLI, EDWIN E. "Traits Differentiating Management Personnel," *Personnel Psychology*, Winter, 1959, pp. 535–44.

SCIGLIANO, ROBERT C. "Trade Unionism and the Industrial Foreman," *Journal of Business*, October, 1954, pp. 293–300.

" 'Upgrading' Foremen with an Ax," *Business Week*, February 11, 1961, pp. 110–12.

WRAY, DONALD E. "Marginal Men of Industry: The Foremen," *American Journal of Sociology*, January, 1949, pp. 298–301.

CHAPTER 16

The Executive and His Roles

THE functions of management are ubiquitous, and so too are the professional managers who are found in business, government, private nonprofit organizations, and even in labor unions. The professional executive is indeed a key figure in our times. He is strategically placed in crucial decision roles, and his actions have such far-reaching influence that some writers have spoken of a managerial revolution.

This chapter explores some facets of the business executive's behavior and personality as they are manifested in his job. Also considered are the intricacies of the role of the executive and the problems he encounters in his climb up the promotional ladder. The following chapter treats some of the broader implications of management practice within the framework of the corporation.

The manager in the business organization is the central focus of this chapter. A good deal of research has been done on executive groups in industry; this chapter draws on much of this work. Most of these studies have divided the executive segment of the organization into four groups for comparative purposes. Lateral studies have been made of line and staff executives. Vertical comparisons have been drawn between various levels of executives in the managerial hierarchy. Since the problems of line-staff relations are considered in previous chapters, they are not treated in detail here. The main distinctions made among executives in this chapter rest on differentiating personality and role characteristics found in the organization strata.

THE JOB

The first step in this discussion of management is to look at the job. This must be done in a generalized way. It is traditional to state that the job of management is planning, organizing, motivating, and controlling. More recently, some writers have viewed management functions as communicating, decision making, and resolving conflicts. All these activities are part of the management process. They are important, but they reveal little of the people who perform them.

Rather than a process, it is more valuable in the context of this book to look upon the manager's job as a role. By knowing something of the dimensions of the role inferences may be drawn regarding the sorts of personalities in it. Every role has a counterpart in a personality. The individual generally will accept the role that he knows best, believes in, and finds rewarding. In other words, the personality of an individual may modify a role to some degree but it is more likely that people are preselected, drifting into roles to which they are readily adaptable.[1] And so it is with the role of the executive and the kinds of people who play it.

It is difficult, if not impossible, to talk of *an* executive role. Higher levels of management comprise no more a homogeneous body than do the foremen. Take the breakdown between middle and top management, for example. A company does not have to get too large before considerable distinctions appear separating middle managers from those on top. Rifts begin to show along several dimensions of the managerial role. Although these distinctions are indeed matters of degree, the degree itself often is of such a magnitude as to make the role barrier between the two groups quite insurmountable for the bulk of lower-level executives.

Facets of Management Roles

The six role dimensions described below are found in all managerial jobs. They are really forms of role expectations which adhere to a greater or lesser degree to all the levels of the executive hierarchy.

TABLE 16–1

COMPARISON OF TIME PERSPECTIVES OF DECISION SITUATIONS
AT FOUR LEVELS OF MANAGEMENT

Time	*Works Manager, Per Cent*	*Division Superintendent, Per Cent*	*Department Foreman, Per Cent*	*Shift Foreman, Per Cent*
Short (0–2 weeks)	3.3	54.2	68.0	97.7
Moderate (2 weeks to year)	46.1	41.4	30.4	2.1
Distant (one year and beyond)	50.0	4.3	1.5	0.0
Total	99.4	99.9	99.9	99.8

SOURCE: Norman H. Martin, "Differential Decisions in the Management of an Industrial Plant," *Journal of Business*, October, 1956, p. 251. Copyright 1956, by the University of Chicago. Used with permission.

The Time Dimension in Decisions. Top management must think in terms of long-run strategies. As one goes down the executive hierarchy the extent of futurity in programs and decisions is shorter. Part of Martin's research, shown in Table 16–1, gives evidence of this phenomenon.

[1] William E. Henry, "The Business Executive: The Psychodynamics of a Social Role," *American Journal of Sociology*, January, 1949, p. 286.

Martin's data reveal that of the total decisions made by managers in the plant studied, the highest percentage of decisions with the greatest futurity is found at upper echelons. From these results one would anticipate that management at levels above the works manager would be involved in even higher percentages of distant decisions.

Besides the span of the time perspective, a qualitative difference is found among the decisions at various organization levels. Speaking of higher management levels, Martin says, "Because the true meaning of an event cannot be ascertained until it is actualized, one of the consequences of being involved in situations of distant time perspective is that the executive is in a difficult position to judge correctly the value and meaning of intervening events."[2] Essentially this means that the longer the time span between the decision and the result the harder it is to appraise the quality or "correctness" of any particular decision. Thus, top management lives in a world clouded by uncertainty. It includes not only uncertainty of the future but also uncertainty of the true success or failure of decisions which are matters of record. This is partially attributed to the complexity of the organizational system, where easy separation of causes and effects is impossible.

As the management scale is descended, the time perspective shortens. It is simpler, consequently, to assign specific results as products of specific decisions. The decisions themselves at lower organizational levels increase in frequency but are more highly structured, dealing with more objective and tangible alternatives.

The decisions made by top management generally are quite subjective. But these decisions will affect the future of the company well beyond the time of an executive's tenure in it. The decisions he makes are fewer but more far-reaching than his subordinates. Down the hierarchy, the tempo of decision making increases. However, the alternatives are more concrete and the results of the decisions are more rapidly forthcoming. Thus, lower management decisions, from the standpoint of the time perspective, do not require the degree of "risk," "vision," or "intuition" demanded of top management.

Sense of Mission. The perception of the proper relation of the company to its environment is fundamental to the role of top management. This facet of the management role requires mature judgment of organizational objectives as they relate reciprocally to social values. Kissinger has underscored the importance of reflective thought and creativity to aid in implementing the perception factor of the management role. Kissinger warns, however, "One of the paradoxes of an increasingly specialized,

---

[2] Norman H. Martin, "Differential Decisions in the Management of an Industrial Plant," *Journal of Business,* October, 1956, pp. 251–52.

bureaucratized society is that the qualities rewarded in the rise to eminence are less and less the qualities required once eminence is reached."[3]

Stress is placed at lower management levels on the so-called technical skills. Such skills are necessary because of the specialized functions prevailing in the lower echelons. The middle manager develops proficiencies in these routines. Technical competence, however, is not necessarily related to the leadership and creative needs required as he moves up.[4]

The Setting of Shorter-Range Goals. Top management sets the targets to make it possible for others below them to interact. Top management stages activities at lower management levels and gives direction to them. Of course, the shorter-range goals are implemented by middle management, and implementation must always be consistent with the over-all objectives or mission. Top management, functioning in a control capacity, insures such consistency. There are dangers here of the sort already discussed in Chapter 12 on bureaucracy.

Stated again, as organizations get bigger it is more difficult for the top manager to preserve consistency between the objectives of programs of different time durations. That is, priority may be given at lower management levels to the accomplishment of short-range goals to the disadvantage of the broader mission. To counteract this possibility, the top executive depends upon subordinates to brief him on policy and performance at lower organizational levels. Out of this situation develops the specialist in briefing, who is frequently given to making biased interpretations. Over-reliance on staff advice can undermine the top executive's judgment and perspective. The chief executive has to maintain some independence from the judgment of lower levels in the organization so that he is able dispassionately to integrate and co-ordinate short-range goals with long-range strategies.

Combining and Utilizing Resources. At any level in an organization, but particularly at the highest levels, co-ordination is a consuming job. Intimate knowledge of mission and shorter-range objectives is the only route to successful co-ordination. But this is far from being the whole story. Top management must balance time. It has to weigh the attention given to internal co-ordination with the demands on it to abstract from the organization and to view the company, in its total context, in relation to its setting. Top management must have the ability to detach itself from

---

[3] Harry A. Kissinger, "The Policy Maker and the Intellectual," *The Reporter*, March 5, 1959, p. 30.

[4] Leavitt and Whisler see the elimination of routine middle management jobs as a result of breakthroughs in information technology. The consequences of the new technologies will be to reduce the number of middle managers. Those remaining will do more creative work of the type associated with top management. See Harold J. Leavitt and Thomas L. Whisler, "Management in the 1980's," *Harvard Business Review*, November–December, 1958, pp. 41–48.

the internal imperatives of co-ordination and to reflect on the general purposes and objectives of the company in its industry and society.

Only top management is required to do this kind of thinking as part of its role. Middle management's scope does not extend greatly beyond the horizons of its activities. So it is expected that middle management attends to internal co-ordinative problems. As a result, much middle management thinking is circumscribed by the boundaries of the company and for that matter even specific jobs. This consideration constitutes a formidable role barrier between middle and top management.

The Socratic Approach.   Top management questioningly evaluates the ideas brought up from below. In this respect, top management is both teacher and judge of subordinates in an ultimate sense. Such a role requires infinite patience and sensitivity to the interactions among people below and the material resources with which they work. Top management, therefore, has the final obligation for training and for structuring an effective staff of executives that will be thoroughly oriented and equipped to carry out the missions and programs assigned to it.

"Aloneness."   Top managers, by the nature of their role, are often detached from outside judgment or objective criteria against which they can appraise their approach to problems, their decisions, and their philosophy. The production worker has a skill accompanied by a tangible output which is a source of justification and a criterion of performance. The foreman's role, though ambiguous, has at least one objective measure in terms of department efficiency. The staff has a high degree of specialized training, and, at times, "professional" standards against which performance is judged. Middle and upper-middle management get into the twilight zone, but here managers can look to numerous colleagues for support and appraisal. Top management enjoys few of the advantages just enumerated for subordinates. Partially, its problem of aloneness stems from the long time span of decision and the subjectivity of the job. Additionally, the number of top managers is limited, restricting the extent of support and critical commentary available from colleagues.

All members of management tend to look to their own reference groups and their immediate superiors for backing and critical appraisal. Top management is not unusual in this respect. Where intangibles, intuition, uncertainty, and subjectivity are involved in action, the manager naturally turns to colleagues facing similar circumstances for vindication of his attitudes and behavior. Middle management finds reference groups within the company. Top management, however, frequently has to turn outside to colleagues at similar levels in different companies to "talk out" problems of philosophy, and to participate in mutual admiration cliques.

Aloneness has a number of behavioral by-products. Several of these are the attitudes of optimism, rationality, realism, and practicality which appear to be ingrained in the American business executive's ideology.[5] These attitudes are probably necessary concomitants of a role which requires decisive action in spite of risks and lack of sources for the justification of the legitimacy of decisions. Such attitudinal expressions are not unlike whistling while walking past a graveyard at midnight.

Quite the opposite of the above attitudes is the contrary aspect of aloneness which frequently forces the individual into assuming a conservative posture. There often is more pressure on an individual when he makes a mistake than when he fails to take advantage of an opportunity. Particularly at higher organizational levels, foregone opportunities are debatable as to whether they *were* indeed opportunities in the first place.[6] Top management must be constantly aware of this human tendency lest valuable alternatives pass by it.

Another by-product of aloneness is the committee, which Kissinger says is often more a spiritual necessity than a decision-making device.[7] The committee offers support and a degree of anonymity to individuals. It is something of a defense against individual responsibility when making decisions for action. The motivations to use the committee tool are complex; many companies have adopted it as a problem solving-morale building device. The committee, however, as a bulwark against aloneness must be considered among the motivations.[8]

Accompanying these aspects of management roles are the pressures or strains which are in evidence in the executive's job. Some of these are outlined below.

Pressures in the Management Role[9]

Pressures for Achievement. The modern executive must compete for success—and compete not only with other companies and their managements but also with colleagues in the executive's company. He usually will compete on the basis of his own specialty, particularly if the executive is in the staff or middle management in the line. As a result—and this often is frustrating—the executive's other talents and interests are allowed to atrophy.

The executive's achievements, or lack of them, are measured against

---

[5] See Francis X. Sutton, Seymore E. Harris, Carl Kaysen, and James Tobin, *The American Business Creed* (Cambridge: Harvard University Press, 1956), chap. 5.

[6] Kissinger, *op. cit.*, p. 31.

[7] *Ibid.*, pp. 31–32.

[8] Once established as part of operational procedures, committees are infrequently abandoned. For a discussion of why U.S. Rubber Company *eliminated* committee management see "U.S. Rubber Moves Ahead," *Business Week*, October 22, 1960, pp. 101–11.

[9] Unless noted otherwise, the following treatment of strains in executive roles is adapted from Sutton *et al.*, *op. cit.*, chap. 16.

those of his associates. This is not say there is no abstract or generalized success criterion. There is. But usually such a criterion is expressed in qualitative terms such as efficiency, profitability, rate of growth, and so on. More infrequently is success measured qualitatively. Thus, size alone is a success criterion and constitutes a claim for achievement.

Pressures for Change.   Change and the quest for novelty are an occupational hazard of managers, with the exception of executives in stagnant organizations. Pressures for change are initiated by competition and by internal demands in the organization. Change is common in a dynamic society and managers must accept it as part of their job. Survival demands an initiative and flexibility without which the executive cannot survive.

Executive adaptation to change requires more than a state of mind predisposed in this direction. It requires a life pattern adjusted to the possibility of frequent movement about the country while moving up the promotional ladder. Not only the executive but also his family absorbs the brunt of change, to say nothing of the community in which he lives as something like a migrant worker.

The Pressures of Uncertainty.   No greater strain exists than that of the uncertain and hostile environment in which the executive must act. This environment creates situations in which there are discrepancies between the effort expended by the executive and the rewards derived. Therefore, considerable effort is often repaid with only marginal success or often complete failure. The executive, however, is judged on outcomes, not effort.

The presence of uncertainty causes most executives to think in terms of the controllable and uncontrollable factors in his environment. The controllables represent some factors over which he has the power to reduce or eliminate uncertainty. Naturally, the executive attempts to increase the scope of his power over these factors. Ordinarily, the uncontrollables in the environment are thought as consumer sovereignty, the government, community acceptance, price and availability of raw materials, and, of course, competition. But even here the efforts of management in advertising, political action, public relations, reciprocal agreements with suppliers, and mergers act to bring these conventional uncontrollables into the sphere of managerial influence. Consequently, the pressure of uncertainty extends the boundaries of the manager's job well beyond the traditional limits of the firm itself.

The Pressure for Conformity.   The vehicle for administrative action is the organization. It is the structure in which executives work. Employment in a company requires the individual to make certain sacrifices largely in terms of his freedom of action and expression. The executive is expected to conform to rules, regulations, and policies. For his sacrifices and contributions to the company the individual receives rewards.

Some writers, like William H. Whyte, Jr., see in the organization a manifestation of all that is evil in the social ethic.[10] He notes that some companies are demanding far more conformity from executives than they have the moral right to expect. The upshot of this evil is the annihilation of the individual's personality.

Whyte and other observers[11] are concerned about the "organization" becoming a monster which converts people into automatons. These protests about modern organizations and their conformity pressures are part of a larger pattern of reaction against the individual's absorption by the group or the collectivity generally. Whyte concludes that the individual executive must *fight* the organization when it attempts to make inroads on his privacy. The manager must fight because it is necessary if he is to retain his individuality and his self-awareness.

Pressure for Role-Conflict Resolution. Often the executive is faced with the necessity of making a decision requiring a choice between conflicting expectation generated by different interest groups. The executive, in other words, is confronted with a dilemma. Suppose the executive is presented with two incompatible alternatives. According to Shull and Miller,[12] he can act in the following ways:

1. Conform to alternative *A*.
2. Conform to alternative *B*.
3. Attempt to compromise between the alternatives.
4. Avoid making a decision.

A decision to act along the first two lines would satisfy one group and disappoint another, with the result being organizational disharmony. Since it may be supposed that both groups are pressuring for a favorable decision, the executive is likely to try the path of compromise. If compromise is out of the question, then the issue might be avoided entirely, in the sense that the executive delays making a decision with the hope that the problem will resolve itself.

Too frequently in organizations conflicts of interest arise among subordinates and have to be resolved by the executive. The temptation is great to compromise these interests for the sake of organizational harmony. The executive, however, has to withstand group pressure and make decisions which are compatible to organizational objectives. At times avoidance and compromise are reasonable tactics. But at other times the

---

[10] William H. Whyte, Jr., *The Organization Man* (New York: Simon and Schuster, 1956).

[11] See, for example, Erich Fromm, *The Sane Society* (New York: Rinehart and Co., 1955); David Riesman, *The Lonely Crowd* (New Haven: Yale University Press, 1950); and C. Wright Mills, *White Collar* (New York: Oxford University Press, 1951).

[12] Fremont A. Shull, Jr., and Delbert C. Miller, "Role Conflict Behavior in Administration: A Study in the Validation of a Theory of Role-Conflict Resolution" (an unpublished paper, 1960).

executive has to be prepared to face the wrath of interest groups which may be inconvenienced by unfavorable decisions.

In spite of the pressures and strains of management, most executives are adjusted to their role. They accept the role's inherent difficulties because they believe in the worthiness of what they are doing. The next section treats the type of personality which seems best equipped to endure the exigencies of the management role.

PERSONALITY AND SELF-PERCEPTIONS OF EXECUTIVES

An hypothesis was forwarded in the last section stating that the role of management is a selection device, attracting people whose personalities are most readily adaptable to it. Some personality modification occurs once the individual occupies the role, but not much because of the pre-selective qualities of the role itself.

FIGURE 16–1

EXECUTIVE CHARACTERISTICS

General

1. Intelligence is higher than population average.
2. Healthier.
3. Has fewer neurotic tendencies.
4. Not introspective—lacks deep awareness of motivations.
5. Essentially a pragmatist.

Values

1. Identifies with company and with immediate superior.
2. Strongly motivated to achieve.
3. Values money and power as symbols of status, not as ends in themselves.
4. Strong reality orientation—revolts against theory.
5. Tends to think about others in black-or-white terms.
6. Highly positive and optimistic attitudes.
7. Apprehensive of failure.
8. Earnestly seeks approbation for his actions.

Source: Adapted from Ephriam Rosen, "The Executive Personality," *Personnel,* January–February, 1959, pp. 8–20; Perrin Stryker, "On the Meaning of Executive Qualities," *Fortune,* June 1958, pp. 116–19, 186, 189; William E. Henry, "The Business Executive: The Psychodynamics of a Social Role," *American Journal of Sociology,* January, 1949, p. 286.

A vast amount of research has been done in the area of executive personality. The scope of the work covers the qualities of managerial leaders,[13] the average executive personality profile, and the deficiencies in

---

[13] Perrin Stryker, "The Rarest Man in Business," *Fortune,* May 1960, pp. 119–20, 210, 212.

personality which cause executives to fail.[14] A composite or profile of the "average" executive is given in Figure 16–1. Although there are many dangers in drawing up a profile, it does point up one rather important observation. The business executive has characteristics or traits which appear to be fairly commonly distributed throughout the population as a whole. But, as Rosen puts it, "He has them *to a stronger degree.*"[15]

Probably more valuable than the listing of typical executive traits are the perceptions of executives themselves in reference to their functions and roles in an organization. The work of Porter and Ghiselli reveals some interesting contrasts between the self-perceptions of middle management compared to those of top management. See Figure 16–2.

FIGURE 16–2

SELF–PERCEPTIONS OF MIDDLE AND TOP MANAGEMENT

Middle Management Sees Itself as:	*Top Management Sees Itself as:*
1. Providing the backbone of the organization.	1. The dynamic brains of the organization.
2. Providing stability through careful analysis and investigation.	2. Not being swayed entirely by objective evidence.
3. Seldom taking rash actions or making hasty, unfounded decisions.	3. Willing to take risks based on personal judgment and faith in its abilities.
4. Not as confident as top management.	4. Confident that its actions will lead to success.
5. Placing reliance on rules and regulations rather than plunging ahead on its own.	5. Action oriented, able to capitalize on opportunities, and self-reliant.
6. Wishing to avoid being controversial and wanting to be thought of as stable and dependable.	6. Confident in social and business relations.

Source: Adapted from Lyman W. Porter and Edwin E. Ghiselli, "The Self-Perceptions of Top and Middle Management Personnel," *Personnel Psychology,* Winter, 1957, pp. 397–406.

The findings of Porter and Ghiselli bear out in terms of the executives' perceptions the descriptions of middle and top management roles given earlier. These authors summarize their findings as follows:

Not only is there a difference in the types of decisions that the different groups see themselves as most capable of undertaking, but there also seems to be a difference in the way in which they arrive at the decisions. The results suggest that top management go more on their own hunches which they think are good, whereas middle management people seem more reluctant to

---

[14] Frederick J. Gaudet and A. Ralph Carli, "Why Executives Fail," *Personnel Psychology,* Spring, 1957, pp. 7–21.

[15] Ephriam Rosen, "The Executive Personality," *Personnel,* January–February, 1959, p. 19.

rely on themselves and inclined to rely on an accumulation of available evidence.[16]

Thus, the role of top management requires that executives operate on such subjective factors as vision, intuition, hunches, and judgment. The self-perception study reported here apparently confirms that top managers see themselves behaving this way. The case is similar for middle management. Its role is more highly structured, using concrete factual data as bases for decisions.

Role and personality go hand in hand. The normal person will usually perceive his role with a fair degree of accuracy and play it according to the rules of organizational policy. All this says is that people have attitudes which are consistent with their actions. It does not mean, of course, that the middle management role is necessarily a strait jacket binding a "middle-management personality" to it. Indeed, the achievement and the change pressures found to some degree in most executive positions establish the channels for role changes, enabling the individual to progress in the company.

PROMOTIONS

Much has been written about the many determinants of career success. For Horatio Alger these determinants were "pluck and luck." Nothing was more important in Algerian idealism than honesty, clean living, and hard work. But even these factors were not sufficient for success because fate, in the form of some lucky break, always lurked in the background to give the hero an extra nudge to success. Modern explanations and scientific investigations of success patterns are far more sophisticated (but not as much fun) as the Horatio Alger approach. One form of analysis is to study the backgrounds of successful executives to find commonalities in them.

The Biographic Approach

Probably the most elementary condition in anyone's background is his social origin. Studies of executive origins have shown that most have fathers who were themselves executives, professional people, or self-employed businessmen of a middle- to upper-middle-class status.[17] But

---

[16] Lyman W. Porter and Edwin E. Ghiselli, "The Self-Perceptions of Top and Middle Management Personnel," *Personnel Psychology*, Winter, 1957, p. 405.

[17] Statistical studies of executive origins relating to this point are offered by Mabel Newcomer, *The Big Business Executive* (New York: Columbia University Press, 1955), chap. 5; and W. Lloyd Warner and James C. Abegglen, *Big Business Leaders in America* (New York: Harper and Bros., 1955), chap. 2. These authors also present a wealth of data relating to other aspects of executive backgrounds such as nationality, religion, education, and wives.

writers like Warner have noted that over the years there has been a tendency toward "freer competition" for top jobs in large organizations.[18] People from humbler origins can aspire and can attain major positions in large companies.

This democratic trend is explainable in two ways. First, the large corporation bases its selection of executives on rationalistic policies.[19] The best trained and most competent for a post are selected. This policy is opposed to the more traditional procedure of selection based on family ties, which perpetuates relatives in executive posts regardless of qualifications. The large, impersonal corporation destroys this form of vested interest.

The second cause of greater democracy in competition for top positions is education. Relatively free access to education has made it possible for those of lower origins on the social scale to become equipped with the knowledge and skills necessary to qualify for managerial jobs. Through the growth of large organizations and widespread educational opportunity, access to the top levels of corporations has become more of a reality for people in all socioeconomic brackets. But *realistically* it must be emphasized that it is still far more probable that the sons of fathers of higher social origins will be future executives than, say, sons of laborers or farmers. So in spite of the democratization process, the probabilities of becoming a top executive still tilt in favor of those born in higher socioeconomic strata.

The biographic approach has turned up other similarities in executive backgrounds. Higher education appears frequently, along with Masonic membership, a favored ethnic composition, membership in "correct" clubs and societies, political affiliation of a conservative nature, judicious consumption and display of material well being, and participation in civic associations and charitable works.[20]

The individual's background helps frame his perspectives. Looking back on the life of successful executives it can be demonstrated how one advancement became their take-off point for further progress through the company. The individual's *level of aspiration* was such that he strove constantly for greater successes. Perhaps the most significant feature of

---

[18] W. Lloyd Warner, "The Corporation Man," in Edward Mason (ed.), *The Corporation in Modern Society* (Cambridge: Harvard University Press, 1960), pp. 106–21.

[19] Stuart Adams, "Trends in Occupational Origins of Business Leaders," *American Sociological Review*, October, 1954, p. 548. This democratization factor stems largely from the bureaucratic characteristic of selection based on the qualification-for-office criterion discussed in Chapter 12.

[20] Charles H. Coates and Roland F. Pellegrin, "Executives and Supervisors: Informal Factors in Differential Bureaucratic Promotion," *Administrative Science Quarterly*, 2 (1957), pp. 204–8; and Melville Dalton, "Informal Factors in Career Achievement," *American Journal of Sociology*, March, 1951, pp. 407–15.

an individual's background is the role it plays in gearing-up a person's aspirational level. All the opportunity a company offers will not get a man to move if he does not aspire beyond a certain point.

Of course, there is more than one way of satisfying aspirations other than vertical mobility in a company. For example, the supervisors in Pellegrin's and Coates' study achieved a small degree of vertical movement up the organization hierarchy. But when they reached the supervisory position they did not appear to aspire further. They were quite content.[21]

This situation is an apparent denial of the psychological theory that achievement at one level of aspiration leads to higher aspirational levels. However, it may well be that the supervisors in this example found satisfactions outside the organization after they reached this management level. Their aspirations probably shifted from a job to a nonjob focus.

In any event, there is no doubt that early experiences, training, and associations play a major part in framing an individual's aspirational level by conditioning him to accept a way of life which stresses a job-success orientation. Consequently, background can hardly be discounted as a determinant of a person's career successes. Obviously, however, it is not the only determinant. People who have had "all" the advantages fail, and those who have had few advantages succeed. Once in the business environment other influences instrumental in advancing or retarding a person's career take over.

Vertical Mobility—Two Points of View

How free is an individual to determine his progress in an employment situation? This is, of course, a relative matter which is reducible to a degree ranging on a continuum of dependence to independence. Naturally, in every organization a person will find he has some latitude to determine his own progress, based upon his abilities and aspirations. He will also discover that he is dependent upon established promotional channels, policies, sponsors, and rituals.

At one end of the dependency continuum is the "American dream"— that a man gets ahead solely on his own merits. In this case, the individual is the primary determinant of his own success. At the other end of the continuum is the notion that in spite of ability, drive, and aggressiveness, the individual is dependent on well-structured organizational channels and methods defined for promotional purposes. One of the main mechanisms in this process is the seniority or tenure-in-job criterion which requires a certain amount of time "in-grade" before moving to the next step. Both these points of view have received a good deal of treatment in manage-

---

[21] Roland F. Pellegrin and Charles H. Coates, "Executives and Supervisors: Contrasting Definitions of Career Success," *Administrative Science Quarterly*, 1956, pp. 513–14.

ment literature. The two "models" presented next express a fairly contemporary approach toward vertical mobility.

The Model of Dependence. Martin and Strauss paint an interesting picture of organizational mobility patterns.[22] In their view, as an organization matures it establishes and evolves career lines which are open to individuals seeking advancement. They describe these lines as branches on a tree, with some terminating at lower management levels, fewer moving through middle management, and still fewer going all the way to top management.

The upward movement of an individual in an organization involves a series of vertical and horizontal steps. Horizontal movement from one function to another is designed to give the executive a broader background in the organization. Vertical mobility, of course, constitutes the real promotion to higher levels of authority and responsibility. Each move, either horizontal or vertical, is considered as a training and testing point where the executive is judged. If he performs well in the opinions of his superiors he is in line for another move, everything else being equal. If he does not live up to expectations his mobility probably is terminated.

The interesting feature of established career progressions is the timetable by which an individual can gauge his progress. Martin and Strauss observe, "Acceptable age ranges are identifiable for the various strata. . . . A person who does not progress in accordance with these age timetables may know . . . that his potential for higher levels of management has been judged unfavorably."[23]

Even within this model of a well-structured promotional system the individual retains some discretion and control over his career. In any organization a person has available to him a number of alternative channels or career lines from which he may select. It is largely up to the individual to appraise these alternatives and select the channel which he feels will be the most beneficial to him in the realization of his ambitions. In the stable organization, however, *he selects from established career lines; he does not make his own.*

Thus far, individual progress is predicated on possession of technical competence, favorable judgment of superiors, and appropriate selection of a career alternative. Another factor emphasized by Martin and Strauss is the role of sponsorship. Sponsorship is the support lent by one person to another in order to facilitate a career. The sponsor, usually an executive higher-up in the chain of command, pulls his protégés up the ladder.

Here again, the judgment of the subordinate executive (the protégé) enters into his promotional pattern. A career often is greatly enhanced

[22] Norman H. Martin and Anselm L. Strauss, "Patterns of Mobility within Industrial Organizations," *Journal of Business*, April, 1956, pp. 101–10.

[23] *Ibid.*, p. 109.

by the happy wedding of a protégé and a powerful sponsor. But there are also dangers in these arrangements. A sponsor may lose ground in company transitions and power shifts, in which case the protégé is placed in an extremely tenuous position. It is not only high-level executives who are affected by organizational personnel changes; also affected are constellations of people, high and low, who have formed alliances.

One consequence of organizational reshuffling is, of course, being fired. However, it often happens that an executive who at one time appeared to be a "hot prospect" in the organization has had his lustre tarnished. Instead of being fired, his failure to perform up to expectation or his loss of power might result in being "cooled out." "Cooling out" is a face-saving device by which the executive is "kicked upstairs" or "banished" to an innocuous position where he can do no damage. The cooling-out process may be only temporary, in the event an executive has moved too fast too soon, or it may represent a terminal point in an executive's upward mobility.

The Model of Independence.   A different emphasis to career progress is given by Dill, Hilton, and Reitman. To them, "Career progress . . . depends greatly on the strategy or heuristics that an individual employs in 'his game' with the organization environment that he encounters at work."[24] The executive's awareness and sensitivity to the environment play an important part in their model.

The large organization, they observe, is indifferent to the advancement of most individuals as personalities. Therefore, it is incumbent on the executive who wants to get ahead to behave with social and political expedience in light of what he finds the tone of his environment to be. He must maintain a detached and objective attitude toward the job situation. The aspiring executive cannot allow himself to be incumbered by alliances with sponsors that might prove fatal in the event of organizational power transitions. He must consider himself as an "active agent" in the promotion of his career. In this respect, the executive should abstract himself as far as possible from the internal machinery of advancement and address himself to the solution of the immediate problems at hand. But always the aspiring executive keeps a wary eye on the subtle human nuances in the job situation and at the crucial time he applies the appropriate tactics which will be effective for his career.

The model posed by Dill and his associates represents the "cold-blooded" maneuvering required if the individual wants to get ahead in an organization which at best is indifferent or at worst hostile to his progress. Such tactics may indeed be appropriate for an executive's struggle to the top of the middle-management jungle. The question might be raised however as to whether these tactics employed by a manager to worm his way

---

[24] William R. Dill, Thomas L. Hilton, and Walter R. Reitman, "How Aspiring Managers Promote Their Own Careers," *California Management Review*, Summer, 1960, p. 10.

through middle management might not produce insurmountable barriers to his progress beyond. Is it the operator and the politician who get to the top?

The two promotional models just discussed are not mutually exclusive. The matter is one of emphasis. The Martin and Strauss model emphasizes a certain dependence on procedural and sponsorship elements in progress through a career line. The Dill, Hilton, and Reitman model stresses independence and self-determination in career progress. Both models underscore two key ideas. First, the typical modern executive's future is related to a rather highly structured organizational environment. Second, it is important that the executive maintain vigilance to extract clues as to the career alternative to select and the appropriate form of behavior necessary to secure advancement.

The Career and Philanthropic Activity

The realities of life and success in a large organization presuppose technical competence in the job. Progress, however, is based also on maneuvers, alliances, cold-blooded situational appraisals, risks, acceptance of setbacks, and many other social, psychological, and political factors which are peculiar to the internal affairs of an organization. Another career determinant worth noting is the rising young executive's acceptance and creditable performance in charitable drives, fund-raising campaigns, and the like. This is the "fifth function" of management— the social service function.

It is almost impossible for executives to avoid participation in foundation or charitable committee work. Not only do large companies have vested interests in charitable campaigns for altruistic and public relations reasons[25] but the public itself expects executive participation; hence, active work in campaigns becomes part of the executive role.[26]

Ross finds support for the hypothesis that the level of participation by an executive in organized collection campaigns corresponds closely to his status in the company where he is employed.[27] One campaign was organized in the following way:

1. Door-to-door canvassers.
2. Team captains.
3. Division captains.
4. Subordinate positions on campaign executive committee.
5. Vice-chairman of the committee.

---

[25] More is said in the next chapter on the motivations for corporate philanthropy.

[26] Roland J. Pellegrin and Charles H. Coates, "Absentee-Owned Corporations and Community Power Structure," *American Journal of Sociology*, March, 1956, pp. 413–19.

[27] Aileen D. Ross, "Philanthropic Activity and the Business Career," *Social Forces*, 32 (1953–1954), pp. 274–80.

6. Chairman of the committee.
7. Special names committee—to canvass potentially large donors.
8. Chairman of the special names committee.

Each of these campaign levels was manned by executives occupying parallel positions in the companies contributing manpower. For example, junior executives filled the lower rungs of campaign positions; top executives were selected because of their prestige to solicit the more important contributors. While cause-and-effect relationships are difficult to establish, Ross concludes that a person's success in campaigns has a positive influence on his business career. Philanthropic activity is a way which an executive can strengthen his hand in competition with others. From these activities the executive is able to establish valuable contracts, give evidence of being a hard worker with level-headed judgment, and demonstrate what kind of organizing and motivating ability he has.

*   *   *

This chapter has surveyed various aspects of executive personality and role. The appendix following gives a somewhat different presentation of these topics as seen through the eyes of the novelist. The next chapter discusses the wider implications and issues in management practice, focusing on the corporate framework and the problems of ethics and social responsibility.

REVIEW QUESTIONS

1. Review the various dimensions of a manager's role. Contrast the differential facets of these dimensions as applied to top management and lower levels of management.

2. Discuss the pressures of the managerial role.

3. What is meant by the notion that people are "preselected" for managerial roles?

4. Contrast the self-perceptions of middle management with those of top management.

5. Why is there greater democracy now in the promotional patterns of organizations? How can the "qualification-for-office" characteristic of bureaucracy be applied in this context?

6. Discuss the function of an individual's aspirational level in career progress.

7. Contrast the independent with the dependent model of vertical mobility.

8. What function does the sponsor perform in an individual's progress?

9. To what extent may the tactics used by an individual to rise in middle management present a role barrier to top management?

10. How is career progress facilitated by philanthropic activities?

SUPPLEMENTARY READINGS

COATES, CHARLES H., AND PELLEGRIN, ROLAND F. "Executives and Supervisors: Informal Factors in Differential Bureaucratic Promotion," *Administrative Science Quarterly*, 2 (1957), pp. 200–15.

DILL, WILLIAM R.; HILTON, THOMAS L.; AND REITMAN, WALTER R. "How Aspiring Managers Promote Their Own Careers," *California Management Review*, Summer, 1960, pp. 9–15.

KISSINGER, HARRY A. "The Policy Maker and the Intellectual," *The Reporter*, March 5, 1959, pp. 30–35.

MARTIN, NORMAN H., AND STRAUSS, ANSELM L. "Patterns of Mobility within Industrial Organizations," *Journal of Business*, April, 1956, pp. 101–10.

PORTER, LYMAN W., AND GHISELLI, EDWIN E. "The Self-Perceptions of Top and Middle Management Personnel," *Personnel Psychology*, Winter, 1957, pp. 397–406.

WARNER, W. LLOYD, AND ABEGGLEN, JAMES C. *Big Business Leaders in America*, chap. 2. New York: Harper and Bros., 1955.

APPENDIX I[1]

The Novelists' View of
the Business Executive

MOST of the information covered in the previous sections of this chapter is based on research by behavioral scientists in the personality and role of the executive. Besides empirical studies, though, there are other sources of insights into the personality and functions of the manager. One such source is provided by the novelists.

As set out by the novelists, the impact of the executive's image on the public mind cannot be underestimated. The written word is a powerful tool for molding opinion. For example, Upton Sinclair's novel *The Jungle* stimulated the administration of Theodore Roosevelt to investigate the meat-packing industry. The result was the passage of the Pure Food and Drug Law.

The modern novelist has a great potential for image building. Many novels find their way into the mass-communication media. For example: John P. Marquand's novel *Point of No Return* was produced as a play on television. *The Man in the Gray Flannel Suit* was made into a movie as were *The Hucksters, Executive Suite,* and *Cash McCall.*

Further, practically all the successful business novels first published in hardback editions are reprinted in the less expensive paperback form. Through reprints and adaptations to the screen and television the message of the novelist has a greater audience than ever before.

The artist—in this case the novelist—frequently is more perceptive of human problems than is the scientist. This sensitivity enables the novelist to relate the complicated picture of personality and interactions more effectively. Thus, the novelist can convey to his readers a fresh perspective in understanding executive character and the environment in which it acts.

---

[1] This appendix with a few minor changes is taken from William G. Scott, "The Novelists' Picture of Management and Managers," *Personnel Administration,* January–February, 1959, pp. 9–19, 34. Used with permission.

THE MODERN FICTIONAL HERO-MANAGER

Howard Upton grasps his literary cudgel in the *Saturday Evening Post* and defends the modern male in the business rat race. The critics of the businessman, relates Upton, feel he has succumbed to three peculiarly American evils—conformity, security, and the "buck hunt." The truth, Upton tells us, is that the Old Rat Race is not as bad as many writers would have us believe. Concluding his article, Upton says:

But those who stay—those who elect to continue in the Old Rat Race— require neither apology nor explanation. They need not rationalize. When you look at the total picture, it is not the militant nonconformist, cultivating a beard and painting seascapes in Sausalito, who is the hero of our age. The real hero is the fellow you see there with the brief case, waiting to catch the night plane to Houston to see what he can do about sacking up that big double-threaded pipe order.[2]

This observation has much insight. However, while Upton thinks conformity to the Old Rat Race is praiseworthy, the novelists feel it is lamentable. The real significance of Upton's article is not what he says but his compulsion to justify modern managerial work and life. Upton rails against the novelists' conception of the hero-manager. Just what constitutes this onerous profile will be taken up next.

The Contemporary Hero-Manager Profile. The modern manager is a hero, not because he does great or daring deeds but because he tolerates grinding mediocrity and conformity. Relative to bank-manager Charley Gray's ability to put up with the business world, Malcolm Bryant, cultural anthropologist, says in the novel:

"Charley," he says, "you've got a lot of guts."
"How do you mean, guts?" Charles asked.
"Saying what you do," Malcolm said, "doing what you do, takes guts. You're a very nice boy, Charley."[3]

The temptation is strong to abstract a profile of the hero-manager from novels and show him as a conforming automaton. Although there would be some accuracy in such a profile it would not be entirely true because there is also a spirit of rebellion in the hero's personality. To be sure, this spirit in some of the heroes is stifled, and in others it boils over. But in most cases, no matter what the hero does in the end, somewhere along the line he rebels.

The hero-manager is a dependent employee. He works for a company in which he occupies a management position somewhere at or above the middle. *He is not at the top or at the bottom of the managerial structure.*

---

[2] Howard Upton, "Had Enough of the Old Rat Race?" *Saturday Evening Post*, December 7, 1957, p. 118.

[3] John P. Marquand, *Point of No Return* (New York: Bantam Books, 1952), p. 51.

The hero-manager actively participates in or is directly affected by committee action. Hence, he is largely divorced from the necessity of making or carrying the responsibility of major decisions. In short, he is a member of a team.

As a team member, priority is given to "getting along with people." The manager should be a relationship expert. He has to "deal" with a large number of people at different levels and in different functions in the organization. The manager must constantly be aware that his actions contribute to the good of the group. If they do not, his managerial abilities are suspected, regardless of his success in performing the technical side of his job.

The amount of standardization, apple polishing, and general banality to which the hero-manager often is subjected is appalling. The organization is a "velvet trap." But although it threatens to vaporize the hero-manager's individuality, it offers security for this price.

And security is important because, like Charley Gray in *The Point of No Return,* many of the hero-managers have gotten themselves submerged by family and time-payment responsibilities. Continued attachment to the organizational umbilical cord is the easy way out for hero-managers. As dependent employees, all they can sell is their brains, their individuality, and their lives.

They sell their lives because the influence of the job extends beyond the eight-hour day at the office. The organization lays down rules, both formal and informal, governing the type of home in which they live, the kind of car they buy, the club to which they belong, and the acquaintances they make. It even determines the ideal mold into which a manager's wife should be pressed.[4]

These observations bring up the subject of conformity.

Conformity. Conformity among the hero-managers of early novels was pragmatic. When it paid to conform, they conformed. They discarded conformity when it was no longer useful. Only Babbitt made conformity a way of life. Today, for many hero-managers security and conformity go hand in hand. And since security seems to be an important work motive, conformity results.

But this is too simple. Conformity arises from the nature of organizational systems. A growing government or business bureaucracy is an

---

[4] The composite is drawn from the heroes of the following novels: Charley Gray —Marquand, *op. cit.;* Abe Rogoff—Ernst Pawel, *From the Dark Tower* (New York; The Macmillan Co., 1957); Victor Norman—Frederick Wakeman, *The Hucksters* (New York: Rinehart and Co., 1946); Tom Rath—Sloan Wilson, *The Man in the Gray Flannel Suit* (New York: Simon and Schuster, 1955); Cleves Barwick—Howard Swiggett, *The Power and the Prize* (New York: Ballantine Books, 1954); Stephen Lowry—Howard Swiggett, *The Durable Fire* (Boston: Houghton Mifflin Co., 1957).

ideal medium for breeding standardization. Bureaucracy could not work without well-disciplined, passive employees. This point is made by Ernst Pawel. In his book *From the Dark Tower* he presents a powerful indictment of a modern business bureaucracy. As he puts it, ". . . the reign of the clerk in all its variations, from the Tower on the Square to the Superstate on the Volga, is dedicated to the extinction of man's awareness of himself."[5]

The Tower, the center of a huge insurance company, is a symbol of the destruction of a person by the organization. Like "Big Brother," the Tower is mother and father to all, offering universal security. The fact that a manager sits at the top of the company or occupies a lowly rank is immaterial. He is a clerk who does the bidding of the organization.

Pawel looks sourly at another aspect of the modern corporation—the committee. The endless amount of committee activity to which managers are subjected is a product of business bureaucracy. Committee behavior is typified by compromise and thus places a premium on conformity. The committee conveniently relieves the individual from responsibility for major decisions. This fact, of course, increases personal security.

Swiggett's novel *The Durable Fire* has an example of such committee behavior. The Continental Industries Corporation was, among other operations, engaged in heavy construction. One such project was a bridge on which the company bid, to be built in Latin America. The bridge was underestimated by $500,000. Who was to blame? Apparently specific responsibility for the error was impossible to ascertain. *Everybody* initialed the estimate; therefore everybody or nobody was to blame, depending on how the situation is viewed.

Wives and Home Life. As suggested before, conformity radiates beyond the company. The novelists see it extending into the manager's home life. The wife of the hero-manager in earlier business fiction was relatively detached from the career of her husband. This situation is not always so in contemporary fiction. The wife frequently is intimately concerned with the progress of her husband in the company.

Nancy, Charley Gray's wife, is a good example of wifely preoccupation with her husband's business fortunes. She is not so much concerned that business success might be a source of satisfaction for Charley. Rather, a promotion means more money and a surer route to the good life.

But what is the good life? Charley Gray is not sure. A better home, a better car, a nicer club, a good education for the children—all appear to be at stake. However, success seems to boil down to giving a man an opportunity to conform at a plusher level. So he gets a promotion! This

---

[5] Ernst Pawel, *op. cit.*, p. 245.

means giving up one set of superficial acquaintances and assuming "friendships" with another set. The standards and values lived by do not change, despite changes in income.

The hero-manager and his family live either in a suburb or what Spectorsky calls an exurb.[6] For the hero-manager, home is like a dormitory; he spends his evenings and weekends there, but large portions of his hours awake are consumed by commuting and working in an urban center. The urban center in the novels is often New York City.

The wife, of course, remains at home in the community during the day. Her life is involved with children, "constructive" community activities, and other wives. These communities are matriarchies. Employed in distant locations, the hero-manager is physically removed from domestic problems. Rearing children and making important family decisions are left to the wife. The wife becomes quite pecuniary minded, since children and other matters associated with running a home and maintaining community status cost money. Naturally, when the husband and wife engage in a little introspection about the pleasure-pain calculus connected with making money, the wife usually is for a lot more "pain."

The wife also has to worry about company as well as community acceptance. Two novels by Howard Swiggett bring out some problems involving wife-organization relationships. Swiggett is engrossed in showing a foreign woman's reaction to American business patterns and an American response to foreign women. In both his novels, *The Power and the Prize* and *The Durable Fire*, the main female characters are European imports. In these novels the hero-manager is involved with a foreigner in some amorous capacity. Stephen Lowry, of *The Durable Fire*, was married to an Estonian. Cleves Barwick, in *The Power and the Prize*, got himself mixed up with a refugee pianist in England. The "carryings on" of these hero-managers with Europeans of "dubious" backgrounds were looked upon with suspicion by the top managers of their corporations. The bosses' worry was that the hero-managers' women might not "fit in" with the company family.

Being able to "fit in" naturally presumes some kind of mold to fit into. The novelists do not spell out the mold pattern. But the ideal (and successful) organization wife is often depicted. She is intelligent, but not too intelligent. She should be a white American of not-too-humble origins. She must dress well. Above all, she should never take a blatantly active part in pushing her husband. Rather, the ideal wife should operate in a "nice" way behind the scenes.

Rebellion. A system which demands identification and personality digestion is bound to cause even the least sensitive of souls to rebel. The novelists' treatment of the rebellious spirit makes an interesting analysis.

---

[6] A. C. Spectorsky, *The Exurbanites* (New York: J. B. Lippincott Co., 1955).

The nature of rebellion is not the same among hero-managers, although the differences may be more of a matter of degree than of kind.

At one end of an extreme is Charley Gray. He feels his life is contrived—something out of a soap opera. Will Junior go to prep school? Will the family get a new car? Everything depends on Charley's promotion. On the way to Tony Burton's house (Tony is Charley's boss) Charley begins to question the values of the whole thing, much to his wife's dismay. The dinner party, given by the Burtons for the Grays, is to be the setting for the "moment of truth" about Charley's promotion. Before the news is revealed Charley really does not give a damn about the new job. He actually feels free for the first time in a long time.

Of course, Charley does get promoted. Burton implies there was never any question of it. But Charley was dangled so long, so unmercifully, he was too numb to appreciate it. Naturally Charley accepts. What else can he do? He is at the point of no return.

Marquand's picture is one of helplessness and frustration for Charley and presumably for others like him. They have virtually no control over their destinies. Charley's rebellion was personal and ineffectual. Charley is caught.

Abe Rogoff, a character in Pawel's *From the Dark Tower*, is at the other end of the extreme. He lives in a suburb dedicated to security, conformity, and the "good life." Abe works for an insurance company dedicated to making money and converting employees to happy, satisfied nonentities. However, he is not about to let this happen to him. Abe is different from most of the hero-managers because he is an intellectual who never quite recovered from his Bohemian past. He is also a Jew, which is definitely against him as far as his company is concerned.

Abe sees his life much the same as Charley Gray—phony and artificial. However, Abe has the courage to chuck it all when the boss offers him a new "challenge" in the company. Abe's rebellion is overt, but he is in a better position to pull out. At least he has certain literary talents which give him some independence. Charley Gray, on the other hand, has nothing to make him more than what he is—a dependent employee for the rest of his life.

There is a large assortment of other characters between the extremes of Gray and Rogoff. They are too numerous for individual discussion. However, Tom Rath, the gray-flannel-suit man, is important enough to receive some attention.

Rath is neither a Gray nor a Rogoff. If any parallels are to be drawn, Rath is kind of a post-World War II edition of Dos Passos' Charley Anderson, to the extent that wartime experiences color his civilian life. The reactions of the two are different though. Anderson was dead set on seeing how fast he could kill himself, whereas Rath wants to return to the quiet secure life.

Tom Rath wants two things—money and security. He never really rebelled against the business system; he was a split-the-difference man. And
he acted quite consistently with this observation in his business career. He
figured $10,000 a year would be sufficient to entice him away from the
foundation for which he was working at the beginning of the story. The
broadcasting company with which he was seeking a job offered him
$8,000; they settled on $9,000.

Tom Rath wanted a job which offered sufficient but not a lot of money.
In turn, he was not willing to take on responsibilities which would separate him too much from his family. About the only rebellion on Tom's
part was his refusal to accept more responsibility.

In this respect, there is an interesting contrast between Tom's and
Hopkins' lives (Hopkins is president of the company). Hopkins' mar-
riage is a failure and his daughter a problem. Reason? Hopkins devoted
too much time in the past to being a success. Tom does not want this to
happen to him and his family. Justifiable? It depends on an individual's
set of values. Yet someone has to sacrifice something for the sake of
success and progress.

The moral of *The Man in the Gray Flannel Suit* is hard to determine.
Probably it is "to each his own." But some writers see business breeding
too many Tom Raths and not enough Hopkinses. The gray flannel suit
has become a symbol and a specter of conformity.

Rebellion against organization has a curious counterpart. In several
novels, the hero-manager has found a valley for himself to which he re-
treats. His valley is an idealized place. The peace, simplicity, and virgin
beauty of "the valley" contrast starkly with the world of business.

Cash McCall has his valley—Aurora. Jim Coutler, in Bernard Lester's
Weatherby Crisis,[7] has a retreat in a valley filled with happy rural folk.
And Abe Rogoff, after he breaks with "the Tower," finds refuge—
where else but in a valley out West. Ayn Rand has John Galt building
a new world in a valley in *Atlas Shrugged.*[8] Although the valley is
quite real for these hero-managers, it also has certain allegorical qualities.
The valley is *too* perfect; the life is *too* good; and the people in it are *too*
kind. The valley is roughly the equivalent of positive mental hygiene
or tranquilizers. Some psychologists might say the valley represents a
retreat to the womb.

A valley, as such, is not present in all the novels. But the fact that it
exists in four lends a certain symbolic significance to it. It is a place to
escape and to sublimate. The "valley" perhaps stands for sanity or a
reality greater than business life. The hero-managers who have their
valleys seem to face life more confidently than those who do not.

---

[7] Bernard Lester, *Weatherby Crisis* (New York: Twayne Publishers, 1956).

[8] Ayn Rand, *Atlas Shrugged* (New York: Random House, 1957).

The Top Executives. As previously observed, the main character in contemporary fiction is usually a man who is located in the lower ranks of the organizational hierarchy. However, the novelists also treat the man at the top of the organization. Even though this man is not a central figure in novels, a few words about him would not be amiss.

These men at times exhibit considerable identification with the organization. Peabody is a case in point.[9] He reveals to Abe Rogoff that a man cannot—absolutely cannot, no matter what his position in a company —lead two separate lives: a private life and a company life. The private life of a manager must always be interpreted and conducted from the standpoint of what is good for the company. This is sound advice for avoiding a split personality but at the same time it cuts off the private life of a manager as a source of expression. In part, Abe Rogoff rebelled against this philosophy.

In quite another vein is the "double-standard" philosophy found among top managers. This philosophy assumes different forms. For example, Salt objected strongly to Cleve Barwick's affair with a European pianist.[10] On the other hand, Salt himself had kept a mistress for years. Apparently Salt interpreted his own actions as not having any effect on the prestige of the company. But Barwick's "indiscretion" might have serious foreign repercussions. The top manager's attitude seems to be that individualism is all right for him, but his subordinates should support a "teamwork" or "group-first" philosophy.

More basic than the foregoing is the double-standard philosophy applied to organization objectives. A knotty problem in Cameron Hawley's *Executive Suite* seems to turn on a double-standard consideration.[11] Don Walling, in his "over-the-goal" speech for the company presidency, emphasizes two objectives. The first is structuring a company in which the men could take pride. The second is growth. These objectives are not incompatible. But together, in Walling's mind, they constitute ends which precede profits in a form that will be returned as dividends to the owners.

This attitude is curious but perhaps not unrepresentative. It could be that Don Walling is voicing the philosophy of an employee–management-centered organization. Growth plus happy workers indeed may be the monument to achievement for the professional top executive. The matter of the double standard comes in when a return to the absentee owners of the corporation is considered. Their place in the structure is apparently vague in Walling's scheme. Management's obligation to the stockholders, according to Walling, is to keep the company *alive*. The subtlety of Walling's argument is the shift in emphasis from the "pure"

---

[9] Peabody is found in *From the Dark Tower*.

[10] Salt is a character in *The Power and the Prize*.

[11] Cameron Hawley, *Executive Suite* (New York: Ballantine Books, 1952), esp. pp. 330–40.

notion of management stewardship for the owners to a philosophy designed for management ego-satisfaction and worker welfare.

The Operators. *Sincerely, Willis Wayde*,[12] by John P. Marquand, is a success story about a man who possesses "classic" administrative qualities. Willis sees the "broad" picture. Much the same is true of Cameron Hawley's character, Cash McCall.[13] The interesting feature about these two men is that each is able to move successfully in the ambivalent business environment which sways between the individualistic ethic and the social ethic. Indeed, they are sensitive enough to this environment to be able to exploit it for their own "unaltruistic" ends. Neither of the two fits the "organization-man" prototype.

Willis Wayde is conservative; he does not drink (to excess), speculate, or endorse notes. Cash McCall and Willis Wayde are smooth. But, more important, they grasp and intelligently apply administrative principles and thus are led to success. Both are professionals at the job of salvaging lost business causes. And although Willis probably identifies more with the firms which employ him this does not prevent him from making changes advantageous to himself and for that matter to the companies.

As a manager, Willis Wayde, is of course, somebody's employee. He is a man who acts in the "best" interest of the owners. But who are the owners? For a while Willis was employed in a mill owned by the Harcourt family—a family he eventually views as parasitical remnants of the capitalistic past. From the Harcourt mill he moves to the huge Simcoe Corporation, undoubtedly owned by many small, noninterfering stockholders. With Simcoe he has his meat. Here he can be a true professional manager unencumbered by a lot of peculiar feelings of loyalty springing from essentially noneconomic sources. As long as Simcoe pays some dividends and grows, Willis has a job.

The attitude of Willis Wayde toward the Harcourt family and the Harcourt mill is a study in the relativism of loyalty. To some of the Harcourts, especially Bess, the mill had sentimental significance. In spite of his promise to do "everything in his power" to keep the mill open after the merger of the Harcourt Company with Simcoe, Willis is forced to shut the mill down. From the Simcoe point of view, Willis must treat the Harcourt mill as a unit in a "broader" picture, and a liability at that. His action in closing this mill is based in economic logic and is derived from his obligations to the Simcoe Corporation. But what of his obligations to the Harcourt family? Willis learned that dual loyalty is fine when one does not have to make a decision. But when a decision is pressing a single loyalty must be paramount. This tenet of decision mak-

---

[12] John P. Marquand, *Sincerely, Willis Wayde* (Boston: Little, Brown and Co., 1955).

[13] Cameron Hawley, *Cash McCall* (Boston: Houghton Mifflin Co., 1955).

ing causes Willis and others like him to ponder the question of just what sincerity is.

Cash McCall is a capital-gains operator. He makes money by buying sick companies, applying his genius to get them on their feet, and then selling out. Cash McCall's motives in this complicated operation are not easy to understand. He himself does not seem to know them. He is nevertheless absorbed with "playing the game"—only the game McCall plays is the sort in which everybody wins. Is your business going on the rocks? Cash McCall will buy you out at an exceptionally good price. He will then reorganize, work a couple of fast shuffles, and ultimately sell—after six months of course—and take capital gains.

In spite of his philanthropy McCall moves in legal and moral "fringe areas." His deals are certainly no more bloodthirsty than are those of the older hero-managers. But they got away with what they did for a long time—and their actions had the moral approbation of many as the "way of business." From the start, a shadow of disreputability hung over McCall's deals.

Cash was never interested in staying with any firm he acquired, at least not until the end of the book. Then, under the mellowing influence of Lory Austin, he begins to worry about all those faceless people affected by his deals. She pleads with him and says that people need him, winning is not everything, and so on.

It is not known whether Cash, after Lory's persuasions, will give up his money-making business and permanently devote his time to one company, making faceless people happy and secure; but there is little doubt that with his superhuman abilities he could be a successful relationship expert if he put his mind to it.

The Hero-Manager of the Future.   Outside of science fiction, few contemporary novelists describe the future. However, in Ayn Rand's *Atlas Shrugged* and in George Orwell's *1984*[14] the future is projected. It is a grim one, indeed. In both these novels Ernst Pawel's "tower" reaches its logical conclusion. Individualism is extinguished; man's awareness of himself is destroyed; bureaucratic power becomes paramount. Man exists for the state while the bureaucrats fatten on their exploitations.

The bureaucrats, of course, are managers. Their system of organization is grossly inefficient in the allocation of resources. But the bureaucrats remain in control through a combination of lip service, social uplift, and police power, plus the creation of crises to develop a "common cause" as an object of wrath to weld together an unthinking populace.

Orwell's world is comprised of three superstates run by such bureaucrats. Theoretically, these states are based on conflicting ideologies. Actually, the philosophy of government, power, and control in these states is

---

[14] George Orwell, *1984* (New York: The New American Library, 1954).

identical. The states are so large and militarily unyielding that no two combined can defeat the other one. Internally, the economy and the government of the states are static.

Orwell offers no solution and no happy ending to the situation he creates. A vague hope is present that a savior in the person of a mythical Goldstein will come as a deliverer. Winston Smith, the hero of *1984*, lives for this occasion. Goldstein never does appear, and Smith is brainwashed. His trace of individualism is destroyed and in the end he loves Big Brother.

Ayn Rand's vision is different. To be sure, the bloated bureaucrats are there. But effective resistance to bureaucratic power is organized by a group of individualists who have retreated to a valley and are constructing a utopian new world. *Atlas Shrugged* is a huge thesis in defense of individualism. After bureaucratic bungling has wrecked the United States the individualistic managers and entrepreneurs return to put things right. The novel is a struggle between good and evil. The bureaucrats are evil and the individualists are good. And in the end, of course, good must win out.

Atlas Shrugged is a business novel unlike any written in the contemporary period. It is reminiscent of novels written in the first three decades of this century. The superhuman qualities of the individualistic hero-manager are reasserted. Although Dreiser, Norris, and Sinclair could see nothing but doom in those days for the individualist, Miss Rand sees triumph for him today.

Just how inevitable is the future that George Orwell and Ayn Rand see? In an essay called *James Burnham and the Managerial Revolution*,[15] Orwell left little doubt that a managerial revolution is *not* inevitable in his mind. Yet the events that Orwell discusses in *1984* seem uncomfortably close.

Depending on the state of one's optimism, Miss Rand's thesis of individualism prevailing ultimately over the bureaucrats can be accepted or rejected. But even Miss Rand's utopia is not an anarchy. Control would become vested in those having financial power. Thus the alternatives of these two novels appear to be a dictatorship by the right or a dictatorship by the left. In the best tradition of "double-think," maybe Freedom *is* Slavery.

THE SEARCH FOR A CONVICTION

The novelists' insights into managerial "manners and modes" are difficult to slot into convenient pigeonholes. The novelists do not present a

---

[15] George Orwell, *James Burnham and the Managerial Revolution* (London: Socialist Book Center, 1946). (Originally published in Polamic 3 as *Second Thoughts on James Burnham*.)

pat or easily understandable picture of the manager. Over the years, the business novels show a kaleidoscope of behavior and work motives.

Certain generalizations, however, are possible about management novels. The first and most important generalization concerns the novelists' reaction to the diminishing expansion factor and the growing collision effect. The novelists in the period of 1900 to 1930 forecasted the end of the expansion factor, accompanied by a decline in the significance of the individualistic ethic.

Some novelists, like Upton Sinclair, sought an answer to the collision effect in socialism. Sinclair apparently visualized socialism as a gigantic human relations program. Other novelists in the early period were not willing to go quite to the extremes of Sinclair to counterbalance the collision effect. Yet the novelists' utopian visions were built around a program based on some form of the social ethic.

This trend has continued into the contemporary period. Some statement of the social ethic has run through most business novels. Recently, however, there have been rumblings of discontent with the social value system as, for example, in Ayn Rand's *Atlas Shrugged*.

The second generalization is a corollary of the first. Many hero-managers of the earlier novels voluntarily behaved according to the tenets of the individualistic ethic. The modern hero-manager, as portrayed in modern novels, is almost forced to accept the values of the social ethic whether he likes them or not. The older hero-manager seemed just to blunder ahead in the face of the "mass" which would not be denied. The modern hero-manager rebels when the conditions of conformity and standardized living become more than he can stomach.

The third generalization relates to the similarity of ethics practiced by the contemporary top hero-managers and the earlier hero-managers. Both the modern and the older hero-managers incorporate the individualistic ethic into their philosophy and their behavior. But the modern top hero-manager's approach to the individualistic ethic is more subtle than his older counterpart's. Individualism is all right for the man on top; his subordinates, however, should be "team men." Swiggett's novels are filled with examples of this double-standard attitude.

The last generalization points to the novelists' portrayal of the managers' quest for a philosophy of life that can be squared with their business environment. Perhaps the modern novelists are more sensitive than were their predecessors to the ideological cleavage brought about by the individualistic ethic and the social ethic. The contemporary hero-manager is often satirized. He is drawn as a rather pathetic figure struggling through a world of conflicting values, hoping to find a faith.

Some of the characters in business novels are hedonists, some are human relationists, some are conformists, others are nonconformists. Despite this diversity of characterization, one thing is fairly clear. The hero-managers move in a world of paradox. Some conflicts they bring on themselves; others are generated by the nature of the business system. The earlier hero-managers seemed to be steadfastly certain that their ethical judgments guiding them in the business world were right. However, more often than not among the modern hero-managers an insecurity of belief is present. The modern hero-manager appears to be searching for a conviction.

CHAPTER 17

Executive Incentives and Constraints in the Corporate Setting

TECHNICALLY, the corporation is an engine of finance. It is a device for the aggregation of capital, spawned by the heavy financial demands of a mass-production and mass-distribution economy. But the corporation is more than a legal and financial instrument. The large modern corporation provides a domicile and a way of life for thousands of executives. Also, because of its peculiarities of structure and social role, the corporate environment makes behavioral demands on executives dissimilar to those made by partnerships or single proprietorships. Further, the corporate executive is circumscribed by influences of a profit orientation in markets characterized by varying degrees of competition for customers and resources. Therefore, what is said in this chapter about attitudes and behavior of the executive in a business corporation should not be taken to apply necessarily to administrators in nonprofit organizations.

The corporation is unique, in the sense that it makes possible a combination of human, financial, and material resources which are quite unlike combinations possible under other legal and economic institutions. Woodrow Wilson said many years ago: "A modern corporation is an economic society, a little economic state—and not always little, even as compared to states."[1] To this might be added that the corporation is indeed more than an economic society. It is also a society which offers social and psychological rewards to participants. And it is a society which exerts political power and influence in relation to other institutions in its quest for survival and growth.

The corporation in this chapter is not considered in its legal or economic manifestations primarily. Instead, the concern here is on the motivations and inhibitions to executive action within the boundaries of corporate organization. Additionally, since the corporation has a pervasive

---

[1] Woodrow Wilson, "Annual Address," American Bar Association, Chattanooga, Tenn., 1910. Cited in William Z. Ripley, *Main Street and Wall Street* (Boston: Little, Brown, and Co., 1927), p. 6.

influence in our society issues of power and responsibility are considered in the concluding sections of this chapter.

THE CORPORATE SETTING

Corporate enterprise is a means for marshalling and distributing a business' resources. Among the many advantages of the corporate device, the most obvious is the opportunity it affords a business to amass large amounts of capital. This method of capitalization involves the relatively simple expedient of selling stock to private and institutional buyers.

The use of the corporation device is extensive. Not only have many businesses elected this method of financial organization but also the largest companies in America have assumed the corporate form.[2] The corporation is a characteristic landmark in American business.

The corporation is often stereotyped as a large organization engaged in a wide range of production and distribution operations. The modern corporation frequently is depicted as an ever-changing, complex apparatus serving the material needs of customers, owners, employees, and the public. These stereotypes are misleading because corporations assume many sizes, shapes, and types, each pursuing objectives with varying degrees of success.

All corporations possess the peculiar legal characteristic which admits the possibility for the separation of ownership from control. That is, the control over a property may be detached from the ownership of the property. Of course in many corporations this possibility is not realized. Such is the case when the stock of a corporation is owned entirely or in large part by one person or a family. However, when the stock of a corporation is widely distributed among a large number of small owners, the occasion for the separation of ownership from control arises.

The issue of separating ownership from control was raised in Chapter 2. This consideration, however, is so pivotal to the main theme of this chapter that it is worth going over again in greater detail.

The nature of property is the basic issue at question in any discussion of corporate ownership and control. Traditionally, the characteristic of property includes the privilege of control over the acquisition and distribution of what is owned. The owner, within limitations, has full power to administer, to gain benefits from, and to dispose of his property in ways he sees fit. Thus, ownership and control are centralized in a single decision source.

The corporation creates the opportunity to change this traditional view of property. The open corporation allows many small investors to gain property rights in it, but at the same time the investor delegates his con-

---

[2] Roughly 130 manufacturing corporations produce half the manufacturing output in the United States.

trol privilege over his property to hired managers. The consequences of this for many American corporations are the centralization of control and the decentralization of ownership.[3]

Conceivably, corporate executives should administer property in the best interests of owners. Regardless of whether or not this is the case in fact, shareholders have precious little chance for satisfaction if they feel their interests are not being served.[4] Their only recourse is to sell their holdings and reinvest in other firms. Therefore, more than anything else the modern investor buys management rather than property.

The management of large, widely held corporations is in a curious position. The common leading symbols of management in these circumstances are associated with the ideas of trusteeship or stewardship. The adequate and dispassionate dispatch of stewardship duties leads directly to the notion of the "professionalization" of management. Like the stewards in the Bible, the modern corporate manager symbolically serves the master—the owner. But these owners, unlike their Biblical counterparts, are not especially powerful or articulate. Further, they are usually small and tend to neutralize each other. Thus, management is left with a fair degree of freedom to do as it likes, within the boundaries of "prudent business practice."

Then, too, it is not an altogether obvious fact that the owners are management's only masters. Indeed, it is questionable whether or not they are the most important among many masters. A case can be made that corporate management treats the owners as one of a number of groups whose interests in the corporation must be balanced. This view is far from the "pure" stewardship notion that management's overwhelming responsibility is to maximize the return on the shareholder's investment. Of course, it may be that in the long run the management which serves the owners best is the management which balances the interests of all parties having claims on the material resources and the human talents of the corporation. But this is getting ahead of the story.

------

[3] The problems posed by this situation are not new. An early treatment of the subject may be found in William Z. Ripley, *Main Street and Wall Street* (Boston: Little, Brown, and Co., 1927). The classic treatment is Adolf A. Berle, Jr., and Gardiner C. Means, *The Modern Corporation and Private Property* (New York: The Macmillan Co., 1933). There are many contemporary studies of the corporation. See, for example, Adolf A. Berle, Jr., *Power Without Property* (New York: Harcourt, Brace and Co., 1959); also Edward S. Mason (ed.) *The Corporation in Modern Society* (Cambridge: Harvard University Press, 1960).

[4] A distinction must be made between *de facto* and *de jure* control rights. Legally (*de jure*) the ownership has control privileges, but in fact these privileges are not operative because of the small amount of ownership interest vested in an individual. Theoretically, many small owners acting in concert could muster sufficient strength to assert their legal control prerogatives if they were dissatisfied with the management of their corporation. Practically, such joint action by the ownership is quite difficult and often impossible.

The corporation has presented a number of abiding problems to those who are interested in matters of executive behavior, power and influence, and responsibility in our society. These problems, outlined below, are treated in greater depth throughout this chapter.

Executive Incentives

Corporate enterprise shatters the traditional owner-manager image. The owner-manager, typical of an earlier era, had direct proprietary interest in his business. For practical purposes the modern manager does not have much, if any, ownership interest in the firm which employs him. Hence, the goals which motivate him might be expected to be considerably different from the ends sought by the owner-manager. But even if the ends of the "professional" and the owner-manager are not substantially apart, it is certain that the modern corporate manager acts in a far more complex environment. The intricate nature of the corporate world is in itself sufficient to produce a "breed" of executives quite unlike those of the past.

The Corporate "Image"

Under the law, the corporation is a person—a legal entity. Unfortunately, the corporation has assumed the attributes of a human being. Common parlance reflects this by statements like "The corporation formulates policy," "The corporation has decided to merge," or it "has decided to introduce a new product," and so on. Actually the corporation decides nothing, because it is an abstraction. It is the management of the corporation which acts. If a corporation "is soulful," or "has a conscience," it is because management has decided that these attributes are worthy of the corporation image. Though this may be a mundane point, all too often favorable or unfavorable judgments are rendered by the public toward an inaccessible corporate image rather toward the praise or condemnation of the management of the corporation.

Legitimacy and Power

The corporate device allows for some concentrations of power. Our society, however, provides only imperfect sanctions for the misuse of power. This is a rather delicate point since our culture insists that the exercise of power be legitimate in the sense that it is responsible to higher authority. For reasons set forth later, the traditional sources of sanctions—the sovereign consumer, the government acting for the public, competition, and of course the owners—have been neutralized in varying degrees as sources of effective control.

Business Goals and Objectives

The freedom to incorporate has been a major factor in the growth of business and the extension of its influence into many aspects of American life. As businesses grow it is more difficult for them to maintain their monolithic role of profit orientation. Instead, large companies take on the semblance of multipurpose institutions with the function of achieving ends that are not directly related to economic activity. This leads, of course, to the question of the capability of managers to make decisions, render judgments, and use corporate power to promote and obtain goals which lie outside the economic order.

The corporation is probably an inevitable product of industrialization, in spite of the issues, dilemmas, and paradoxes raised by it. Technology requires large capital aggregations, mass employment, and many investors ready and willing to become "people's capitalists;" and this makes for a situation in which corporations with centralized control emerge and thrive.

Although there are many criticisms of the corporations, these criticisms are paralleled by statements extolling the virtues of corporate enterprise and professional management. Issues appear which make interesting and stimulating copy. But whether these issues are straw men or real is a matter which cannot be easily determined.

The corporation (and hence corporate management) is a complex affair. The corporation is so thoroughly integrated in American culture that fundamental changes in it would undoubtedly modify the fabric of society. In this respect, it has been said that if by divine decree the corporation is eliminated as a legal fiction, the corporation itself would continue to exist and fulfill its functions with very little change in structure and executive behavior. Nothing short of general catastrophe could persuade society to cast off that which it has deemed so essential to its well-being.

Social need alone, however, is not sufficient justification for power, particularly for those who feel that power in all forms must have restraints. Since corporations are really the creatures of those who run them, it is apparent that management must ultimately become the focus of consideration when matters of responsibility are discussed. The pressure on management and the incentives for action in the corporate environment are really the motivating and constraining forces which eventually cause the managers to shape the "corporate personality." Consequently, it is relevant to present some of the incentives, both positive and negative, which prompt executive action.

EXECUTIVE INCENTIVES

Financial Incentives

Making money is supposedly the cause for going into business. Ideally, profits are the guiding criterion for judging the correctness of business decisions; and they are the incentive necessary to entice people to perform an economic function. The role of profits for the owner-manager of a relatively small concern is clear and unambiguous. They constitute his reward for successful practice.

Like most else in the corporate world, profits and their role are not so forthright. Profits frequently are means rather than ends for the professional manager. As such, they are only loosely correlated with executive incentives. Certainly the management of a corporation cannot disregard profits as a minimum expectation necessary to ensure passive stockholders and directors. But beyond this, it is a moot question whether executives seek every rational economic alternative to enlarge profits. Instead they may pursue other alternatives, such as personal power, organizational stability, organizational growth, consumer respect, social philanthrophy, and employee welfare.[5]

Personal Financial Success and Corporate Financial Success. The owner-manager is directly dependent on his own wit in running his business for the income it returns to him for his efforts and on his investment. Ultimately, of course, the financial success or failure of a corporate enterprise will also affect the livelihood of its management. However, in the usual course of events the managements of large, relatively stable corporations are not faced with the extreme circumstances of stupendous successes or dismal failures of the companies which are immediately translated into earning fluctuations.

Instead, corporate executives have relatively stable basic salaries which are fairly detached from corporate earnings. Methods of executive compensation take numerous forms beyond the basic salaries, however. Bonuses, pensions, and stock options are typical of short- and long-range deferred-income plans.

Some parts of executives' total incomes are more sensitive to corporate earning fluctuations than others. For example, bonuses move quite closely with earning changes over short periods. The decisions of executives to exercise stock options are also intimately related to the current earnings of the company. However, salaries are just moderately responsive to earning fluctuations, while pension programs are relatively insensitive to earning movements.[6]

Another important feature of executive compensation is its relative stability compared with other occupational categories. The owner-manager thrives or perishes as a result of short-range conditions which are frequently beyond his control. The operative employee and the foreman

---

[5] Robert Aaron Gordon, *Business Leadership in the Large Corporation* (Washington: The Brookings Institution, 1945), p. 327.

[6] One facet of executive compensation plans is that as an executive builds up a substantial interest in profit sharing and retirement programs he becomes less and less inclined to move from his company. If he did leave the loss of participation rights would result in a considerable financial penalty. Thus, executives tend to think twice about moving from their jobs even though attractive opportunities are available elsewhere. See Arthur H. Cole, *Business Enterprise in Its Social Setting* (Cambridge: Harvard University Press, 1959) pp. 92–93.

are susceptible to layoffs due to seasonal and cyclical business conditions. The executive, however, is fairly immune to serious income difficulties caused by short-run economic adjustments.[7] Executives are retained to the bitter end in economic adversity in anticipation of better times to come. A company would be hard put to replace its executive cadre constantly.[8]

From this it may be concluded that executive income exhibits a fair degree of inflexibility when related to corporate earnings.[9] This leads Gordon to observe that, "This system of incentives is far removed from the classical method of remunerating business leadership in a private enterprise economy. The particular reward of business leadership is supposed to be profits which link the businessman's remuneration directly and completely to the success or failure of the firm's operation."[10]

Thus a direct coupling between executive compensation and earnings does not prevail. The question now is what else besides profit provides incentives for executive action. Perhaps a partial answer is found in growth.

Incentives Stemming from Growth

It will be recalled by readers of the appendix to the last chapter that Don Walling, hero of *Executive Suite*, felt that growth and employee pride were ends which preceded making profits. However, profits in Walling's mind were necessary as means to achieve these salutary ends. This view is hardly atypical.

Managers are led to pursue objectives which are attractive to them as managers, not as owners. The interests of owners and managers need not be incompatible, of course, but they may differ as to the scale of size on one hand versus the amount of return on investment on the other. Nevertheless, owners may be content to forgo high returns if they realize an enhancement in the value of their property. Since appreciation is associated with a growth policy, the objective of management to expand finds a desirable mate with the objective of many investors to experience capi-

---

[7] For an example see "Top Pay Resists Slump," *Business Week*, May 20, 1961, pp. 63–68.

[8] Knauth observes: "Management looks upon salaries as a means of building up a corps of elite personnel that will carry on its essential policies. Each member acquires specialized knowledge that might be sacrificed were he to leave the organization. His value to it is disproportionately large in comparison to his market value. . . . The objective of management is to assure continuous functioning and the amount paid in salaries is a small part of total expense. It is natural, therefore, that salaries should be named for a long period and should be on the liberal side." See Oswald Knauth, *Managerial Enterprise* (New York: W. W. Norton and Co., 1948), p. 156.

[9] Katona says, "It has been found . . . that moderate increases in corporation profits rarely have a direct effect on the executive's remuneration or on the assurance with which they hold their positions." George Katona, *Psychological Analysis of Economic Behavior* (New York: McGraw-Hill, 1951), p. 197.

[10] Gordon, *op. cit.*, p. 296.

tal gains. This may explain why owners are happy with limited returns in the face of large retained earnings; but it does not get to the core of the issue of why management finds incentives in growth.

Many executives claim "we grow because we have to." In essence, they mean that growth is thrust upon them by the exigencies of their environment. Preservation of the *status quo* is not the way a progressive management meets the challenges of competition and the insatiable demands of the consumer. There can be no doubt that growth is necessary for survival for many firms. And there can be even less doubt that conditions external to a company make growth policies the only feasible long-run strategy for management.

Management, however, is not composed simply of passive actors responding to external stimuli. The growth of the firm offers executives forms of material and egoistic satisfactions which are not available through any other corporate incentive. Some of these satisfactions are explored below, running from the simple and obvious to the less obvious and complex.[11]

1. Growth makes more opportunities available for promotion.

2. Salaries are often dependent more on the size of a department or the size of a company as a whole than on profitability. Given the maintenance of a standard of efficiency and profitability, salaries are geared to such considerations as volume of sales, number of people employed, and volume of manufactured output. This is the same as saying salary is linked more to an executive's responsibilities than to profitability. As an organization grows there is no assurance its *rate* of profit will increase, although its absolute dollar profit might. However, increasing size generally carries increasing responsibility which provides a basis for higher compensation.

3. The third growth incentive is called the "instinct of workmanship" (for lack of a better title). Man has certain cravings for the personal satisfaction connected with a well-done job. This desire is no less evident among managers than among master carpenters. However, the satisfaction an executive derives from his work is more intangible—although no less real—than the concrete satisfactions produced by the creation of a beautifully carved cabinet.

A growing and efficient organization is both a tribute and a monument to managerial ability. Also, the chance to develop a vital organization is an outlet for the creative mind of an active personality. The fact cannot be discounted that "doing a good job" as reflected in organization growth is an incentive underlying management action. Rewards forthcoming from successful accomplishments along these lines have very few substitutes in the business world.

---

[11] Most of the satisfactions in this section are adapted from Clare E. Griffin, *Enterprise in a Free Society* (Chicago: Richard D. Irwin, Inc., 1949); esp. chaps. 5, 6.

4. Growth to a respectable size is prestige building in a business setting. Prestige, for reasons peculiar to our society, is associated with magnitudes of influence over large numbers of people and control of considerable quantities of resources. The ancient and often-cited characteristic of materialism is concerned with measuring success quantitatively rather than qualitatively.

It might be argued that a manager derives as much satisfaction from the quality of his operations or products as he does from the net worth, volume of sales, or the number of employees in his company. But size per se has a prior claim in support of the legitimacy of a business which quality does not possess. A hint of this is found in advertisements calling the public's attention to the point that this motion picture or this circus is the *biggest* and the best offered yet.

The objection might be raised that a company's growth is predicated on the quality of the goods and services offered, plus adherence to high standards of internal operations. This poses something of a chicken-egg problem which becomes helplessly entangled when the question of executive motivations is considered. Does management pursue quality and service objectives as means which eventually will produce a large and successful company? Or does management seek quality and service objectives as intrinsic values in themselves which may have the happy byproduct of giving a firm a commanding position in an industry?

These questions do not admit generalizations. At best, answers to them must consider management's personal goals and the situational character of the corporate setting. But one thing is fairly certain. An executive's affiliation with a large and successful organization is frequently sufficient in itself to reflect considerable prestige on the individual.

Prestige is bestowed from a number of sources which tend to give size a high priority in their value system.

a) Prestige is internally bestowed by fellow employees. The manager of a large department has a high stature because responsibility for a department of considerable magnitude implies a high degree of competency.

b) Prestige is externally bestowed by colleagues in other businesses.

c) Prestige is bestowed by the stockholders upon the management of influential companies.

d) Prestige is bestowed by the public because of awe-inspiring size and contributions to community well-being resulting from corporate influence in community affairs.

e) Prestige is bestowed by customers as a result of the provision of products and services which are available only through large companies.

Thus, size commands the respect and recognition of others. It is natural, therefore, that management should adopt organizational growth policies leading to increased size which will ultimately resolve themselves in the satisfaction of executives' prestige incentives. As expected, organization size goes hand in hand with power. Indeed, power and prestige are quite inseparable.

Power is socially defined. The culture of a society stakes out those institutions which are more favored as sources of power. Then it is up to the individual to affiliate with that institution which he appraises as yielding him the greatest opportunity to achieve personal power (if indeed power is an objective in an individual's life).

Many institutions have power potential—the church, government, the military, education, and business. Those people who are so disposed will gravitate to the institution which offers the greatest opportunity to exert power. In the Middle Ages the church offered careers which provided power incentives sufficient to attract the talented and the ambitious. The military in the Prussian state offered to the impoverished aristocracy the major outlet for their power drives. In our society the corporation of today has a good deal of potential in the power realm. Of course, not all of those who elect a career as a corporate executive will accumulate much personal power. But nevertheless the opportunity is there, and it is more or less democratically available to people from many different backgrounds.

Business yields power in a number of ways of which the most apparent is the production and command over wealth. But in addition, large corporations have other power incentives to offer their executives. Among these are influence over people, control over resources, and control over the machinery of organization. Another important adjunct of corporate power is the opportunity it gives executives to make decisions favorable to themselves as a management group. More is said of this later in the chapter.

Power is useful to perpetuate interests already vested in an organization. An established top management is usually sufficiently in control of proxy machinery that it seldom has to worry about retaining its position in face of discontented minorities or corporate raiders.

The corporation as a device for marshaling resources also makes possible the marshaling of power. As Latham points out, "A mature political conception of the corporation must view it as a rationalized system for the accumulation, control, and administration of power."[12] Management by expanding corporate power also expands the prestige and influence which go with it. Of course, as corporate power is extended the power of the individual executive is comparably expanded. Thus in a growing corporation the executive finds a setting offering sufficient opportunities for the satisfaction of his power drives.[13]

---

[12] Earl Latham, "The Body Politic of the Corporation," in Edward S. Mason, *op. cit.,* p. 220.

[13] The individual advances his power interests two ways: by promotions through the organizational hierarchy and by affiliating with a growing concern. Obviously,

So far two forms of executive incentives have been treated in their various ramifications. These are the financial incentives and the satisfactions obtained from company growth. Other motivations for participation in a corporation are indirectly associated with both the financial and the growth incentives.

Social Approval

Personal power and prestige are derived from occupying high status positions in the management of a large corporation, whereas "social approval" implies society's recognition of the worthiness of the activity itself.[14] Key men in criminal syndicates do not enjoy social approval, but they have considerable power as well as prestige in their immediate circles.

Historically, businessmen did not have a great deal of social approval. There is not much glamor about the self-seeking pursuit of wealth, even though wealth is supposed to be the reward for providing vital goods and services to the community. There has always been a deep-seated sentiment in our culture that the pursuit of wealth is not the noblest of man's endeavors. But the sentiment against business as such is wearing down for reasons enumerated below.

First, as a dominant institution in our society business claims the attention of the public. Size and influence often carry grudging social approval as long as they are not used to transgress loosely defined boundaries of propriety. Further, the owner-manager and the independent farmer are no longer social influentials. The executives of medium-sized and large corporations are now the spokesmen of free enterprise and individual liberty. These modern torchbearers are far differently situated than their predecessors.

As indicated earlier in this chapter, managerial financial incentives are not so rigid that the pursuit of wealth alone necessarily enjoys a singular or even a top-priority position on the index of an executive's work motives. Other objectives become more important—or at least equally important—than the attainment of wealth itself. Thus, the "uncouth" pursuit of profit is tempered by the executive's interest in more socially acceptable objectives.

Second, associated with these transitions in personal goals are changes which have taken place in business objectives.[15] It is frequently pointed

---

it is more to the advantage of the individual with strong power drives to associate with an expanding organization and work his way up than to attempt to work up through a fairly stable company.

[14] Griffin, *op. cit.*, p. 81.

[15] Dent observes that, "Not only do larger businesses subscribe to public service more than smaller ones, but growing businesses likewise mention public service more frequently than declining ones. . . ." James K. Dent, "Organizational Correlates of the Goals of Business Managements," *Personnel Psychology*, 1959, p. 389.

out that the corporation is a quasi-public institution in the sense that it has major objectives beyond the economic which make claims on its resources. The corporation, therefore, can be thought of as a multipurpose institution. Such objectives as industrial peace, community development, philanthropic activities, and employee well-being extend into areas which are sensitive to social approval or disapproval.

And third, in recognition of their quasi-public nature and their social visibility, large corporations have intensified public relations activities to sell the community on the idea that they are aware of their social obligations and are discharging them. Public relations programs are frequently directed toward building the image of good corporate citizenship and corporate responsibility.

The large corporation, in general, has succeeded in improving its position in public esteem.[16] Also, by the process of osmosis the smaller corporation is able to participate in the reflected glories of the larger. Flowing from this, management has grown in stature as an honorable and worthwhile "profession." Both established executives and young executives starting their careers are fairly assured that their choice of occupation will carry with it greater social approval today and in the future than it has in the past. Still, however, the corporate executive does not enjoy the approval usually given to doctors, clergymen, or lawyers. In fact, other less honorific occupations like teaching, social service, and governmental service, carry more approval, at times, than the management of a business. Consequently, the search for social acceptance by corporate management constantly goes on.

The Quest for Approval

There can be no question of the modern corporation's impact on the processes of American society. The extensiveness of corporate influence makes it difficult to talk of the corporation and corporate management as instruments of economic rationality. The corporation is a way of life for its members and for people outside it who come within its orbit of influence.[17]

The executives employed in a corporation carry into their communities the corporate image, either directly as agents of "good corporate works" or indirectly by the mere fact of affiliation with a particular company. It is because of the high degree of visibility of both the corporation and its executives that management is concerned with promoting an acceptable image.

----

[16] Now and then the polished image of the corporation becomes a little tarnished. The recent antitrust proceedings against large manufacturers of electrical products did not do much to advance the cause of good corporate citizenship.

[17] Carl Kaysen, "The Social Significance of the Modern Corporation," *American Economic Review*, May, 1957, p. 319.

Image slogans—such as the corporate conscience, the soulful corporation, and good corporate citizenship—have become popularized. The fact that such anthropomorphic characterizations are quite absurd does not seem to be a matter of much concern.[18] In reality, what is meant is that the management of a corporation is soulful, has a conscience, and accepts the responsibility of citizenship.

Achieving these high levels of managerial nobility as a matter of fact and not as a matter of public relations is a difficult affair, involving built-in paradoxes. For example, a corporate management would be socially conscious and a good citizen if in times of recession it would expand its capital investments, and if in times of prosperity with inflationary overtones it would contract its capital investments. However, most businessmen would say that such decisions do not make sense *from the standpoint of the company*. Probably they are right. The point is that decisions which are beneficial to society as a whole often may be detrimental to the firm in particular.

Management is faced with this same paradox when it moves into the political sphere of activity, when it moves into action on social issues, and when it sees fit to move into the areas of education and aesthetics. The dilemma is always one of organization good as opposed to social good. The nature of private enterprise forces American management to give priority to the company, although management sometimes makes good copy with decisions which simultaneously promote the interests of the firm and the welfare of society.[19]

Executives as chief actors in the economic order are forced to balance the need for social approval with the needs of their company. A management of a corporation does not win social approval by committing antisocial acts even if these acts are in the best interests of the firm. But at the same time, business ideology has it that the primary aim of management is economic rationality, at least in the long run. Also, society is perverse enough to punish those companies which do not live up to the obligations imposed by undertaking a business enterprise.

So management must somehow reconcile the demands of society for socially conscious behavior with the demands of economic rationality also expected by society. This situation would present an impossible dilemma were it not for two circumstances:

1. Social consciousness and economic rationality need not always be antithetical.
2. Social consciousness and economic rationality are not "either-or" alterna-

---

[18] See Earl Latham, "Anthropomorphic Corporations, Elites, and Monopoly Power," *American Economic Review*, May, 1957, pp. 303–10.

[19] Recognizing the inherent discrepancies which exist between society's aims and the aims of independent companies within society, the apocryphal statement, "what is good for General Motors is good for the country," makes little sense.

tives. Between these two alternatives, management has a range of discretion in which the social demands of the moment and the future can be balanced with short- and long-range economic goals.

The difficulties created by the dilemma just considered are on a rather high level of abstraction. The difficult issues of the social good and the individual good do not have wide appeal. Hence, the problem of social consciousness is geared down to a more mundane level. In this respect, some suppose that management dispatches its social obligations by contributions to worthy causes, thereby obtaining social approval.

Corporate giving as a means of gaining social approval is too large to be ignored. Richard Eells, one of the major exponents of corporate giving, states that management must use some funds for philanthropic purposes in order to insure the survival of the corporation. He points out that corporate philanthropy is not a capricious diversion of assets. Rather, the corporation strengthens its positions socially and economically by contributions to deserving beneficiaries.

Philanthropic activities, according to Eells, are related to a company's long-range, broadly-conceived social objectives. Corporate giving also has a crucial role in business strategy because an intelligent program enhances corporate power, prestige, and influence in a competitive situation. But a philanthropic program must be rationally conceived in a sense that the corporation must give in sufficient amounts to individuals and private organizations who are most influentially placed for granting approval and support to the management of the corporate donor. The recipients of grants should be in a position to respond with favorable opinions of the corporation which will percolate to the greatest extent possible through society. The salutary corporate image created by philanthropy facilitates the accomplishment and acceptance of other corporate goals like profitability and market domination. Thus, the guiding principle of corporate philanthropy is enlightened self-interest.[20]

A program of corporate philanthropy uses a number of channels for giving. Contributions are made to individuals for research and education; grants are bestowed on universities for either unrestricted uses or in support of specific research projects; and private research organizations benefit from corporate donations. In addition, corporations also contribute to charitable fund drives and community cultural and recreational programs.

Eells has an interesting statement pertaining to the philosophy of selecting grant recipients:

A corporation would not only be justified in supporting *research* into the whole problem of corporate survival in varying degrees of restraint on freedom of association; it should go further, and give *active support* to the vital private sectors in its immediate environment that work for the principle

---

[20] See Richard Eells, *Corporation Giving in a Free Society* (New York: Harper and Bros., 1956), p. 7.

of freedom of association and represent that principle in practice. This includes not only economic groups, but also health, recreational, educational, religious, professional, scientific, artistic, and other associational efforts to serve human needs.[21]

Although it might seem ungrateful, corporate philanthropy—and, indeed, the whole matter of corporate social responsibility—has not gone unchallenged. For example, Levitt claims that the major responsibility of business is to perform an economic function for a profit. The issue of social responsibility serves only to confuse the goals of business.[22]

Levitt notes that most advocates of the social responsibility doctrine admit, under close questioning, that they are motivated by cold cash. It is good business to be responsible. But still, there has been considerable talk about the altruistic motives behind corporate giving as a way to meet social obligations. Levitt feels the subtle danger is that executives will begin to believe their public relations image and accept the idea that their philanthropy is out of the pure love of man. Levitt concludes by saying, "Business will have a much better chance of surviving if there is no nonsense about its goals—that is, if long-run profit maximization is the one dominant objective in practice as well as in theory."[23]

Levitt's basic point is that management should stick to what it is able to do best—run a business. Management should not dabble in functions where it is on shaky ground—social responsibilities. This argument is extended by the notion that management ultimately makes its greatest social contribution through the operation of an efficient, profitable economic enterprise.

This issue is carried still further by questioning the predisposition and adequacy of management to judge the inherent value, objectives, and performance of nonbusiness undertakings which presumably fall within the scope of management's social responsibility.[24] According to Eells, in his statement quoted above, management should be interested in supporting health, recreational, educational, religious, professional, scientific, and ar-

---

[21] *Ibid.*, p. 103.

[22] Theodore Levitt, "The Dangers of Social Responsibility," *Harvard Business Review*, September–October, 1958, pp. 41–50.

[23] *Ibid.*, p. 49.

[24] Thorndike questions the role of businessmen as "keepers of public morality" in a shrewd article from which the following quotation is taken. "The virtues and services the world needs from producers, merchants, owners, and managers are not just the same as those which it needs from priests or teachers. The primary service of the former is to satisfy human wants; the primary service of the latter is to improve them. The cardinal virtues of the former in their capacity as economic agents are to maximize production, minimize waste, and distribute goods and services so they will be used to the maximal advantage of the human species. . . . Many farmers, miners, manufacturers, and merchants who do first-rate work for the world in their present states of mind would probably be confused and misled if they tried to behave as trustees for the public." Edward L. Thorndike, "The Psychology of the Profit Motive," *Harpers*, September, 1936, pp. 431–37.

tistic groups as long as they conform to principles of freedom of association.

More is at stake here than freedom of association. Certainly business is concerned with this important aspect of freedom. Educational institutions, and religious, scientific, and artistic groups are predicated on freedom of association but they thrive on freedom of expression as well. There are two dangers connected with corporate giving. The first is that socially valuable undertakings may not receive needed support because they do not ascribe to business ideological standards of philosophy and performance. The second, and more disasterous consequence, is that voluntary associations may modify *their* objectives and temper their freedom of expression to conform to business requirements for the receipt of support.

Eells' enlightened self-interest policy of giving is tricky because it leads to satisfying just those social obligations which produce the greatest material and ideological returns to the corporation. Other obligations are ignored. In this philosophy, the altruistic enhancement of social good is not the criterion of giving at all.

If the principle of corporate giving is accepted, then the issue resolves to what is the best means for making financial allocations for the advancement of social good. There are three other alternatives in addition to direct corporate giving:

1. *The government.* Presently the federal government encourages corporate giving by tax advantages. Supposing these advantages were removed, would the government make a better and more impartial agency for the distribution of funds derived from increased tax revenues? Or would anything be gained from retaining tax advantages but permitting the government to designate organizations to which contributions are acceptable or not acceptable for tax purposes?

2. *The stockholders.* In the short run, stockholders are deprived of some part of their dividends by a corporate giving policy. Would it be better for the corporation to withhold all contributions and distribute them to stockholders? Then stockholders could use this extra income as they see fit.

3. *Trusteeships or foundations.* This alternative centralizes giving but at the same time it does not have the onerous connotation of a government dole. It overcomes at least two objections which can be raised to the other alternatives. Thus, would it be an adequate solution to corporate giving to do so through a private agency, distinctly removed from the influence of the management of the corporation or corporations which have established it?

It is not without a reason that these alternatives have been stated in the form of questions. The whole matter of corporate giving and the motives of management underlying it is highly debatable. Ultimately, the reader must decide for himself the appropriateness of corporate giving in our society. If he decides it is appropriate he must then consider the most effective means for the distribution of funds.

The Profit Incentive

One aspect of the profit incentive has already been touched on in this chapter. It is the relationship between executive income and the profitability of the firm. The conclusion of this discussion, it is recalled, is that profit in itself is insufficient as an incentive to explain executive motives in the corporate setting. The question of profit as an incentive factor is reopened now to explore some of its other dimensions.

It is wise to make a distinction, following Drucker, between profitability and the profit motive. Profitability, according to Drucker, is an *objective* principle of social action. It is a measure of economic rationality and a criterion of success of a business enterprise in performing economic functions. The profit motive is a subjective facet of human motivation.[25] People pursue profits in order to gain personal satisfaction.

From the standpoint of the owner-manager, the profit motive and profitability are clearly inseparable. The owner-manager satisfies his personal material needs directly through the profitability of his firm. The case of the hired professional manager is not so simple. The manager's material wants are satisfied through a fairly stable salary and employment situation. As a first approximation, it could be said that the corporate manager is motivated by profit and seeks profitability to satisfy the needs of others having claims on the company.[26]

Perhaps the best place to begin talking about the profit issue is with the various claimants to corporate gross income. Gross income is apportioned among six claimants: suppliers, government, employees, maintenance, depreciation-obsolescence, suppliers of capital, and surplus.[27]

The last two items in this list require further explanation. Suppliers of capital as claimants include bondholders and stockholders. In the latter case, while it is not accepted accounting practice, some corporations have treated stockholder dividends as fixed charges implemented by a level dividend policy. Such a policy allows management to retain a high percentage of earnings in good periods for expansion purposes and to provide a bulwark against poor earning periods. From a strong position of retained earnings management is also able to pay the "usual" dividends regularly, thus keeping stockholders satisfied during times of lower-than-average earnings.[28]

---

[25] Peter Drucker, *The Concept of the Corporation* (New York: The John Day Company, 1946), pp. 234–36.

[26] The distinction is not so neat, however, because as indicated earlier there is a relationship between profitability and the gross income of managers.

[27] Knauth, *op. cit.*, pp. 149–50.

[28] *Ibid.*, pp. 145–46; pp. 159–60.

As for the last item, that which is left over after the claimants to the corporation's gross income have been taken care of is called loosely profit or surplus. Now, profit has claimants, too. These claimants are the government (more taxes), employees (fringe benefits and incentive rewards), stockholders (extra dividends), the public (social beneficences), and finally management itself (bonuses and other amenities). Management occupies the unique, and at times uneasy, position of both participant in and dispenser of corporation profits. The allocation by management of gross income, but particularly profit, to claimants underscores management's need to balance the distribution of assets among the several groups having legitimate claims.

The Problem of Retained Earnings. "Plowing back" earnings into a company is a fundamental part of American business ideology. Sutton and his associates observe that, "So enchanted is the business creed with the social beneficence of plowing back that in some circumstances it is reluctant to count retained earnings as profits at all."[29]

Probably the roots of the philosophy of plowing earnings back into the business are traceable to the period in history when America was a capital-poor nation. During this time Europe supplied some capital for the development of railroads. In general, however, businessmen came to rely on self-financing as the most reliable source of funds for expansion purposes. Over time the notion of financing growth out of internal capital resources became ingrained in business mentality.

One would expect, however, that as this country moved from a capital-poor to a capital-rich nation the reliance on internally generated funds to support expansion would give way to the use of funds available externally in the capital market. But apparently any vast shift from internal to external financing is not discernible, or not in this century at least. Lintner says:

> The relative shifts in the reliance on internal or external funds as the level of business activity, profits, and total financial requirements change have been remarkably stable over a full half century, and the ratio of internal to external funds has been approximately the same in years of comparable level and rate of change of activity.[30]

The classical rationale behind the decision to retain earnings for self-financing or to pay them as dividends is simple and straightforward. According to the theory, if the directors and management of a corporation are to act in the best interests of the stockholders they must reinvest earnings in the business or pay dividends in conformance with marginal principles governed by the ruling rate of interest. Management should act as

---

[29] Francis X. Sutton, Seymore E. Harris, Carl Kaysen, and James Tobin, *The American Business Creed* (Cambridge: Harvard University Press, 1956), p. 85.

[30] John Lintner, "The Financing of Corporations," in Edward S. Mason (ed.), *op. cit.*, p. 184.

if it feels stockholders' potential dividends will earn more if plowed back into the company than these dividends would command by being paid to owners and then employed in other investment channels.[31]

In practice, data to support such marginal calculations are extremely difficult to come by. It is really impossible to say whether a retained-earnings policy best serves the interest of the stockholder and the free enterprise system or results in a misallocation of capital resources.

In spite of this, the use of retained earnings for expansion does have some interesting implications which focus on the profit incentive as a managerial motivation.

First, "the plowing in of earnings on the part of business corporations is another means of securing predominating influence for the groups in control. . . . Self-financing . . . is an expression of the general tendency of modern business management to work for the business as such and not for the capitalists and creditors."[32] Beckerath's observation points up a key idea often cited in management literature. The typical corporate executive identifies with the company and finds his relevant reference group among other executives. He does not usually identify with others having interest in corporate affairs.[33]

Making profits coupled with the opportunity of keeping a sizeable chunk of them allows for a managerial flexibility in the decision area which will strengthen the company and insure its expansion. Additionally, corporate growth, continuity, and affluence are essential to the perpetuation of incumbent management, affording it an opportunity to enhance power and prestige. Hence, there is a very happy wedding between managerial objectives and retained earnings policies which is not entirely explainable by the marginal logic relative to the "ideal" distribution of corporate profits.

Second, "plowing-back insulates the expansion projects of existing firms from the test of the market . . . plowing-back enables the management to go ahead with its investment projects . . . even if the appraisal of the market is that the funds could be better used elsewhere."[34]

Self-financing frees management from the possible limitations that could be imposed by having investment plans subject to the veto of the capital market. By detaching itself from this constraint management can make investment decisions which may be good for the firm, but without

---

[31] Norman S. Buchanan, "Theory and Practice of Dividend Distribution," *Quarterly Journal of Economics*, 1938, pp. 70–78.

[32] Herbert Von Beckerath, *Modern Industrial Organization* (New York: McGraw-Hill Book Co., 1933), pp. 68–69.

[33] On the point of managerial identification see C. Addison Hickman, "Managerial Motivation and the Theory of the Firm," *American Economic Review*, May, 1955, pp. 549–50; and Katona, *op. cit.*, pp. 196–97.

[34] Sutton, *op. cit.*, p. 88

prior endorsement of the affair as a socially useful undertaking. Freedom from the capital market allows management to present corporate "outsiders" with a *fait accompli* in an investment sense.

This discussion should cause the reader to realize that the opportunity to make a profit invokes a very complex set of motives in corporate management. Retained earnings are obviously based on profits. These earnings are used for a variety of purposes, such as expansion, freedom from market tests, securing the future of the corporation and its management, and making possible a continuous and level dividend for stockholders. Also, corporate profits force management to make balancing decisions in terms of distribution to various claimants. In this role management is at once a distributor of profits and a claimant of them. Management then must be cautious of the returns it allocates to itself relative to the other parties.

All of this should not obscure the fact that there is a profit orientation, pure and simple, to which corporate management subscribes. Whether this orientation is one of maximization or something else is highly debatable. It is certain, however, that management does not seek profits for the sake of directly improving its personal fortunes (although this may be the happy result over a moderately long period of time). Also, there is doubt that management seeks profits for the owners alone.

It is fair to conclude that management seeks profits so that corporate well-being is assured, thereby satisfying those who have stakes in it. A vital corporation is a monument to management. That such a corporation is also profitable is a necessary fact of life. But by no means is profitability the only incentive, or even the main incentive, for management action. It is a means to an end.

The various incentives and their implications provide some insight into the reason for executive action. Limitation on executive behavior is also apparent in the corporate setting and must be treated to round out the discussion. Therefore, constraint on management is the topic that follows.

EXECUTIVE CONSTRAINTS

The constraints on executive action are no less important than the incentives which promote action in the corporate environment. It could be said that even the incentives have built-in limitations. For example, organization growth may bring new people to the organization and result in a dilution of the power and influence of established executives. Profits or market domination might create adverse public reaction and cause antitrust proceedings to be instituted by the federal government. Stockholders may rebel on the issue of management stock options. Thus, the incentives are not absolute in any sense.

This section, however, does not examine the limitations which logically adhere to executive incentives. Rather, it explores some other limitations imposed on executive behavior by sources both internal and external to the corporation.

Internal Sources of Constraints

The constraints treated under this heading flow from limitations to executive action generated by the interpersonal and organizational dynamics found within the firm. The internal constraints are dwelt upon at length. Many of the following considerations have been analyzed in other chapters; for example, the constraints of organization, both formal and informal, have been discussed in Chapters 7 and 8. Most of the issues appearing below are simply applications in a specific context of ideas covered elsewhere.

Formal Internal Limitations. The limitations in this classification are derived from classic organization theory. It is obvious that in a military, chain-of-command type of organization the behavior of subordinates is circumscribed by the demands of superiors. Authority, responsibility, and accountability are the formal devices which limit executive behavior to a certain extent. Re-enforcing the authority structure of the formal organization are policies, procedures, and rules which provide quasi-automatic regulations that the individual accepts by curbing his inclinations and modifying his behavior to accord with formal company requirements. Submission of the individual to these internal controls is prerequisite to his continued participation in a firm.

Formal constraints, of course, do not cover all possible behavior patterns. And they are not always effective in the cases they do cover. Formal constraints set out the ground rules for behavior. Far from being comprehensive these rules allow individuals and groups considerable latitude for unregulated behavior.

Quasi-Formal Constraints. Many behavioral codes never find their way into written, formal company policy. These constraints are real nonetheless, and they limit an individual's freedom to behave as he likes. These codes range from relatively innocuous prescriptions like the manner of dress, modes of transportation to and from work, and the pecking order in executive dining rooms, to matters of policy vital to the firm. The methods of executive promotion discussed in the last chapter are also included in this area.

The quasi-formal constraints can be described best as customary behavioral forms which have developed historically. They are traditions to which executives better conform in order to avoid embarassment and trouble. They are the how-we-do-it-here codes which are not committed to writing but are generally known and accepted by the executives in a company.

Informal Constraints. Informal organizations among executives often spell out the power groups influential in directing the destiny of a company. Like most informal organizations they possess the characteristics of social control, sociometric structuring, informal leadership, and the like. In other words, there is a certain universality about the characteristics of the informal organization as it is found throughout all levels of the company. But the stakes of informal association are higher in upper-management levels. The influential informal organization of higher management is perhaps more rigorous in its selection of membership. At the same time, the individual member must be more cautious in his alliances and in the way he behaves once an alliance has been contracted.

In bureaucratic theory, the informal groups are often referred to as centers of influence in the organization. Through such groups an individual can gain considerable personal power, if he receives the necessary group support. But if support is withheld or withdrawn an individual's power aspirations may be doomed. An executive must keep one eye on the formal aspects of organization and the other on their sources of internal support for programs. No executive can remain aloof from power alignments, because they provide him with valuable assistance for the implementation of his programs and for support in his position. An executive is constrained in his actions by the expectations of his informal associations in the organization. He must service these expectations or be faced with the consequence of the denial of group support. The seriousness of group denial for an executive is situational. It depends on the degree of independent, personal power, and prestige of an executive; it also depends on the structure and magnitude of group influence.

Committees. It is difficult to categorize the type of constraints that result from committee activities. In a real sense, the constraints they imposed are of a form combining all three of the restraints mentioned previously. First of all, the committee is a formally constituted body within the structure of a company. As such it is endowed with power and limitations much as with any other formal activity. These limits to authority circumscribe the behavior of the membership of the committee. Second, committees, particularly standing committees, develop over time folklore and rituals all their own. These traditions delineate acceptable and unacceptable forms of behavior. Third, the element of informal pressure is active in committees. The group decision-making process is a powerful force for bringing into line recalcitrant individuals.

A variation on this same theme is noted by Cyert and March.

There is a reasonable amount of evidence to support the prediction that an individual with an attitude at variance with his perception of the group's attitude will tend . . . to adjust his "public" position to conform to the position he expects the group to take. Such behavior may be exhibited even in the limiting case where all members hold a position at variance with their common perception of the group standard.[35]

---

[35] R. M. Cyert and J. G. March, "Organizational Structure and Pricing Behavior in an Oligopolistic Market," *American Economic Review*, March, 1955, p. 133.

The committee is an excellent spot for the display of interpersonal dynamics. As a body of the formal organization the committee allows for the "legitimate" interplay of personalities. The chances for power maneuvering, discrediting adversaries, and building one's personal prestige are rife in these situations. The committee offers an excellent stage for organizational gamesmanship.

That the group demands conformity is fairly well established. But there is doubt that conformity to a group decision in the committee setting will result in individual conformity to this decision outside the committee room. Whether or not an individual conforms depends on company philosophy[36] and the sanctions he might anticipate from a deviation from a group decision.

Much more can be said of the internal constraints on management. Role theory could be restated along with administrative problems of communication, morale, and balance. But since these matters have received attention earlier it serves no purpose to go into them again in this section. The reader should be able to list a dozen more internal constraints on executive behavior after a cursory review of the analytical areas in Part II. The issues associated with the external constraints are treated next.

External Sources of Constraints

Woodrow Wilson said in 1910, "We have witnessed in modern business the submergence of the individual within the organization, and yet the increase to an extraordinary degree of the power of the individual—of the individual who happens to control the organization."[37]

Twenty-two years later Berle and Means observed, "In its new aspect the corporation is a means whereby the wealth of innumerable individuals has been concentrated into huge aggregates and whereby control over this wealth has been surrendered to a unified direction. The power attendant upon such concentration has brought forth princes of industry, whose position in the community is yet to be defined."[38]

Speaking of the corporation in 1960, Rostow asks ". . . has it become a free collectivity, divorced in its business life from significant public or private control, save the will of the small group which happens to have inherited its management?"[39]

These quotations represent abiding problems of the corporation which thoughtful writers have focused upon throughout the century. The first problem is corporate economic, social, and political power. The second

---

[36] See Drucker's concept of the "chief-executive" team which stresses joint deliberation but individual decision. Peter Drucker, *The Practice of Management* (New York: Harper and Bros., 1954) pp. 176 *ff.*

[37] Cited in Ripley, *op. cit.*, p. 1.

[38] Berle and Means, *op. cit.*, p. 2.

[39] Eugene V. Rostow, "To Whom and for What Ends is Corporate Management Responsible?" in Edward S. Mason, *op. cit.*, p. 50.

problem is the role of management in the exercise of this power. And the third problem is the source of external control over this power. This last provides the theme for this part of the chapter.

Power and Responsibility. Deeply ingrained in American tradition is the notion that power must be responsible. Those who possess power have to give account to others of the way in which it is used. Only because of accountability is power considered legitimate in our society. Thus, power is granted when controls over it are available. Theoretically, corporate power is tolerated in the name of economic necessity; but more importantly power is tolerated because society accepts existing external constraints as sufficient to render management of the corporation responsible. Four traditional constraints on the power of corporate management are reviewed next.

Traditional Constraints. 1. *Property.* Stockholder participation in the affairs of the company is a classic solution to managerial autonomy. But efforts in this direction are doomed. The dispersion of ownership makes effective stockholder participation hopeless.[40]

2. *The consumer.* The sovereignty of the consumer is another frequently cited traditional element of control over managerial autonomy. Businessmen are careful to point out that competition for consumer "votes" in the form of dollars is a real constraining force. Therefore, business must follow the lead of the consumer. That consumer tastes are molded by advertising and sales promotion is somewhat in opposition to the claims of consumer sovereignty. Sutton and his associates make the interesting observation that the more businessmen attempt to condition consumer behavior the more they proclaim the doctrine of consumer autonomy.[41]

3. *The public.* The public's capability for imposing restraints on management assumes three forms. The first is as a mass capable of violent reaction by force against misdeeds; revolution, in short! The second form is an orderly expression through representatives of sentiments that are eventually manifested as new government regulations or enforcement of existing regulations. The third form is spontaneous public reaction to irresponsibility through various communication media such as the press and the organs of voluntary pressure associations. These methods of expression and others constitute the verbalization of the restrainng force of public opinion.

Public sentiment as a means of constraint operates with varying degrees of effectiveness. Discounting revolution as a likely possibility, public opinion and government regulation remain. The efforts of public relations to create a favorable image are at least in apart an attempt to neu-

---

[40] For Rostow's position on this point see *ibid.*, pp. 53–56.
[41] Sutton, *op. cit.*, pp. 360–62.

tralize the sovereignty of public opinion.[42] It has been sagely suggested by a businessman, however, that the harping of public relations departments on corporate social responsibility has raised public expectations of corporate behavior. A misdeed that might have been passed off years ago by the public as, "Well, what more could you expect from businessmen?" now elicits severe critical judgments.

Government regulation has traditionally been negative in that it prescribes what a corporation cannot do in the interest of public well-being. Typically, it has not been positive by encouraging and supporting those groups that have stakes in a company; it has not backed the efforts of those wishing participation in corporate affairs. Chayes points out that regulatory "nay-saying" has proven ill-adapted to answer the question of corporate power.[43]

4. *The economic system.*[44] The role of the "unseen hand" of competition in classical economic theory secured the responsible allocation of resources despite ignoble intentions and actions of individual businessmen. This automatic regulating force was something of a reality for a nineteenth-century economy which approximated a purely competitive system more closely than the twentieth-century market structure.

That this impartial force is potently operative today is generally discounted. However, some writers who speak of uncertainty under oligopolistic conditions and of countervailing power make the case that these situations result in a form of "workable competition" which achieves outcomes not unlike those created in highly competitive economic systems.

The alternative models to the "invisible hand" of competition do not give as tightly reasoned explanations for the allocation of resources as does the model of pure competition. Management has such a wide range of discretion under imperfectly competitive situations that if it does behave responsibly it is not because it is reacting to an impersonal and impartial market force. It is for other reasons which must be sought outside the economic order.[45]

The discussion so far has highlighted the shortcomings of the traditional constraints on management. The preceding should not obscure the fact that these four constraints are still operative with varying degrees

---

[42] For an interesting commentary on public relations see Bernard D. Nassiter, "Management's Cracked Voice," *Harvard Business Review*, September–October, 1959, pp. 127–33.

[43] Abram Chayes, "The Modern Corporation and the Rule of Law," in Edward S. Mason (ed.), *op. cit.,* p. 45.

[44] The problem of retained earnings discussed earlier may be reread in connection with this section. The propensity of the capital market to supply or withhold funds for business is another aspect of constraints imposed by the economic system.

[45] See Edward S. Mason, "The Apologetics of 'Managerialism'," *Journal of Business,* January, 1958, pp. 1–11.

of effectiveness. The constraints, however, have been diluted, leaving regions in which management can act without being accountable for its behavior.

The gaps created by the breakdown of classical constraints allow for two forms of management behavior. They are managerial exploitiveness and managerial morality.

Exploitive Behavior

A number of years ago James Burnham's thesis of the managerial revolution caused quite a stir. George Orwell, commenting on Burnham, summarizes his thesis.

> Capitalism is disappearing, but Socialism is not replacing it. What is now arising is a new kind of planned, centralized society which will be neither capitalist nor, in any accepted sense of the word, democratic. The rulers of this new society will be the people who effectively control the means of production: that is, business executives, technicians, bureaucrats, and soldiers lumped together by Burnham under the name of "managers." These people will eliminate the old capitalist class, crush the working class, and so organize society that all power economic privileges remain in their own hands. Private property rights will be abolished, but common ownership will not be established.[46]

Orwell's interpretation of Burnham is not altogether accurate. The managerial expropriation of the working class is overstated. But the central theme of Burnham's thesis is indeed the idea that neither capitalism nor socialism will survive. These systems will be replaced by "managerialism," which is similar in spirit to technocracy.

Burnham does say that the managerial economy will be exploitive. However, he carefully qualifies his meaning of "exploitation." Since Marx, exploitation in an economic sense has meant the gouging of classes by a ruling class. Of exploitation, Burnham says it "is . . . simply an economy wherein one group receives a relatively larger share of the products of the economy than another. . . . All class economies are exploiting . . . and the managerial economy will be exploiting."[47] Thus, because of their strategic location in industry managers will be able to get for themselves more than their "rightful" share of the fruits of the economy. However, this does not mean that managers will necessarily be predatory.

While much of Burnham's thesis can be dismissed, one facet of it remains of vital concern. As the power of managers in key decision-making situations increases the question must be raised as to how prone they will be to subordinate their interests, collectively or individually, to the inter-

---

[46] George Orwell, *James Burnham and the Managerial Revolution* (London: Socialist Book Centre, 1946), p. 1.

[47] James Burnham, *The Managerial Revolution* (New York: The John Day Co., 1947), p. 123.

ests of the groups they are supposed to serve. Exploitation is a continuum. At one extreme are rewards which "naturally" accrue to groups because of their position in society; at the other extreme are socially burdensome advantages which favorably situated groups extract because they have the opportunity to do so.

Managerial Morality

The Burnham thesis imputes to management two reasons for being responsible. The first is that managers, like all good technocrats, work for the efficiency of the industrial system as a value in itself. The second reason is that managers stand to lose their exploitive advantages if the system fails to function effectively.

This thesis sounds foreign to American business folkways because nowhere in it is the notion of simple morality as an underlying reason for responsible behavior. Out of the considerable literature dealing with American business ethics and morality one is able to extract the leading idea that, deep down, management is of good and kind disposition.

But it is not even necessary to go to the literature to find support for this point of view. Public sentiment largely reflects the attitude that management is basically responsible. And this attitude has a rather firm foundation in fact. On the whole, management does behave responsibly in the sense that decisions which have moral and social implications are made in accord with prevailing social values and public policy.

This affirmation of faith in the basic morality of businessmen hardly answers the question of why management is responsible even in situations where society cannot impose direct sanctions. Perhaps part of the answer is found in a notion of positive and negative reasons for morality.

Management has a genuine concern for mass opinion and its latent potential of being felt in government and in the market place. Unfavorable public sentiment can be expressed through more intensive regulation of business. All in all, the public can modify the existing system by legal means. This ability is a deterring force that prevents gross irresponsibility. Management feels it has more to lose than gain from risky acts that might stir up public opinion. It is better to be comfortably assured of what one can get under the *status quo* rather than risk substantial lose.

There is another negative explanation for managerial responsibility. Many corporations, particularly the large ones, are in oligopolistic industries where firms are uncertain of the decisions of other firms. There is no assurance under these circumstances that all companies in a particular industry will act irresponsibly at the same time; so the management of any particular company hesitates to take the risk of being the first to have the spotlight turned on it. What results is a kind of responsibility vacuum, which each firm's management fears to be the first to fill with irresponsible acts.

A positive type of morality is motivated by a sincere feeling of social responsibility. Positive morality is a product of professionalization and is manifested as the pure notion of managerial stewardship.

Masons' alternatives regarding managerialism are excellent for summarizing the thoughts developed in this section. He says it is possible that:

1. The economy is not so managerial. It is still subject to classical constraints.
2. The economy is managerial, but not enough is known about it to explain why managers act responsibly in the public interest.
3. Managers do not generally behave in a responsible manner.[48]

Of the three alternatives, the second appears to be the most promising for two reasons: it accords with the intuitive feelings of many who are directly or indirectly concerned with corporate enterprise; and it opens up an avenue of research, evaluation, and critical judgment which may either support or prove the error of public opinion.

REVIEW QUESTIONS

1. How does the separation of ownership from control relate to the unique position occupied by management in the modern corporation?

2. In what respects does the incentive of profit differ for the modern manager as compared with the owner-manager?

3. Discuss the relationship between a manager's personal financial success and corporate financial success.

4. How is growth a managerial incentive? How does growth relate to personal power and prestige?

5. What factors underlie management's quest for social approval? What paradoxes are inherent in this quest?

6. Evaluate the self-interest concept of corporate philanthropy.

7. Discuss the allocative decisions management must make in respect to gross income and profits. What problems are posed by retained earnings in the allocative sense?

8. "Deeply ingrained in American tradition is the notion that power must be responsible." Discuss in reference to corporate management.

9. What are the shortcomings of the traditional restraints on corporate power?

10. "All class economies are exploiting . . . and the managerial economy will be exploiting." Analyze Burnham's thesis in reference to modern management.

SUPPLEMENTARY READINGS

GORDON, ROBERT AARON. *Business Leadership in the Large Corporation*. Washington: Brookings Institution, 1945.

LATHAM, EARL. "Anthropomorphic Corporations, Elites, and Monopoly Power," *American Economic Review*, May, 1957, pp. 303–10.

---

[48] Edward S. Mason, "The Apologetics of 'Managerialism,' " *op. cit.*, p. 9.

LEVITT, THEODORE. "The Dangers of Social Responsibility," *Harvard Business Review*, September–October, 1958, pp. 41–50.

MASON, EDWARD S. "The Apologetics of 'Managerialism'," *Journal of Business*, pp. 1–11.

ROSTOW, EUGENE V. "To Whom and for What Ends is Corporate Management Responsible?" *The Corporation in Modern Society* (ed. EDWARD S. MASON), pp. 46–71. Cambridge: Harvard University Press, 1960.

CHAPTER 18

Leadership

F EW areas in the behavioral sciences have attracted as much research and speculative activity as leadership. In the past, theories of leadership gained ascendancy only to give way eventually to newer postulates. Even now there is hardly a coherent body of doctrine which may be labeled *the* theory of leadership. In spite of this difficulty most students of the subject agree that they address themselves to seven major questions, with varying degrees of emphasis, in their research and writing. These questions are:[1]

1. Why do people subordinate themselves to a leader?
2. What are the sources of the leader's power?
3. How and why do leaders arise?
4. What motivates leaders to lead?
5. What are the functions of the leader?
6. What determines leadership effectiveness?
7. Are there any common denominators of leadership behavior and leadership characteristics?

This chapter reviews and appraises some of the work in the behavioral sciences and management which has sought answers to these questions. It is not the objective of this chapter to propose a theory of leadership. Rather, its objective is to acquaint the reader with some problems and issues in this area and to direct him to research sources which may provide him with additional insights into the mystery of leadership.

VARIOUS APPROACHES TO LEADERSHIP

Historically, a number of leadership theories have enjoyed popularity. Some of these theories have been discredited, others have been retained in modified forms, and still others are emerging as research in the behavioral sciences continues. The types of leadership theory discussed in this section are found in current literature. They are not all acceptable to the many schools of leadership thought, however. (For example, the traitist approach to leadership finds limited approval among those who are com-

---

[1] Warren G. Bennis, "Leadership Theory and Administrative Behavior: The Problem of Authority," *Administrative Science Quarterly*, Vol. 4 (1959–1960), p. 261.

mitted to the situational theory.) In any event, there is value in outlining the various strands of contemporary leadership thinking.[2]

The Traitist Approach

The traitist approach deals exclusively with the personal abilities of leaders; it represents one of the earliest attempts to organize a coherent theory of leadership. At the start, leaders were associated with extraordinary powers—the "great man" idea. Somewhat later this view gave way to simple descriptions of traits which a good leader should have. Reviewing some of these trait lists recalls Boy Scout days; they admonish the leader to be helpful, friendly, courteous, kind, and so on.

While the traitist approach finds little favor among the more sophisticated scholars of leadership it is surprising how frequently it appears in management and marketing literature in reference to desirable qualities of salesmen, sales managers, and administrators in general.

The Modified Traitist Approach

Usually, the unsophisticated lists of traits which describe characteristics of "good" leaders are based on intuition of the writer or questionable research. The recent traitist approach is different. Traits are not arbitrarily selected. They are derived from carefully designed tests and from research methodologies which continuously refine the processes of data collection. Out of these research efforts have come two or perhaps three generalized traits.

Conscientious researchers are not given to making vast claims for the generality of their findings, especially in the behavioral sciences. But the traits of intelligence (abstractive ability), communication, and the ability to perceive group values come as close as anything presently recognized as common personal qualities found among leaders in widely diversified activities. More is said of these traits later.

Basic to research of this type is the methodological problem of the initial separation of study groups into leaders-nonleaders, or good-not-so-good leaders. Categorizations of these types require judgments. Obviously, the researchers must have systems of values in mind when they designate "leaders" and "nonleaders" for study. These values in themselves defy empirical validation.[3]

The traitist approach rests in the nature of personal qualities. However, it can be objected that traits are not only personal qualities but are necessities generated by the situation in which they appear. In this respect, leadership is situational.

---

[2] This discussion follows Alex Bavelas, "Leadership: Man and Function," *Administrative Science Quarterly*, March, 1960, pp. 491–98.

[3] *Ibid.*, pp. 492–93.

The Situational Approach

The situational view of leadership has many exponents. This approach is based on the notion that traits are not the main determinant of who will rise in a leadership setting; rather, the situation or the environment is the relevant variable. Thus, a leader in one situation may not be a leader in a different situation regardless of the traits he possesses.

The situational approach is valuable because each organization has a certain uniqueness in spite of the fact that organizations have structural similarities as well. The uniqueness of an organization corresponds to its personality. Research following the situational approach focuses on the personality of the organization as a whole as well as on its parts.

The functional character of leadership is closely allied to the situational approach. It is possible for almost anyone to become a leader if circumstances allow him to perform activities designated by the situation. Hence, if the situation is one of emergency a leader might arise to fulfill the functions demanded in this case. And the individual who appears in this role might not ordinarily be the same one who carries out leadership functions over the group in stable situations.

The functional aspect of leadership requires researchers to investigate how leadership activities are distributed in an organization. It requires, further, a probe of the organization's power structure to determine why one individual, out of a number of presumably qualified individuals, is propelled into a leadership role.[4]

Generalizing on the status of the situational and traitist approaches to leadership, Bavelas says:

> The status of trait and situational leadership research can be summed up in this way: (1) The broad similarities which hold for a great number of organizations make it possible to say useful things about the kind of person who is likely to become a leader in any of these organizations, and (2) the unique characteristics of a particular organization make it necessary to analyze the situational factors that determine who is likely to become a leader *in one particular organization.*[5]

---

[4] An interesting sidelight on this matter is revealed by a study of the Nazi elite. Lerner states, "The conclusion we draw is that in the Nazi Party, despite its being a revolutionary movement, leadership came chiefly not to those of propagandist brilliance or charismatic qualities but to those with the more bureaucratic qualities of loyalty and seniority—traits the administrator showed." Most Nazi administrators were of plebian origin; they joined the movement later than other groups; and they were generally disappointed in earlier attempts to make a middle-class career for themselves. Thus because of a peculiar combination of events the bulk of the Nazi elite was composed of frustrated administrative types projected to their status positions in the party by the nature of the situation combined with the function they had to perform. See Daniel Lerner, *The Nazi Elite* (Stanford: Stanford University Press, 1951), pp. 39–59.

[5] Bavelas, *op. cit.*, p. 494.

DEFINITION OF LEADERSHIP

Although it is impossible to find a definition of leadership which is generally accepted, it is useful to examine several that have been offered. These definitions were developed largely out of research projects and they contain certain common elements which are discussed in this section.

Stogdill defines leadership as ". . . the process of influencing the activities of an organized group in its efforts toward goal setting and goal achievement."[6]

He points out that in a definition of leadership three elements are presumed to constitute minimum social conditions. The first is the presence of a group; second, a common task or group objective; and third, a differentiation of responsibility. Leadership, to Stogdill, is a segment of group organization. Organization as such is based on the division of functions which must be performed. The distinctions among organizational roles, founded on functional differentiation, are essential to the existence of leadership. Without the separation of activities there is no opportunity for the leader to co-ordinate the efforts of group members toward accomplishing an objective.

Gibb looks on leadership as ". . . a concept applied to the personality-environment relation to describe the situation where one, or at most a very few, personalities are so placed that his or their 'will, feeling, and insight direct and control others in the pursuit of a cause.' "[7] Gibb feels leadership is not a trait but a quality of a role within a group structure. Along Stogdill's line, Gibb believes that a group structure implies different directions of individual action requiring a leader to weld them into a co-ordinated attack on problem solving.

Bennis sees leadership as ". . . the process by which an agent induces a subordinate to behave in a desired manner."[8] He describes five elements contained in this definition.

1. *The agent*—an actor in a leadership role.
2. *The process*—sanctions, incentives and moral suasions by which the leader induces action.
3. *The subordinate*—the agent must perceive what needs the subordinates wish satisfied, and he must control the means for granting satisfactions.
4. *Induced behavior*—the process of influence implemented by sanctions and incentives.
5. *The manner*—the avenues of obtaining a goal.

---

[6] Ralph M. Stogdill, "Leadership, Membership and Organization," *Psychological Bulletin*, January, 1950, p. 4.

[7] Cecil A. Gibb, "The Principles and Traits of Leadership," *Journal of Abnormal and Social Psychology*, July, 1947, p. 267.

[8] Bennis, *op. cit.*, p. 295.

Bavelas observes that leadership acts are those which enable the group to achieve its objectives by giving assistance in making choices. From this point of view, "Organizational leadership consists of uncertainty reduction."[9] Alternatives in a decision setting range on a continuum of increasing uncertainty and importance. At some levels in this range management reserves the decisions for itself. "Precisely where a management draws this line defines its scope."[10] At this point it assumes the responsibility and risks inherent in directing a group toward objectives.

These definitions have several common elements which are stated explicitly or are implied. They are:

1. *Differentiation of functions.* Without a division of labor in a group the leader is deprived of the opportunity to assert his co-ordinative abilities to promote group solidarity in the pursuit of a goal. Further, it is recognized that the leadership function itself is a differentiated activity which arises out of group processes.[11]

2. *The necessity of the group.* While it may be evident that leadership cannot exist where there are no people to lead, it is not so obvious that the group often supports the leader, defines objectives, and serves as the source of effort for goal accomplishment. Many definitions of leadership stress the role of the group, its culture and "personality," as the most significant variable in the situational approach to leadership activities.

3. *Objectives.* Most groups arise to solve problems, and in this respect the goals or the ends sought by the group are important to the people in it. The leader should be able to perceive these ends and direct the group to al-

---

[9] Bavelas, *op. cit.*, p. 495.

[10] *Ibid.*, p. 496.

[11] Some interesting lessons may be learned in this respect from experiences with the so-called "structureless group." Use of the structureless group as a selection device for army officers is traceable to German military psychology in the 1920's. The process works rather as follows. A small group of officer candidates is assembled after the initial phases of selection are completed. They are brought together with no other apparent purpose than to discuss areas of common interest. At first the group flounders because of its hazy goal and lack of organization. But during the meeting an individual appears who directs the group into channels of fruitful analysis. The leader who arises actually "structures" a previously unstructured situation and reduces the group's uncertainty about the direction it is to proceed in the session.

During these activities the formal conference director, who usually remains passive throughout the proceedings, observes the group's and the leader's behavior. The expression of attitudes by individuals which are most desired in military leadership are carefully noted and credited to these persons' behalf when the final choice of candidates for officer training is made. It might be added that the traits looked for by observers are carefully identified and validated against the traits evidenced by successful military leaders. See H. L. Ansbacher, "German Military Psychology," *Psychological Bulletin*, June, 1941, pp. 370–92; and, by the same author, "The History of the Leaderless Group Discussion Technique," *Psychological Bulletin*, Vol. 48 (1951), pp. 383–91.

There are many modifications of this approach in modern executive selection and training methods. However, the idea behind the use of these techniques remains much the same as developed by the German psychologists. This idea is to allow normal group processes to identify potential leaders.

ternative choices of action which are the most efficient for the accomplishment of these objectives.

4. *The leader.* A leader is not a passive actor in the sense that group opinion regarding goals dominates the setting. The leader interacts with the group, modifying goals and courses of actions so that a mixture of his opinions and wishes and the group's opinions and wishes result. In this regard, the generalized traits of the leader are relevant because he must be able to communicate to the group and be intelligent and sensitive enough to perceive group needs.

These, then, are the basic elements in a leadership definition. But as Stogdill relates, they do not necessarily involve such problems as the number of leaders who may arise in an organization, the extent to which a leader's influence over a group is continuous or intermittent, or the quality of leadership from the standpoint of welfare and effectiveness of group members.[12] These matters are considered in the following sections of this chapter.

LEADERSHIP BEHAVIOR: SOME RESEARCH FINDINGS

Seven questions noted in the introduction to this chapter refer the reader to some of the basic leadership problems which researchers in the behavioral sciences are attempting to solve. This section discusses some of the research and its findings. No attempt is made to treat the questions in the sequence presented in the introduction. Rather, the analysis is arranged thusly: the process of leadership selection is discussed first, followed by some elements of leader behavior; then the leadership role and finally leadership patterns are considered.

On Becoming a Leader

There are two polar conceptions of how an individual emerges into a leadership role. The first is that the group thrusts up one of its members. The second is that an individual takes over the role, through the use of power and influence, when he senses the circumstances to be appropriate for his move. The first extreme emphasizes the group as the main determinant of the leader. The other stresses the individual's ability and motivation to assume a leadership position.

Taking more of a middle position between these two extremes, but leaning toward the first, Gibb notes that groups can propel individuals into a leadership capacity, and the choice of the specific individual is more dependent on the nature of the group than on the personality of the individual. But the main determinant of the leader rests on the relationship between the group and the individual at a particular time.[13]

---

[12] Stogdill, *op. cit.*, pp. 4–5.
[13] Gibb, *op. cit.*, p. 268.

Nothing is found in the leadership concept to suggest that it is an enduring role. The organization, however, may be structured to support individuals in a leadership position after they have lost effectiveness. In this case, leadership becomes domination.

It is wise at this point to distinguish between the "natural" and the designated leader.[14]

The natural leader may well achieve this role primarily as the result of group interaction. In this process the group selects one of its own members to serve in a leadership capacity. The person so selected, according to the theory, is one who represents and articulates group values to those outside and, indeed, to members of the group themselves.

The designated leader is one who is appointed to serve in a formal leadership capacity. Such appointments to executive positions in a conventional line organization are based on authority. They result in supervisory or executive *headships,* but not necessarily in leadership.

Hence, as a first approximation, those who serve as true natural leaders have gained *group acceptance.* Needless to say, leaders who are selected by the process of group consensus have acceptance behind them. However, there is nothing in this theory to preclude an individual who is designated to a *headship* from gaining *leadership* over the group in time.

Regardless of whether leadership falls to an individual as a result of his own initiative or as a result of group processes, the role presumes a readiness on the part of the individual. In other words, the individual needs certain personal qualities which permit him to function in a leadership capacity.

Personal Qualities Associated with Leadership

Although the traitist approach has limited value, refined research methodologies appear to have uncovered three personal qualities which show up frequently in studies of leaders. These qualities, as already mentioned, are intelligence, communicative skill, and the ability to sense group goals.

These characteristics are not at all absolute; they are relative to the group. Thus leaders are often found to be more intelligent, better communicators, and more sensitive *relative to other members of the group.* This point underscores the situational character of leadership.

Further, these three qualities are combined in a personality configuration. It is not sufficient, for example, for an individual to have high intelligence relative to the group if he is not also aware of group thinking. Or he may be sensitive to group values but he may not be able to articulate them. Thus, as one study points out, the leader is one who knows the thinking of the group best and is able to verbalize it. Leadership refers to

---

[14] For a discussion of natural versus designated leadership see *Leadership and Supervision,* (U. S. Civil Service Commission, Personnel Management Series #9, 1955), pp. 48–50.

the ability to *abstract* relevant determinants of group behavior in order to move the group to action.[15]

A fourth quality, observed by Hollander and Webb, is interesting as it refers to the relationship between leadership and followership.[16] They note that leadership and followership nominations, sociometrically derived, are closely related in a positive direction. The more desired followers tend to be at the upper extremes of leadership distribution. That good leaders also are good followers makes sense in a business organization because of its hierarchial structure. Managers must look to others above and below themselves for decisions and performance, respectively.

The ways by which an individual becomes a leader and the traits he may possess are preliminary to the consideration of the leadership activity itself. A person occupying a leadership position, either formal or informal, has a role to play which is differentiated from other roles in the group. A role, it is remembered, is a composite of rights, duties, and obligations which an individual must discharge to satisfy the expectations of those who rely on the functions that the actor performs.

Leadership Roles

The role of the leader is difficult to play to the satisfaction of all members of a group. Not only is the leader faced with conflicting expectations originating from within the group, he also finds, often enough, that the expectations of his group as a whole conflict with the demands of outside groups.[17] This situation is particularly evident in business organizations where a foreman has demands placed on him from above which may run counter to the expectations of the group he leads.

Commenting on the problem of role conflict in formal organizations Stogdill says:

> Leadership is concerned with problems of human performance and interaction. . . . The leader in any actively operating organization is constantly confronted by discrepancies between the demands of organization and performance of organization. This means that the leader is concerned with the co-ordination (restructuring) of interactions and performances as necessary in order to accomplish the tasks at hand.[18]

---

[15] C. G. Browne and Richard P. Shore, "Leadership and Predictive Abstracting," *Journal of Applied Psychology*, April, 1956, pp. 112–16. See also Kamla Chowdhry and Theodore M. Newcomb, "The Relative Abilities of Leaders and Non-leaders to Estimate Opinions of Their Own Groups," *Journal of Abnormal and Social Psychology*, January, 1952, pp. 51–57.

[16] E. P. Hollander and Wilse B. Webb, "Leadership, Followership and Friendship: An Analysis of Peer Nominations," *Journal of Abnormal and Social Psychology*, March, 1955, pp. 163–67.

[17] Ralph M. Stogdill, Ellis L. Scott, and William E. Jaynes, *Leadership and Role Expectations* (Ohio State University: Bureau of Business Research, Research Monograph #86, 1956), p. 5.

[18] Ralph M. Stogdill, *Leadership and Structures of Personal Interactions* (Ohio State University: Bureau of Business Research, Research Monograph #84, 1957), p. 3.

Co-ordination has been noted already as a basic activity of a leader. Relating to co-ordination, however, are nine other leadership acts used to direct the group toward a goal:

1. Integration—acts which tend to increase co-ordination.
2. Communication—acts which tend to increase understanding and transmission of information.
3. Production emphasis—acts oriented toward volume of work done.
4. Representation—acts which promote group representation with outside organizations.
5. Fraternization—acts which make leaders part of the group.
6. Organization—acts which lead to the differentiation and prescription of duties.
7. Evaluation—acts which pertain to distribution of rewards and punishment.
8. Initiation—acts which result in changes of group activities.
9. Domination—acts which disregard the ideas or persons of group members.[19]

These leadership functions represent the content of the leader's role. In an organizational setting the group expects the leader to take the initiative in performing these activities. In fact, the more highly oriented the group is toward an authoritarian type of leadership the more intense this expectation is.

Berkowitz, in a study of shared leadership, observed that the groups analyzed indicated a general expectation that the designated leader should be the sole behavioral leader. The groups had an expectation of role differentiation. When the leader did not perform as expected other members of the group took over and filled the vacuum. However, leadership sharing, in these instances studied, was accompanied by a *decrease* in group solidarity and satisfaction.[20]

A distinction was made earlier between leadership and headship. The basis of this distinction rests in the group's acceptance of an individual in a leadership role. The relationship between the group and the leader is reciprocal. The leader has to perceive group needs and to direct the group toward their gratification. In turn, the group must feel that the leader is adequate in this role. Under such circumstances, group support of the leader should be forthcoming. The environment determines what a group's needs are and who will be the leader.

In a study of naval recruits, Henning and Economos observed three forms of behavior associated with an individual's takeover of an informal leadership role.[21] The first type was one in which the leader was thrust up

---

[19] Ralph M. Stogdill and Alvin E. Coons, *Leader Behavior: Its Description and Measurement* (Ohio State University: Bureau of Business Research, Research Monograph #88, 1957), pp. 8–9.

[20] Leonard Berkowitz, "Sharing Leadership in Small Decision-Making Groups," *Journal of Abnormal and Social Psychology*, April, 1953, pp. 231–38.

[21] Kenneth K. Henning and Gus L. Economos, "Patterns of Natural Leadership: A Research Study of Informal Organizations" (an unpublished manuscript, 1962).

by the group to serve in what was perceived to be an emergency situation. The second type was the leader who took over the role on his own initiative; his tenure persisted as long as the group recognized him. The third type of leader planned his strategy "behind the scenes" and made his play for leadership when he felt the group was ready. It is interesting that of the second and third types of leaders, the most durable in resisting challenges were those who accepted the formal goals of the Navy.

It might be hypothesized from this study that informal leaders who arise in stable formal organizational settings and who accept the goals of the formal organization tend to remain in leadership capacities longer. They are best equipped to help the group reconcile its own needs with those of the formal organization. This is a key function because groups in military or business surroundings often have few alternatives but to conform to the strictures of the environment. The individual is most likely to persist in a leadership role if he is able to direct the group through formal organizational and technological mazes, showing it how to gain some satisfactions at the same time. In this respect, there is no inherent conflict between formal and informal leadership.

Commenting on this point, relative to an assembly-line situation, Whyte says:

> The technological environment is so overwhelming that nothing the foreman can do would really make the workers like the work they do. Nevertheless, it is possible for him to modify to a degree the impact of this environment upon the workers. To the extent that he does so, he can build favorable sentiments toward himself.[22]

Patterns of Leadership

Persons who are delegated headship roles in formal organizations often are not chosen because of their leadership qualities or group acceptance. Headships are frequently given to the best technician or to the best tactician in organizational power plays. But regardless of why an individual ends up in a headship, he finds that once there it is necessary for him to get things done through other people.

Prescriptions have been offered in management literature for years as to the best ways for motivating subordinates.[23] The scholars working in the areas of bureaucracy and classical organization theory often neglected the human variable. They assumed that a division of work and a rational structuring of an organization along functional and scalar lines would result in a system where people could almost automatically accomplish objectives and derive their personal satisfaction from so doing.

The neoclassical treatment of organization theory stressed the human variable; and out of this orientation came a unique approach to leadership.

---

[22] William Foote Whyte, *Men at Work* (Homewood, Ill.: The Dorsey Press, 1961), p. 197.

[23] For an excellent summary of leadership thought see Bennis, *op. cit.*, pp. 262–87.

The neoclassical doctrine of leadership emphasizes the *consent* of those led. By the same token, it plays down the authoritarian form of leadership based on domination. The human relations approach to leadership has a number of labels, including "democratic," "participative," and "permissive" leadership. The most frequently used is "democratic leadership" and this is adopted in the following pages for uniformity.

For many years, and particularly since the end of World War II, democratic leadership has been accepted as the appropriate *and* the most effective pattern of leader behavior for employee motivation. Its doctrine carries force because it has been supported by research findings and it has the additional advantage of moral suasion. How can a leadership pattern be denied if it results in higher productivity, greater human happiness, increased group solidarity, *plus* conformance with the democratic ideals of American society?

Recently, however, there has been a strong reaction against democratic leadership. Writers taking this position have made substantial cases. The next two sections develop the points of view for and against democratic leadership patterns.

The Case for Democratic Leadership. Endorsements for democratic leadership are not difficult to find in either management or behavioral science literature. The general theme of these endorsements is that people work better, are happier, and are more apt to accept change in an environment when they are allowed to have some say in matters that affect them directly. The opposite of the democratic philosophy is the autocratic where individuals are permitted little if any chance for self-determination.

The contrasts which Laird and Laird draw between these leadership patterns are shown in Table 18–1.

TABLE 18–1

Autocratic versus Democratic Leadership

Autocratic Subclasses of Behavior	Democratic Subclasses of Behavior
Authoritarian	Equalitarian
Dictatorial	Facilitative
Leader centered	Group centered
Production centered	Worker centered
Restrictive	Permissive

Source: Donald A. Laird and Eleanor Laird, *The New Psychology for Leadership* (New York: McGraw-Hill Book Co., Inc., 1956), p. 44.

The essential feature of democratic leadership philosophy is its orientation toward those led, particularly the group. Laird and Laird's choice of descriptive words and phrases is particularly good for highlighting the basic philosophy of democratic leadership. They succinctly illustrate the ideas of group centeredness, the atmosphere of permissiveness, and the consideration which pervade the democratic organizational environment. In short, the philosophy of democratic leadership rests on allowing the expression of the collective will. It disclaims any part of organizational "cults of personality."

Now, of course certain problems arise when democratic leadership is applied to organizations which are authoritarian in concept and structure, like business organizations. Obviously, a company in which the decision process is democratic from top to bottom is not tenable. Consequently, democratic leadership has to undergo some modifications to be appropriate for business.

The instrument regarded as the most satisfactory for introducing democratic leadership into a business setting is *participation*. In its extreme, participation allows employees to share in all decisions which affect them; that is, they may decide on goals and on methods to reach the goals. In its less extreme form—designed to protect the authority of the designated leader—employee participation applies to sharing in the decisions relating to the *alternatives* open for the accomplishment of the objective. Thus, the objective is given by the boss; employees participate in deciding on the methods to achieve it. This latter form of participation is naturally more acceptable to business.

There have been numerous variations on the participation theme which management has found attractive. Bottom-up management is an example.[24] This type of participation permits junior executives to experience setting top policy. It gives them the chance to "get the feel" of making high-level decisions. If they make mistakes it is not fatal because top management reserves the right to veto any lower-level actions. Bottom-up management is at once a training and morale-building device. It is supposed to produce better-qualified executives who have feelings of greater involvement in company affairs.

Democratic leadership in a business organization involves far more than participation. Democratic leadership implies a "climate" where employees have a chance to grow and develop, where formal supervision is considerate and the application of sanctions is not arbitrary, and where employee attitudes are sincerely respected and solicited. Thus, democratic leadership is a "state of mind" in which the management of a company is committed to the recognition of the dignity of employees as men and not merely as factors of production. That such a state of mind is peculiar to a democratically led organization is not completely obvious. In fact, one writer feels that the benevolent autocracy is capable of such a noble expression.

---

[24] See William B. Given, *Bottom-Up Management* (New York: Harper and Bros., 1949).

The Case for Authoritarian Leadership. One of the strongest cases for autocracy is made by Robert N. McMurry. His feeling toward democratic management is clear and straightforward. The "cold reality" of democratic leadership is simply that it will not work. His reasons behind this are:

1. Every business has its "goldbrickers and wise guys" who are encouraged by a permissive environment.
2. The business climate is unfavorable to democratic management. Its principles are not accepted throughout the organization.
3. The current need for policy uniformity and position structuring requires more centralization of decisions in companies.
4. Democratic leadership is not compatible with bureaucratic traditions of large, stable organizations.
5. Participation in practice by lower levels may actually be limited to kibitzing and gripe sessions where dissatisfaction is expressed about top-management decisions.[25]

In addition to these points, McMurry goes on to question the merit of the group decision making process, which is one of the main tools of democratic management. He points out that group decision making stimulates individual dependence rather than independence on the group. The individual often develops a fear of the group. The truly different person with valuable ideas can be neutralized by group pressure. Further, group decision making is slow and conservative. All in all, group decision making tends to replace individual autocracy with group autocracy.[26]

The substance of much of McMurry's argument is similar to that of a number of writers who fear the growing tendencies toward groupism and collectivism in business. He feels that democratic leadership has had a chance but has failed. McMurry commends the benevolent autocrat to the leadership role because the rule of the strong but benign man is more suitable to the business environment.

The basic feature of the controversy between democratic and authoritarian leadership is ideological. Democratic leadership contains elements which are incompatible with systems built on authority and the privilege of exercising sanctions. While democratic leadership stresses equalitarianism, all men are not equal by definition in organizations. In fact, all those characteristics of autocratic leadership mentioned in Table 18–1 flow naturally from and are quite consistent with the scalar structure of formal organizations. Right or wrong, the use of authoritarian leadership is generally the easy way out for an executive or supervisor.

Although democratic leadership does not conform to the nature of formal organizations this does not mean that some of its principles and

---

[25] Robert N. McMurry, "The Case for Benevolent Autocracy," *Harvard Business Review,* January–February, 1958, pp. 82–83.

[26] *Ibid.,* pp. 84–85.

techniques cannot be successfully applied. But in general, the philosophy of democratic leadership runs against the grain of a typical formal structure.

Management Leadership Problems

The debate over democratic-authoritarian leadership patterns appears rather academic to the operating executive; which works best is of more interest to him. However, the answer, "It depends," may not have any appeal at all. But according to contemporary leadership theory this is the only reasonable answer to such a generalized question, because the effectiveness of any leadership pattern *depends* on the situation.

Neither democratic nor authoritarian leadership is inherently good or bad *if one's frame of reference is organizational effectiveness*. Therefore, an executive's selection of a leadership pattern is not a matter of moral judgment but simply a case of practicality. The trick, however, is for the executive to be sensitive enough to the environment and the group so that he introduces the leadership approach most fitting to the situation.[27]

Thus, the real test of leadership in a business environment is group effectiveness.[28] How the leader goes about obtaining this and whether or not the group is happy in the process are conditions of secondary importance to the accomplishment of organizationally defined goals.

This statement will no doubt conjure up many invidious implications for the perceptive reader. Are there no limits on the leader in obtaining group effectiveness? Since when does the end justify the means? Is not job satisfaction one objective of human relations? These are valid questions but fortunately they usually do not pose serious obstacles in operating situations, because of three factors.

First, every organization has policies, rules, regulations, and unwritten proprieties which constrain the actions of leaders. The Machiavellian can circumvent these limitations and pursue his own methods for obtaining objectives. If he is successful, his group may out-perform others. If he is caught contravening organizational conventions and brought to justice, he is not a very good manipulator and must accept the penalties.

Second, as an ethical principle the means-end argument is valid. But in concrete administrative circumstances it is often most difficult to decide what is a means and what is an end. This problem is disregarded when it comes to leadership practice because it is not resolvable.

Third, few executives would agree that human satisfaction on the job is any higher a goal than the satisfaction of consumers, owners, and the

---

[27] For a discussion of this point see Robert Tannenbaum and Warren H. Schmidt, "How to Choose a Leadership Pattern," *Harvard Business Review*, March–April, 1958, pp. 95–101.

[28] See Fred E. Fielder, *Leader Attitudes and Group Effectiveness* (Urbana: University of Illinois Press, 1958).

public. If anything, job satisfaction of employees is an objective which must be balanced with other primary objectives.

Generally, people in a work situation are sufficiently attuned to the "habits of industry" that they expect a certain type of leadership pattern to predominate in a situation. A case in point is an interesting study of leadership patterns among research scientists conducted by Baumgartel. His findings indicate that,

> . . . while conformity of the chief to the preferences of subordinates has the most consistent positive influence on the scientist's attitude toward him, this leadership factor makes little difference in the motivation sense of progress of the group toward its goal—at least in this scientific organization.[29]

Thus, while these research scientists might *prefer* a leader who is likeable and considerate, this attitudinal preference does not appear to be the relevant leadership variable in goal accomplishment. Rather, the main determinant of group effectiveness is a supervisor who himself shows high scientific performance and motivation as a research leader.[30]

Baumgartel's findings can be generalized to other types of leader-follower relationships in organizations. Argyris comments that people feel a dependency on a leader, whether designated or natural, no matter how democratic or permissive he may be. This dependency arises from the nature of organization itself as it is structured on superior-subordinate relationships. The leadership pattern is merely a tool which either increases or diminishes group effectiveness.[31]

This fact of organizational life is undoubtedly the main determinant behind the results of experiments in shared leadership cited earlier. That is, where the designated leader fails to perform his functions adequately leaders will be generated by the group. But the result of this phenomenon is a decline in group effectiveness and satisfaction. People expect an individual to assume a leadership role, and they expect to follow him. In some cases, the methods used by the leader may appeal to the followers. But because of the leader's technical competence, or because of the followers' perception of and sympathy toward the difficulties of the leader's role, or because of the respect the followers have for the status of the leader, they will support him in the task of goal accomplishment. The *degree* of support, however, may be a function of the ability of the leader to apply human skills.

The central assumption of the democratic-leadership school is that optimum group effectiveness is achieved if people regard the accomplishment of organizational objectives as the best route to the satisfaction of

---

[29] Howard Baumgartel, "Leadership, Motivations, and Attitudes in Research Laboratories," *Journal of Social Issues*, Vol. 12 (1956), p. 31.

[30] *Ibid.*, p. 30.

[31] Chris Argyris, *Executive Leadership* (New York: Harper and Bros., 1953), p. 40.

personal needs.[32] This is the idea of mutuality of interests all over again. Obviously, if people perceive they can satisfy their own ends by pursuing organizational ends there would hardly be a need for motivation as a management function, and much less a need for leadership except as it would serve in an advisory capacity. But as a matter of fact this axiom of democratic leadership is not applicable to the realities of organizational life in business. It is not possible for the ends of individuals and the ends of business organizations to be altogether harmonious. Nor is it entirely clear that harmony of this sort constitutes an ideal goal toward which executive leadership should try to strive.

Few are so unsophisticated (and those who are soon learn) as not to know that some sacrifice of self-determination must be made if they are to realize the rewards coming from participation in an organization. Democratic leadership and participation are soothing influences that make this sacrifice more palatable; and by so doing they *may* promote more job satisfaction and group effectiveness than if they were withheld. However, no matter the form the use of leadership tools is a method whereby the executive as an agent of an organization accomplishes its ends. The tools do not change the basic character or anatomy of the structure.

A BROADER PROBLEM OF ORGANIZATIONAL LEADERSHIP

In part because of the collectivistic tendencies in our society, and in part because of the zealous efforts of the proponents of democratic leadership, the personal leader is becoming an anachronism. He is supplanted for decisions and actions by the committee, the group, and the team. Numerous writers look upon this development as dangerous. Bavelas cites two specific manifestations of this trend.

1. Although many occasions arise for the high expression of personal leadership in organizations, the commitment by the individual is not made because of the risks involved.
2. The submergence of the leader in the group is likely to produce mediocrity of performance for the sake of personal feeling of safety and security.[33]

Much in the same vein, Jennings remarks that, "Risk and initiative have been taken out of leadership by our present demand for chairmen, co-ordinators, facilitators, diagnosticians, and therapists."[34]

No doubt the reader has noticed while studying this chapter the amount of emphasis placed on the group in current leadership theory and research.

[32] David A. Emery, "Managerial Leadership through Motivation by Objectives," *Personnel Psychology*, Spring, 1959, p. 67.

[33] Bavelas, *op. cit.*, p. 497.

[34] Eugene E. Jennings, *An Anatomy of Leadership* (New York: Harper and Bros., 1960), p. 16.

The group and the situation are the dominant variables; the personal leader is given little attention. The reader may ask, justifiably, what has become of the man who can shape the situation to suit himself and who can give objectives and direction to a group without first taking its pulse to determine its needs. Similar questions are asked throughout the critical literature of management. And indeed such questions are also found in the more probing treatments of contemporary American culture.

The central strand of this analysis and criticism constitutes a rebellion against collectivism. The plea of many of these writers is for a return of the personal leader—one who assumes responsibility for his decisions even though they involve unpleasant changes or risky undertakings.

The personal leader must be willing to do more than accept risks. Plenty of adventurers are rambling through enterprises today, intent on the manipulation of people and organizational machinery for their own ends. The need is for leaders in business, labor, and government who have both a vision of organizational purpose and sufficient integrity and courage to identify with the decisions they make in pursuit of those purposes.

This is more than a brave statement useful in ending a chapter. It is a central issue in management. The modern leader cannot be a mirror of the nineteenth-century individualist any more than he can be a collectivist who submits all major decisions to a group.

Instead, the leader is one who reduces the risk others see in their environment by shouldering the burdens attendant with decisions involving people's welfare. In a real sense, leaders must consider their private well-being and the well-being of their organizations as linked to the fate of society as a whole. The leader personally and his organization can accomplish their ends only to the extent that these ends also contribute to the corporate welfare of society. Thus, the leader must be an individualist who is willing to assume the lonely and dangerous task of accepting the consequences of his programs and actions. And if he must assume these responsibilities he has to be sufficiently "visible" as a symbol around which his followers can rally and support. But in addition to this the leader needs to be a collectivist in the sense that he frames his programs and pursues them in a fashion which corresponds to social ideals.

REVIEW QUESTIONS

1. Discuss the following approaches to leadership:
   a) The trait approach.
   b) The modified trait approach.
   c) The situational approach.

2. Outline and describe the key elements which appear to be necessary in a definition of leadership.

3. What are the two polar conceptions relating to how an individual assumes a leadership role?

4. Distinguish between leadership and headship.

5. Identify the three personal qualities which often appear in leadership studies. Discuss the notion that these qualities are combined in a personality configuration.

6. Analyze the various aspects of the leadership role.

7. Evaluate the cases made for authoritarian and for democratic leadership.

8. What is participation? How is it adapted to the business environment?

9. Why does the real test of leadership in a business environment reduce to a question of group effectiveness?

10. What is the status of the concept of the personal leader? Why is this concept a crucial issue in modern business?

SUPPLEMENTARY READINGS

BAVELAS, ALEX. "Leadership: Man and Function," *Administrative Science Quarterly*, March, 1960, pp. 491–98.

BENNIS, WARREN G. "Leadership Theory and Administrative Behavior: The Problem of Authority," *Administrative Science Quarterly*, 4 (1959–1960), pp. 259–301.

GIBB, CECIL A. "The Principles and Traits of Leadership," *Journal of Abnormal and Social Psychology*, July, 1947, pp. 267–84.

JENNINGS, EUGENE E. *An Anatomy of Leadership*. New York: Harper and Bros., 1960.

McMURRY, ROBERT N. "The Case for Benevolent Autocracy," *Harvard Business Review*, January–February, 1958, pp. 82–90.

TANNENBAUM, ROBERT, AND SCHMIDT, WARREN H. "How to Choose a Leadership Pattern," *Harvard Business Review*, March–April, 1958, pp. 95–101.

CHAPTER 19

Management Training in the Behavioral Sciences

Very little of what has been discussed in the preceding pages of this book is of much value to management unless it filters through to executives at all levels of organization. The function of training and education is to relate the concepts and findings of the behavioral sciences in a way as to have *operational* significance for practicing managers with the ultimate effect of changing behavior. The emphasis in the last sentence is on "operational" for good reason. Being confirmed pragmatists, management is not likely to accept theories which do not have practical applications to the business of running an organization.

Since the Hawthorne studies, management has been interested in human relations as a legitimate field in which training should be carried on. Management gets things done through people, so the saying goes. If this is the case, then it is expedient that managers sharpen their "human skills." The hope has been in the past that by the use of appropriate training techniques managers would find out something about why people act the way they do. But what is more, training has also carried the promise of improving management's ability to deal with people.

Much has happened in the human relations training area since the end of World War II. The 1950's can be considered as the "golden days;" during this period programs in human relations were abundant. They were held with equal frequency on the premises of business firms and on the campuses of universities offering executive-development programs. Managers participating in these development activities had the chance to learn a little bit about the sociology of the informal organization, something about psychology, and often a considerable amount about leadership. These programs combined several techniques of presentation. The lecture-conference method was employed to cover the content of the subject matter. The case approach and role playing were used to give participants an opportunity to experience the ideas they had learned.

Late in the 1950's, management's interest in human relations training waned—and *not* because management felt that "good human relations practice" was no longer important. Rather, the causes were many and complex. Some of them are noted below.

First, human relations training had assumed the proportions of a fad. The management of many companies went into programs of this general nature without a very clear idea of the training needs of the participants. Motivations were strong to get on the bandwagon, and as a result human relations programs were hastily conceived. Then the recession of 1957 prompted the management of many companies to cut back on these programs. While sitting out the recession management had the chance to reflect on the nature of its executive-development activities. The upshot was the elimination of weak programs and the planning of future ones on a sounder base.

Second, the objectives of early human relations training programs were none too clear. Advised by researchers doing studies in democratic-participative leadership, management felt that somehow conferees in programs should be made more permissive toward their subordinates. Also, management felt that participants in these programs would profit from a general understanding of human motivation and group behavior. This type of knowledge helped, it was felt, to round out the education of the executive. Finally, management thought that simulation of human relations problem situations through case analysis and role playing would give program participants an opportunity to develop their human skills in a setting where mistakes in relating would not carry serious on-the-job repercussions. From this experience it was hoped that the participants would learn something they could carry back to their jobs to make them better human relations practioneers. In short, most human relations programs had the objective of improving the executives' human skills.

Third, human relations programs were endorsed enthusiastically by management and they were vigorously implemented. But little if any follow-up was attempted to discover whether or not the program met its objectives. Lack of control over results was a serious deficiency. This absence of adequate control was attributable to a number of factors: (1) the nature of human relations itself is pretty nebulous; (2) since the objectives of human relations programs were rather fuzzy it was difficult to set tangible standards to provide the basis for control; and (3) the effects of training on participants often would be delayed. Tangible improvements in the individual's ability to manage might not appear for a considerable period of time. And even if improvements were noted they would be difficult to attribute to the program alone. Thus, because of the inadequacy of effective control measures over human relations programs, management had to be content generally with the "warm glow of satisfaction" when the program was over, knowing that it had done all it could to improve the ability of the participants "to relate" successfully with others.

Management has had the opportunity to reappraise its policies on human relations training in the light of its rather spotty success with past programs and in the light of the newer developments in the behavioral sciences and training techniques which have matured in the last four years. These changes have subordinated the skills approach to training in human relations to reach a more sophisticated level of abstraction regarding human behavior and a more sensitive one regarding an individual's role in a social system.

Before trends in management development in the behavioral sciences are dwelt on at length, some ideas pertaining to the philosophy and scope of training are considered.

PHILOSOPHY AND SCOPE OF TRAINING

Training Defined

The phrase "industrial training" has many meanings. To some writers in the field of personnel management training means developing manpower for particular jobs.[1] Other writers interpret industrial training more broadly, including training for adequate job performance *and* extending an employee's intellectual range through general education.[2] Still other writers speak of an over-all area called development which they divide into education and training. Training in this instance means fitting the man to the job, whereas the purpose of education fits the man to his environment off and on the job.[3]

Searching management literature for an operative definition of management training in the behavioral sciences is quite futile. By its nature, such programs crosscut the definitions of training and education given above. In one sense, an understanding of the behavioral sciences at the skill level and at the level of concept fulfills the requirement of the training definition because the presumption is that knowledge and ability in this area will help a manager do a better job. In another sense, a knowledge of the behavioral sciences is essential for the executive from the standpoint of its educative overtones. An awareness of the scientific findings relating to organization theory and the theory of personality is essential for executives who are moving in complex social and business environments.

These remarks provide a background for an operative definition of management training programs oriented toward the behavioral sciences. *Training in the behavioral sciences is an activity of line and staff which has as its goal executive development to achieve greater individual job*

---

[1] Dale Yoder, *Personnel Management and Industrial Relations* (4th ed.; Englewood Cliffs: Prentice-Hall, 1956), chap. 9.

[2] William W. Waite, *Personnel Administration* (New York: The Ronald Press, 1952), pp. 219–40.

[3] Arthur M. Whitehill, Jr., *Personnel Relations* (New York: McGraw-Hill Book Co., 1955), pp. 121–51.

effectiveness, improved interpersonal relationships in the organization, and enhanced executive adjustment to the context of his total environment.

This definition may be broken into three parts for purposes of explanation. The first part of the definition indicates that training is a function of line and staff management. The line organization retains the ultimate responsibility for training; the staff provides the technical assistance to aid the line in performing this function.

The second part of the definition, relating to individual job effectiveness and improved interpersonal relationships, states the immediate objective of a program in the behavioral sciences. By necessity, training must be aimed at facilitating the accomplishment of company goals. It is the purpose of training in the behavioral sciences to equip executives with the knowledge and attitudes toward human behavior necessary to maintain an effective departmental organization. *In short, training must result in a change in behavior of the trainee.*

A balanced program in the behavioral sciences focuses on the trainee's attitudes regarding human behavior; additionally, it imparts knowledge, derived from scientific sources, pertaining to human behavior. In summary, training needs to be based in solid content and must be geared to create an awareness and sensitivity in the individual toward human problems in concrete business situations.

The third part of the definition refers to a more distant aim of training in the behavioral sciences. This goal ties into the broad function of education and its role in executive development. The modern executive is concerned with a wide range of social relationships which extend beyond his job. He cannot be content with fairly simple human relations formulations. His skills should include the ability to generalize from basic research information and to perceive interconnections among a variety of behavioral forms.

Four Aspects of Training in the Behavioral Sciences

Like most forms of training, programs in the behavioral sciences aim to transmit information, develop attitudes, and improve skills.[4] Another facet of training, representing a fairly recent shift in emphasis, is the marked interest in the development of managerial conceptual abilities in the behavioral sciences. Each of these training facets is next discussed in turn, but it should be recognized that there is a considerable amount of overlapping among them.

Transmitting Information. The essential element in most training programs is content. The purpose of training is to impart to the trainees in-

---

[4] See Herbert J. Chruden and Arthur W. Sherman, Jr., *Personnel Management* (Cincinnati: South-Western Publishing Co., 1959), pp. 153–54.

formation drawn from a body of knowledge. Training in the behavioral sciences, therefore, transmits to participants information relating human personality and motivation, the process of communication, organization theory including small group processes, leadership, and so on. Fields like sociology, psychology, social-psychology, and anthropology are relied upon by the program developers and conference leaders to supply the material.

Development of Attitudes. Closely linked to imparting knowledge, in human relations training programs, is the development of attitudes. Actually, it is more accurate to say *changing* the attitudes of participants. People go into training programs with certain preconceived ideas about leadership, the grapevine, the function of status, and the informal organization. The attitudes management trainees have regarding these factors and others in the organization environment determine executive effectiveness as a leader.

Experts in behavioral science training feel it is not sufficient just to impart knowledge in these fields. It is also necessary to work on changing the participants' attitudes on human behavior. Thus, the training aspect of attitude development is an important part of human relations training programs. It is, however, the most difficult to execute effectively.

Development of Skills. Assume that in a given training program a considerable amount of information has been transmitted to participants, and that in the process of training their attitudes have been changed so that they accord more closely with objective guidelines for "effective leadership." In other words, the first two aspects of training were accomplished well. Is the program then a success? The answer probably is "no," because the trainees have not yet had an opportunity to develop "human skills" in the application of the material imparted to them. Consequently, the next logical phase of training is skill development.

Some argue that the development of skills in the use of human tools derived from training must come from on-the-job experience. Classroom simulation of human problems through case studies and role playing, it is claimed, is inadequate even when conducted under the supervision of a training expert. Nevertheless, those in the training field are constantly working on new devices and techniques which endeavor to fill the need for realistic forms of classroom experiences where skills can be developed. More is said about this facet of training later in the chapter.

Conceptual Level. The notion that training or education in the application of the behavioral sciences to management practice should be conducted on a higher level of abstraction is a fairly recent development. The objective is to move training a step or two beyond direct application to a level of greater generalization. The idea is to develop managers who can *think* in behavioral science terms.

The impetus for this reorientation stemmed from the Ford and Carnegie appraisals of business-school curricula around the country.[5] The result has been for colleges of business to take greater interest in the role of the behavioral sciences in their programs.

Concluding Remarks on the Four Aspects of Training

Training in the behavioral sciences has been under the influence of the clinical school of human relations philosophy for many years. This approach, it is recalled, stresses concrete application of "human tools and human data to solve human problems." Therefore, it is not surprising to find that training-program orientation has been in the direction of attitude change and skill development, coupled with the minimum of content necessary for providing an elementary understanding of behavior.

The lack of sophistication in the treatment of the behavioral sciences could very well be a cause for the disenchantment with human relations training programs. The emphasis in training on permissive and considerate attitudes along with techniques for using human relations tools is not a complete substitute for adequate grounding in the behavioral sciences.

In recent years, much more research information is available and many behavioral scientists are taking an interest in the application of their disciplines to management problems. Additionally, progress has been made in the development of such fields as decision theory and cybernetics which of necessity require the integration of information coming from the behavioral sciences.

The advances in the behavioral sciences themselves and their application to business are forcing changes on industrial training programs. Such improvements as they have introduced will ensure that the behavioral sciences are represented in depth and are meaningfully transmitted to executives. This is the role of the conceptual level of training discussed above.

The clinical approach to human relations training probably never will go completely out of style. Indeed, this approach can be vitalized by a more substantial foundation in the basic sciences which apply to behavior.

TRAINING METHODS

The various techniques described in this section have wide industrial acceptance. They are also the most frequently used devices in human relations training programs.

---

[5] See Robert Aaron Gordon and James Edwin Howell, *Higher Education for Business* (New York: Columbia University Press, 1959), pp. 166–70, 382–83. See also Frank C. Pierson, and others, *The Education of American Businessmen* (New York: The McGraw-Hill Book Co., 1959), pp. 250–51, 326–28.

The Lecture Method

The lecture method is quite familiar to educators and trainers. Basically, the lecture is a one-way means of communication where the trainer presents the course content with a minimum of audience participation. The lecture method is convenient for training large numbers of people in a short time.[6]

The lecture has limitations. A major risk in the lecture technique is the danger of going over the heads of trainees when presenting rather abstract subjects. The lecturer has no real check on how well the course content is being absorbed by the trainees.

The lecture does not invite participation and it discourages trainee involvement in the subject. Since the lecture is one-way the trainees do not take an active part in the development of subject matter. The lecture encourages a passive audience that tends to become detached from the material presented.

The Panel Discussion

Using a panel is another method of training large groups in industry. The panel consists of a board of experts who express opinions on a topic. This technique is often effective when a subject is controversial. A panel is useful when several opinions are desired.[7] The panel technique has shortcomings similar to the lecture since trainees are required to sit passively through a program.

The Phillips-66 Method

Lecture and panel methods of training are useful for large groups but, as stressed before, they lack trainee participation. The Phillips-66 method is an attempt to achieve widespread participation with large training groups. Although there are many variations on the theme, the basic training pattern is to divide an audience into groups of six and let each group discuss a problem posed by a lecture for six minutes. Each group elects a spokesman who carries the group's opinion on the problem to the audience after it reassembles. This method attempts to get individual participation in situations involving many trainees.[8]

The Conference Method

The conference method is a widely used training technique in management-development programs and consequently warrants rather close ex-

---

[6] For a discussion of the lecture method see Earl G. Planty and J. Thomas Freeston, *Developing Management Ability* (New York: The Ronald Press, 1954), p. 149.

[7] M. F. Stigers, *Making Conference Programs Work* (New York: McGraw-Hill Book Co., 1949), pp. 12–13.

[8] Norman R. F. Maier, *Principles of Human Relations* (New York: John Wiley and Sons, 1952), pp. 73–76.

amination. The conference method is not new in industry. It is used extensively by management for trading ideas on business problems. Modern training techniques, however, have put the conference method to a different use. In this respect the conference technique is modified so that the leader is responsible for directing participants to the acceptance of predetermined principles and conclusions.

Stigers identifies two forms of conference—the straight conference and the directed or guided conference.[9] In the straight conference the leader does not make an effort to guide the conferees to any predetermined conclusions. Presumably, the solutions to a problem are not known or are poorly defined before such a conference is called. This type of conference is somewhat similar to the structureless-group concept discussed in the last chapter. However, problem solving through discussion was incidental in this situation; the conference was used as a selection device to pick army officers.

The directed conference is just what its name suggests. It relies on the leader for stating the problem, stimulating group discussion, and skillfully channeling the contributions of the conferees along planned lines of thought.

Many authors have stressed the value of the directed conference as an training method in executive-development programs.[10] These writers state quite a few advantages of this method. Their opinions are summarized as follows:

1. The directed-conference method simulates the actual business-decision and policy-setting processes. Hence, the conference establishes a realistic setting familiar to businessmen for problem solving.

2. The directed conference promotes participation by all members of the group. It encourages individual development through sharing in the ideas and experiences of others. The conference appeals to practical men who wish to contribute their knowledge to develop the subject under consideration.

3. The directed-conference method appears well adapted for use in programs stressing the behavioral sciences and human relations. The content of these subjects lends itself readily to methods using the discussion technique.

The conference method does have pitfalls. One problem is overzealous efforts of the conference leader to "guide" the conferees to a conclusion. True group discussion ends under these circumstances and actually only the leader's opinion prevails. Razzledazzle methods of conference leadership serve to antagonize the participants. The manipulation of the conferees' ideas and statements to the leader's ends is a dangerous practice and can undermine the usefulness of the method.

---

[9] Stigers, *op. cit.*, pp. 9–10.

[10] For examples see Henry W. Busch, *Conference Methods in Industry* (New York: Harper and Bros., 1949); Alfred M. Cooper, *How to Conduct Conferences* (New York: McGraw-Hill Book Co., 1946); and Thomas Fansler, *Creative Power through Discussion* (New York: Harper and Bros., 1950).

The directed conference has great value for covering information requiring progressive and developmental thinking. As such it is useful for implementing conceptually oriented programs in the behavioral sciences.

The four methods of training just discussed focus heavily on the imparting-knowledge phase of training, although the directed-conference method has been cited as useful for attitude development as well. The following training methods center more on attitude and skill development.

The Case Method

The case approach is a method whereby conferees are given a narrative of a business problem which is then discussed and analyzed with a view to reaching a decision on a course of action.[11] The case, is generally in the area covered by the subject matter of the training program. The program participants are assigned a case ahead of time for study and analysis. The case is discussed in group meeting where emphasis is placed on free exchange of ideas. The leader plays a passive role in these sessions, leaving the conferees responsible for discussion and contributions.

The case approach stresses problem identification, analysis, and decision. This method trains participants to apply principles and to frame their own decisions within the area of a practical situation. Each member of the group makes his own proposals. Through the give and take of ideas the participants actively engage in problem solving and are exposed to a number of views.

The Incident Method

The incident method is an adaptation of the case-problem technique. The leader reads or distributes a short statement of an incident which has or is about to cause a problem. The mechanics of this device follow along these lines. The discussion leader possesses all the facts about the incident he has distributed. The conferees get the facts behind the incident by questioning the leader for a specified period of time, usually ten to twelve minutes. At the end of the question period the leader outlines the key points brought out by the trainees. Next each member of the group jots down a decision relating to the incident, and the group then evaluates them. Finally, the group considers how the incident can be prevented.[12]

The incident method is a rapid-fire technique for gaining group interest in a problem. It has the advantage of presenting a short situation

---

[11] A review of the case method is found in Malcolm B. McNair and Anita C. Hersum (eds.), *The Case Method at the Harvard Business School* (New York: McGraw-Hill Book Co., 1954).

[12] B. J. Speroff and A. K. Heydick, "The Incident Method; Its Use with Buzz Groups and Filmstrips," *Advanced Management*, October, 1954, p. 170.

which, unlike the case approach, pinpoints a particular problem within an area the conference leader wishes to stress. The incident method also gives trainees an opportunity to sift facts, formulate issues, and weigh evidence leading to a decision. The members of the group have the chance to work independently and co-operatively in a problem-solving situation.

Role Playing

Role playing has been described as "reality practice." It involves trainees in playing the parts of other people. Dr. J. L. Moreno first gave prominence to role playing under the name of "psychodrama."[13] Role playing was originally used as a therapeutic procedure in treating the mentally ill. Later role playing was adapted to the educational field, and it finally found its way into industrial training. Role playing in industrial training does not follow rigid procedures; its main purpose is to achieve spontaneous interaction among trainees.

Generally, a few preliminary steps are necessary before role playing begins.[14] A situation must be developed by the conference leader so that trainees have parts to play. The situation briefly gives the setting and problem, but ends at this point. The trainees themselves supply the rest of the script by ad-libbing from the point where the written problem stops. Frequently in role playing the conferees are given data on the character of the personality they are to play. The trainee must project himself into the type given him.

At times the role-playing problem is resolved; but just as often a solution is not obtained. Solving problems, however, is somewhat incidental to the major role-playing objective: to give trainees practice in interpersonal relationships.

Role playing demonstrates effectively how the interplay of personalities conditions the outcome of a problem situation. Usually two different groups playing the same situation will come to different conclusions. Role playing has the advantage of being the most realistic device for application and appraisal of principles in a classroom or training setting. It allows trainees to reflect their personalities by their behavior in a role-playing session. Trainees can make mistakes and have the opportunity to evaluate their shortcomings where serious consequences will not result.

The training techniques described in this section are basic vehicles for accomplishing the objectives of a program in the behavioral sciences. There are many modifications of these devices as well as a welter of lesser-known and used techniques.

---

[13] L. Moreno (ed.), "Inter-personal Therapy and the Psychopathology of Inter-personal Relationships," *Sociometry* (July and October, 1937), pp. 9–76.

[14] For a detailed account of role-playing techniques see Alan F. Klein, *Role Playing in Leadership Training and Group Problem Solving* (New York: Association Press, 1956).

Most training programs apply a combination of the devices discussed in the preceding pages. A typical pattern is found in the MDP-I program for group supervisors in the Internal Revenue Service. In this program the mornings are devoted to a form of the directed conference where content is covered. "Breakout" groups are set up in the afternoons for case analysis and role playing. This combination of techniques allows for coverage of all training phases—content and concept, attitude development, and skill development.

A REVIEW OF TRAINING IN THE BEHAVIORAL SCIENCES

There probably have been hundreds of industrial programs in human relations in which thousands of executives at all management levels were trained in the last twelve years. These programs have run the gamut in techniques, formality, and degree of sophistication. They have been held on company premises, in special locations outside the company, and on university campuses. A report covering these programs in terms of objectives, content, and presentation techniques would be a heroic, but exceedingly dull, undertaking. Consequently, the appraisal of human relations training that follows must be generalized as far as possible. Examples of programs are utilized when they serve to illustrate points. First, foreman training in leadership and human relations is discussed, then training higher levels of management is considered.

Foreman Training in Human Relations

Of all management levels, none has suffered as extensive training in human relations as has first-line supervision. The reasons for concentrated foreman training in human relations need not be dwelt upon because they have been considered in Chapter 15. The results of foreman training in the behavioral sciences are inconclusive. Appraisal of program effectiveness depends on clearness of objectives and adequate follow-up of performance. Both these requirements are conspicuously absent in human relations training, at least from the standpoint of the reports available in management literature. The case is not altogether hopeless, however. A good deal of information is available on a foreman training program run by International Harvester in the early 1950's. Attention is directed to this material because it has clues pointing to certain strong points and weaknesses inherent in human relations training at this organizational level.

The Harvester Program. The Harvester program for works foremen covered a wide range of subject matter of which a large part was human relations oriented. The program was quite ambitious. Around 5,000 first-line supervisors participated in it. The course content is shown in Figure 19–1. Also indicated is the training time spent on each subject as a reflection of the weight assigned to various topics. The basic program for foremen was centralized in a special Harvester school in Chicago. Some months after the main program a follow-up program was given at the plant where the foremen are employed.

The Ohio State Appraisal of the International Harvester Program.[15] The Personnel Research Board of Ohio State University studied the results of the works-foreman program. Some of the works foremen at the plant studied had taken the training program; those who did not were used as a control group. The objective of the study was to see how long foremen retained and practiced leadership and human relations principles after exposure to them.

The Ohio State researchers developed leadership dimensions which they felt represented dominant leadership characteristics. These characteristics provided the objective criteria against which the attitudes and leadership practice of the foremen were cast. The characteristics are *consideration* (identified as friendship, mutual trust, and warmth between leader and group), and *initiating structure* (identified as well-defined patterns of organization with emphasis on schedule and getting the job done).[16] The consideration factor was stated explicitly in the study as the more desirable leadership pattern, since an analysis of workers' attitudes indicated they would rather work under a "democratic" foreman.

The immediate impact of the training program on the foremen in the study group was to increase their consideration attitudes and decrease their initiating-structure attitudes. This effect was observed while the foremen were still on the site of the training program. But once back in the work environment this same group of foremen was noted, upon further study, to show a drop in consideration and an increase in initiating structure. In other words, the program did not achieve the objective of producing democratic or consideration attitudes among the foremen trained.

Two reasons are offered by the study group for why a change "for the better" was found directly after completion of the program and why the foremen reverted to their former ways after returning to the job. First, foremen were made more aware of their role in management by the program. From experience, foremen developed the notion that management appreciated and rewarded the initiating-structure type even though this attitude ran counter to the philosophy of the program they just experienced. Second, foremen tended to reflect the leadership characteristics

---

[15] The technical aspects of this study are reported in Edwin A. Fleishman, Edwin F. Harris, and Harold E. Burtt, *Leadership and Supervision in Industry* (Columbus: The Ohio State University, 1955).

[16] There is a rough correspondence between the leadership factor of consideration and democratic leadership, and between the initiating structure factor and authoritarian leadership.

FIGURE 19–1

OUTLINE OF THE INTERNATIONAL HARVESTER WORKS-FOREMEN

TRAINING PROGRAM

Topic	Time
1. Introductory sessions......................................	3 hours
2. Personal development:	
a) Effective speaking.......................................	10 hours
b) Everyday writing.......................................	4 "
c) Planning and organizing................................	3 "
d) Logical thinking.......................................	4 "
Subtotal.......................................	21 hours
3. Human relations:	
a) Human behavior.......................................	14 hours
b) Industrial relations....................................	9 "
c) Industrial organizations and control..................	2 "
d) Application of human relations.........................	4 "
Subtotal.......................................	29 hours
4. Economics:	
a) Economics—our standard of living.....................	8 hours
b) Harvester's financial structure.........................	4 "
Subtotal.......................................	12 hours
5. Company operations:	
a) Supply and inventory..................................	1 hour
b) Public relations in the plant community..................	2 hours
c) Product distribution...................................	2 "
Subtotal.......................................	5 hours
6. Tours..	6 hours
7. Concluding sessions..	5 hours
Grand total....................................	81 hours

Source: Education and Personnel Department, International Harvester Company, *Outline Course for Works Foremen* (Chicago: Mimeographed Publication Cl-15, N. D.), pp. 1–4.

of their boss. So a foreman returning to an initiating-structure leadership climate would adopt this approach regardless of his attitudes toward consideration derived from the program.

Further Observations on Foreman Training. The Harvester program, though more elaborate, is fairly typical of many foreman training programs which have enjoyed industry popularity. The human relations phases of these programs tend to be psychology oriented; that is, they stress the structure of human personality. Very little time, if any, is devoted to small-group processes and group-individual interactions. Another element of similarity among human relations programs is their emphasis on the leadership topic and their predisposition toward a democratic-permissive leadership pattern.

It is especially significant to note in the Harvester program that the desired changes in behavior were not forthcoming as a result of training. Indeed, some foremen were found to be more authoritarian after taking the training than they were before. The Ohio State researchers attributed the failure to the "leadership climate."

This state of affairs is not peculiar to the Harvester program. Hariton noted similar results in an appraisal of the Detroit Edison program.[17] He also concluded that the foreman's leadership pattern and attitudes are far more sensitive to those of his boss than to the ideas he learns in a training program. On the basis of this evidence, one might be tempted to recommend appropriate training for the foreman's boss, the boss' boss, and so on, with the expectation of changing the whole leadership climate. While such a decision would be profitable for training consultants it probably would not accomplish the desired result for the reason that the nature of the work supervised still has not changed.

When work is paced by the impersonal timing of a machine or an assembly line it is extremely difficult for supervision to assume a leadership pattern which is not ultimately oriented to a schedule. Situationally, an authoritarian pattern is more or less dictated by the nature of production-line work routines. In other situations where work is not so rigidly geared to a schedule, such as maintenance, a democratic approach to leadership is feasible and implementable.

It appears that human relations training programs have the objective of making foremen better leaders so as to facilitate the accomplishment of a job. This objective is predicated on these assumptions:

1. Foremen can be trained in leadership principles.
2. These principles, based in a philosophy of democratic leadership, are sound.
3. A training program is a sufficiently powerful device to effect a permanent change of attitudes and behavior.[18]
4. A training program can teach foremen "human skills" which are reenforced through job experience.

That these assumptions are rather tenuous is attested to by the indifferent success which has accompanied foreman training in human relations.[19] However, it is conceivable that as content and training methods improve, and as the nature of the foreman's role changes, future programs will succeed in achieving improved foreman leadership practice.

MANAGEMENT DEVELOPMENT AND TRAINING

One product of the post-World War II boom economy is executive development. A factor significantly contributing to management's pre-

---

[17] Theodore Hariton, "Conditions Influencing the Effects of Training in Human Relations" unpublished doctoral dissertation (University of Michigan, 1951). The Detroit Edison program was fairly similar to the Harvester program in terms of leadership philosophy and human relations orientation. If anything, the Detroit Edison program had more intensive work in human relations.

[18] This assumption is based on the policy of follow-up programs which refresh leadership principles learned in a basic course.

[19] See James N. Mosel, "Why Training Programs Fail to Carry Over," *Personnel*, November–December, 1957, pp. 56–64. Mosel offers an interesting appraisal of the shortcomings of foremen training.

disposition toward training is the rapid growth in numbers of executives, staff specialists, scientists, and engineers in relation to total employment in business. In other words, more and more people are assuming positions of administration, and it is felt that these people need training to improve their executive abilities.

The reason for the increase in executive and technical personnel is a matter of some dispute. Certain writers have suggested it may be due to "Parkinson's Law." Others have pointed to automation, company growth, reorganization of established firms, process and product innovation, and new administrative practices.

Regardless of the specific causes for the growth of executive and technical personnel it is fairly evident that the prevailing situation calls for more effective utilization of highly talented people. It is difficult to develop a climate conducive to making people of this caliber creative and happy in the work situation. Supervisory skills and training concepts which work well enough for operative employees are not always the most appropriate for dealing with people on the professional and managerial levels of companies.

It is obvious that the more brainpower employed by companies the greater is the demand for more thoroughly and broadly trained top executives. Experience alone is not a wholly adequate teacher for top and middle management. Thus the need for executive development is evident. But the question is: what constitutes the most meaningful route to accomplish the end of developing mature executives who have a sense of organization purpose and a sensitivity for the human problems in a firm?

Executive-development programs have one overriding objective: to change the behavior of trainees so that they may perform their jobs more effectively. Since 1946, executive-development programs have proliferated. These programs have used a multitude of training techniques to cover a vast range of subject matter. Many programs were in-company activities, although quite a few have been—and are—conducted on university campuses throughout the country.

The content of existing and defunct programs is something of a potpourri including principles of management, labor-management relations, business-government relationships, speed reading, speech, marketing, humanities, and human behavior. All sorts of training methods are represented, but there is an inclination toward the use of the case approach in business problems for the simulation of realistic situations.

Because of the diversity of topics it is difficult to generalize on the nature of the work done in the behavioral sciences in executive-development programs. It can be said with some assurance that popular topics are human motivation, communication, leadership, and small-group behavior. Also, cases are used to develop specific human problems for discussion and solution by the executive trainees. The usual pattern of executive-development programs has been to include human relations and the behavioral sciences in a curriculum encompassing a variety of other subjects having relevance for practicing executives. Thus, most appraisals of executive-development programs relate to the entire curriculum rather than to the human relations sessions.

Appraisal of Executive-Development Programs

Shortly after the second World War some fervent advocates of executive training sold their programs as panaceas for all the ills faced by management. Many such programs were grasped by frustrated managements as the answer to their "people problems." All too frequently these expectations were not fulfilled. The results management assumed would be forthcoming often did not, and indeed realistically could not, materialize. Hence it was to be expected that during the recession years of 1957 and 1958 the expenditures for executive-development programs would become subject to close examination. As a consequence, many programs were discontinued.

Currently there is a major need for management to be appraised of what it can reasonably expect from development programs and what conditions are necessary to insure maximum effectiveness for the programs that are installed.

Expectations. Probably the greatest block to the progress of sound management development is the fact that programs often are instituted for reasons quite apart from their avowed goals.[20] Management must be thoroughly committed to the aims of the program if any beneficial change in the behavior of participants is to be experienced on anything like a permanent basis. This is especially true if the program is oriented toward the behavioral sciences and attitude development in human relations and leadership.

In addition, management has to understand the ends it hopes to achieve by the program. It is hardly sufficient to say, "We want a well-rounded man to come out of the program." If the individual is not "well-rounded" in the first place, three weeks or even six months of executive development is not likely to do the trick.[21]

Expectations have to be more specific. If they are, then the objectives of the program will be clear and appraisal of program effectiveness will be eased. For example, if improvement of executive leadership is the objective sought, program content and presentation methods should be wholly devoted to securing this end. The shotgun approach to executive

---

[20] E. K. Taylor, "Management Development at the Cross-roads," *Personnel*, March–April, 1959, pp. 9–10.

[21] Except in the exceptional cases of programs which are so enlightened that participants are motivated to continue their development after the program terminates.

development is likely to give way to programs with less ambitious goals than the development of the "complete executive." As the scope of programs narrows, the likelihood of accomplishing what management expects of them increases.

Effectiveness. The ultimate guide to program effectiveness is, of course, the degree of behavioral change it is able to secure in the participants' on-the-job performance. However, effectiveness is predicated on concrete program *objectives, well-planned* content and presentation techniques, a training *organization* built around qualified instructors, *motivated* participants who are convinced their training needs will be satisfied by the program, and *control* or follow-up and appraisal of training results.

The motivation and control factors are probably the most forsaken of all the above conditions underlying program effectiveness. Too often programs are structured not to meet the training needs of participants but to reflect the prejudices of training officers. Nothing undermines a program's effectiveness more than the feeling on the part of the participants that their training serves little purpose from the standpoint of their development.

The lack of adequate appraisal of a program's impact on behavior has been noted already as a symptomatic shortcoming of human relations training. Standards for the appraisal of program effectiveness should be developed as part of the program *plan*. As far as possible, standards should be tangible enough to allow an objective comparison between them and the trainee's performance after he has experienced the program.[22]

But this is not the last step. A counseling and interviewing program should be an integral part of executive-development activities. Counseling is necessary when evidence shows that individual performance and training standards do not compare favorably. Interviewing all trainees provides information on the strengths and shortcomings of the program. Both counseling and interviewing are necessary parts of control activity.

Counseling is undertaken with varying degrees of formality. It exists between the superior and the subordinate trainee, or between the trainee and a staff counselor. Another approach which is recommended is evaluation of individual performance in a group of one's peers. A form of "peer counseling" is valuable to the extent that the individual is made to see his shortcomings without the embarrassment of appraisal by his boss or a professional counselor.

---

[22] Much work along these lines has been done by Likert. See, for example, Rensis Likert, "Motivational Approach to Management Development," *Harvard Business Review,* July–August, 1959, pp. 75–82. For a discussion of evaluation techniques see Frank A. DePhillips, William M. Berliner, and James J. Cribbin, *Management of Training Programs* (Homewood, Ill.: Richard D. Irwin, Inc., 1960), chaps. 15, 16.

Through the use of personal interviews or written questionnaires, data are gathered from all trainees pertaining to the impact of the program on them. It is essential in evaluation measures like these to glean information relating to trainee changes in attitude and behavior. Asking whether or not trainees liked the program or are satisfied with the content is relatively useless. Most responses to such questions show a positive bias. The only real measure of program effectiveness is the extent to which it changed behavior.

The function of training appraisal also serves as a check on the standards of the program. It is possible that standards conceived in the planning stage will be modified by renewed planning activities as the company has experience with the program. Thus, counseling and interviewing serve several purposes:

1. They implement the control function.
2. They provide criteria for redesigning program content, presentation methods, and performance standards.
3. They are essential in helping the individual trainee see his failings and strengths in light of the program's philosophy.
4. They re-enforce the principles and practices to which the trainee is exposed in the program.

Additional Elements in Program Effectiveness. Andrews, in a discussion of management training, indicates five conditions beyond those mentioned above which have bearing on the effectiveness of development programs.[23]

First, effectiveness depends in part on the length of the program, the amount of trainee participation in the subject matter, and the extent of the trainee's effort. Short programs (less than a week) or programs with sessions spread over a long period of time reduce effectiveness. Also, trainee involvement in the program is essential. As mentioned before, reliance on the lecture technique lessens effectiveness because it discourages participation.

Second, effectiveness of the program is heavily dependent on the qualifications and performance of the instructors.

Third, program content is likely to have its greatest impact on participants who are specialists rather than "generalists." Hence, technical staff executives stand a better chance of profiting from development programs than executives who have a wider range of responsibility.

Fourth, the more insulated program participants are in their companies from other companies and industries the greater will be the impact of the program on them.

And fifth, in order to be effective the program content must have specific meaning to the participants in terms of their career objectives.

[23] Kenneth R. Andrew, "Is Management Training Effective?" *Harvard Business Review*, January–February, 1957, pp. 87–88.

Up to this point, the discussion has been concerned with executive-development activities in which training in the behavioral sciences may constitute only one part of the curriculum. Now it is necessary to focus on a training development devoted exclusively to the behavioral sciences and the improvement of trainees' interpersonnal skills.

Sensitivity Training

Sensitivity training is a fairly recent innovation in executive development. It has grown out of the work of applied group dynamics[24] and is often associated with the program of the National Training Laboratory in Group Development.[25] The training approaches developed by researchers in these activities have been applied to industrial programs in a number of forms.[26] The objectives of sensitivity training, however, are basically the same.

It has been repeatedly observed in this chapter that the purpose of training is to change behavior. In the realm of human interrelationships as in no other sphere of human interest are attitudes fixed and loaded with explosive content. The aim of most human relations training is both to make executives more effective in their ability to relate to others and to accomplish organizational goals through the efforts of people. It is something of a self-evident truth that executive behavior in human undertakings is a matter of attitudes which are effective or ineffective from the standpoint of motivating people. Therefore, human relations training attempts to change attitudes so that ultimately behavior itself will change. However, human relations programs in the past enjoyed a rather low level of success in effecting anything like a lasting or even initial change in attitudes.

Sensitivity training attempts to accomplish the end of behavioral change through a philosophy and technique of training which are not oriented in the same direction as most human relations programs. Perhaps the difference in orientation is best described as a concern with "how"—how a trainee appraises himself, how a group behaves, how another would react in a given situation. In short, sensitivity training has as its purpose the development of an executive's *awareness* of himself, of others, of group processes, and of group culture. In addition, it proposes to develop

---

[24] See D. Cartwright and A. Zander (eds.), *Group Dynamics: Research and Theory* (Evanston, Ill.: Row, Peterson and Co., 1960).

[25] See National Training Laboratory in Group Development, *Explorations in Human Relations Training: An Assessment of Experience, 1947–1953* (Washington: National Education Association, 1953).

[26] For example see Irving R. Weschler, Marvin A. Klemes, and Clovis Shepard, "A New Focus in Executive Training," *Advanced Management,* May, 1955, pp. 19–22; and Michael G. Blansfield and W. F. Robinson, "Variations in Training Laboratory Design: A Case Study in Sensitivity Training," *Personnel Administration,* March–April, 1961, pp. 17–22, 49.

in trainees specific skills in interpersonal relationships and behavioral adaptability to changing human situations.[27]

Tannenbaum, Weschler, and Massarik point out five elements which characterize sensitivity training.[28]

First, sensitivity training is process rather than content oriented. That is, trainees direct their attention toward feelings and attitudes which are the essence of personal and group interactions. They learn to become aware of their own sentiments and those of others. Writers who subscribe to the sensitivity-training approach feel that experiences of this type are far more effective in changing attitudes and behavior than the conventional method of learning content.

Second, the design of a sensitivity training program is partly unstructured. A good deal of freedom is allowed trainees to decide for themselves what they want to discuss.

Third, as a result of the unstructured nature of parts of the sensitivity training program, frustration is often caused among the trainees. Proponents of sensitivity training feel that some uneasiness is necessary because it shakes the trainee out of his complacency and forces him to reexamine his concept of himself.

Fourth, the core of sensitivity training is the small group. Within these groups (sometimes called т-groups) a high degree of participation and involvement is encouraged. From interacting within the small-group structure the trainee is able to get an insight into himself and an awareness of the motivations of others.

Fifth, a permissive atmosphere is essential to the success of sensitivity training. Permissiveness in this sense is a condition where trainees are free to express themselves and to listen to opinions of others in the group. It is an environment in which the discussion leader does not try to force his own values and goals on the trainee.

Sensitivity-training programs do not all have the same degree of unstructuredness. A certain amount of time, depending on the program, is allocated for lectures and the use of more conventional training methods like role playing, case studies, and training films.

THE FUTURE OF THE TRAINING IN THE BEHAVIORAL SCIENCES

Responsibility for training executives in the behavioral sciences cannot devolve entirely on business. The responsibility must be shared by universities.

In a paper given before the Academy of Management David G.

---

[27] Robert Tannenbaum, Irving R. Weschler, and Fred Massarik, *Leadership and Organization: A Behavioral Science Approach* (New York: McGraw-Hill Book Co., 1961), pp. 124–31.

[28] *Ibid.*, pp. 132–34.

Moore discusses the role of the behavioral sciences in management philosophy.[29] He points to the need for executives to have the conceptual ability to visualize organizations as systems, and the skill to structure and to work effectively within the context of the system. From this it is clear that executive-training needs exist both at the conceptual level and at the level of human skills, attitudes, and behavior. Precisely how the responsibility for training in concept and skill will be divided between businesses and universities is a difficult matter to predict. However, if the problem is one of emphasis, which it seems to be, then it appears that colleges in their business curricula should stress the behavioral sciences at the conceptual level. The training in this field offered under company sponsorship should stress skills and attitude change.

The nature of training and education in the behavioral sciences should be considered as a wedding between concepts learned in college programs and attitudinal and behavioral developments which accrue to the individual during his work experience and participation in company training activities.

It seems reasonable to leave to university business schools the obligation to improve the individual's conceptual abilities in the behavioral sciences. Universities are disposed to work along the line of generality more than practice. Business in its turn must pursue the pragmatic undertaking of the development of specific skills which are closer to being immediately translatable into improved job performance. A less haphazard union between business and universities in behavioral science training would be repaid fully by greater individual effectiveness in this complex and difficult segment of industrial affairs.

REVIEW QUESTIONS

1. Discuss the reasons which caused management to re-examine its efforts in the area of human relations training.

2. Distinguish between education and training.

3. Outline the elements in the operational definition of training in the behavioral sciences.

4. Discuss the four functions of training in the behavioral sciences.

5. Describe the various training techniques used to impart content. To improve skills.

6. Evaluate the proposition that the success of any training program in human relations is dependent, in part, on the leadership climate to which the trainee returns.

7. What factors account for the popularity of executive-development programs after World War II?

---

[29] See David C. Moore, "Contributions to Management Philosophy from the Behavioral Sciences," *Proceedings of the Academy of Management,* December, 1960, pp. 10–16.

8. Discuss the various determinants underlying the effectiveness of executive-development programs.

9. What are the objectives of sensitivity training? How does sensitivity training differ from other training approaches in the behavioral sciences?

10. How can business and universities more effectively combine their resources for the development of executives?

SUPPLEMENTARY READINGS

ANDREW, KENNETH R. "Is Management Training Effective?" *Harvard Business Review*, January–February, 1957, pp. 85–94.

FLEISHMAN, EDWIN A.; HARRIS, EDWIN F.; AND BURTT, HAROLD E. *Leadership and Supervision in Industry*. Columbus: The Ohio State University, 1955.

LIKERT, RENSIS. "Motivational Approach to Management Development," *Harvard Business Review*, July–August, 1959, pp. 75–82.

MOSEL, JAMES N. "Why Training Programs Fail to Carry Over," *Personnel*, November–December, 1957, pp. 56–64.

TANNENBAUM, ROBERT; WESCHLER, IRVING R.; AND MASSARIK, FRED. *Leadership and Organization*, pp. 124–31. New York: McGraw-Hill Book Co., 1961.

CHAPTER 20

Conclusion

I NVARIABLY, when the last chapter of a textbook is reached, the "so what" factor is paramount in the reader's mind. What is the significance of the content in the "real world"? More specifically, what is the role of the behavioral sciences today and in the future of management practice? Another short digression into history is necessary for an answer to this last question. This time some observations are made on the matter of power.

Power in this context refers to the ability of individuals to influence the direction of social action by means of the control and allocation of resources. Obviously, in one sense, most active participants in any culture have a modicum of power. But the concern here is with elites in a society who possess sufficient power to frame the destinies of the many by commanding allegiance to their decisions. Whether this allegiance arises from domination or spontaneous acclaim is not the issue. What is, is the fact of power and the way it is justified by the elite. Thus, the source of power is not the focal point of this discussion; rather it is the way which power is rationalized that draws attention.

Now, naturally a subject of this sort could occupy volumes. But in spite of its potential for heroic proportions, one observation emerges which is deceptively simple when first stated. The justification of power has changed in the past, and future changes may be anticipated. In the past, and today, power is sanctioned because it is thought of as granted by a superauthority which prescribes rules of conduct.

Thus, kings ruled by virtue of divine right; dictators seek goals following the abstract principles of state supremacy; presidents enjoy power after a periodic expression of the "collective mind" of the electorate. In another sphere, commercial giants reigned because they survived in the game of social Darwinism, enabling them to participate in the rewards bestowed by an economic system indifferent to all but the successful in the competitive struggle.

It is fairly clear that in the process of justifying power, elites, either financial or political, looked outside themselves and their administrative organizations to superauthorities for the legitimacy, and indeed the source, of their power. At a particular time, these external authorities might have been God, the state, the masses, the competitive economic system, or a combination of any or all of these authorities. Given some ultimate but unapproachably abstract entity, endowed with ideal qualities manufactured to suit the tenor of the times, principles of human conduct are deducible to serve as practical, day-to-day standards of behavior.

Behavior, so considered, is evaluated by comparison with the ideal standards of the ultimate authority. The ideal standards serve as reference points against which behavior is plotted and socially desirable rewards are either given or withheld. All in all, the power of kings or economic leaders appealed to sources external to themselves for justification. Power always had outside reference to mystical ultimates from which principles of "proper" behavior were derived.

Today, however, it is not completely apparent that the idea of "power looking outside itself for justification" is as relevant as formerly. To be sure, administrators and politicians make much of the external sources of justification for the power they have. But as a principle of social action, power may well be the source of its own justification. While this notion is nothing new, it commands more credibility today because of the evolving nature of monopolistic organizations in which power is generated, perpetuated, and exercised.

Indeed, many modern organizations, both political and economic, command sufficient resources in a protected environment so as to insulate them from external influences which could challenge their behavior. Under such circumstances the justification of power is the organization itself and not much else. Thus, a president or board chairman need not look to God, the state, or society for the justification of the power he possesses which flows to him from his position in a large corporation. The state and society must tolerate vast power aggregations because their loss would be a blow that society and the state could not afford to sustain.

All that this means is that the modern administrative organization is the source of its own justification. The fact that the organization exists and possesses substantial resources is enough in itself to endow the administrators of the organization with power. In turn, the administrator does not have to look much farther than his own organizational system for personal justification of the power he exercises.

In summary, it has been conventional to seek external justifications for personal and organizational power. However, the modern administrative organization has achieved such a dominant position in society that it is able to supply, by internal generation, the justification for its existence. And, of course, those who run the organization can tap these internally created justifications to rationalize the power they possess personally. These generalizations must not be taken in an absolute sense, however. Society is not entirely composed of monolithic organizations completely protected from external sanctions. But at the same time, organizations, private and public, economic and political, have achieved a stage of development giving them greater potential for self-justification than ever before. This capability, naturally, devolves upon the individuals charged with the responsibility for setting organizational policy and running organizational affairs.

Much of what has been said so far here is implicit in earlier material covering organization theory and executive behavior. Certainly, the matter of power is a theme which runs through the Chapters on Executive Incentives and Constraints and Bureaucracy. Far from being passive actors responding to satisfy externally dictated needs, modern administrators are in a position to impose their will and policies on society by the use of organization power.[1]

These observations do not imply value judgments. But there are many who would rebel at the notion of our society being dominated by administrative machineries which are relatively less hampered by external constraints today than, say, 50 or 100 years ago. Regardless of personal prejudices in the matter, this is the way things are. Given this setting, where do the behavioral sciences fit in?

It has been observed often that management needs relationship experts. What does this mean? It means that management should attract to its ranks people who are able to abstract beyond the performance of a single function to the system as a whole. That is, modern management needs those who have the abstractive ability for visualizing the organization as a totality of variable interacting parts. But beyond this, the "relationship expert" must have more than an abstractive inclination. He also needs the concrete skill to administer the relationships of an organization effectively. It is through his conceptual and concrete skills that the manager contributes to organizational stability and progress.

This view of executive qualification is rather new. While, of course, conceptual skill always worked in the favor of the administrator, few would deny that in the past emphasis was placed on the concrete or functional attributes of executive behavior. Does not the manager need to plan, organize, motivate, and control? While it is a sophistry to claim the absence of a need for conceptual expertness in the successful performance of these functions, nevertheless the treatment of these activities in the literature has been weighted heavily toward concrete applications with lip-service given to their abstractive demands. It is a recent development that the abstractive nature of managerial activity has been given the emphasis it deserves.

One among the many reasons for the current stress given to the ability for conceptualization is the evolution of organizations and the demands arising therefrom. History shows the growing size and evolving com-

---

[1] For further discussion see Reinhard Bendix, "Bureaucracy and the Problem of Power," *Public Administration Review*, Summer, 1945, pp. 194–209.

plexity of organization. The size of organization does not provide the main index. Rather the complexity of organizational relationships does. Complexity stems from numbers of people and the "geometric" progression of their interrelationships, but this is not the whole picture. Specialized activities add functional complexity. With functional complexity comes sophisticated technology and highly trained "professionals" to operate it. In addition to this, powerful modern organizations are not single-purpose institutions but embrace numerous goals. Organizational ends and purposes contribute their part to complexity. Thus, organizational evolution is qualitative and quantitative, and its qualitative aspects are crucially important, as they are manifested in complexity of organizational form and objectives.

Evolution is the point to be emphasized as the characteristic of the modern organization. Organizational development through the evolving of higher types of complex systems is a form of adaptation to a changing environment. However, the evolution of human organizations does not guarantee stability; quite the contrary is true. Side by side with organizational evolution grows the propensity of organizations to become increasingly sensitive to disrupting internal influences which run counter to the evolutionary processes. These antievolutionary forces may be people, obsolete processes, decaying technology, density of internal relationships, or 101 other causes that multiply not only in number but in potential to disturb the delicately balanced mechanism of the administrative system as it gets larger.

So it seems that within the context of one activity, the organizational activity, two opposing forces exist: the uphill force of evolution projecting organizations to higher degrees of complexity and differentiation opposed by downhill forces acting to degrade, offset, or undermine evolutionary achievements. The manager stands in the midst of these forces, on the one hand doing what he can to facilitate the evolutionary and adaptive processes, and on the other hand trying to minimize the natural tendencies toward deterioration. To work effectively in a situation like this, management needs the abstractive ability to appraise the consequences of change on the total organization. Management needs the conceptual insight necessary to discriminate between transformations which will positively contribute to the adaptive process from changes which will be detrimental to it. A management successful in this undertaking preserves the organization.

Unequivocally, the primary role of the behavioral sciences in management practice is to supply conceptual schemes to administrators for organizational maintenance and adaptation. This statement has objective and subjective implications. The formal organization is a centralized system of abstract relationships. In an objective sense, the modern manager who perceives the subtlety of these relationships and acts effectively on them helps preserve organization integrity and helps insure its progress. Subjectively, the person, or persons, who are able to maneuver in and influence the system are in a position to employ strategies for attracting power to themselves. Thus, the behavioral sciences have a significant role in management practice, both for their objective contributions to the organization as such and for their subjective contributions to the achievement of the personal power goals of managers.

The specific objective applications of the behavioral sciences to organizational processes are considered at length in Part II and need not be dwelt on here. However, the relation of the behavioral sciences to the subjective problem of the accumulation of personal power merits more thought.

If the premises set forth in this chapter are accepted—[2] that is (a) if organizations are growing increasingly capable of self-justification resulting in administrators' not having to look beyond the boundaries of their own organization for the legitimacy of their power, (b) and if an expertness in the behavioral sciences is a key element in a manager's personal strategy to attract internally generated power to himself then some interesting questions arise. These are:

1. What is the position of the behavioral scientist in this setting?
2. Can he continue in the pursuit of pure scientific achievement divorced from normative considerations?
3. Is there an "ethical vacuum" created by the lack of concern with normative matters on the parts of the scientist and the administrator who uses his findings?
4. If so, how is this vacuum to be filled?

Loren Baritz, in his provocative book *The Servants of Power*, traces historically the employment of behavioral scientists in business.[3] As the title suggests, the behavioral scientists who have "sold out" to industry as full-time employees or part-time consultants are pawns in the games of managerial power consolidation. Baritz feels that these individuals cannot be termed "scientists" at all because they are under the influence of powerful interest groups, and consequently are not free to pursue scientific inquiry no matter where it leads. Further, the contributions that behavioral scientists do make to management are used for ignoble purposes of human manipulation, which casts an additional cloud over their status in industry. For as Baritz says, "Many managers have not hesitated to make explicit the point that their use of social scientists and their skills is for the purpose of human control."[4] The general sense of the Baritz thesis is that "human control," refined by the behavioral sciences and ap-

---

[2] As general statements of tendencies.

[3] Loren Baritz, *The Servants of Power* (Middletown, Conn.: Wesleyan University Press, 1960).

[4] *Ibid.*, p. 207.

plied by managers in an industrial setting, is an unmitigated evil with which self-respecting behavioral scientists should have no association.

This issue, though important, is duly noted and will not be pushed further here. Let it suffice to say that Baritz has turned up evidence of extensive employment of behavioral scientists in industry who are being used, he thinks, to enhance the power position of managers. Through the devices of human manipulation, installed by the behavioral scientists, managers are in a better position to tap and control the internal sources of organization power.

One might complain, in response to this point of view, that industry has *not* employed enough behavioral scientists, or has not engaged in "human research" on a sufficiently broad plane, or has, indeed, not given wide enough credence to the behavioral sciences to make the problems of human manipulation and control less a phantom and more a reality. Even Baritz notes that there are large gaps in business acceptance of the behavioral sciences. Many managers still feel there is something "fishy" about them and, therefore, are suspicious of their value and also the people in the behavioral disciplines.

But the problem is larger than simply the industrial employment of behavioral scientists for whatever reasons they and their skills are used. Hundreds of scientists in the behavioral disciplines engage in research and experimentation which has no connection or just remote connection to business. And many behavioral scientists, while working in a business setting, consider it merely a laboratory for their research. In other words, the study of the social and psychological nature of man in organizations goes on, data accumulates, and generalizations are made on human behavior without reference to normative or practical applications of these findings for managers, or for that matter anyone else.

In this respect, the behavioral sciences are similar to other sciences which independently seek the truth about phenomena existing in the environment of man. The goal of science is knowledge which contributes to a predictive facility. The way this facility is used is not its concern, regardless of whether the science is in the natural order or in the behavioral order.

In part, as a result of this "value-free purety" in research, the behavioral sciences have made progress toward higher levels of scientific achievement in terms of methodology, predictions, and generalizations. While the degree of sophistication in these three respects varies considerably from discipline to discipline, and among areas within disciplines, there is no doubt that the policy maker, in business, government, and other institutions, has at his hand powerful tools for decision and control purposes. It may be that the function of behavioral scientists in industrial employment, and also professors in colleges committed to a strong behavioral science program for administrators, is to provide a liaison between the pure scientist and his findings, and the executive who needs information of scientific accomplishments for the ultimate objective of application.

Four questions asked above prompted part of the discourse in these last few pages. Given that the behavioral sciences can be a tool of power, what should be the scientists' position on the normative issues posed by this situation?[5] A scientist, *qua* scientist, cannot concern himself with the ethics of application of the information he uncovers.[6] Ethics governing the use of scientific findings is peculiar to the province of policy and decision making. If he does entangle himself in this sphere of activity, it is likely that his science will become sterile. But, at the same time, the absence of normative considerations in the use of science on the parts of the scientist and the administrator *does* create an ethical vacuum. There remains, therefore, the question of how this vacuum is to be filled.

One alternative, of course, is to ask the administrator to be aware of the ethical implications of his acts. That is, he should be concerned with the consequences of his use of the behavioral sciences in respect to the dignity of his fellow employees. He should not be a cynical, self-seeking manipulator. He should not use people for his selfish ends or for the accomplishment of the abstract ends of the organization only. He should instead promote the goals actively sought by mankind which involve the preservation and rational development of groups and individuals.

Some may feel that this is idealistic. The reasons for this attitude lie, perhaps, in:

1. A recognition of the pragmatic character of administration.
2. An acknowledgement that administrators are not disposed to being philosophers or moralists.
3. An acceptance, in fact, of the self-justifying capabilities of organizations enabling administrators to set and cause acceptance of their own rules of conduct.

---

[5] That is, the power to influence behavior toward the accomplishment of goals (either personal or organizational) which have not been sufficiently justified by any authority other than the organization or its administrators.

[6] This is not to say that the behavioral scientist is, or can be, completely removed from the realm of ethics, goals, values, and policy. In the first place, the culture and the mores of a society are *data* to be objectively analyzed by the scientist. In the second place, the scientist often is a part of and a participant in the phenomena he is studying, if only in the sense that he has certain prejudgments of it flowing from his own experiences. Thus, the behavioral scientist brings to a research situation a set of values which condition, consciously or unconsciously, his approach to the analysis and his interpretation of the findings. This is particularly evident in "value loaded" research settings like interpersonal relationships in business. Thus "pure objectivity" is extremely difficult for the scientist to maintain. And even if he has success in doing so, it is hard for him to convince others that his approach to the situation is as objective as he, himself, feels it is. For interesting discussions of this problem see Philip M. Hauser, "Social Science and Social Engineering," *Philosophy of Science*, July, 1949, pp. 209–18; and, Benedict M. Ashley, "Social Science Founded on a Unified Natural Science," in James A. Weisheipl (ed.), *The Dignity of Science* (River Forest, Ill., The Thomist Press, 1961), pp. 475–80.

In the face of these objections, is it not, indeed, idealistic to expect a relatively enlightened and altruistic use of the behavioral sciences in administration? The answer is not all, if the conditions of a second alternative are approached.

It is characteristic of our society, and our culture, to develop concepts having complementary antitheses.[7] For example, *body* has been paired with *soul, responsibility* with *accountability,* and *power* with *regulation.* The last couplet, though ingrained in American tradition, is becoming less an operative reality for reasons discussed in this chapter and in Chapter 17. Thus, power without appropriate restraints, while condemned on ideological grounds, is still a growing phenomena in our society. A matter of major concern to some social theorists is how a better balance can be re-established between power and regulation.

This far-reaching topic must be restricted here to the behavioral sciences as an instrument of administration. The subject is relevant nonetheless if the premise is accepted that the behavioral sciences are useful for those wishing to augment personal and organizational power.

It seems necessary that there has to be interposed between the behavioral scientist and the administrator a third vital party of interest. The attributes of this party are an intimate appreciation of administration and also the disciplines of the behavioral sciences contributing to it. This party need not know in detail the technical aspects of either area of endeavor. But it must have a taste for the implicit values of administration and the relationship of the behavioral sciences to these values, taken in the context of society's cultural and moral heritage.

For lack of better language, this party may be called the social philosopher or social critic. In any event, it appears that a real need exists for some individuals to work independently of the world of the behavioral disciplines and administration, and, in a sense, judge or criticize the activities of both with norms not necessarily derived from either.

Of course, this is not an appeal to set up some almighty source of final judgment in which the critics reign supreme. It is, however, a suggestion that more attention, support, and acceptance be extended to those sitting outside the "sacred cow" of science and the practical arts of administration, scratching their heads asking, "Just what does all this mean?" It is this lack of recognition of independent work of modest proportions that prompts Whyte to observe, in his successful critical study *The Organization Man,* that there is "money, money everywhere . . . but not a cent to think."[8]

In more explicit terms, the critic is an external constraining source on power because he articulates values which he perceives society holding

---

[7] A. L. Kroeber, "The Superorganic," *American Anthropologist,* April–June, 1917, p. 163.

[8] William H. Whyte, Jr., *The Organization Man* (New York: Simon and Schuster, Inc., 1956), p. 237.

or needing to hold. He justifies his existence when he sees and exposes practices which run counter to these values. In the "pure state" he is found in journalism and education, where he serves to communicate social values to practitioners who might have never known them or forgotten them. He is the medium for verbalizing the conscience of society in regard to *ends* or *goals*.

The critic also serves in a less noble capacity by pointing out to administrators the inherent idiocy of certain fads and fancies which crop up from time to time. More generally speaking, the critic can give "advice" to the policy maker on what is good and useful and what is irrelevant in scientific research as *means* to ends.[9] That independent judgment on policy goals and means is socially valuable, there can be no question. Whether or not it is wanted is another matter.

Metaphorically, the administrator is the ultimate consumer of the product of critical judgment.[10] The administrator, in a mixed world where his power is far from absolute but substantial, actually thirsts for "outside" opinion regarding the ethical implications of his decisions. In this respect, critical judgments certainly are wanted. However, it seems that such judgments are wanted more for assessment of the relative worth (practically and ethically) of various *means* to ends, rather than for an assessment of administrative ends themselves. It should be clear that the social critic could not justify his role if it was restricted to the estimation of means. The critical function must be recognized as including evaluations of means *and* ends.

The second alternative discussed in the foregoing pages is an expression of faith in the positive consequences that critical work would have in filling the "ethical vacuum." The rush to scientism on the one hand and to administrative practice on the other needs a moderating influence which can only come through "third party" critical effort. This is because neither the behavioral sciences nor the administrative organization has an absolute need for critical self-appraisal based on external normative standards.[11]

But the critic cannot carry the load by himself. The administrator should also cultivate a critical bent. While a case can be made for an

-----

[9] The matter of irrelevancy from the standpoint of the critic must meet more than pragmatic tests. A method to achieve action or control might be pragmatically valuable in an administrative setting, but at variance with values which the critic perceives as worth maintaining. In this case, the critic would be required to advise the policy maker against the use of a particular method as a means to achieve an end.

[10] Of course, the social order would be the final beneficiary of the critical-administrative relationship.

[11] This is another way of stating the matter of self-justifying power growing as the monopolistic position of the organization grows. Obviously, the weaker the organization, the more it must look to external sources to justify its existence and to lend it support. But, again, this is a relative notion.

amoral behavioral science, it is not so easy to disregard the ethical aspects of the process of administration as it is implemented through the private judgments and actions of managers. More than ever, the leadership of society is devolving on individuals operating within large organizations. These people cannot assume a posture of bureaucratic "neutrality" in regard to external values and still produce an enlightened form of leadership. They must, instead, be sensitive and responsive to goals which exist outside themselves and their organizations.

As stated in Chapter 17, as the power of administrators in key policy-making positions increases, the question always resolves to how prone these people will be to subordinate their interests, collectively or as individuals, to the interests of the groups they are supposed to serve. The answer must relate back to the power-regulation couplet. The stakes are too high to rely on the benevolent despot for perceptive personal leadership. External regulation still exists and has reactive potential in most power arenas. Because of the rather technical nature of the behavioral sciences as instruments of power, it appears that the critic performs a vital regulative function in this area. But, more generally, external systems of regulation do persist, and they should be nurtured and fulfilled.

Indexes

Name Index

Subject Index